This Catalogue is presented as a benefit of your membership. The exhibitions and programs of the Los Angeles County Museum of Art would not have been possible without your support.

Doug. Merry Christmas!

Love.
Always. Mom & Joe

2011

CALIFORNIA DESIGN 1930–1965

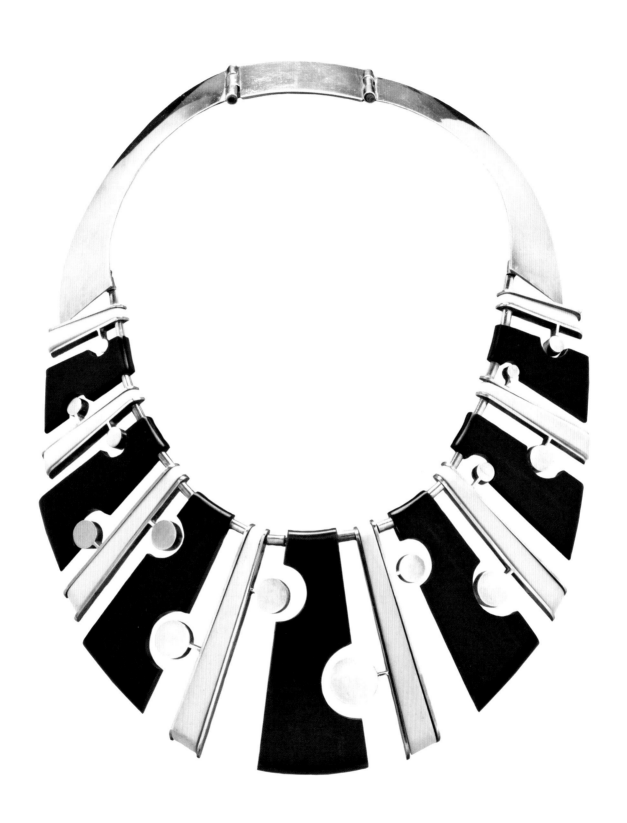

Published with the assistance of the Getty Foundation

Wendy Kaplan, Editor

Wendy Kaplan and Bobbye Tigerman, Curators

LIVING IN A MODERN WAY
CALIFORNIA DESIGN 1930–1965

with contributions by
Glenn Adamson
Jeremy Aynsley
Wendy Kaplan
Pat Kirkham
Melissa Leventon
Christopher Long
Nicholas Olsberg
Staci Steinberger
Bill Stern
Bobbye Tigerman

Los Angeles County Museum of Art
The MIT Press
Cambridge, Massachusetts, and London, England

This book was published on the occasion of the exhibition *California Design, 1930–1965: "Living in a Modern Way,"* on view from October 1, 2011, through March 25, 2012.

 An initiative of the Getty with arts institutions across Southern California.

Presenting Sponsors The Getty   Bank of America

The exhibition was organized by the Los Angeles County Museum of Art and funded through a lead grant from the Getty Foundation. Corporate sponsorship was provided by *Barbie*.

Additional funding was provided by the Henry Luce Foundation, Debbie and Mark Attanasio, Martha and Bruce Karsh, and LACMA's Decorative Arts and Design Council.

Copublished by the Los Angeles County Museum of Art, 5905 Wilshire Boulevard, Los Angeles, CA, 90036, lacma.org, and MIT Press, 55 Hayward Street, Cambridge, MA, 02142.

MIT Press books may be purchased at special quantity discounts for business or sales promotional use. For information, please email special_sales@mitpress.mit.edu or write to Special Sales Department, The MIT Press, 55 Hayward Street, Cambridge, MA, 02142.

Library of Congress Cataloging-in-Publication Data

California design, 1930–1965 : living in a modern way / Wendy Kaplan, editor ; Wendy Kaplan, Bobbye Tigerman, curators ; with contributions by Glenn Adamson ... [et al.].
p. cm.
Published on the occasion of an exhibition held at the Los Angeles County Museum of Art, Oct. 1, 2011–Mar. 25, 2012.
Includes bibliographical references and index.
ISBN 978-0-262-01607-0
1. Decorative arts—California—History—20th century—Exhibitions. 2. Modernism (Aesthetics)—California—Exhibitions. I. Kaplan, Wendy. II. Tigerman, Bobbye. III. Adamson, Glenn. IV. Los Angeles County Museum of Art.
NK835.C3C35 2011
745.09794'0904—dc22
2011015580

For the Los Angeles County Museum of Art:
Head of Publications: Nola Butler
Editor in Chief: Thomas Frick
Editor: Nancy Grubb
Design: Michael Hodgson, Ph.D, A Design Office
Production: The Production Department
Publications Administrator: Monica Paniry
Proofreader: Dianne Woo
Indexer: Susan Burke
Supervising Photographer: Peter Brenner, with Steve Oliver
Rights and Reproductions: Cheryle T. Robertson, with Stephen Forsling

This book was set in Gotham Book and Medium, and was printed and bound in China.

Front:

Adapted from original design by Saul Bass for Capitol Records. *Frank Sinatra Conducts Tone Poems of Color*, 1956. Cat. 19
Inset: Thomas Dolliver Church. Donnell Ranch pool, Sonoma County, 1948. Cat. 42

Back, top to bottom, left to right:

Raymond Loewy for Studebaker Corporation. *Avanti* automobile, designed 1961, manufactured 1963–64, photo c. 1962
La Gardo Tackett for Architectural Pottery. Garden sculpture, c. 1955
Gilbert Adrian. Two-piece dress from *The Atomic 50s* collection, 1950. Cat. 5
Dan Johnson for Hayden Hall. Desk, 1947. Cat. 139
Byron Wilson. Necklace, c. 1956. Cat. 313
Greta Magnusson Grossman. Interior of Grossman House, Beverly Hills, 1949. Photo by Julius Shulman, 1949
Charles Eames and Ray Eames. Eames House (Case Study House #8), Pacific Palisades, 1945–49

Endsheets:

Adapted from original design by Alvin Lustig for Laverne Originals, *Incantation* textile, c. 1947. Cat. 194

pp. 2–3: Buff, Straub & Hensman. Recreation pavilion, Mirman House, Arcadia, 1958. Photo by Julius Shulman, 1959
p. 4: Dan Johnson for Hayden Hall. Desk, 1947. Cat. 139
p. 5: Charles Eames and Ray Eames. Elephant, 1945. Cat. 74
p. 6: Rupert Deese. Cocktail pitcher, c. 1950. Cat. 59
p. 7: Greta Magnusson Grossman for Ralph O. Smith Manufacturing Company. Left: floor lamp, c. 1952. Cat. 117. Right: lamp, c. 1949. Cat. 116
p. 8: Byron Wilson. Necklace, c. 1956. Cat. 313
p. 9: Claire Falkenstein. Model for garden gate, Peggy Guggenheim Collection, Venice, Italy, 1961. Cat. 89
p. 10: Dan Johnson for Dan Johnson Studio. *Gazelle* lounge chair, c. 1959. Cat. 138
p. 11: Don Smith for L. Anton Maix Fabrics. *Fish Fair* textile, c. 1953. Cat. 263
p. 12: Margit Fellegi for Cole of California. Woman's swimsuit and jacket, c. 1950. Cat. 93
p. 13: Harrison McIntosh. Covered jar, 1961. Cat. 213
p. 14: Fujiye Fujikawa. *See Evil, Hear Evil, Speak to the FBI*, c. 1942. Cat. 108
p. 15: Deborah Sussman for the Los Angeles County Museum of Art. *Six More*, 1963. Cat. 280
p. 16: Levi Strauss & Co. Pants and top, c. 1955. Cat. 177

Contents

Foreword

In 1947 the acclaimed industrial designer Henry Dreyfuss asked, "Is California, where youthful thinking and new ideals are encouraged and fostered, destined to become the world's new design center?" *California Design, 1930–1965: "Living in a Modern Way"* affirms that the state did indeed become mid-century America's most important source of progressive architecture and furnishings and explores how California's innovations in consumer goods helped transform modern American life. It takes the California of our collective imagination—a democratic utopia where a benevolent climate permitted life to be led informally and largely outdoors—and demonstrates how this image was translated into a material culture that defined the era.

By the 1930s European émigrés like R. M. Schindler and Richard Neutra had established avant-garde ideas on the West Coast, and Asian and Mexican influences permeated the design culture. Two factors were fundamental to shaping the state's economic future after 1945: the population boom that continued unabated throughout the Great Depression and World War II, and the resourceful application of war-developed materials and production methods to peacetime use. The explosive growth of California's population led to an unprecedented need for housing and, with the state's distinctive embrace of the new, a burgeoning demand for "contemporary" furnishings. The heart of this exhibition focuses on the furnishing of the modern domestic interior, famously characterized by open plans and indoor/outdoor living. In addition to providing new insight into work by familiar figures such as Charles and Ray Eames, Sam Maloof, Rudi Gernreich, and Edith Heath, the exhibition introduces museum audiences to dozens of previously unheralded designers who played an integral role in creating what, in 1951, the *Los Angeles Times* called "The California Look."

The five years of research for *California Design* were directed by Wendy Kaplan, Department Head of Decorative Arts and Design, and Bobbye Tigerman, Assistant Curator. Wendy Kaplan applied the same exemplary scholarship and interpretive skills to organizing this exhibition as she did in her groundbreaking work on the Arts and Crafts movement, which culminated in a

Pierre Koenig. Bailey House (Case Study House #21), Hollywood Hills, 1958. Photo by Julius Shulman, 1959

John Kapel. Chair, c. 1958. Walnut, leather, 46¾ x 30½ x 26½ in. (118.8 x 77.5 x 67.3 cm). LACMA, Decorative Arts and Design Council Fund. See cat. 145

historic exhibition here in 2004; her deft editing of the catalogue ensures that it will be the standard reference for years to come. In the first major exhibition of her career, Bobbye Tigerman was crucial to the project's success, providing astute curatorial skills, adroit direction of the ambitious research plan, and inventive installation ideas.

While organizing this complex exhibition, the curators have significantly expanded LACMA's permanent collection of modern California design. Thanks to their determination and the support of many design aficionados, LACMA now has the preeminent assemblage of mid-century California furniture, ceramics, lighting, textiles, and industrial design. As the largest encyclopedic museum in the West, one that has long demonstrated a deep commitment to California art, LACMA is the ideal institution to house this collection and to organize the first comprehensive exhibition about California design.

California Design would not have been possible without the outstanding support of the Getty Foundation, which invited LACMA to take part in Pacific Standard Time: Art in L.A. 1945–1980. The Getty Foundation's grants funded the research and substantially contributed to the installation of the show and the publication of the catalogue; it is an honor to be part of this unprecedented collaboration of more than sixty cultural institutions across Southern California. We deeply appreciate a grant from the Henry Luce Foundation American Art Program and the generous support of Debbie and Mark Attanasio, Martha and Bruce Karsh, and LACMA's Decorative Arts and Design Council. Finally, we gratefully acknowledge Barbie, a quintessential product of mid-century California, as the lead corporate sponsor of this important exhibition.

Michael Govan
CEO and Wallis Annenberg Director
Los Angeles County Museum of Art

Corporate Sponsor's Statement

Mattel, Inc., was founded in 1945 in a Southern California garage-workshop by Ruth and Elliot Handler and Harold "Matt" Matson. Today, it is the worldwide leader in the design, manufacture, and marketing of toys and family products, with many best-selling brands, including Barbie, the most popular fashion doll ever made. The very first Barbie doll, named after the Handlers' daughter Barbara, was unveiled at the New York Toy Fair in 1959—wearing her famous black-and-white bathing suit, which was inspired by California beach culture and the sophisticated glamour of 1950s film stars. The Ken doll, Barbie's boy-friend (named after the Handlers' son), was introduced in 1961. Barbie's first Dream House came soon after, designed in a mid-century modern style with Barbie-size furniture and decorative accessories. An iconic figure, reflecting the style, trends, and architecture of the last five decades through her fashion and accessories, Barbie remains the world's most popular doll and a powerhouse brand among girls of all ages. With a rich history rooted in Southern California, the Barbie brand is thrilled to partner with the Los Angeles County Museum of Art to tell the story of California's role in shaping the design history and culture of the United States and beyond, and is proud to be the lead corporate sponsor for *California Design, 1930–1965: "Living in a Modern Way."*

Lisa McKnight
Vice President of Marketing for Barbie

Los Angeles Times
Home
★ MAGAZINE ★
OCTOBER 21, 1951

See Page 18   *Harry H. Baskerville Jr. color photo; arrangement by Richard Petterson*

IN THIS ABSTRACT ARRANGEMENT ARE THE GLOWING COLOR, ORIGINALITY OF TREATMENT AND SIMPLICITY OF DESIGN THAT TYPIFY THE CALIFORNIA LOOK.

What Makes the California Look

1

Introduction: "Living in a Modern Way"

WENDY KAPLAN

"What Makes the California Look"? asked the *Los Angeles Times*, a question so pressing it was posed on the cover of the newspaper's "Home" magazine for October 21, 1951 (1.1). The answer was so obvious that it was immediately supplied with this image and its caption: "In this abstract arrangement are the glowing color, originality of treatment and simplicity of design that typify the California look."[1]

The cover depicted the most recognized characteristic of California culture—indoor/outdoor living—and many of the objects assembled have become icons of California

1.1. "What Makes the California Look," *Los Angeles Times*, "Home" magazine, October 21, 1951, cover design. Since the state's benign climate permitted the great outdoors to be incorporated as an extended living room, the photograph highlights objects intended to be used either on a patio or in the living room: a planter by Architectural Pottery and a cord-and-metal lounge chair by Van Keppel-Green. The blurring of boundaries is emphasized with the prominently featured grill and the garden lamp, both by Hawk House, placed among the interior furnishings. New industrial materials—a fiberglass chair by Charles and Ray Eames and a plastic screen by Spencer Smilie—are displayed with traditional handicrafts, evidence of other ways that boundaries were fluid. The bright yellows, burnt oranges, and vivid greens of sunny climes prevail, as does a stripped-down, casual aesthetic that was the essence of California modern style.

The essays in this book explore how "The California Look" was established, idealized, and disseminated at mid-century. It became synonymous with a modern way of life and, as the "Home" magazine article observed, a symbol of "the willingness to experiment and be different, to solve problems in California's way."[2] Such paeans to California exceptionalism were ubiquitous until the late 1960s—one of the most oft-repeated quotations about the Golden State is writer Wallace Stegner's 1959 observation that California is "America, only more so."[3] If the United States symbolized the land of opportunity for immigrants, California was the repository of the most intense longings for reinvention. Odes to California's endless capacity for growth, inventiveness, and individuality, coupled with its rejection of conventions, permeated the popular press of the era. As industrial designer Henry Dreyfuss, who moved from New York to Pasadena in 1944, wrote three years later: "On the Pacific Coast there are fewer shackles on tradition. There is an unslackening development of new thought. There is a decided willingness to take a chance on new ideas."[4] More recently, the California dream has been exhaustively and eloquently studied by historians such as Kevin Starr; many books and innumerable articles have been devoted to the image of California and the state's history of incessant boosterism.[5]

These associations are persistent because so many of them ring true. This volume explores the California modern aesthetic, analyzing how the general qualities associated with the state (optimism and democracy, fearless experimentation, and a love of new technology) and those specific to design (an affinity for light and brilliant color, an openness to Asian and Latin influences, and an embrace of fluid spaces and cross-disciplines) made the state's best products distinctive. None of these qualities, however, was unique to California, and all had important precedents before the 1930s, when this account begins.

The characteristics now associated with the mid-century home had first developed with the Arts and Crafts movement at the turn of the last century, particularly in the work of Frank Lloyd Wright. In the Prairie houses, he created interior spaces that were not enclosed in the traditional sense. Barriers between the dining room, living room, and porch were abolished, establishing

Wendy Kaplan

1.2. Gerrit Rietveld (1888–1964). Interior, Schröder House, Utrecht, the Netherlands, 1924–25. Photo by Kim Zwarts, 2005

interpenetrating spaces and freeing the walls to define distinct areas rather than enclose them. This startling innovation became widespread with its application to the inexpensive bungalow, which, though built throughout the country, has always been associated with California. The bungalow's open interior, one-story plan, prominent porch, and overhanging roof offered the ventilation and protection from the sun appropriate to the state's climate, and its rapid assembly, affordability, and informality made it particularly well suited to a mobile society.

In the 1920s, revolutionary experiments in modern living were taking place throughout Europe and elsewhere in the United States, most famously in Germany at the Bauhaus and in Holland with the De Stijl group of architects. Gerrit Rietveld's Schröder House in Utrecht (1924–25)—with its open plan, sliding walls for flexible room configurations, built-in furniture, and large, uncurtained windows—is widely considered to be the first truly modern house (1.2). Truus Schröder's convictions about what a house should provide were prescient: "She wanted to experience consciously the changes of nature from within her own house. . . . She felt that life should be transparent and elementary," a view commonly shared by California architects and their clients twenty years later and half a world away.[6] That the defining characteristics of California design had originated decades earlier and very similar innovations

1.3. R. M. Schindler. Pauline Schindler's studio, Kings Road House, West Hollywood, 1921–22. Photo by Grant Mudford, c. 1981

1.4. A. Quincy Jones and Frederick E. Emmons, Quincy Jones House, Brentwood, 1955. Photo by Julius Shulman, 1955
The sliding glass doors, made possible by steel-frame construction, connected the kitchen and the patio. The size of the glass panels was made possible by new technology developed during World War II.

had occurred elsewhere does not negate the state's remarkable achievement. In fact, the house that architect R. M. Schindler designed for his family and another couple in West Hollywood (1.3)—with sliding canvas doors, glass panels, and gardens that functioned as unroofed living rooms—was earlier (1921–22) and arguably even more adventurous (although at the time much less known) than the indefatigably promoted Schröder House.

The utopian dreams of European modernists (at least those that pertained to the health and freedom of indoor/outdoor living) could be realized most fully in California for one simple reason—the benevolent climate—and many complex ones. Californians could actually come close to living in the open air, which was not possible for even the sturdiest Northern Europeans. (Schindler did have to enclose his rooftop "sleeping baskets," since California weather is not *always* salubrious.) With their sleeping porches, pergolas, and patios, the bungalows of the previous generation had already demonstrated the pleasure of living close to nature. What became the distinctive vocabulary of the California house and its furnishings at mid-century resulted from a natural evolution, accelerated by new construction techniques and new domestic applications for materials such as steel, which, by completely freeing the wall, allowed the floor-to-ceiling windows that made space more permeable (1.4).

1.5. Carlos Diniz for Ladd & Kelsey,
Architects. Monarch Bay Homes, Laguna
Niguel (outdoor dining terrace), 1961.
Cat. 69
**Expert delineator Carlos Diniz evoked
the casual ease of outdoor dining in a
rendering used to promote Monarch
Bay, an upscale housing development.**

The climate and the culture of California provided the ideal environment
for modernism to take root and flourish, but in its own particular way. Like
European modernism, it was functionalist, anti-ornament, and utopian in the
conviction that design and technology could transform society. California prac-
titioners, however, were committed to solutions appropriate to California. They
adhered to a looser, warmer, more ad hoc modernism, one almost exclusively
domestic in scale (1.5). Schindler's rejection from the Museum of Modern Art's
defining *Modern Architecture* exhibition of 1932 and its accompanying catalogue, *The International Style* (so influential that its title named the style),
highlights the qualities that made California different. Stung by his exclusion,
Schindler wrote to the exhibition organizers, "I am not a stylist, not a functionalist, nor any other sloganist," and he protested "rational mechanization" at the
expense of responding to particular circumstances.[7]

While embracing new technology, innovative materials, and a language of
reductive geometry, California modernists still retained the individuality of the
Arts and Crafts movement, of being particular to a place, of being joined to
nature. In contrast, the International Style by its very name was opposed to
localism, to being rooted to its surroundings, and instead championed a pre-
scription for architecture and design that would follow a universal language of

form.[8] California modernism became a different, and hugely influential, model for the rest of the country and was widely admired abroad because it reflected the way people really wanted to live (1.6).

This volume examines California modern at mid-century, particularly the furniture, ceramics, metalwork, fashion and textiles, graphic design, and industrial design that defined the California home, with architectural drawings and photographs selected to illuminate how these spaces were used. Four themes provide the leitmotifs of the book and the exhibition it accompanies: Shaping California Modern; Making California Modern; Living California Modern, and Selling California Modern. The term "California Modern" was commonly used by the 1930s. However, when a critic in the *Decorative Furnisher* described a room installed at the 1939 World's Fair in San Francisco (the Golden Gate International Exposition) as "in the new 'California Modern' style" or when the influential designer Alvin Lustig wrote an article entitled "California Modern," they were referring not to a single aesthetic but to a loose, albeit clearly recognizable, group of ideas.[9] Therefore, our overarching goal is to elucidate the 1951 quote from émigré Greta Magnusson Grossman incorporated into the title: California design "is not a superimposed style, but an answer to present conditions. . . . It has developed out of our own preference for living in a modern way."[10]

Shaping California Modern

In the 1920s boom economy, California experienced an extraordinary population growth, and these new denizens flocked to the state's urban areas, changing the image of the state as a bucolic Eden of relatively uninhabited mountains, desert, and shoreline. Los Angeles exemplified this development: the population of Los Angeles County more than doubled in the 1920s, from little more than 900,000 to over two million by the end of the decade. The county also expanded its boundaries and, with the demand for subdivided land, assumed its characteristic sprawl. By the late 1920s undeveloped space began to fill in with single-family houses and low-scale commercial buildings (1.7 and 1.8). By 1930 most Los Angeles residents lived in single-family homes (94 percent— higher than anywhere else in the country).[11] All these people needed houses and furnishings: the "Shaping" theme focuses on the 1930s because that is when buildings and products started to be made in modern ways and in modern styles. By the end of the decade, postwar paradigms about California would already be in place. As San Francisco architect Ernest Born stated in a 1941 issue of *Pencil Points* dedicated to California architecture: "One trait is evident in all our work: an unselfconscious adaptation of new architectural forms and concepts for use in informal and rational houses . . . scaled to everyday use for everyday people."[12] (See, for example, houses by Gregory Ain and George Agron [2.31] and Harwell Hamilton Harris [2.32].)

1.6. *Built in USA, 1932–1944*, Museum of Modern Art, New York, 1944. Cat. 344 **This survey of contemporary American architecture featured Bay Area architect John Funk's Heckendorf House on the cover. MoMA curator Elizabeth Mock praised the state's regional style as "amazingly fresh to a modern eye."**

WILSHIRE *and* FAIRFAX
1922

ROBERTSON BLVD.

FAIRFAX BLVD.

WILSHIRE BLVD.

WILSHIRE BLVD.

SPENCE
Air Photos
F 4041

Bringing with them a passion for experimentation and the most progressive design training, the early émigrés who came from Central Europe in the teens and 1920s (for example, Kem Weber, R. M. Schindler, Richard Neutra, and J. R. Davidson) were critically important to the formation of California modern. These seekers of new professional opportunities were joined in the 1930s by other, equally influential émigrés who had fled Nazi persecution. Particularly in Southern California, they often found patrons for their work in other émigrés— for example, Neutra with director Josef von Sternberg (see 4.2) and Davidson with writer Thomas Mann—a creative synergy made possible because, as critic Mike Davis has observed, "Since the 1920s [Los Angeles] has imported myriads of the most talented writers, filmmakers, artists and visionaries."[13] The luxurious lifestyles of successful actors also provided a steady stream of work for émigrés: Hungarian-born Paul László's obituary called him "architect to celebrities" (Cary Grant and Barbara Stanwyck were among his clients); Danish silversmith Philip Paval's self-aggrandizing account of his life was entitled *Autobiography of a Hollywood Artist.*[14]

Transplants from other parts of the United States as well as native Californians such as Millard Sheets also played a key role in defining California modern. In addition to being an architect and California's leading regionalist

Text on image: WILSHIRE and FAIRFAX 1930, WESTWOOD, ROBERTSON BLVD, OLYMPIC BLVD, SAN VICENTE BLVD, WILSHIRE BLVD, FAIRFAX BLVD, FAIRFAX BLVD

painter, Sheets was head of the Art Department at Scripps College between 1932 and 1955 (and thereafter director of the Otis Art Institute). He also directed the Art Department at the Los Angeles County Fair (1931–57), organizing annual exhibitions of California art, crafts, and design. Sheets's multifaceted career embodies many of the characteristics of California modern: the resonance of place; the development of design- and crafts-based art education to prepare students for commercial careers; and, through exhibitions such as the 1954 *Arts of Daily Living* at the county fair, the cultivation of a broad audience for design.[15]

Sheets was also director of the Federal Art Project (FAP) for Southern California, part of the New Deal government-spending program that was instrumental in pulling California out of the Great Depression. With more than 20 percent unemployment, California, like every other part of the country, was profoundly affected by the Depression, although its still prosperous oil, agriculture, and film industries ensured that it fared better than most regions. While many gained employment from the FAP, tens of thousands more found jobs with huge government infrastructure projects such as the building of the San Francisco–Oakland Bay Bridge in 1936. Projects like this were immediately incorporated into images of modern living, as on the cover of *Sunset* magazine later that year (1.9). Berkeley designer Lanette Scheeline created a fabric

1.7. Spence Air Photos. View of Wilshire and Fairfax, Los Angeles, 1922. Cat. 270

1.8. Spence Air Photos. View of Wilshire and Fairfax, Los Angeles, 1929; printed 1930. Cat. 271

decorated with views of the bridge that, placed between streamlined furnishings and her painted view of the bridge, "makes this staged photograph look like a room on San Francisco's Nob Hill."[16]

Such federal intervention was imperative: what finally succeeded in ending the Depression in California was the huge government investment in shipbuilding in the North and the airplane industry in the South to prepare the nation for the impending global conflict. After war was declared in December 1941, the FAP was refocused to support increased industrial production.[17] And very soon, millions of people came to California, where, as the Hollywood Writers Mobilization asserted, production lines were battle lines (1.10).

Making California Modern

After 1945 the United States became the world's strongest industrial, military, and cultural power. California played a key role in this development, having dominated defense and aerospace production during World War II. After the war, this escalated production had a galvanizing effect on the design and manufacture of consumer goods in the state. Fiberglass, molded plywood, wire mesh, and synthetic resins were only some of the materials developed in the early 1940s that would be imaginatively adapted to peacetime use (1.11 and see p. 5). The Cold War, the escalating U.S.-Soviet arms race that followed, and the Korean War (1950–53) ensured that the military would continue to be a crucial part of the state's economy as well as of its intellectual capital. (Again, Mike Davis provides interesting commentary: "Since the 1940s, the Southern California aerospace industry and its satellite think-tanks have assembled the earth's largest concentration of PhD scientists and engineers."[18]) However, California's material culture was shaped by the imperative to apply innovative wartime materials and production methods to peacetime use.

Charles and Ray Eames's work for the U.S. Navy in molded plywood and fiberglass, resulting in their now-legendary chairs made with these materials, is a well-known story, one recounted with new details later in this volume. But there are many other emblematic tales, and one that particularly captured the public's imagination was the flying car developed by Convair (Consolidated Vultee Aircraft) (1.12). In 1944 the industrial designer Henry Dreyfuss was brought in to work with the company's engineers on this project, a strategic effort to develop new products as the end of the war (and the contracts dependent on it) approached. Completed in 1947, the successful fiberglass design (with detachable wings for the plane) was, as Dreyfuss biographer Russell Flinchum noted, "far ahead of its time in terms of its aerodynamic envelope and efficiency." Unfortunately, the prototype was destroyed in a freak accident in 1947 and the car never went into production, but "its carryover of the wartime 'can-do' attitude into the postwar period is indicative of the aspirations, achievements, and failures in the world of design in the 1940s."[19]

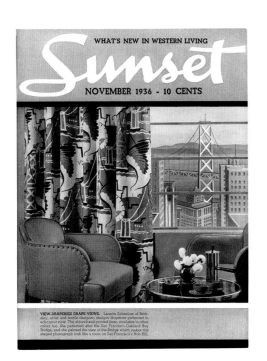

1.9. *Sunset*, November 1936, cover. Cat. 349

1.10. Chester Cobb for Division of Information, War Production Board, Office for Emergency Management. *Production Lines Are Battle Lines!*, c. 1942. Cat. 46

PRODUCTION LINES *are* BATTLE LINES!

POSTER ISSUED BY DIVISION OF INFORMATION OF W.P.B. AND O.E.M.
MATERIALS COURTESY AERO TOOL CO, BURBANK, CALIF..   DESIGNED, CONTRIBUTED BY CHES COBB OF THE
HOLLYWOOD WRITER'S MOBILIZATION..   ...   ..W.P.A. SO. CALIF. ART PROJECT

Demountable Mural by Grace Clements

PLYWOOD FOR WAR...LATER FOR PEACE

DESIGNS for post-war living will call for an ever expanding use of plywood, which today we are furnishing in vast quantities for vital military uses . . .

when war orders have been filled the George E. Ream Company, having aided step by step in the development of plywood, will continue as the prime source of supply in the Southwest.

California artists working in traditional craft media also responded to the spirit of modernism and experimentation and tried to adapt new methods of production to make their work more accessible to the new middle classes. Margaret De Patta used molds for one line of her jewelry, declaring, "I am proud of the fact that the popularly priced piece is indistinguishable from the 'one of a kind' piece" (although this claim of interchangeability was not quite true).[20] Ceramist Glen Lukens was a forceful advocate of crafts that "must harmonize with machine-made things."[21]

The concept of the designer-craftsman, though not unique to California, was most successfully realized there, particularly in ceramics. This achievement was analyzed by designer Don Wallance in his 1956 publication, *Shaping America's Products*. In his chapter "The Small Manufacturer as Designer-Craftsman," he wrote that California's ceramic production was characterized by small potteries that had frequently "grown from an artist-craftsman's experiments." He particularly praised Heath Ceramics because "the design directions pioneered by such enterprises have in turn influenced the mass produced wares of larger plants"[22] (1.13 and see 7.8).

The critic John Mullins praised Architectural Pottery, a progressive company known for its mass-produced indoor/outdoor geometric planters (seen on the

1.11. Advertisement for George E. Ream Company, Los Angeles. From *Arts and Architecture,* February 1944, p. 5

1.12. Henry Dreyfuss and Theodore P. Hall (1898–1978) for Convair. *ConvAIRCAR* Model 118
The flying-car prototype is shown during a test flight in California, November 1947.

1.13. Edith Heath for Heath Ceramics. *Coupe* dinnerware, 1947. Cat. 129

1.14. David Cressey for Architectural Pottery. *Glyph* screen wall for California state government building, Sacramento, c. 1963. Cat. 50

Los Angeles Times "Home" cover), as "one of the pioneers in this field of designer-craftsmen on a production basis." Their artist-in-residence program was cited for helping "to bridge the gap from the one-man one-object to the one-man many-objects."[23] Even though this program soon morphed into a single, successful line, David Cressey, the studio potter discussed in Mullins's article, made a wide range of work: cast production pieces, individual commissions, and something in between, such as the *Glyph* tiles illustrated in the article, which were made by pressing into a sand mold a large slab of clay that was cut at intervals to form unique patterns (1.14).

Whether handmade or industrially produced, the goal was to provide well-designed homes and furnishings for the millions of newcomers to California who craved them. The commitment of most designers and craftspeople to accommodate this was imbued with a passion that far exceeded the simple desire to earn a living. While evidence for this sense of mission can seem exaggerated in period magazines and newspapers (which might have had a vested interest in promoting this outlook), recent conversations with many of these designers and their families, as well as transcripts in the Archives of American Art and many other kinds of documentation, attest to its core truth.[24] Alvin Lustig, for example, completely embraced the ideal that well-designed objects

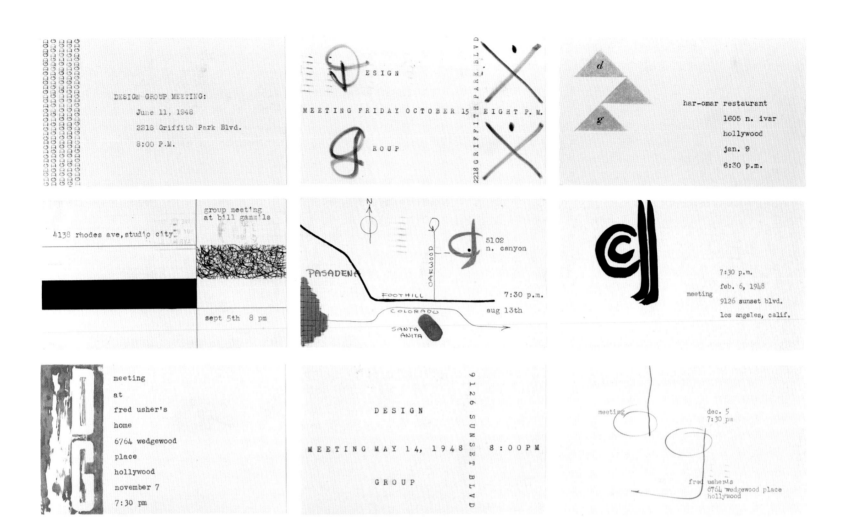

....

1.15. Frederick A. Usher Jr. Design Group invitation cards, 1947–48. Cat. 294
Inspired by the discussions in Lustig's Art Center courses, several of his students formed an extracurricular Design Group, which met monthly to share work, discuss the design process, and plan their annual exhibitions in Griffith Park.

....

1.16. Alvin Lustig. Book covers, c. 1944–45, for the New Classics series published by New Directions. Cat. 195

would function as art in everyday life. In a posthumous tribute to Lustig, *Print* magazine wrote that he had chosen to design book jackets because "he had had his great vision of a new realm of art, of a wider social role for art, which would bring it closer to each and every one of us, out of the museums into our homes and offices, closer to everything we use and see."[25] In his inspirational teaching at Art Center School, Lustig had urged his students to adapt this more holistic approach to design, and he put this philosophy to work, as did many of his followers (1.15). Beyond the design of books and their covers, he created every kind of graphic art as well as textiles and furniture (1.16 and 1.17; see endsheets, 9.8, 9.10, and 9.13)—even a helicopter. Fluidity, openness, experimentation, the abolition of boundaries: the same qualities that characterized the modern California home equally applied to the modern California designer.

Living California Modern

California design flourished in large part because of the critical need for housing— first, for the millions of workers who moved to the state to take jobs in the ship, airplane, and munitions industries during World War II. These workers urgently required housing just when materials to provide it had been severely curtailed. This challenge, however, provided opportunities for local architects,

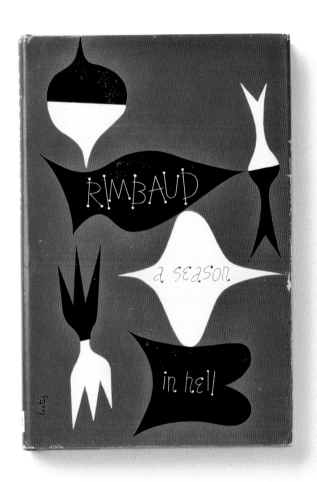

RIMBAUD a season in hell

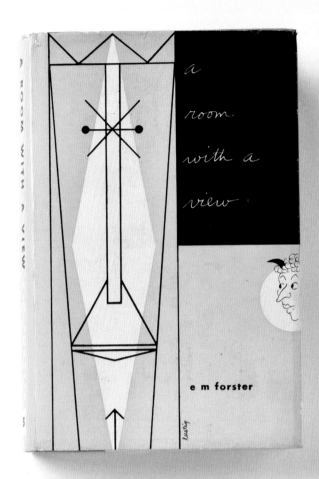

a room with a view

e m forster

a handful of dust

evelyn waugh

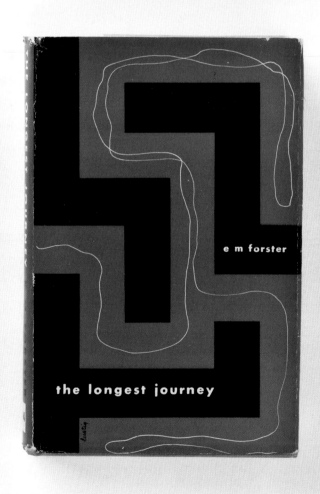

the longest journey

e m forster

1.17. Alvin Lustig. Coffee table from the Max and Fanya Finkelstein House, c. 1948. Cat. 188

....

1.18. William Wilson Wurster. Alterations to Defense Housing Project (elevations), Carquinez Heights, Vallejo, 1947. Cat. 323

Wurster designed the 1941 Carquinez Heights development in the naval town of Vallejo so that units could be easily relocated after the war. This drawing demonstrates how removing every other home could convert the densely packed workers' housing into an idyllic postwar suburb with freestanding homes and spacious yards.

....

1.19. Alvin Lustig for the Housing Authority of the City of Los Angeles. *Homes for Heroes*, 1942. Cat. 193

who were hired by government agencies such as the Farm Security Administration (FSA) and the Division of Defense Housing to come up with creative solutions to the problems (1.18 and see 4.8).[26]

Federal and local governments promised soldiers that upon their return from war, as a reward for their sacrifices to the nation, they would receive new homes with all the latest modern conveniences. The Housing Authority in Los Angeles, for example, guaranteed "Homes for Heroes"[27] (1.19). A state government report, *Postwar Housing in California* (1945), asserted that these homes should be single-family dwellings built for "people who came west to enjoy a garden or to live more out of doors."[28] And millions came to claim them, including about 850,000 returning GIs, who, as Kevin Starr observed, had experienced the allure of California when they trained there or passed through en route to the battlegrounds of the Pacific. With the subsequent baby boom, it is not surprising that "between 1940 and 1950, the population grew from 6.9 million to 10.6 million, a gain of 53%."[29] The need to accommodate these new residents was nothing short of an architectural emergency, and the prefabrication techniques and new materials developed during the war would be applied immediately to alleviate the situation.

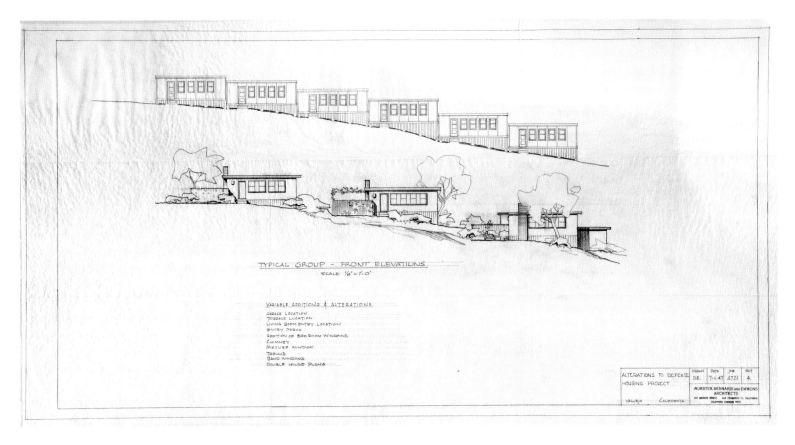

The aftermath of the war and the housing crisis is an exceptionally important topic, but it is one that has been well documented in other exhibitions and publications. What has not yet been addressed is the way this population explosion produced an attendant need for furnishings and, assisted by the GI Bill of Rights and California's exemplary state college and university system, the skills to execute them. The focus of the "Living" theme is the content of the California interior, though architecture cannot, of course, be excluded. As Virginia Stewart noted in her "Home" magazine articles, "The houses we build and the way we live in them set the pattern for our furnishings."[30] The presentation drawings, photographs, and housing brochures illustrated in this volume have been selected to highlight the way the spaces were animated rather than to provide a survey of California's architectural achievements.

For example, the kitchen in the house that A. Quincy Jones designed for his own family embodies casual living (see 1.4). The dining room is no longer a separate space, and the kitchen table was formed simply by extending the cooking range. The tableware perfectly suits this informal conflation of function, with simple single-color earthenware by Gladding McBean placed on the cotton place mats that replaced the more formal tablecloths of an earlier era. That such factory ware shared counter space with a covered jar by studio potter Marguerite Wildenhain attests to the easy commingling of all kinds of production in a California modern home. The family will sit on mass-produced steel wire and vinyl chairs by the Eameses, with an Eames fiberglass chair in the corner just like the one (but in a different color) displayed on the "Home" magazine cover (see 1.1 and 6.16). The dining area flows out to the patio through a sliding glass door, blurring the distinction between indoors and out and allowing the Joneses to keep a watchful eye on the children playing by the pool.

Pierre Koenig's Bailey House displays another kind of permeable space—between the kitchen and carport—demonstrating the new centrality of the automobile in California life (1.20). The settings at the Eames table are simple to the point of austerity, without place mats or any suggestion of decoration. This harmonizes well with the pure geometry of the steel-and-glass structure: the flowers on the table are the only nonutilitarian touch, serving as a visual link to the Architectural Pottery planters outside. (See page 20 for another view of this house.) Like most of the interiors illustrated in this volume, the Jones and Koenig images were staged for publicity purposes. This does not discount them as visual evidence, but any reader must take into account that photographs in magazines, newspapers, and company literature served as agents of persuasion—to purchase a product, a home, a lifestyle, or all three. Jones's wife, Elaine Sewell Jones, was a publicist, and she arranged for the photograph of their kitchen to be illustrated on the cover of the magazine section of the *Los Angeles Examiner*.[31]

The Bailey House was photographed as part of the famous Case Study House Program that editor John Entenza conceived and published between 1945 and 1966 in his magazine *Arts and Architecture*. The influence of these houses—low-cost prototypes made with modular, standardized parts—was enormous, not only because they were presented in one of the leading avant-garde journals of the time (and used as a sourcebook by architects in Europe as well as the United States) but also because at certain times they were open to the public.[32] Since there were only thirty-six designs (and a few of those were never built), not many people had the opportunity to live in a Case Study House and experience what architectural historian Esther McCoy considered "the answer to the need for well-designed two-bedroom houses that were easy to maintain without servants."[33]

However, successful developers—such as Joseph Eichler, who hired leading progressive architects to build more than 11,000 homes (the majority in Northern California), and Robert and George Alexander, who did the same with over 2,200 houses in the area around Palm Springs—provided moderately priced modern houses for the middle classes. Yet even though tens of thousands of people did live in the glass-walled, open-planned homes that were the subject of such intense discussion, most of what was produced in California and the rest of the country was not "modern." Then as now, progressive

1.20. Pierre Koenig. Kitchen with view to carport, Bailey House (Case Study House #21), Hollywood Hills, 1958. Photo by Julius Shulman, 1958 or 1959

architecture and design garnered the most critical attention and acclaim, but they were by no means typical of what was made. Nor did the products for these modern homes always reflect the democratic ideals espoused by Charles Eames, who declared, "[Our objective was] to get what is ultimately the most of the best to the greatest number of people for the least."[34] Many craftspeople did try to provide an alternative to expensive, one-of-a-kind pieces, but others found that producing multiples impeded their personal artistic fulfillment. And no architect or designer would turn down a special commission.

The Donnell Ranch in Sonoma exemplifies what could be achieved when a wealthy client committed to living in a modern way. The ranch is a Gesamt-kunstwerk, where the gardens, buildings, and furnishings form a completely integrated work of art. In 1948 Dewey and Jean Donnell commissioned Thomas Dolliver Church to create what historian Marc Treib considers to be "a theatre for outdoor living and a showpiece of modernity in landscape design" (1.21). Rejecting any historical precedent, the Church office—working closely with the family and responding both to the specific requirements of the site and to the influence of abstract art by Jean Arp, Joán Miró, and others—built the first kidney-shaped pool, surrounding it with biomorphic forms that dissolved any distinc-tion between the garden and the surrounding hills and marshland (1.23).[35]

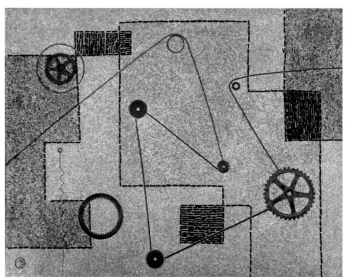

Wendy Kaplan

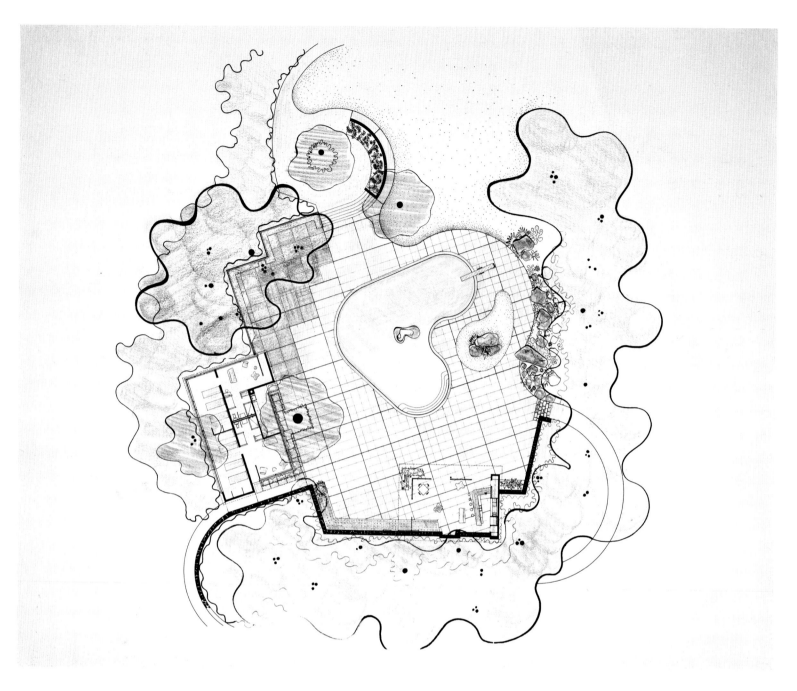

1.21. Thomas Dolliver Church. Donnell Ranch pool, Sonoma County, 1948. Photo c. 1948. Cat. 42

1.22. Margaret Bruton. Mosaic, c. 1935–40. Cat. 33
Although not one of the built-in mosaics for the Donnell Ranch, this mosaic is an excellent example of Bruton's unusual work with terrazzo.

1.23. Thomas Dolliver Church, Lawrence Halprin, and George T. Rockrise. Donnell Ranch pool, bathhouse, and lanai (plan), 1948. Cat. 43
Working in Church's office, Halprin was the project designer for the landscape architecture, and Rockrise designed the buildings around the pool.

1.24. Don Smith for James Kemble Mills. *Windmobiles* wallpaper from the bathhouse, Donnell Ranch, c. 1948. Silkscreen. Collection of Sandra Donnell and Justin Faggioli
Used in the entrance to the women's changing area in the Donnell bathhouse, this wallpaper was also displayed in the 1949 *Design in the Kitchen* exhibition at the San Francisco Museum of Art.

1939
WORLD'S FAIR
ON SAN FRANCISCO BAY

GOLDEN GATE INTERNATIONAL EXPOSITION

The structures around the pool had dressing, sleeping, and living areas with sliding glass doors and other features for easy access to the outdoors. All of their furnishings (and those for the main house, built a few years later) were specially commissioned by the Donnells from leading, mostly Northern Californian, designers and craftspeople. For example, as Jean Donnell recalled in a letter decades later, Dorothy Wright Liebes made the blinds; Peter Voulkos, the lamps; and Margaret Bruton (1.22), the terrazzo counters.[36] Don Smith's bio-morphic design for the bathhouse wallpaper (1.24) provided another link with both the shape of the pool and the sculpture by Adaline Kent that anchored it.

"Living in a modern way" could mean many things. For silent-film-star-turned-decorator William "Billy" Haines, modern meant an updated classicism that appealed to the wealthy clients who visited his Beverly Hills office. *Interiors* magazine described this showplace, furnished with sleek, richly upholstered red leather chairs, as "a design that combines working efficiency with a lush, almost regal air—the better to impress the clients with"[37] (1.26). The designer George Nelson wrote of Paul László that since his "personal taste did not include austerity . . . [he] pursued a path whose directions led towards the merger of the qualities of the old and the new."[38]

California modern encompassed a wide variety of styles and influences, particularly from Asia and Mexico. For example, the theme of the 1939 Golden Gate International Exposition (1.25) was "A Pageant of the Pacific." With extensive exhibitions of contemporary Mexican art and with Diego Rivera painting the mural *Pan American Unity* on site, the fair emphasized California's strong ties to Latin American as well as to Pacific Rim countries.[39] After the war, one of the most successful marketing campaigns (spearheaded by Harry Jackson at his chain of Jacksons furniture stores in the Bay Area) was for "Pacifica," which *House and Garden* described as "a new mood in decorating" inspired by "the islands of the Pacific and the countries bordering it."[40]

Ironically, there was a disconnect between wanting ethnic art and design in the home and accepting ethnic diversity in daily life. Latinos, Asians, and African Americans were mostly marginalized from participation in the California good life (modern or otherwise), and this is reflected in their small representation as designers and craftspeople in this volume and the exhibition it accompanies. There are several notable exceptions (including Carlos Diniz, Fujiye Fujikawa, Tony Hill [1.28], Doyle Lane [1.27], Marion Sampler, Kay Sekimachi, and Jade Snow Wong), but discriminatory practices and sentiments made success far more difficult to achieve. African Americans were generally barred from the bounty of the GI Bill, and racially restrictive housing covenants were as common in California as they were in other parts of the country.[41] Even though some developers, like Joseph Eichler, would not accept racial covenants, progressive social policy did not necessarily accompany progressive design.

1.25. Shawl, Nyeland, and Seavey. *1939 World's Fair on San Francisco Bay,* 1937. Cat. 257

1.26. William "Billy" Haines. Chair for the William Haines, Inc., conference room, 1954. Cat. 123

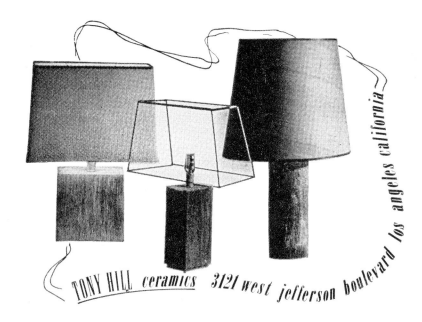

1.27. Doyle Lane. Vase, c. 1960. Cat. 161
The work of Los Angeles studio ceramist Doyle Lane was featured in exhibitions designed to raise the profile of African American artists, such as *California Black Craftsmen*, Mills College Art Gallery, 1970, as well as in broader surveys, including the *California Design* exhibitions at the Pasadena Art Museum.

1.28. Advertisement for Tony Hill from *Arts and Architecture*, January 1951, p. 42
From his studio in South Central, ceramist Tony Hill (1908–1975) promoted his line of lamps and accessories through prominent Los Angeles decorators and stores, gaining a national market through advertisements in *Designs* and *Arts and Architecture*. His success fostered that of succeeding African American artists.

1.29. *House Beautiful*, April 1951, cover. Cat. 332

Selling California Modern

Through exhibitions, newspapers and magazines, specialty and department stores, and film, California design was disseminated across the entire country as well as abroad. The idea of "selling" is so central to all the other themes that it permeates every essay in this volume. And since the final essay is dedicated to exploring this phenomenon, just a few examples demonstrating how some of the objects discussed earlier were promoted will suffice here.

The renown of the Donnell Ranch attests to the power of publications. Even though its pool and garden were enjoyed by only one family, incessant coverage in books and magazines made it hugely influential: the pool became the progenitor of free-form, kidney-shaped swimming pools throughout the country and indeed, the world. Its pride of place on the cover of *House Beautiful* (1.29) demonstrates its pervasiveness in popular American shelter magazines, and within a few years articles were written about it in France ("Jardin en Californie" in *L'Architecture d'aujourd'hui*, 1954), and it was prominently featured in international surveys such as Peter Shepheard's *Modern Gardens: Masterworks of International Garden Architecture* (London, 1954).[42]

This essay began with the alluring assemblage of "The California Look" on the cover of the *Los Angeles Times* "Home" magazine (1.30 and see 1.1). This image, arranged by ceramist and Scripps professor Richard Petterson, exemplifies the central role of exhibitions in promoting California design. Working under Millard Sheets, Petterson had organized the arts and crafts section at the 1951 Los Angeles County Fair, where many of the objects on the cover had been displayed and seen by hundreds of thousands of people. Some of these

House Beautiful

APRIL 50c

55¢ IN CANADA

objects were then included in the touring exhibition *California Crafts*. Sponsored by the American Federation of Arts, *California Crafts* was organized by Petterson and a team of jurors from the county fair, and it was shown in New York, Boston, Honolulu, and other cities in 1951–52.[43] The *Los Angeles Times* reported that still other objects illustrated in that particular issue of "Home" magazine received international exposure as part of "an exhibition of American design which is now touring Europe under government auspices to promote cultural relations."[44] The exhibition referred to was almost certainly *Design for Use, USA*, which traveled between 1951 and 1953 to many European cities, particularly in Germany. Heath dinnerware and a teapot were also included in this exhibition (see 1.13 and 7.8), as was the Van Keppel-Green lounge chair on the cover.[45] The "Home" cover demonstrates not only how California modern design was touted as the model for the good life in the state but also how it was displayed nationally and internationally, taking part in a larger Cold War initiative by the U.S. State Department to promote the American way of life with the superiority of its domestic goods.

Descriptions of California between the 1930s and the 1960s portray the state either as a larger-than-life reflection of the country as a whole or as a portent of America's future; they are usually characterized by a relentless, giddy optimism: "What America is, California is, with accents, with italics."[46] "California is the mirror of America as it will become."[47] Wallace Stegner's famous observation that California was "America, only more so" belongs to the former category and came from his account of a 1958 conference in Carmel that posed the question, "Has the West Coast an Identifiable Culture?" A serious conference attended by leading scholars and opinion makers, it was free of the overt boosterism that dominated so much of the popular press, yet its conclusion was much the same. Stegner summarized the views of everyone there: "Contribute regionally to the national culture? We *are* the national culture, at its most energetic end."[48]

In 1962 California surpassed New York as the country's most populous state, and by 1967 it had the world's sixth-largest economy. But confidence in an untrammeled destiny would soon be shaken by regional and national upheavals. Opposition to the Vietnam War and the escalating struggle for civil rights were by no means unique to California, but the Free Speech Movement at Berkeley (1964–65) and the Watts Riots in 1965 were galvanizing events that resonated throughout the country. They reinforced the belief that California was a microcosm of the nation and cast doubt on the future of both.

These traumas contributed to the growth of a counterculture sensibility that would profoundly affect California modernism. While the counterculture belief in the primacy of individual expression would lead to extraordinarily creative objects, it would also erode the designer-craftsman ideal of working with

The Cover

IDENTIFICATION of the articles appearing in the cover photo and their designers appears below. Numbers in the text refer to the numbers on the reproduction of the cover photo at the top of this column.

Several of the ceramic articles and fabrics shown in this issue of Home Magazine have been selected for a traveling exhibition of California crafts by the American Federation of Arts. This exhibition will be shown in New York City, Boston, Honolulu, Stanford University and other cities during 1951 and 1952. In addition, other articles illustrated here have been selected for an exhibition of American design which is now touring Europe under government auspices to promote cultural relations.

1, 2—Cord and metal lounge chair and ottoman designed and manufactured by Hendrick Van Keppel and Taylor Green of Beverly Hills.

3, 4—Brazier with skewers on rack, and garden candle lamp by Stanley Hawk of Los Angeles.

5—Tufted rug by Joseph Blumfield of Los Angeles.

6—Architectural planting pot by John Follis and Rex Goode of Pasadena.

7—Molded plastic and fiberglas lounge chair by Charles Eames of Venice.

8—Curved plastic screen designed and made by Spencer Smilie of Los Angeles.

9—Hand-woven drapery by Maria Kipp of Los Angeles.

10—Drapery fabric designed and hand woven by Alfred Richard Barkley of Beverly Hills.

11—Drapery fabric designed and woven by Maxwell Hawker of Beverly Hills.

12—"Walking Cats" and

13—"Caged," drapery fabrics designed and hand printed by Eric Erickson of Los Angeles.

14—Stick drapery designed and woven by William Webb of Pasadena.

15—On the shelf, ceramic salt shakers, Rupert Deese, Claremont; animal, John Caruthers of Los Angeles; martini mixer by Deese.

16—Shelf contains ceramic bottle by Harry McIntosh of Claremont; covered dish by Harold D. Strawn of Los Angeles.

17—On this shelf, fish (ceramic sculpture) by John Caruthers.

18—Shelf contains silver water pitcher by Allan Adler of Beverly Hills; porcelain tableware by Gabriel of Pasadena; square crystal and gold plate by Alice Petterson of Claremont.

19—Shelf holds ceramic bottle by Marc Hancon of Van Nuys; ash tray by Deese; crystal plate by Alice Petterson; silver flatware by Lewis A. Wise.

20—Blue bowl by Harry McIntosh; bowl by Don Schaumburg of Claremont; enamelware by El-lamarie Woolley of San Diego.

21—Footed pot by Laura Andreson of Los Angeles, and three other ceramic pieces by John Polikowsky of Claremont.

1.30. Key to the "What Makes the California Look" cover, *Los Angeles Times*, "Home" magazine, October 21, 1951

industry to improve furnishings for middle-class consumption. Most important of all, the idea of consumption itself was called into question.

In 1976 Stegner wrote another, more ambivalent variant of his famous aphorism: "Like the rest of America, California is unformed, innovative, ahistorical, hedonistic, acquisitive, and energetic—only more so." He bemoaned the ecological fallout of unbridled ambition: "Having welcomed unlimited growth, the state has the most acute growth problems anywhere."[49] The greatest number of freestanding single-family houses in the country resulted in uncontrollable sprawl; the highest automobile ownership per capita in the world produced asphyxiating smog.

These consequences, however, do not diminish the profound and lasting contributions of California design at mid-century, nor the real achievements resulting from its democratic ideals. The period between 1930 and 1965 was one of exhilarating innovation, and the objects in this survey tell that story. The 1930s set the stage for a uniquely Californian manifestation of "living in a modern way." After 1945 a burgeoning, newly prosperous population—intoxicated by the power to purchase after the deprivation of the Great Depression and the wartime rationing of goods—turned the state into America's most important center for progressive architecture and furnishings, influencing how people lived across the nation and around the globe.

The poster for a movie about two American surfers traveling the world is both emblematic and, coming at the very end of our period, elegiac (1.31). Surfing is a quintessential California activity, arising from the matchless weather, proximity to Hawaii (where the sport originated), and the development of fiberglass technology during World War II. For millions of people, California represented "The Endless Summer," and the poster's promise of "that perfect wave which may be forming just over the next Horizon" provides an apt metaphor for the entire state.

1.31. John Van Hamersveld for Bruce Brown Films. *The Endless Summer,* poster designed 1963, printed 1965. Cat. 297

The Endless Summer

On any day of the year it's summer somewhere in the world. Bruce Brown's latest color film highlights the adventures of two young American surfers, Robert August and Mike Hynson who follow this everlasting summer a-round the world. Their unique expedition takes them to Senegal, Ghana, Nigeria, South Africa, Australia, New Zealand, Tahiti, Hawaii and California. Share their experiences as they search the world for that perfect wave which may be forming just over the next Horizon. **BRUCE BROWN FILMS**

NOTES

I am greatly indebted to Staci Steinberger and Jennifer Munro Miller for their invaluable assistance with research for this essay and to Debbie Attanasio for her meticulous review of the text.

1   *Los Angeles Times*, "Home" magazine, October 21, 1951, cover.

2   Virginia Stewart, "The California Look," ibid., 6.

3   Wallace Stegner, "The West Coast: Region with a View," in Wallace Stegner, *One Way to Spell Man* (New York: Doubleday, 1982), 108. This essay was first published in the journal *Saturday Review*, May 2, 1959.

4   Henry Dreyfuss, "California: World's New Design Center," *Western Advertising*, June 1947, 60.

5   Kevin Starr, *Endangered Dreams: The Great Depression in California* (New York: Oxford University Press, 1996). Kevin Starr, *The Dream Endures: California Enters the 1940s* (New York: Oxford University Press, 1997). Kevin Starr, *Embattled Dreams: California in War and Peace, 1940–1950* (New York: Oxford University Press, 2002). Kevin Starr, *Golden Dreams: California in an Age of Abundance, 1950–1963* (New York: Oxford University Press, 2009). See also Kirse Granat May, *Golden State, Golden Youth: The California Image in Popular Culture, 1955–1966* (Chapel Hill: University of North Carolina Press, 2002).

6   Bertus Mulder and Ida van Zijl, *Rietveld Schröder House* (New York: Princeton Architectural Press, 1999), 6.

7   Schindler, quoted in August Sarnitz, *R. M. Schindler, Architect: 1887–1953* (New York: Rizzoli, 1988), 209. The correspondence between Schindler and Philip Johnson, co-curator of the *Modern Architecture* exhibition at MoMA, is reprinted in Sarnitz's book.

8   For more on this argument, see Wendy Kaplan, "Building Utopia: Pioneer Modernism on the American West Coast," in *Modernism in Design*, ed. Paul Greenhalgh (London: Reaktion, 1990), 101–23.

9   "Decorative Art at the Golden Gate International Exhibition," *Decorative Furnisher*, April 1939, 25. Alvin Lustig, "California Modern," *Designs*, October 1947, 7–10.

10 Grossman, quoted in Rose Henderson, "A Swedish Furniture Designer in America: An Interview with Greta Magnusson Grossman," *American Artist*, December 1, 1951, 56.

11 Michael Dear, "Peopling California," in *Made in California: Art, Image, and Identity, 1900–2000*, exh. cat., ed. Stephanie Barron (Los Angeles: Los Angeles County Museum of Art; Berkeley: University of California Press, 2000), 56.

12 Born, quoted in Charles Magruder, "Words about California," *Pencil Points*, May 1941, 292.

13 Mike Davis, *City of Quartz: Excavating the Future in Los Angeles* (New York: Vintage Books, 1992), 17.

14 "Paul László, 93, Dies; Architect to Celebrities," *New York Times*, April 8, 1993, D20; Philip Paval, *Autobiography of a Hollywood Artist* (Hollywood: Gunther Press, 1968).

15 Sheets also designed more than forty buildings in Los Angeles and was the author of many books, particularly about the culture of Mexico. See Janice Lovoos and Edmund F. Penney, *Millard Sheets: One-Man Renaissance* (Flagstaff, Ariz.: Northland Press, 1984). For more on Sheets's role as an educator, see Paul J. Karlstrom, "Art School Sketches: Notes on the Central Role of Schools in California Art and Culture," in Stephanie Barron et al., *Reading California: Art, Image, and Identity, 1900–2000* (Los Angeles: Los Angeles County Museum of Art; Berkeley: University of California Press, 2000), 97–98, 102–3.

16 *Sunset*, November 1936, cover. See also "What's New in Western Living" in this issue, 13.

17 Bruce Bustard, *A New Deal for the Arts* (Washington, D.C.: National Archives and Records Administration, 1997), 126–27.

18 Davis, *City of Quartz*, 17.

19 Russell Flinchum, *Henry Dreyfuss, Industrial Designer: The Man in the Brown Suit*, exh. cat. (New York: Cooper-Hewitt Museum, Smithsonian Institution; Rizzoli, 1997), 96–97.

20 Margaret De Patta, "De Patta," *Arts and Architecture*, July 1947, 30.

21 Glen Lukens, "The New Handcraftsman," *California Arts and Architecture*, December 1934, 13.

22 Don Wallance, *Shaping America's Products* (New York: Reinhold Publishing Company, 1956), 93.

23 John Mullins, "From the Craftsmen," unidentified clipping, c. 1964, 17. This clipping comes from David Cressey's personal notebook, copy in LACMA's Decorative Arts and Design Department research files.

24 Since this project began in 2006, the curators have had many discussions with designers and their families about this issue, including Louis Danziger, Elaine Lustig Cohen (widow of Alvin Lustig), and Eames Demetrios and Lucia Dewey Atwood (Charles and Ray Eames's grandchildren). See also: Paul László, "Designing with Spirit," interview by Marlene L. Laskey, 1984–85, Oral History Program, University of California, Los Angeles; Max and Rita Lawrence, "A Better World through Good Design," interview by Teresa Barnett, 2000, Oral History Program, University of California, Los Angeles; Merry Renk, "Oral History Interview with Merry Renk," interview by Arline M. Fisch, January 18–19, 2001, Archives of American Art, Smithsonian Institution.

25 James Laughlin, "Book Jackets of Alvin Lustig," *Print*, October 1956, 52.

26 Greg Hise, "Building Design as Social Art: The Public Architecture of William Wurster, 1935–50," in *An Everyday Modernism: The Houses of William Wurster*, exh. cat., ed. Marc Treib (San Francisco: San Francisco Museum of Modern Art; Berkeley: University of California Press, 1995), 146.

27 For analysis on the effects of the war, see Donald Albrecht, ed., *World War II and the American Dream: How Wartime Building Changed a Nation*, exh. cat. (Washington, D.C.: National Building Museum; Cambridge, Mass.: MIT Press, 1995). See especially Donald Albrecht, "Introduction," xvii–xxiii, and Peter S. Reed, "Enlisting Modernism," 2–41. For promises that companies made to soldiers and civilians about the material abundance that awaited them after the war, see John Morton Blum, *V Was for Victory: Politics and American Culture during World War II* (New York: Harcourt Brace Jovanovich, 1976).

28 Starr, *Embattled Dreams*, 205.

29 Ibid., 193–94.

30 Stewart, "California Look," 6.

31 "Pictorial Living," *Los Angeles Examiner*, March 31, 1957, cover. The magazine is part of the publicity notebooks compiled by Elaine Sewell Jones, now in the collection of Steve Cabella. I am grateful for his generosity in sharing his research materials.

32 Reyner Banham, "Klarheit, Ehrlichkeit, Einfachkeit . . . and Wit Too! The Case Study Houses in the World's Eyes," in *Blueprints for Modern Living: History and Legacy of the Case Study Houses*, exh. cat. (Los Angeles: Museum of Contemporary Art; Cambridge, Mass.: MIT Press), 183–95, especially 186–89.

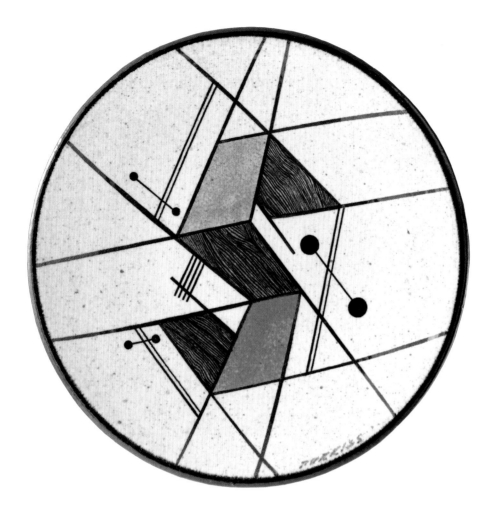

1.32 Myrton Purkiss. Plate, c. 1950. Cat. 235

33 Esther McCoy, "Remembering John Entenza," in *Arts and Architecture: The Entenza Years,* ed. Barbara Goldstein (Santa Monica: Hennessey and Ingalls, 1998), 13.

34 Charles Eames made similar declarations many times in his career. This variant was taken from the transcript of an interview with Charles and Ray Eames on the television show *Discovery*, produced by the San Francisco Museum of Art for KPIX, a CBS affiliate, aired December 17, 1953. Charles Eames and Ray Eames Papers, box 7, Manuscript Division, Library of Congress, Washington, D.C. I am grateful to Daniel Ostroff for sharing this research.

35 Marc Treib, *The Donnell and Eckbo Gardens: Modern Californian Masterworks* (San Francisco: William Stout, 2005), 17 and 16–97.

36 Jean Donnell to her daughter Nancy Donnell (Lilly), May 31, 1974. Courtesy of Sandy Donnell.

37 O.G., "Haines Headquarters," *Interiors*, December 1949, 74.

38 George Nelson, introduction to *Paul László, Industrial Designer A.S.I.D*, n.d. This is one of

three volumes that László self-published, each with an introduction by a leading designer; copies on file in the LACMA library.

39 *Golden Gate International Exposition San Francisco: 1940 Official Art Catalogue* (n.p.: Recorder Printing and Publishing Co., H. S. Crocker Co., Schwabacher-Frey Co., n.d.), 105–9.

40 "Pacifica: A New Mood in Decorating," *House and Garden*, April 1952, 99.

41 Restrictive covenants were "agreements between buyers and sellers of property, which took the form of an appendix or article in the deed not to sell, rent, or lease property to minority groups, usually blacks, but also, depending on the part of the country, Jews, Chinese, Mexicans, or any non-Caucasians." Michael Jones-Correa, "The Origins and Diffusion of Racial Restrictive Covenants," *Political Science Quarterly*, Winter 2000–2001, 541–68.

42 Treib, *Donnell and Eckbo Gardens*, 83, 84, 97.

43 "Home" magazine, 18 (key to cover illustration). That this tour did take place is confirmed in the brochure *American*

Federation of Arts Traveling Exhibitions, 1951–52, archives of the AFA, New York.

44 "Home" magazine, 18.

45 Gay McDonald, "The Advance of American Postwar Design in Europe: MoMA and the Design for Use, USA Exhibition 1951–1953," *Design Issues*, Spring 2008, 15–27. For Heath ceramics at this exhibition, see Charles L. Venable et al., *China and Glass in America, 1880–1980: From Tabletop to TV Tray*, exh. cat. (Dallas: Dallas Museum of Art; New York: Abrams, 2000), 482.

46 This statement by journalist Farnsworth Crowder is quoted in Carey McWilliams, *Southern California Country: An Island on the Land* (New York: Duell, Sloan and Pearce, 1946), 370.

47 "California: A State of Excitement," *Time*, November 7, 1969, 60.

48 Stegner, "West Coast," 106.

49 Stegner, quoted in Philip L. Fradkin, *Wallace Stegner and the American West* (New York: Knopf, 2008), 154.

2

The Rise of California Modern Design, 1930–41

CHRISTOPHER LONG

In September 1929, barely a month before the stock market crash, Bullock's Wilshire department store opened in Los Angeles. The gleaming new temple of commerce—"it is a sacrilege," one critic wrote, "to call it a store"—bore witness to California's ambitions and confidence.[1] It also presented a powerful image of the new modern design. Many noted artists provided works, among them Sonia Delaunay, Léon Jallot, and Herman Sachs, but the store's lavish interiors were mostly the work of designer Jock D. Peters, who collaborated with decorator Eleanor Le Maire and others.[2]

2.1. Jock D. Peters. Sportswear department in Bullock's Wilshire, with the mural *The Spirit of Sports*, by Gjura Stojano. Photo by the Mott Studios, 1929

Peters was born in Germany and trained as a stonemason before going to work for architect Peter Behrens in Berlin. He arrived in Los Angeles in 1923, and for a time he worked as an architect and art director for the Famous Players–Lasky Corporation (later Paramount Pictures). Chafing under the restrictions of the studio system, he left in 1927 to start his own design firm with his brother George. They called their firm Peters Brothers Modern American Design,[3] but most of their work still drew from European—especially German and French—precedents. Peters's sumptuous interiors for Bullock's, which included an intricate inlaid table in the sportswear department (2.2), restated the geometric forms of the prewar German Jugendstil and postwar French modernized classicism. Peters also borrowed from an array of other sources—from the visual ideas of Frank Lloyd Wright to the pure, undisguised lines of the Bauhaus masters. His penchant for the language of the new age was on display everywhere. Most impressive, perhaps, was the great room of the sportswear department—featuring an enormous mural, *The Spirit of Sports*, created by Serbian-born artist Gjura Stojano—which conveyed the energy and dynamism of the best of 1920s design (2.1). But absent was the imprint of a specifically Californian aesthetic. What Peters forged in Bullock's was a transplanted modernism: he had installed the new style in California, but it was not yet *of* California.

Peters was by no means alone: at the end of the 1920s, the handful of modernist designers working in Southern California and the Bay Area were still searching for ways to express the special conditions and culture of California—its mild climate, its relaxed and informal lifestyle, its deep influences from Mexico and East Asia, its pervasive optimism. All that would change in little more than a decade: by the time the United States entered World War II, California would emerge as one of the most important generators of modernist design, and it would become the laboratory for a new aesthetic, one that was vibrant, original, and distinctive. Through their probings of daily existence, the California modernists would remake the entire setting for contemporary living, recasting everything from tableware to the house itself. And that new design, in the years after World War II, would have a decisive impact on the course of modernism around the world.

Many of the early founders of the new California modernism were, like Peters, recent immigrants from Central Europe. One of the first arrivals was Kem Weber (born Karl Emanuel Martin Weber, in Germany). Weber, too, had come from a crafts background: he had trained as a cabinetmaker in Berlin, but he went on to study architecture with Bruno Paul at the Berlin Unterrichts-Anstalt des königlichen Kunstgewerbe-Museums (Royal School of Applied Arts). He arrived in the United States in the summer of 1914 to oversee construction of the German pavilion at the Panama-Pacific International Exposition in San Francisco, planned for the following year. When World War I erupted in Europe, Weber was unable to return home. He opened a studio in San

2.2. Jock D. Peters. Table from Bullock's Wilshire department store, Los Angeles, c. 1929. Cat. 231

Francisco, and later in Berkeley, but found little interest in modern design; after several years of eking out a living with odd jobs, he moved to Santa Barbara. For a time, he had success crafting period furniture and interiors for wealthy families there and in nearby Montecito, but in 1921 he moved to Los Angeles, lured by an offer from Barker Brothers, then the largest furniture retailer in the United States, to serve as the store's chief designer.[4]

From the start, Weber hoped to introduce modern design to the store. But in the early 1920s, Californians, like Americans in general, were still wedded to historical styles, and Weber was forced to rely on his designs for Spanish colonial and other revivalist idioms. Finally, in 1926, he convinced the store's owners to allow him to open a "modern department" on the third floor of Barker's eleven-story building in downtown Los Angeles. The new "store-within-a-store," which Weber christened "Modes and Manners," became the first outlet for modern furniture and accessories in Southern California and one of the first such shops in the country (2.3).[5]

The opening of "Modes and Manners" came precisely at the moment when interest in Art Moderne, awakened by the 1925 Paris Exposition Internationale des Arts Décoratifs et Industriels Modernes, was beginning to gain a foothold in the United States. What Weber presented was a restated version of the jagged forms, startling colors, and frenzied patterns that had dominated the Paris exposition. Barker Brothers made most of the pieces at its sprawling twenty-acre factory and warehouse complex in East Los Angeles.[6] After launching the new department, Weber continued to churn out scores of designs. By the end of 1927, however, weary of having to advocate for his ideas with the store's management, he left and opened his own design studio in Hollywood.

At the time, only a few other local architects and designers were working in a modernist vein. In the late 1910s and 1920s Frank Lloyd Wright undertook a number of projects in Southern California, developing a Maya-inspired aesthetic based on his newly invented system of precast concrete blocks, molded with his own geometric designs.[7] More important for shaping a distinctively Californian modernist aesthetic, though, was the work of his son Lloyd, who had moved to San Diego in 1911. A few years later he relocated to Los Angeles, and after assisting his father with his projects there, he began to pursue his own commissions. Lloyd's fantastical designs for the Sowden and Navarro Houses, both completed in 1927, presented an arresting blend of the new Art Deco and European functionalism. Far more influential than the specific forms of his early designs, however, was his attitude toward the outdoors and the landscape. His houses, and later his commercial buildings, such as the Yucca-Vine Market (1928), embraced the ideals of openness, transparency, and plein air living that would become indispensable ingredients of the new California lifestyle.[8]

Another important early modernist was R. M. Schindler. After studying with Otto Wagner and Adolf Loos in his native Vienna, Schindler had worked for Frank Lloyd Wright in Chicago for nearly five years before arriving in Los Angeles in 1920 to supervise construction of Wright's Hollyhock House for Aline Barnsdall on Olive Hill.[9] Soon he opened his own practice, and one of his first projects, his own house on Kings Road (1921–22) in what is now West Hollywood, charted a novel direction (see 1.3). Inspired by the area's mild climate, Schindler sought to reduce the separation between indoor and exterior space, merging the two into an almost seamless zone for living. Despite his use of massive concrete slab walls, which were poured on the ground and tilted into place, he managed—through the imposition of a series of wood-framed sliding doors (their form borrowed in part from traditional Japanese design) and outdoor "rooms," complete with fireplaces—to erode the barrier between inside and out. Schindler also fashioned the house's minimal furnishings, which relied on a simple planar vocabulary, reiterating Wright's basic forms as well as the lines of Constructivism and De Stijl. But Schindler's goal was to forge an indigenous California modernism. Years afterward, he wrote: "My early realization that a house is not an international but a local product meant for local use, lead [*sic*] towards the exploration of the character of California. Therefore I abandoned the 'modern' as imported from Europe . . . and tried to develop a contemporary expression of California."[10]

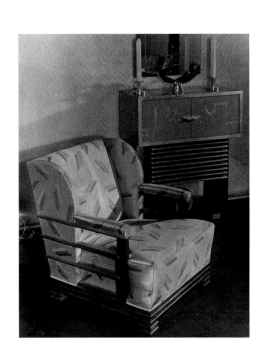

2.3. Kem Weber. "Modes and Manners" showroom, Barker Brothers, Los Angeles. Photo c. 1926

Though Schindler's Kings Road House went mostly unnoticed at the time, it established what would become the ground rules for much of the new California design: its focus became the single-family house and the small shop or office, and the preoccupation of its makers became the investigation of a relaxed mode of living and working, a way to enhance, expand, and ultimately redefine leisure. Throughout the 1920s Schindler would pursue the notion of a specifically Californian modernism. But he also explored the possibilities of a language of complex geometries, relying more and more on jutting, angular forms, as in his interior for the Henry Braxton Gallery (1928–29) in Los Angeles (2.4).

With a little more than a million inhabitants, Los Angeles in the late 1920s was already a large city in terms of population. But the rapid expansion of the suburbs meant that much of the industry, business, and housing in the Los Angeles basin lay outside the urban core, spread over an enormous area.[11] Many of the new modernists' clients came from the film industry—especially recent transplants from New York and from the English, French, and German colonies of actors, writers, producers, and technicians who had been lured to the city by the promise of work. Yet as late as 1929 finding modern design in California was still challenging. Aside from Barker Brothers and the tiny number of modernist architects, designers, and craftspeople who worked for individual clients—most of them in downtown Los Angeles or in Hollywood (and an even smaller number in the Bay Area)—there were few outlets for the new aesthetic. When the movie studio executive Glendon Allvine and his wife, Louise, decided to build and furnish their own modern house in Long Beach (on a trip to Paris in 1927, they had discovered the work of Le Corbusier and Robert Mallet-Stevens), they were unable to find the modern furnishings they wanted on the West Coast. To assemble the interiors of their new house in 1929, they turned instead to New York designers, acquiring pieces and fabrics from Jules Bouy, Donald Deskey, Paul T. Frankl, Ruth Reeves, and Walter von Nessen.[12]

The situation changed as Peters, Weber, and Schindler gained visibility and commissions. Several other Los Angeles–based young designers also started to draw attention. Richard Neutra, another Viennese émigré who, like Schindler, had studied with Loos and worked in Frank Lloyd Wright's office (in Neutra's case, for only a few months), opened a joint office with Schindler in 1926.[13] But he also pursued his own projects, among them a house in Los Angeles for the health columnist and naturopath Philip Lovell. Neutra was one of the earliest advocates in California of the concept of applying industrial materials and finishes to his houses. His Lovell Health House (1927–29) reflected this interest: it was among the first steel-framed houses in the United States and an early example of the use of gunite, or sprayed-on concrete. In another example of the possibilities of industrial production, Neutra positioned two Ford Model A headlights in the house's main stairwell, and he employed factory-made metal window assemblies throughout.[14]

2.4. R. M. Schindler. Henry Braxton Gallery, Los Angeles, 1928–29. Photo by Ernest M. Pratt and Viroque Baker

Neutra's ability to experiment with new forms and construction methods owed much to the fact that in California he came across, as he later wrote, "people who were more 'mentally footloose' than those elsewhere."[15] The other early modernists also found surprising acceptance for their ideas and works at a time when their counterparts in other regions of the country faced difficulty in locating willing clients.

Not all of those working in Los Angeles at the time, however, were as committed to forging a local idiom. J. R. Davidson, another recent immigrant, was much more closely wedded—at least in his early career—to European modernism. Born in Germany, he had spent time in Paris, London, and New York before arriving in Southern California in 1923.[16] Davidson's aesthetic sensibility had been strongly shaped by his work on sophisticated Parisian interiors: what he developed in his residential and commercial projects was a sleek, refined look dependent on flush details, indirect lighting, and polished contemporary materials.[17] The Bachelors' Haberdashery in Los Angeles, which he designed in 1935, for example, featured panels of Makassar ebony set into aluminum frames, brown and tan carpeting laid in strips, and high-quality pigskin upholstery (2.5). It was suave and urbane, but it was an aesthetic that was, in most respects, more in tune with European and East Coast design than the California reality.

In the early 1930s that charge could still be leveled at many of the California designers. By 1933, though, Schindler and Weber in particular (Peters, who had long been in poor health, died the following year) had begun to probe the idea of a more informal and relaxed style. Throughout this time, Schindler continued his experiments with simple planar forms, using long, straight redwood, birch, or plywood boards to fashion furniture and various built-ins for his buildings. Weber, too, investigated the possibilities of casual, unaffected furniture, developing his *Bentlock* line, which did away with traditional mortise-and-tenon joints and relied instead on rounded-over, machine-made members, bolstered with an oval spline of solid wood.

By then Weber had influenced the new California design in another way: he was the first on the West Coast to introduce the idea of streamlining—the application of smooth, rounded forms to furniture and other objects. His initial attempt had come in 1928, with the apartment he designed for John Bissinger in San Francisco (2.6). The chairs and beds he created for the bedroom, with a clarified design vocabulary that relied on soft, curving lines, encapsulated his new style, one that was eloquent and sophisticated.

The idea of streamlining had grown out of contemporary research in aviation and ballistics, which sought to make aerodynamic shapes that would move through the air efficiently. Most of the early adherents of streamlined design— Norman Bel Geddes, Donald Deskey, Raymond Loewy, and Walter Dorwin Teague—were based in New York, but Weber and soon others working in California adopted it. It was a stylistic idiom particularly well suited to the

2.5. J. R. Davidson. The Bachelors' Haberdashery, Los Angeles, 1935. Photo by Will Connell, 1935

2.6. Kem Weber. Bedroom, Bissinger Apartment, San Francisco, c. 1928

Southern California landscape. The visual representation of speed captured the realities of the new automobile culture: on the nearly endless boulevards of the Los Angeles region, the appearance of innumerable low horizontal buildings, with smooth, rounded surfaces, underscored the flowing rhythms of a changing lifestyle. The sweeping forms became a hallmark of Hollywood set designs as well as of common household objects—some useful, some not.

In about 1935 the Opco Company in Los Angeles debuted its ice gun (2.7). Patterned after the ray guns in the *Buck Rogers* comic strip (a spring-loaded trigger crushed a single ice cube and forced it through a hole in the bottom), it introduced the new style to the cocktail hour. Another example of these streamlined designs was one of the first digital clocks, the *Zephyr*, made by the Lawson Time company in Pasadena, in about 1938 (2.8). Not only did its rounded form suggest the flow of time, but, as one of the company's advertisements announced, its numerical readout enhanced legibility: "*Exact* time at a glance. Here is modern time . . . No hands pointing uncertainly. No old-fashioned faces with hard-to-see calibrations . . . streamlined for instant perception."[18]

The impress of streamlining was manifest, too, in one of California's most recognizable products: the Oscar statuettes awarded annually, beginning in 1929, by the Academy of Motion Picture Arts and Sciences (2.9). The design

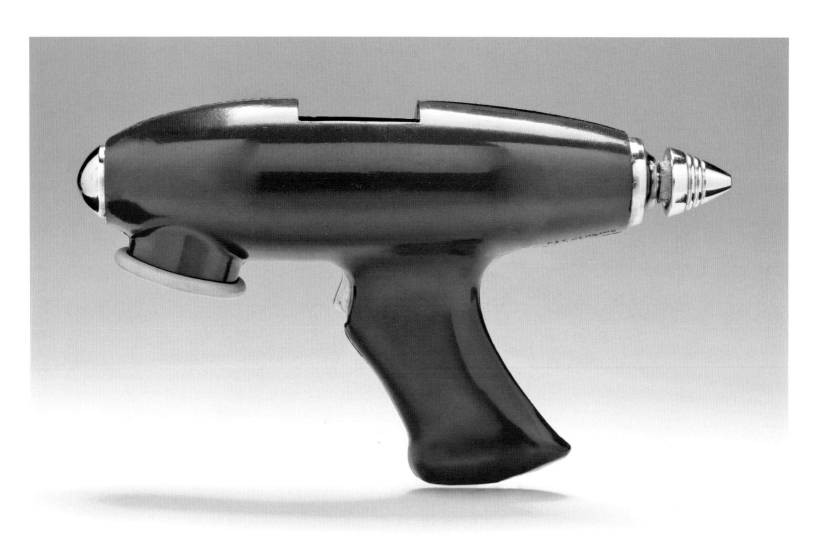

2.7. Opco Company. Ice gun, c. 1935.
Cat. 226

2.8. Lawson Time. *Zephyr* clock, c. 1938.
Cat. 167

The form and the mostly metal housing
of the *Zephyr* clock drew from streamlined airplanes and trains of the 1930s,
but its sleek lines also suggested a new
relationship to time, one tied to efficiency and rapid change.

was the work of Cedric Gibbons. Gibbons was among the most important tastemakers in Hollywood: as art director for hundreds of films, including *Grand Hotel* (1932) and *The Thin Man* (1934), which featured dramatically lit spaces, luxurious materials, and sharp, uncluttered lines, he helped to invent and disseminate to the world the image of modern Hollywood style and refinement. He responded to the Academy's request for a suitable award with a statuette of a streamlined knight standing on a reel of film gripping a crusader's sword—an unmistakable depiction of the strength of the motion picture industry and, by virtue of its smooth, machined surfaces, its embrace of modernity.

The new streamlined aesthetic also had a decided influence on furniture and interior designers throughout the 1930s—even those working in a more hard-edged modernism. Neutra, for example, merged elements of streamlining with the new International Style. But his reliance on minimal forms and industrial materials, including prefabricated metal parts and assemblies, remained an exception at the time. More common was the approach taken by Weber, who sought to foster the look of the machine age without relying on modern materials or radical reduction. Weber's *Airline* chair, designed in about 1934–35, gives the appearance of speed, taking its contours from contemporary aircraft design, even though it was constructed mostly of wood and with traditional methods (2.10). Yet the *Airline* chair offered a novel solution to furniture design in another way: it was among the earliest examples—if not the first—of furniture intended to be sold disassembled (it came in a box roughly three feet by three feet by eight inches); the customer could put it together at home without any construction knowledge or special tools.[19] To ease the task of assembly, Weber reduced the chair to a few simple parts: two leg frames, consisting of four wooden pieces, with eased-over edges, glued together with dowels; back and front wood supports, which connected the two leg frames; and an adjustable leather seat, which was affixed to the rear bar with straps. It was such a revolutionary departure from what had come before that it was too advanced for the marketplace, and Weber was unable to find a manufacturer to mass-produce it; in the end, only a few hundred were ever made.[20]

For many California designers, streamlining became simply a means to foster an immediate impression—a sort of visual shorthand of the new age. Some, though, were more innovative than others. Davidson designed an end table and lamp in about 1940 that make use of the usual softened outlines (2.11), though the table lacks the rigorous formal compression—the stripping away of both materials and mass—that typifies Neutra's or Weber's best works. Even those, like Schindler, who generally did not rely on streamlining in their work occasionally made recourse to it. A chair he designed for Sardi's Restaurant in Hollywood, for instance, presents a stripped-down, futuristic silhouette (2.12). Like the Opco ice gun, the banded armrests drew from science fiction cartoons and one-reelers—as if the chair itself offered a glimpse of things to come.[21]

2.9. Cedric Gibbons, designer, and George M. Stanley, sculptor. Academy Award of Merit statuette, 1927–28. Cat. 113
Cedric Gibbons won this award for his art direction of *The Bridge of San Luis Rey* (1929).

Schindler's design discloses another feature of much of California design in the 1930s: a complex, "difficult," and composite look, with its various parts—frame, armrests, seat, and back—set in formal tension. Rather than depending on a single, continuous curving form, Schindler employed each structural element—be it bent or straight—independently, as if the chair were made up of sundry parts. In studied contrast to the European avant-garde (or even the growing ranks of modern designers in New York), whose works more often than not strove for an impression of unity and directness, he, like many of the California modernists, appropriated from a broad palette of styles and ideas, freely mixing and matching them.

Schindler was also interested in the standardization of wooden furniture. In the early 1930s he developed his idea for *Schindler Unit Furniture*, a system that relied on mass-made parts that could be assembled and reassembled in various configurations.[22] A dresser he designed for the Shep House in Silver Lake, in the mid-1930s, exhibited the reductive logic and straightforward geometry of his earlier designs (2.14). Its overall form, though, was based on the stacking of individual modules—sections of drawers—to which he attached a large three-way mirror.[23] It was a system well suited for mass manufacturing, but other than the Sardi's chairs, he had little success in getting his pieces produced beyond commissions for individual houses. Weber and Davidson, on the other hand, were able to make a more or less seamless transition to large-scale manufacturing.[24] Both men nonetheless continued to design handmade furnishings and other objects, moving back and forth between industry and craft, a situation that would define much of California production even after World War II.

The belief in the importance of craft as a generator of modern design had a rich history in California, extending back to the 1890s. Even though the Arts and Crafts movement as a stylistic ideal had begun to wane about the time of the U.S. entry into World War I, craftspeople in California—particularly those engaged in ceramics, metalwork, and textiles—continued to fashion beautiful and well-made objects. During the 1920s many of them were wedded to the Spanish and Mexican colonial revivals or other traditional styles. But by the end of the decade, a number had made the transition to modernism. The silversmith Porter Blanchard, for example, began crafting modern silver and pewter bowls, trays, and other objects, including an elegant gold-plated clock for his daughter (2.13). And, in the mid-1930s, Margaret De Patta, who had trained as a painter, began making functionalist flatware that blurs the lines both between precious and base metals (her design mixes silver and copper—with stainless steel for the knife blade) and between craft and machine production (the circular bowl of the spoon and the cylindrical forms at the base of the handles suggest the precision of machine parts, but they are, in fact, entirely handmade) (2.15).

Many of the craftspeople tried to express a regional—a specifically Californian—identity in their work. This was also true of certain artists and

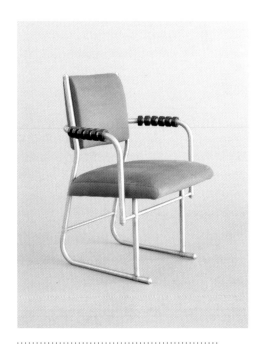

2.10. Kem Weber. *Airline* chair, c. 1934–35. Cat. 308

2.11. J. R. Davidson. Lamp and table, c. 1940. Cats. 55 and 56

2.12. R. M. Schindler. Chair from Sardi's Restaurant, Hollywood, 1932–33. Cat. 253

graphic designers. Millard Sheets, the foremost California regionalist painter, experimented with folded screens in an effort to bring together his two main interests—painting and the decorative arts. A large screen in six sections that he painted in the 1930s offers a modernized (and romanticized) scene inspired by the rocky windswept coast of Northern California (2.16).

Most influential for the emerging California modern aesthetic was the development of commercial product design—in particular, mass-produced solid-color pottery. In the early 1930s several of the state's commercial potteries, which until then had been making utilitarian pieces for the kitchen and garden, turned to dinnerware. To compete with established manufacturers in the East and Midwest, they devised new shapes and finishes. Durlin Brayton, who owned the Brayton Laguna Pottery in Laguna Beach, created a line featuring simple, irregular shapes and dramatically raised handles. Brayton Laguna— or perhaps the Catalina Pottery in Avalon; it is unclear which—originated the idea of employing bright, solid colors for their new designs, setting off a trend that would soon spread across the country (2.18 and see 2.35).[25] Made of earthenware hand-pressed into molds, which gives a slightly uneven surface, they suggest a direct link to "peasant art," but their smooth, uncluttered contours are resolutely modern. These new, inexpensive, and wildly popular wares "expressed a kind of pottery populism," as Bill Stern has written, "an early example of the American propensity for allowing commercial or 'low' culture to rise to the level of art, although it would be more than a half a century before California pottery was recognized as such."[26]

Each of the "Big Five" pottery producers in Southern California—J. A. Bauer Pottery Company, Pacific Pottery, Metlox Potteries, Gladding McBean, and Vernon Kilns—plus Garden City Pottery, in Northern California, devised its own distinctive forms and glazes. Several found direct creative stimulus in the traditional pottery of Mexico, not only the bright, saturated colors that characterized that country's earthenware but also their shapes. Another important producer, Catalina Pottery, adapted the Mexican *molcajete*—the lava-stone mortar used for grinding corn, seeds, and spices—for the base of its shrimp cocktail dish (2.19).[27] Others investigated quirky forms: for his *Ultra California* pattern, Daniel Gale Turnbull, at Vernon Kilns, had the novel idea of inverting the standard handle form (in the process, defying its function as a device for pouring), which yielded a line that was both original and visually arresting (2.20).

Yet even as the large pottery manufacturers were enjoying unprecedented success, studio pottery was gaining new impetus. In the 1930s and early 1940s the field for fine modern ceramics was still small, dominated by a few figures working in relative isolation. F. Carlton Ball, in the Bay Area, and Glen Lukens, Laura Andreson, and William Manker, in Southern California, were among those advancing modernist ideas. Manker, known for his experiments in color and his mastery of cast production, founded the ceramics department at Scripps College

2.13. Porter Blanchard. Clock, c. 1938. Cat. 27

2.14. R. M. Schindler. Dresser with mirror from the Milton and Ruth Shep commission, Silver Lake, c. 1934–38. Cat. 250

2.15. Margaret De Patta. Flatware, c. 1936. Cat. 62

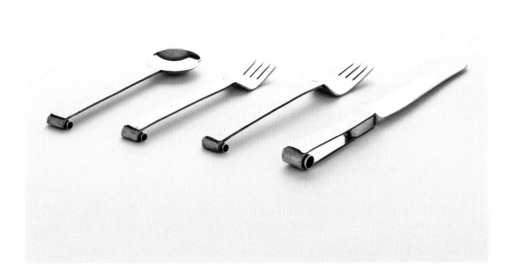

in Claremont. His works, such as a large earthenware vase he made in the 1940s, were noted for their elegant and restrained forms and colorful glazes (2.21).[28]

Lukens, who taught at the University of Southern California (USC), also emerged as a leader in ceramics, working with Manker on statewide surveys of work in the medium. More than any other craftsman in the 1930s, he developed an aesthetic specific to his West Coast locale. His rough shapes, with their thick, cracked glazes, were radically different from sleek European modernist pottery; their melding of parched and glassy surfaces spoke instead of the California desert landscape (2.22).[29] Lukens was also most unusual for an American potter of the time: he explicitly framed his work in modernist terms. He railed against run-of-the-mill traditionalism—"Too many are just going on and on happily but fatuously doing the same old things in quite the same manner of five, ten, or more years ago"—and voiced a theoretical position that might have come from a Bauhaus manifesto: "Let us produce genuine, sincere things that can be taken into machine-made houses and live there on friendly terms with fine machine-made utensils and appliances. Let us find in this new space-beauty our opportunity and an incentive."[30]

In the 1930s, however, many of the important younger modernist designers emerged not from the crafts but from architecture and industrial design. The decade saw the swift development of design education in California. The departments of architecture at Berkeley and USC, the Chouinard Art Institute (which would later become part of the California Institute of the Arts), and the California College of Arts and Crafts (now the California College of the Arts) helped to spread the new doctrine. The most innovative of these schools, though, was the Art Center School (now the Art Center College of Design), founded in 1931 in downtown Los Angeles (2.17). One of the first institutions in the country to offer a full course of studies in modern industrial design, it had the goal, as one of the school's catalogues expressed it, of teaching its students to make "mechanical products work"—everything from "washing machines" to "fountain pens."[31] Weber served as the program's first director, and Davidson and Schindler were among those who taught there.[32]

The various schools turned out a host of young designers, but many of the new figures on the scene in the 1930s had come to California from elsewhere. The Los Angeles area, in particular—which fared better during the Depression than most of the rest of the country because of the booming film, oil, and aircraft industries—attracted many of the transplants. Perhaps the most influential of the new talents was Austrian émigré Paul T. Frankl, who, in 1934, opened his Frankl Galleries on Wilshire Boulevard, along the so-called Miracle Mile, the hub of upscale shopping in West Los Angeles.

One of the preeminent modern designers in New York City, Frankl had visited Los Angeles the year before to teach a summer course in industrial design at the Chouinard Art Institute; taken with the weather and the healthier

2.16. Millard Sheets. Screen, 1930s. Cat. 258

2.17. Art Center School. Course catalogue, 1937. Cat. 325

2.18. Durlin Brayton for Brayton Laguna Pottery. Dinnerware set, c. 1930. Cat. 32

2.19. Left: Catalina Pottery. Shrimp cocktail dish, c. 1934. Cat. 39. Right: Louis Ipsen and Victor F. Houser for J. A. Bauer Pottery Company. Stacking storage dishes, c. 1932. Cat. 134

2.20. Left: Daniel Gale Turnbull for Vernon Kilns. *Ultra California* coffeepot, c. 1937. Cat. 289. Right: Pacific Clay Products, Pacific Pottery division. *Hostess Ware* cocktail mixer, c. 1935. Cat. 228

2.21. William Manker. Oil jar, 1940s. Cat. 200

2.22. Glen Lukens. Bowl, c. 1937. Cat. 181

economy, he decided to relocate there permanently. At first, what he sold through his gallery was a slightly amended version of his elegant New York style. Soon, though, he began to recast his pieces, seeking to adjust them to the benign climate and the more leisurely pace of life. His breakthrough came in 1936, while working on a house for one of his former East Coast clients in Palm Beach, Florida. For the informal living spaces, he wanted to use rattan furniture. Frustrated at finding nothing suitable on the market, he decided to create and manufacture his own designs.

Frankl's new pieces took full advantage of the flexibility and strength of rattan. In his dramatically shaped chairs and sofas, he stacked individual frames to form the bases, and for the arm assemblies, he twisted the rattan into his soon-to-be-familiar "square-pretzel" shape (2.23). He also altered the way the pieces were finished. In lieu of the then-standard dark, shiny lacquer, Frankl had workers hand-rub beeswax into the surface, retaining the fine-grain pattern and, at the same time, making the furniture suitable for both indoor and outdoor use. When he unveiled the new designs at his gallery, they became an immediate sensation: many of the Hollywood elite—Charles Boyer, Charlie Chaplin, Ronald Colman, and Charles Laughton—became his customers.[33]

Frankl also began to make and sell bamboo furnishings—including dining room sets and occasional tables—sometimes adding teak or other tropical woods. Regardless of material, he made no distinction, in terms of either design or finish, between pieces intended for interior use and those destined for the outdoors. In an article in 1937, he insisted that the dissolution of traditional notions of inside and out "marked the greatest advancement toward a truly modern architecture." We are "beginning to comprehend what the Japanese have practiced for centuries. At last, the modern house has found its *raison d'être*. It is coming to life by opening up and letting life flow from the outside."[34]

East Asian design had a decided impact on Frankl's developing aesthetic. With its growing Asian population and its close trade links to the Far East, California was ideally suited, Frankl thought, for the application of Asian motifs, ideas, and materials (such as rattan and bamboo). The spare, understated interiors he devised for his many clients, such as the house of actress Patricia Detring in the exclusive Los Angeles neighborhood of Bel-Air in 1941, exhibited direct borrowings in the spirit of East Asian design, with simple lacquered and bamboo tables he based on Chinese examples and the uncluttered look of Japanese spaces (2.24).

Frankl's new manner had a direct and significant impact on other Los Angeles designers. Paul R. Williams, one of the few successful African American architects on the West Coast, drew on Frankl's tropical idiom for the recreation room he designed for Bill "Bojangles" Robinson in 1937 (2.25). And Hungarian immigrant Paul László, who opened a shop immediately across from Frankl's new store on Rodeo Drive in 1940, made and sold similar rattan chairs and long,

2.23. Paul T. Frankl. Chair, c. 1936. Cat. 105

Christopher Long

2.24. Paul T. Frankl. Living room, Patricia Detring House, Bel-Air, 1941. Photo by Maynard L. Parker, 1941

2.25. Paul R. Williams (1894–1980). Recreation room, Bill "Bojangles" Robinson House, Los Angeles, 1937. Photo by Maynard L. Parker, 1939

low Asian-inspired sofas, chairs, and tables.

Others examined the possibilities of a different kind of relaxed modernism. Weber's design for the new Walt Disney Studios in Burbank, built between 1938 and 1940, was based on both standard modernist ideas—several of the buildings he designed bore a direct resemblance to the works of the contemporary German avant-garde—and a more casual and eclectic approach rooted in an understanding of the California lifestyle. The massive complex, which covered much of the fifty-one-acre site and included more than a dozen buildings, was a tour de force of the new design—the most complete modernist ensemble realized in California in the interwar years. Weber undertook the planning of the entire studio, including the layout of the site, the architecture, and the signage. He also designed all of the furnishings and interiors, meticulously adapting them to the Disney company's needs.[35] In addition to special "animators' desks" arranged to facilitate the work of making the thousands of drawings and cels required for full-length feature cartoons, he created an array of other furnishings, including low upholstered chairs, graceful occasional tables, and simple bookcases (2.26).

Frankl's gracious stylings and Weber's playful, unaffected modernism were only two of many interpretations of the new California aesthetic. What stood out in the later 1930s was the pluralism of modern design in the state, evident not only in its architecture—which ran the gamut from the crisp International Style to a modernized traditionalism that incorporated both historical styles and pared-down forms, massing, and ornament—but also in its products, whether handcrafted or machine made.[36]

2.26. Kem Weber. Walt Disney Studios, Library Reading Room, Burbank (presentation drawing), c. 1939. Cat. 306

2.27. William "Billy" Haines. "Desert Living Room" from the Golden Gate International Exposition, San Francisco, 1939

At the 1939 Golden Gate International Exposition in San Francisco, the decorative arts display organized by the young textile designer Dorothy Wright Liebes offered a full spectrum of modernist interpretations, encompassing, as one observer wrote, both the "functional and the fantastic."[37] Liebes's selection of works by a sizable and representative group of Californians—among them, De Patta, Lukens, and Manker—as well as by many of the leading artists and craftspeople from Europe and elsewhere in the United States, made a powerful case for fine craftsmanship in the modern design movement.[38]

Most evocative of the emerging California lifestyle was a series of room installations. In addition to spaces by Frankl, Neutra, and the San Francisco decorator F. Eldon Baldauf, there was a group of simple "popular" modernist designs by Brown-Saltman, of South Gate, one of the first companies on the West Coast to mass-produce modern furniture and, at the other extreme, an exquisite, romanticized "Desert Living Room" by actor-turned-designer William "Billy" Haines (2.27).

Haines's space exuded Hollywood glamour. Every element, from the sheer mohair curtains and felt-and-leather sofa to the buckeye-burl-and-rawhide coffee table and leather-and-parchment floors, was intended to arouse the senses. He also wanted the materials and art to "speak" about the experience of the West. Over the minimalist fireplace—framed by a simple metal surround—was a painting by Georgia O'Keeffe, and the walls were made of California Joshua wood.[39] But Haines also made a statement about modern materials, using Lucite (an early clear plastic) for the room's backgammon pieces and light fixtures. The space offered what was to become Haines's signature look, one he would replicate in his interiors for George Cukor, Jack Warner, and many others, and it was a harbinger of what was to become a significant interpretation of modernism in the post–World War II years, a refined and polished version of the new design that would appear over and over in the homes of the state's well-to-do.[40]

Equally prescient was Weber's installation, which he described—tongue in cheek—as a "naughty version of a bachelor living room"[41] (see p. 345). It featured—in addition to an "inviting" day bed, one of his *Airline* chairs, and a small wood sculpture by Isamu Noguchi—several of his newest designs, including a coffee table and a desk and chair (2.28).[42] The table, which he had also used for the Disney offices, suggested new ways of using materials (Bakelite with wood) and new combinations of forms (curved legs apposed to a squared top). These same ideas also informed his design of the desk and chair, but here Weber went further, employing varied geometries (the straight lines of the desk; the soft, bending contours of the chair), materials (exotic woods, chrome, and aluminum), and asymmetries (in the arrangement of the massing, the shelves along its back, and the canted metal leg) to contrive a new design language, one that presaged the freer forms of the post–World War II era.

The Golden Gate Exposition was a watershed. Almost all of those whose

works were shown belonged to an older generation of designers, who had begun practicing in the 1920s or early 1930s.[43] But by the eve of the American entry into World War II, a large cadre of mostly younger figures appeared on the scene. Hendrik Van Keppel, who had started making furniture from scrap metal in San Francisco, moved to Los Angeles in 1937 and formed a partnership with Taylor Green; together, they developed an entire line of metal furnishings made specifically for indoor/outdoor use. Swedish-born and educated Greta Magnusson Grossman moved to Los Angeles in 1940 with her jazz bandleader husband, Billy Grossman. And Charles Eames and his wife, Ray (a California native), who had met at the Cranbrook Academy of Art in Michigan, moved to Los Angeles in 1941.

Another group of emerging young designers apprenticed with Schindler and Neutra. Among them were Gregory Ain and Raphael S. Soriano, who had both attended USC, and Harwell Hamilton Harris, who had started his studies at Pomona College, in Claremont, and at the Otis Art Institute (now the Otis College of Art and Design) in Los Angeles before entering Neutra and Schindler's employ.

Neutra had a particularly strong influence on Ain and Soriano.[44] What they took from him was his affinity for pure, clear forms and lines and his absorption with extreme reduction. For Neutra, the essence of a design resided in how it was shaped and joined, how its materials related to one another. Each piece—like the cantilevered chair he designed in 1931 and then used in his own home, the VDL Research House in Silver Lake—was an essay on slimming or eradicating formal and structural elements (2.29). But Neutra was also deeply concerned with how the user interacted with the design, both physically and emotionally. For his chair, he paid particular attention to the haptic qualities of its materials. The upholstered leather seat and the "warm" wooden arms were an attempt to offer comfort and solace, while the metal support at the rear of the seat (part of a spring system that provided elasticity and stability) was an acknowledgment of the new machine age. Here, as elsewhere in Neutra's work, he sought to express modern reality, the requirements of mass production and aesthetic unity, at the same time offering a way to remake the most basic events of living—sitting, sleeping, eating, and relaxing.

In the later 1930s and early 1940s Ain, Soriano, and Harris, each in his own way, added to these ideas. Ain, who grew up in a California cooperative community, launched a practice designing modest homes for less affluent clients, seeking to solve "the common architectural problems of common people."[45] He was especially attentive to the problem of diminishing the separation between inside and out: in the Daniel House in Los Angeles (1939–40) and his other commissions of the later 1930s and early 1940s, he investigated new strategies for free-flowing space and indoor/outdoor living (2.31). Soriano, inspired by Neutra's application of industrial materials, began to explore the use of prefabricated steel and aluminum in his designs for the Latz Jewish Center (Los

2.28. Kem Weber. Desk and chair, c. 1938, exhibited at the Golden Gate International Exposition, San Francisco, 1939. Cat. 305

2.29. Richard Neutra. Chair, 1931, made for the Richard Neutra VDL Research House, Silver Lake, 1932; this example made c. 1941. Cat. 219
Neutra designed this chair for his own home, but he also patented the design, hoping to put it into production. He was unsuccessful, however, and only a few were ever made.

Angeles, 1939), the Glen Lukens House (Los Angeles, 1940), and other works.[46] Harris, too, engaged these problems, but he offered a more upscale version, paying great attention to materials, finish, and comfort. More than Ain or Soriano, he was influenced by a California vernacular informed by Arts and Crafts principles regarding materials and fidelity to place. His living room for the Havens House in Berkeley (1939–41)—which brought together built-in redwood bookshelves and paneling with overstuffed sofas, bentwood chairs, and two Chinese-inspired coffee tables—presented a deluxe California modernism, one that was at once gracious and casual (2.32).[47]

The newly renamed *Arts and Architecture* magazine (formerly *California Arts and Architecture*), which was edited by John Entenza beginning in early 1940, became the principal organ of the new California modern design, featuring projects and works by Ain, De Patta, Charles and Ray Eames, Harris, Neutra, Soriano, and many others.[48] Entenza assumed a prominent role in promoting and popularizing California design. The view he fostered, though, was specific, limited to the more severe and determined reformers.

Others, intent on shaping a more informal version of the new aesthetic, also promoted the spread of the new California lifestyle just before the war. In Northern California, William Wilson Wurster was at the forefront of what would become a widespread movement to develop a regional modernism, making use of indigenous materials and a straightforward design language suited to climate and place. Wurster's fondness for commonsense solutions and his aversion to ostentation led him to a design style that emphasized open, flowing spaces; spare, minimal furnishings; and matter-of-fact arrangements. His Saxton Pope House #2, completed in Orinda in 1940, was an especially strident announcement of his belief in humble materials (much of the house was constructed of concrete block and corrugated metal sheathing) and the importance of leisure (2.30). Regardless of budget or scale, Wurster sought to offer his clients an environment that met the requirements of everyday living simply and directly; eventually, after the war, his lexicon of ideas—his belief that modernism should be ordinary and practical—became part of the California mainstream.[49]

Ultimately, however, the most successful figure in disseminating ideas about the new lifestyle was Cliff May. Raised in San Diego, May was a sixth-generation Californian and descendant of an early Spanish family. His great-great-great-grandfather was José Maria Estudillo, a member of the family that built the Casa de Estudillo there; it deeply influenced him, as did the buildings of the Rancho Santa Margarita y Las Flores, in northwestern San Diego County, where May often spent weekends and summers as a boy.[50] Throughout the 1930s he built houses in Los Angeles and San Diego that took from the western ranch house and Hispanic hacienda forms. By decade's end he began to combine these ideas with elements of modernism.

2.30. William Wilson Wurster. Atrium, Saxton Pope House #2, Orinda, 1940. Photo by Roger Sturtevant

2.31. Gregory Ain and George Agron (1913–1985). Living room, Daniel House, Los Angeles, 1939–40. Photo by Julius Shulman, c. 1940

2.32. Harwell Hamilton Harris. Living room, Havens House, Berkeley, 1939–41. Photo by Wayne Andrews, c. 1950. Cat. 126

2.33. Cliff May. Cliff May House #3, Brentwood, 1939. Photo by Maynard L. Parker, c. 1944

Here, in a carefully staged photograph, the May family is shown enjoying the courtyard space of their new house. Such casual outdoor living became integral to the new California lifestyle.

2.34. Paul T. Frankl. Living room, Cliff May House #3. Photo by Maynard L. Parker, c. 1944

Cliff May House #3, which he built for his family near Sunset Boulevard on the Riviera Ranch in Los Angeles in 1939, adapted the courtyard form of the early Spanish houses. But the sprawling building was more relaxed and open; its extended wings framed two large courtyards, given over to outdoor living (2.33).[51] He devoted special attention to eliminating the barriers between inside and out so that the courtyards became an extension of the house. Rather than industrial materials and polished surfaces, May relied on smooth adobe construction and long, low wood-shingled roofs—all in an effort to generate an easy and acceptable modernism. The interiors, executed by May's friend Paul T. Frankl, blended old and new pieces, further underscoring May's desire to forge a style that was both traditional and modern (2.34). It was the inaugural expression of the "ranch style," but, more than that, it was a glimpse of a new lifestyle. "His passion," wrote Paul C. Johnson, one of the editors of *Sunset* magazine, in 1946, "was not so much architecture as the way people wanted to live. He watched families use his houses—watched them give parties, prepare meals, use the patio for outdoor entertaining. Every idea that gave delight was picked up, worked over, improved in the next house he built."[52] In the postwar era, May would go on to design or build more than a thousand "ranch" homes and commercial properties, and his plans were used to construct more than eighteen thousand more.[53] The many developer-built ranch-house models he inspired, replicated over and over in the state's burgeoning suburbs, would become synonymous with California.

May's mitigated modernism and the more radical designs of the new vanguard shared a defining feature: they were individual and direct expressions of a modernism rooted in California culture and conditions. They were not simply a rehashed version of the European aesthetic but a new way of describing and framing modern life. Harwell Hamilton Harris later offered a succinct summary of this development: "In California in the late Twenties and Thirties modern European ideas met a still-developing regionalism." What the designers there found to be useful, they simply incorporated, and they cast off what was neither meaningful nor relevant.[54] In seeking to respond to the specific features they found around them, the California modernists shaped an aesthetic that articulated a clear regional identity; they devised a new and singular form of modernism. But more than that, they laid the foundation for a new, modern way of living.

NOTES

I would like to thank Wendy Kaplan, Bobbye Tigerman, Glenn Adamson, Bill Stern, Ilene Fort, Maddie Sadofski, and Daniel P. Gregory for their helpful comments and suggestions.

1   Margaret Leslie Davis, *Bullocks Wilshire* (Los Angeles: Balcony Press, 1996), 10.

2   Ibid., 49–67.

3   Natalie Shivers, "Modern Commercial Design and the Industrial Arts," in Victoria Dailey, Natalie Shivers, and Michael Dawson, *LA's Early Moderns: Art, Architecture, Photography* (Los Angeles: Balcony Press, 2003), 182–83.

4   Biographical files, Kem Weber Collection, Architectural Design Collection, University Art Museum, University of California, Santa Barbara.

5   Ibid.

6   *Furnishing for Public Service* (Los Angeles: Barker Brothers, 1929), 66–72, sales brochure in the author's collection.

7   On Frank Lloyd Wright's California designs, see Thomas S. Hines, *Architecture of the Sun: Los Angeles Modernism, 1900–1970* (New York: Rizzoli, 2010), 120–65; and Robert L. Sweeney, *Wright in Hollywood: Visions of a New Architecture* (Cambridge, Mass.: MIT Press, 1994).

8   See Alan Weintraub, Dana Hutt, and Eric Lloyd Wright, *Lloyd Wright: The Architecture of Frank Lloyd Wright, Jr.* (London: Thames and Hudson, 1998).

9   On Schindler's early years, see Judith Sheine, *R. M. Schindler* (London: Phaidon, 2001), 11–33; and Esther McCoy, ed., *Vienna to Los Angeles: Two Journeys* (Santa Monica: Arts and Architecture Press, 1979).

10   Schindler to Elizabeth Mock, August 10, 1945, Rudolph M. Schindler Collection, Architectural Design Collection, University Art Museum, University of California, Santa Barbara.

11   David Gebhard and Harriette von Breton, *Los Angeles in the Thirties: 1931–1941* (Los Angeles: Hennessey and Ingalls, 1989), 17–23.

12   *Furniture from America's First Modernistic Home: The De Lorenzo Collection* (New York: Christie's, 1980), 6–7, 10–23.

13   On Neutra's early years, see Thomas S. Hines, *Richard Neutra and the Search for Modern Architecture* (New York: Oxford University Press, 1982); McCoy, ed., *Vienna to Los Angeles;* and Dione Neutra, *Richard Neutra: Promise and Fulfillment, 1919–1932:*

Selections from the Letters and Diaries of Richard and Dione Neutra (Carbondale: Southern Illinois University Press, 1986).

14   For an excellent discussion of the Lovell House, see Hines, *Richard Neutra*, 78–91.

15   Richard Neutra, *Life and Shape* (New York: Appleton Century-Crofts, 1962), 207.

16   Biographical files, J. R. Davidson Collection, Architecture and Design Collection, University Art Museum, University of California, Santa Barbara; Hines, *Los Angeles Modernism*, 517–18.

17   Shivers, "Modern Commercial Design and the Industrial Arts," 184–85.

18   *Lawson Time . . . Exact Time at a Glance* (Alhambra: Lawson Time), undated advertising brochure, courtesy of Toni Greenbaum. The clock has long been attributed to Kem Weber, but a 1938 Lawson Time brochure that includes this clock states "designs by Ferher and Adomatis"; *Lawson Time-Table Time: Creations for 1938* (Los Angeles: Lawson Time, 1938), courtesy of Kevin Tucker.

19   "Wrap It Up and Take It Home," *Retailing*, May 13, 1935.

20   Weber offered the *Airline* chair design to a number of firms, including Thonet, in New York, and the Johnson Furniture Company, in Grand Rapids, Michigan, but all the companies declined, citing the poor consumer market of the Depression years. Weber also launched a publicity campaign, speaking to various groups and newspapers (see, for example, Carleton Cady, "Kem Weber Tells What He's After in Modern Furniture," *Grand Rapids Herald*, July 3, 1936), but in the end his efforts failed. He established his own firm, the Airline Chair Company, to manufacture them, but only about two to three hundred of the chairs were made, the great majority of them for the Walt Disney Studios in Burbank. Files, Kem Weber Collection, Architectural Design Collection, University Art Museum, University of California, Santa Barbara.

21   Pamela Post, "Sardi's Restaurant, 1932–1933," in *The Furniture of R. M. Schindler*, exh. cat., ed. Marla C. Berns (Santa Barbara: University Art Museum, University of California; Seattle: University of Washington Press, 1996), 118.

22   See, for example, Richard Guy Wilson, "Schindler's Metaphysics: Space and the Modern Machine," in *The Architecture of R. M. Schindler*, exh. cat., ed. Elizabeth A. T. Smith and Michael Darling (Los Angeles: Museum of Contemporary Art, 2001), 130–33.

23   Jo Lauria, "Shep Commission, 1934–1938," in *Furniture of R. M. Schindler*, 131–37.

24   Aside from his *Airline* chair, Weber, in particular, had great success in finding companies to mass-produce his furniture designs, including the Berkey and Gay Furniture and Haskelite Manufacturing companies, both in Grand Rapids, Michigan, and the Lloyd Manufacturing Company, in Menominee, Michigan. For a full list of Weber's clients, see David Gebhard and Harriette von Breton, *Kem Weber: The Moderne in Southern California, 1920–1941*, exh. cat. (Santa Barbara: Art Gallery, University of California, Santa Barbara, 1969), 37–46.

25   Bill Stern, *California Pottery: From Mission to Modern* (San Francisco: Chronicle Books, 2001), 49–50.

26   Ibid., 17.

27   Ibid., 52.

28   Hazel V. Bray, *The Potter's Art in California, 1885 to 1955*, exh. cat. (Oakland: Oakland Museum, 1980), 52.

29   Susan Peterson, "Glen Lukens 1887–1967," *Craft Horizons* 28 (March–April 1968): 22–25; Bray, *Potter's Art*, 23–25; and *American Studio Ceramics, 1920–1950*, exh. cat. (Minneapolis: University Art Museum, University of Minnesota, 1988), 25–35.

30   Glen Lukens, "The New Handcraftsman," *California Arts and Architecture* 46 (December 1934): 13.

31   *The Art Center School* (brochure) (Los Angeles: Art Center School, 1941), 29.

32   Ibid., 52–59.

33   Christopher Long, *Paul T. Frankl and Modern American Design* (New Haven, Conn.: Yale University Press, 2007), 120–25.

34   Paul T. Frankl, "In California Every Room a Sun Room," *California Arts and Architecture* 51 (June 1937): 18–19.

35   "Disney Productions Occupy New Home," *Architect and Engineer* 14 (October 1940): 58; "Disney Studios, Burbank, Calif.," *Architectural Forum* 81 (September 1944): 123–28; "Walt Disney Studios," *California Arts and Architecture* 58 (January 1941): 26–27.

36   See the many examples in Gebhard and von Breton, *Los Angeles in the Thirties*, especially 93–165.

37   Shepard Vogelgesang, "Rooms," in *Decorative Arts: Official Catalog, Department of Fine Arts, Division of Decorative Arts, Golden Gate International Exposition, San Francisco, 1939*, exh. cat. (San Francisco: San Francisco Bay Exposition Company; H. S.

Crocker, Schwabacher-Frey Co., 1939), 11.

38 Among the notables represented in the show were Raoul Dufy, Alberto Giacometti, and Tommi Parzinger (who all contributed ceramic vases); Simon Gate, Edward Hald, and René Lalique (who provided "modern glass"); and Georg Jensen, Peter Müller-Munk, and William Spratling (who contributed "modern silver"). For a full list of exhibits, see *Decorative Arts: Official Catalog.*

39 Peter Schifando and Jean H. Mathison, *Class Act: William Haines, Legendary Hollywood Designer* (New York: Pointed Leaf Press, 2005), 88; Vogelgesang, "Rooms," in *Decorative Arts: Official Catalog*, 13.

40 Schifando and Mathison, *Class Act*, 25.

41 "Progress in Wood: Furniture Design Exhibited at the World's Fair of the West," *Hardwood Record*, March 1939, 17.

42 *Decorative Arts: Official Catalog*, 13.

43 The same was true of the East Coast and international designers, the great majority of whom already had established reputations in their respective fields. See *Decorative Arts: Official Catalog.*

44 See Hines, *Los Angeles Modernism*, 430–83.

45 Anthony Denzer, *Gregory Ain: The Modern Home as Social Commentary* (New York: Rizzoli, 2008), 45.

46 Hines, *Los Angeles Modernism*, 457–67.

47 On the Havens House and Harris's other works of the 1930s and early 1940s, see Lisa Germany, *Harwell Hamilton Harris* (Austin: University of Texas Press, 1991); and Lisa Germany, *Harwell Hamilton Harris*, exh. cat. (Austin: Center for the Study of American Architecture, School of Architecture, University of Texas at Austin, 1985).

48 On John Entenza and his role in defining and disseminating California modernism, see Barbara Goldstein, ed., essay by Esther McCoy, *Arts and Architecture: The Entenza Years* (Santa Monica: Hennessey and Ingalls, 1998).

49 See Marc Treib, ed., *An Everyday Modernism: The Houses of William Wurster*, exh. cat. (San Francisco: San Francisco Museum of Modern Art; Berkeley: University of California Press, 1995).

50 Daniel P. Gregory, *Cliff May and the Modern Ranch House* (New York: Rizzoli, 2008), 28.

51 Ibid., 41–48.

52 Paul C. Johnson, ed., *Western Ranch Houses by Cliff May* (Menlo Park: Lane Books, 1946), 7.

53 Gregory, *Cliff May and the Modern Ranch House*, 20.

54 Harwell Hamilton Harris, "Liberative and Restrictive Regionalism" (address to the Northwest Chapter of the American Institute of Architects, Eugene, Oregon, 1954), quoted in Treib, ed., *William Wurster*, 37.

2.35. Catalina Pottery. *Trojan* tea set, c. 1935. Cat. 40

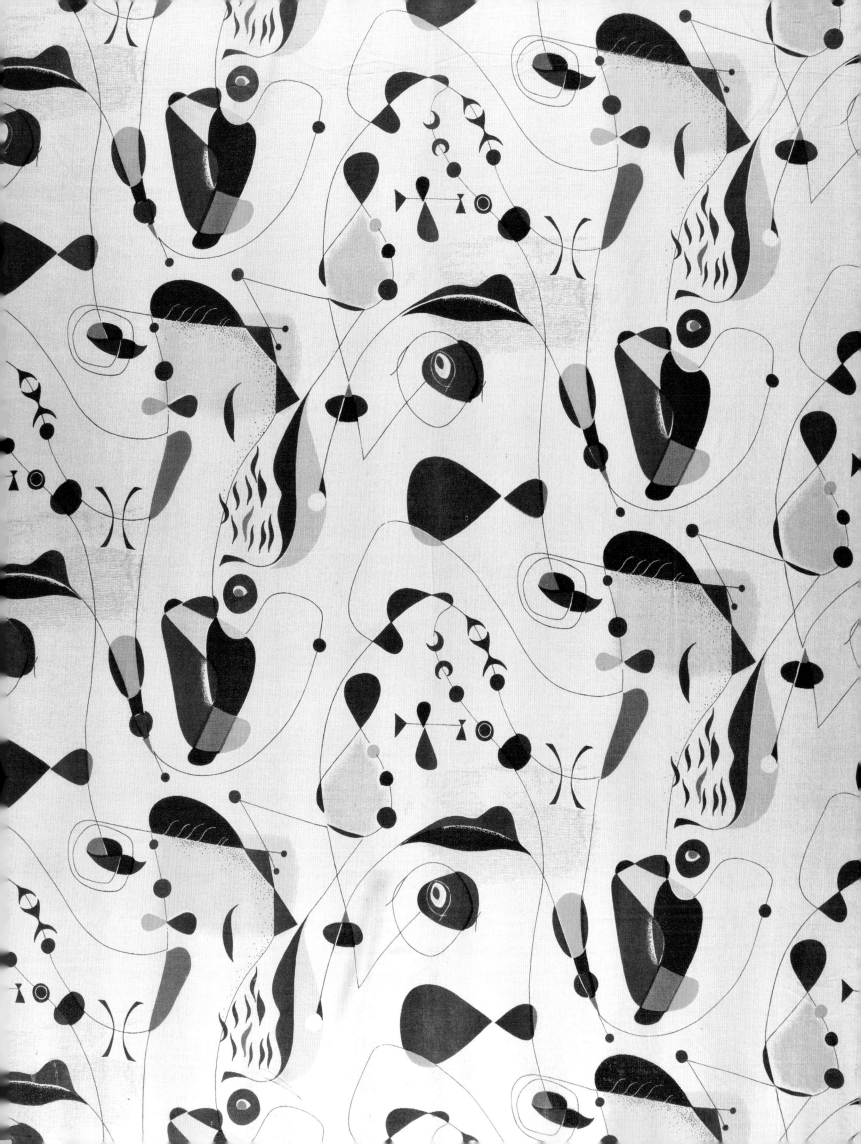

3

Fusing Old and New:
Émigré Designers in California

BOBBYE TIGERMAN

The legend goes that on the first day Hungarian-born and Vienna-trained designer Paul László arrived in Los Angeles in 1936, he rented an apartment in Beverly Hills, bought a car, ate lunch at the Hollywood hangout the Brown Derby, and joined the Beverly Hills Tennis Club.[1] Within fourteen weeks, he had completed the remodeling and refurnishing of five departments in Bullock's Wilshire, the premier department store in Los Angeles.[2] But not all émigrés to the United States leapt from the starting block with such aplomb; for most, the process of assimilation and adaptation to American culture was a prolonged struggle.

3.1. Paul László. *Paul Laszlo's European Group* textile, 1954 or before. Cat. 164

The architects and designers who arrived in California just before and during World War II came at a time of intense growth, when the war was creating significant demand for innovative products and housing. They would have known of earlier émigrés such as Kem Weber, R. M. Schindler, and Richard Neutra, all of whom had received extensive press coverage and professional accolades by the late 1930s. Although their approaches differed, Weber, Schindler, and Neutra sought a uniquely Californian modernism, adapting a modernist design language to suit the benign climate and informal living of California—a model that many of the wartime émigrés emulated. And like that earlier generation, they struggled to reconcile their European training and experience with the distinctive lifestyle and environment of California.[3]

The central questions regarding émigrés concern their modes of assimilation. To what extent did they remain outsiders, and in what ways did they assimilate? How did their position on the margins of society help or hinder their professional success? How did their status as foreigners and the fact that English was not their first language affect their careers? How were their attitudes about assimilation and American culture revealed in their work? And how was their work shaped by the specifically Californian culture that surrounded them? Scholars currently understand assimilation and the experience of "becoming American" as dynamic processes fueled by the interaction of mainstream and immigrant cultures. While the focus of most studies has been on group rather than individual identity, this pluralist model can be applied to individual cases to understand how émigrés define their cultural and ethnic identity after settling in a new place.[4] Applying these ideas to architects and designers, William Jordy posited "acceptance of the new situation, but resistance too: this is usually the fruitful formula if the displaced creator continues to be creative."[5]

A significant and growing literature on émigré artists and intellectuals has emerged in the past four decades, with an increasing emphasis on the reciprocal relationship between the displaced individuals and the American culture that received them. Many books have devoted entire chapters to the émigré experience in Southern California, and several have focused on the Los Angeles émigré community alone, but none has yet taken into account the role and influence of the émigré architects and designers working there.[6] Ultimately, the latest scholarship concludes that each creative figure adapts to a new culture in a unique way, due to a very personal blend of character and circumstance. Using the objects and words of the émigrés themselves, this essay will elucidate how they were shaped by the culture they encountered and how, in turn, they helped to define the design culture of postwar California.

Overall view of site for Pond Farm Workshops.

POND FARM WORKSHOPS

Architects and designers came to California in the late 1930s and early 1940s for a variety of reasons, but most common was the need to escape persecution as National Socialism spread throughout Europe. Following the Anschluss on March 12, 1938, Gertrud Amon and Otto Natzler began the process of immigration to the United States, seeking sponsorship by Otto's cousin Adolf, who had settled in Los Angeles in the early 1930s.[7] After traversing the dense Austrian bureaucracy, they boarded an Italian freighter from Trieste, sailed through the Panama Canal, and arrived in the Southern California port of San Pedro on October 28, 1938.[8] For other émigrés, the journey was not so direct. Marguerite Wildenhain, who taught at the Stadt Halle–Kunstgewerbeschule Burg Giebichenstein (Halle City School of Fine and Applied Arts) in Halle an der Saale in Germany, was asked to resign in 1933 (the year Hitler became chancellor of Germany) because of her Jewish background. She moved to Putten, in the Netherlands, where she opened a ceramic studio. When the Nazis invaded Poland in 1939, she made her way to New York and ultimately to Northern California.[9] Metalsmith and jeweler Victor Ries was born in Germany and emigrated to Palestine in 1933, teaching and operating a workshop there before moving to California in 1947.[10] Teaching opportunities drew several designers to California, particularly Wildenhain, Ries, and Trude Guermonprez, who were all

3.2. Pond Farm, Guerneville. *Arts and Architecture*, December 1949, p. 25. Photo by Otto Hagel, 1949

recruited to teach at the School of the Pond Farm Workshops in Guerneville (3.2). And the benign climate was also an attraction. Some émigrés lamented the perpetual sunshine—Thomas Mann wrote that "the oleander . . . blooms very beautifully. Only I have a suspicion that it may do so all year round"[11]—but many new arrivals had either moved to California because of the mild weather or, having experienced it while visiting, decided to search no further for a new home.

The California émigré social circles are well documented by both first-person narratives and scholarly accounts. In the 1930s and early 1940s, writers, composers, musicians, and intellectuals gathered at the homes of such figures as actress Salka Viertel or writer Lion Feuchtwanger and his wife, Marta, to make connections with other émigrés, share news of political developments in Europe, commiserate about adjustments to life in America, and find comfort in the company of compatriots.[12] Neutra was a frequent guest at these elite gatherings, but for the most part, the designers considered here moved in less lofty circles.[13] It is likely that some of them chose to socialize with their language peers, but those gatherings were not recorded for posterity. The scant evidence from figures such as Victor Gruen and Paul László indicates that many of their early clients were German-speaking or of Viennese descent. László, in particular, had many fellow émigrés as clients, including the shoe-store owner Walter Loewendahl and the movie producer Heinz (later Henry) Blanke.[14]

The philosopher Theodor Adorno observed that the émigrés' alien status allowed them to see American culture in relief and to comment critically on it, and that in order to retain their analytical perspective, they had to resist assimilation.[15] This essay divides the émigrés into three categories that reflect different approaches to assimilation: those who continued to put into practice ideas and methods learned during their European training, those who combined elements of European training with the relaxed modernity of California lifestyle, and those who established a new cultural identity and developed a language of architecture and design entirely different from their prewar work. Theoretical extremes—such as the total disavowal of the past or the complete adoption of American culture—are rare in reality, so all of these figures fall along a spectrum of assimilation, and the three categories are used not to establish precise distinctions but to highlight different degrees of adoption or rejection of American culture. All of the émigrés absorbed some aspects of the American way of life, but the differences lie in what aspects of European influence or training persisted in their work, how thoroughly they assimilated local influences, and how they represented themselves to the public.

The potter Marguerite Wildenhain led the ceramic workshop at Pond Farm, an art school and studio/residence for practicing artists founded in 1949 by Gordon and Jane Herr. Born in Lyon, France, to a German-French father and a British mother, Wildenhain studied drawing, painting, and sculpture at the Kunstgewerbeschule (School of Fine and Applied Arts) in Berlin. She enrolled at the Bauhaus in 1919 in the pottery course directed by two masters: Max Krehan, an experienced potter who taught the technical skills of throwing, glazing, and firing; and sculptor Gerhard Marcks, who instructed on aspects of form, line, and expression.[16] Krehan taught the students in the manner of a traditional apprenticeship, emphasizing diligent practice and repetition. Only after students had mastered form making did Marcks play a larger role in their education.[17]

Wildenhain believed in the necessity of mass production, declaring that "though the manufacture of things no longer means the making of things by hand, nor is it possible to meet contemporary demands by such means, it is essential that we keep alive the human values and individual responsibility in work which are lost to us under methods of mass production alone."[18] At the same time, she believed that "only a designer-craftsman . . . thoroughly versed in his craft, can create pottery designs of lasting value for factory production."[19] Her ideal scenario would have craftspeople with tactile knowledge of the material responsible for the design of mass-produced goods. Even though her California output (3.3) diverged from the Bauhaus ideal of affordable mass production, the lessons that she taught at Pond Farm were modeled after those of Krehan and Marcks, emphasizing dedicated practice and offering honest yet measured critique.[20]

In Germany, Wildenhain designed a tea service for the Staatliche Porzellanmanufaktur (KPM, State Porcelain Factory) in Berlin, applying the craft techniques she had learned to mass production (3.4). After arriving in the United States, Wildenhain made all her pots on the wheel and did not embark on any production ventures again. She did, however, continue to produce utilitarian forms, as exemplified by her hand-thrown tea set (3.5), which won an award for the best ceramic design suitable for mass production at the *Eleventh National Ceramic Exhibition* at the Syracuse Museum of Fine Arts in 1946.[21] This tea set was governed by the same requirements as the earlier factory-made version; in essence, both comprised a group of implements for preparing and consuming tea. The difference between them was due to a change not in function but in materials and techniques. Using a California clay body and local glazes, and with access only to a potter's wheel, Wildenhain created the later tea set using the resources available around her.

In a statement of principles about Pond Farm Workshops, she said, "We want to educate young people to honest creative work based on sound knowledge in their craft and to prove their own talent."[22] The course description for Wildenhain's pottery course at Pond Farm included instruction in selecting suitable materials; using coil, slab, and wheel methods; studying the components of functional ceramics, like handles, lids, and spouts; glazing and decorating; jiggering and casting; and the loading and firing of kilns. These technical aspects of pottery making reflected her education under Krehan. At the same time, her students also learned about form, surface, and clay behavior, and the potential of clay as an expressive medium, reflecting ideas imparted by Marcks. Wildenhain also taught how to develop forms for mass production from handmade models, showing her continuing concern for the widespread application of the techniques she was teaching.[23]

Even though her teaching philosophies hewed closely to the lessons of the Bauhaus, Wildenhain cut off nearly all contact with friends and colleagues in Europe, with the notable exception of a lifelong correspondence with Marcks. The combination of a traumatic divorce from Frans Wildenhain, her geographic remoteness in Guerneville, and a fervent desire to focus on her own artistic development compelled her to turn away from her past. She wrote to Marcks in 1976 that her early life "was such a long time ago, and I began such a whole new life when I came to the U.S. that I hardly thought of those people. ONLY YOU, Gerhard and Maria, have remained an important part of my life, even here."[24]

The question of why Wildenhain chose to make unique pots rather than design for industry is an important one. Ultimately, she felt that in order to create good designs, one must have a physical relationship with the clay. She taught that "you need a more direct knowledge of the material; you must learn its possibilities and its limitations; know the whole process of the production."[25] A "ceramic designer" who creates only with pencil on paper does not have a sense for how clay behaves on a wheel or in a mold. Knowledge of the material was crucial before mass-produced design could be considered, and Wildenhain felt that the best possible pots would be those made by her own hands, not produced in a factory, no matter how sensitive or sophisticated the manufacturing. She harbored no antagonism to designers working for industry, even writing, "I have found that cooperation with industry is a very challenging and excitingly interesting affair and should like to advise every student to work in a pottery factory for a substantial period."[26]

The Pond Farm Workshops offered opportunities to two other German-born émigré craftspeople—weaver Trude Guermonprez and metalsmith Victor Ries. Guermonprez's professional trajectory closely followed Wildenhain's. Born in Danzig, Guermonprez attended the City School of Fine and Applied Arts in Halle an der Saale, where she met Wildenhain and Marcks. She studied weaving with Benita Otte, who had trained at the Bauhaus and emphasized abstraction, form, and color in textile designs.[27] Like Wildenhain, Guermonprez moved to the Netherlands in the mid-1930s; she designed woven textiles there in the years leading up to and during World War II. She survived the war in hiding, obtaining false papers and working as a nanny for Dutch friends.[28] In 1947 Guermonprez joined her family at Black Mountain College in North Carolina and studied with weaver Anni Albers, eventually taking over her classes while the latter was on sabbatical. At Wildenhain's invitation, Guermonprez moved to California in 1949 to help found Pond Farm Workshops.[29] There, Guermonprez emphasized the importance of acquiring handcraft skills for the design of both

3.4. Marguerite Wildenhain, form designer, and Trude Petri (1906–1968), decoration designer, for Staatliche Porzellanmanufaktur (KPM, State Porcelain Factory). Teapot, creamer, and sugar, model no. 13944, 1929–30. Porcelain, teapot, height: 4⅞ in. (6.4 cm); diameter: 8 in. (10.2 cm). The Wolfsonian–Florida International University, Miami Beach, Florida, The Mitchell Wolfson, Jr. Collection

3.5. Marguerite Wildenhain. Teapot, creamer, and sugar, c. 1946. Cat. 310

unique and production work. She stressed that the aim of the weaving course was "to develop contemporary-craftsmen designers. The versatility of the hand-loom allows for a development in fabric construction which can contribute a wider variety of design to industrial production. Hand-weaving re-establishing the link between artistic study and progressive technical development—or as a means of expression for individual creative ability."[30] Similar to Wildenhain's teaching philosophy, Guermonprez's approach focused on acquiring basic skills that could be applied in modern ways, whether through industrial or unique production. She admitted that "my thinking within weaving is very much influenced by Bauhaus training," referring to the emphasis on building a basic weaving skill set.[31] Guermonprez often worked on commission, and her sample curtain design for Rodef Sholom Synagogue in San Rafael features the geometric rigor typical of Bauhaus work (3.6).

Following her marriage in 1951, Guermonprez moved to San Francisco and joined the faculty of the California College of Arts and Crafts (now the California College of the Arts), a position she held for the rest of her life. Over the course of several decades at the college, Guermonprez produced a vast body of work, ranging from functional furnishing textiles to fiber art. Although never engaging with the off-loom techniques that some of her contemporaries

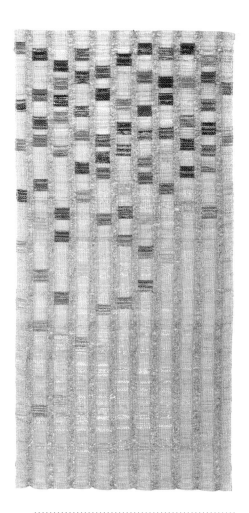

explored, Guermonprez did experiment with textile graphics and warp printing. Like Wildenhain, she continued to emphasize the need to learn basic techniques before engaging in creative expression, but unlike her potter friend, she encouraged students to respond to contemporary developments in art and weaving. Guermonprez found inspiration in the California landscape, taking her Pond Farm weaving classes to the beach to record the structures and textures of rocks, shells, and driftwood, which would be incorporated into textile designs.[32] In an obituary, textile artist Ed Rossbach wrote that "her work constantly reflected the discipline of her European textile training while responding to current happenings in the art world."[33] As she put it, "I felt that what I was able to bring over here in the way of tradition, could be made livelier, more up to date in fusing it with what ever progress had been made in this country."[34]

The metalwork instructor at Pond Farm was Victor Ries, who was born in Germany in 1907 and completed a silversmith apprenticeship and fine arts training in Berlin. When Hitler came to power in 1933, Ries immigrated to Palestine, where he opened a metalworking studio and taught briefly at the Bezalel School of Arts and Crafts in Jerusalem. While there, Ries executed several commissions for architect Erich Mendelsohn. Wanting to improve his ill health and hoping for more opportunities in the United States, Ries immigrated to San Francisco in 1947, in large part due to encouragement from Mendelsohn, who had already settled there.[35] Shortly after arriving in San Francisco, Ries met Jane and Gordon Herr, the founders of Pond Farm, who invited him to teach and work in Guerneville. He stayed until the school's dissolution in 1952 and later set up a studio in the Bay Area, executing commissions for synagogues and churches, and making ritual objects and jewelry.[36] Though best known for his ecclesiastical metalwork, Ries made secular objects as well. His candelabrum (3.7) formally resembles a large-scale outdoor sculpture that he created for Sacramento's Temple B'nai Israel in 1955 (3.8), demonstrating how a design motif could be adapted to different scales and uses. He executed commissions for small metal objects and jewelry, too, and his necklace from about 1969, with its Shakespearean couplet, demonstrates his renowned skill at forming metal letters, which also could be executed at varying scales (3.9).

Like Wildenhain and Guermonprez, Ries strongly believed in acquiring basic drawing and design skills and learning proper technique as important prerequisites to working as a professional craftsperson, and he attributed this grounding in basics to his European education.[37] Ries taught metalwork courses throughout his life, with his longest tenure at the California College of Arts and Crafts from 1953 to 1975.[38] His curriculum for the metalwork course at Pond Farm included instruction in executing working drawings; basic techniques of chasing, mounting, and soldering; experience with a variety of metals and their integration with other materials such as wood and stone; plus some background in the history of metal craft.[39] The education was clearly intended

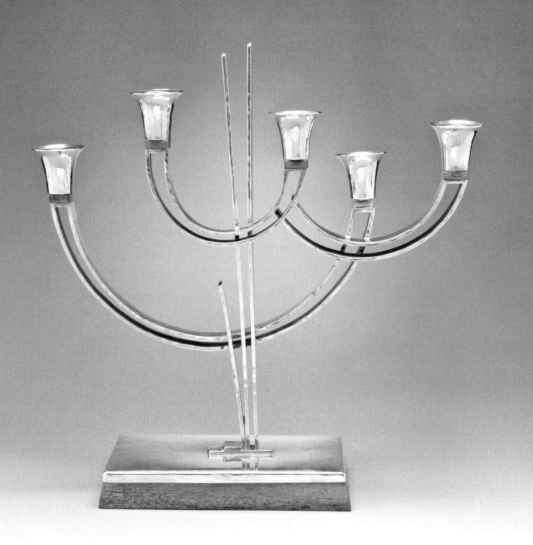

to give the student all the tools to be a self-sufficient craftsperson. Ries was always intent on imbuing his objects with both functionality and spirituality, writing that "the main problem of all creative work [is] how to fuse into the chosen object and through the special medium that individual feeling and the human experience of the craftsman."[40]

Many other émigré designers, such as Greta Magnusson Grossman, synthesized old and new, amalgamating their European training with the culture and lifestyle of California. Theirs was a pragmatic approach, one that allowed the greatest leeway to interpret the client's needs. Grossman herself emphasized the way she skillfully combined old and new, proclaiming in a 1951 profile that "so many old things mix in very well. So many good things are timeless."[41] A house that combined familiar forms with a concern for modern living would be a source of spiritual and physical comfort to homeowners, and Grossman sought to strike this balance.

Some émigré designers capitalized on their European backgrounds, and Grossman was no exception. Designers native to Austria or Germany would not have drawn attention to their country of birth during the war, but Grossman was effective in using her Scandinavian heritage as a selling point. She was

3.7. Victor Ries. Candelabrum, c. 1957. Cat. 243

3.8. Temple B'nai Israel, Sacramento, with sculpture by Victor Ries, 1955

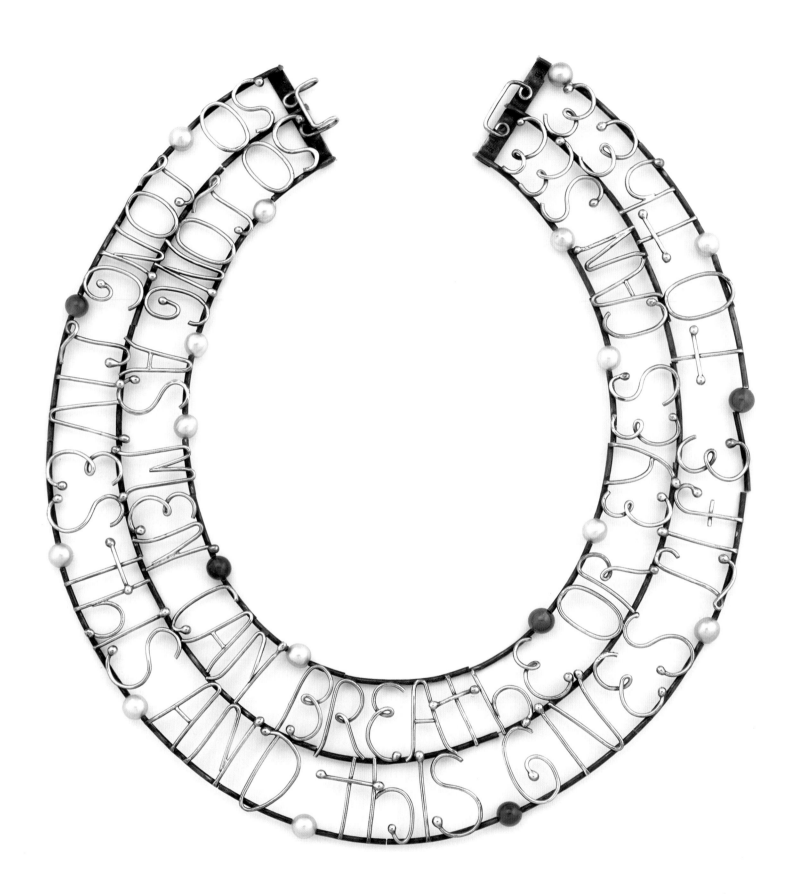

often described in the press as a Swedish designer, suggesting that she was a worldly heir to a long design tradition. One article proclaimed that she "offers the California design field her talent for interiors with the Swedish Modern touch of light and air, of cheerfulness and practicality."[42] Grossman encouraged this association, which attracted clients and helped distinguish her from competitors. She had, in fact, descended from a family of Swedish cabinetmakers and studied furniture, metalwork, and textiles at the School of Industrial Design, and then architecture at the Royal Academy of Technology, both in Stockholm.[43] With the outbreak of World War II, she and her British husband, who was Jewish, fled Sweden and settled in Los Angeles, where she swiftly began advertising her architecture and design services (3.10).[44]

Her 1952 desk for Glenn of California exemplifies the way she combined Scandinavian and Californian design influences (3.11). It is part of the *'62 Series*, so named because it was intended to be a portent of the future. Grossman's forms and silhouettes drew inspiration from and were designed for the progressive architecture that was rising in Southern California at the time. Likewise, her juxtaposition of light and dark, preference for asymmetrical forms, and use of Formica contribute to the modern aesthetic of the desk. But her choice of iron and walnut and the skillful way she engineered the desk also reveal an interest in traditional materials and the craftsperson's training she had received in Sweden. The line for Glenn was designed twelve years after Grossman immigrated to the United States—long enough for her to have absorbed the essence of the California lifestyle. She was not relying solely on Scandinavian forms, but her respect for solid wood construction and traditional joinery is evident in this group of furniture, in contrast to the work by some of her contemporaries who were actively engaged in experimentation with new materials. What is remarkable about this furniture is not the technological developments it represents, but the way it modulates a modern aesthetic with more familiar elements in order to make it acceptable to a wider range of tastes. Indeed, other furniture from the *'62 Series* embodies the same combination of modernism and comfort. Grossman said that "comfort was a prime consideration, as well as functional character that comes from the elimination of the nonessentials."[45]

Grossman employed the same integrative approach in the interiors she designed for herself in Southern California. The first, in Hollywood in 1943, was described as "a back-to-nature kind of Modern that sees sermons in stones and good in everything" (3.12).[46] She designed biomorphic upholstered furniture, contrasted the texture of a rough stone wall with a luxuriously thick rug and unstained woods, and liberally added plants, even creating a bamboo window screen draped with ivy to conceal an offensive view. Her split-level house built in Beverly Hills in 1949 was Grossman's first opportunity to act as both architect and interior designer (3.13). In the living room and dining area, she

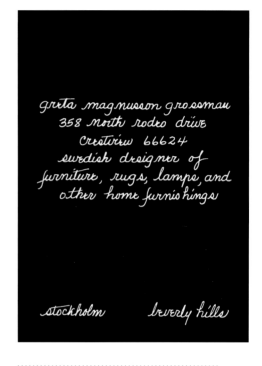

greta magnusson grossman
358 north rodeo drive
Crestview 66624
swedish designer of
furniture, rugs, lamps, and
other home furnishings

stockholm   beverly hills

3.9. Victor Ries. Necklace, c. 1969. Cat. 244
This necklace features a couplet from William Shakespeare's sonnet 18, "So long as men can breathe or eyes can see, so long lives this and this gives life to thee."

3.10. Greta Magnusson Grossman. Advertisement in *Arts and Architecture*, February 1941, p. 7

3.11. Greta Magnusson Grossman for Glenn of California. Desk (with storage unit), 1952. Cat. 114

3.12. Greta Magnusson Grossman. Interior of Grossman's house, Hollywood, 1943. Photo by Maynard L. Parker, 1943

Opposite 3.13. Greta Magnusson Grossman. Interior of Grossman House, Beverly Hills, 1949. Photo by Julius Shulman, 1949

juxtaposed floor-to-ceiling glass windows and modern furniture of her own design with organic and tactile elements like wood ceiling beams, throw rugs, plants, and a slate floor. With its redwood, elm, and mahogany paneling and stone fireplace, the house made a prevailing impression of a rugged modernism. The studied contrasts between the organic materials and the metal and glass deliver what a period journalist called "rusticity improved"—a deliberate combination of modern and traditional forms and materials.[47] Grossman described it as "Nordic," which connoted a Swedish modernism. Her roots were clearly reflected in the kitchen accessories, which she imported from Sweden, and in the wooden chest that had descended in her family, which she placed in the entryway.[48]

Like Grossman, the ceramists Gertrud and Otto Natzler were grounded in a European training that they adapted to the local taste and to the availability of materials. They studied ceramics in Vienna with potter Franz Iskra; after just a year of part-time classes, they furnished a rented studio space with a potter's wheel, kiln, and raw materials and experimented extensively, selling their work in Viennese gift shops.[49] They fled Vienna in 1938 and took what materials they could to Los Angeles, where they set up a studio.

The Natzlers frequently emphasized that they were self-taught and minimized both the importance of their early study in Vienna and the influence of the California landscape and lifestyle on their work. Nonetheless, Gertrud's throwing skills and Otto's knowledge of glaze chemistry, both acquired in Vienna, were critical to their success in California. As two among just a handful of West Coast potters who knew how to throw on a wheel (another was Marguerite Wildenhain), the Natzlers taught many influential California potters this fundamental skill, including Beatrice Wood and Laura Andreson. Many glaze formulas that Otto used were developed after his arrival in California, and he expressed a preference for native and local ingredients.[50] He noted that his and Gertrud's palette evolved and became more elaborate because of their exposure to "the subtle colors of the desert and the High Sierra."[51] And even though Gertrud consistently strove for a classical balance and proportion in her pots, destroying many vessels that did not meet her exacting standards, she derived inspiration from nature and kept a collection of found objects such as seedpods, pebbles, wood, pinecones, and shells in the studio.[52] A bowl that Otto described as one of his all-time favorites demonstrates the subtle way that nature influenced their work, with its "grey lava" glaze juxtaposed with the bright turquoise overflow, much like the contrast of earth and water (3.14).[53]

The versatile designer Walter Landor drew on his British art training, adapting it to the exigencies of his new situation. Born in Munich, Landor moved to London in 1931 to study at the Goldsmiths College School of Art. One of the founding members of the Industrial Design Partnership in London, he traveled to New York in 1939, ostensibly to assist with and report on the New York World's Fair for British publications but most likely hoping to immigrate to the United States.[54] Sensing great opportunity, he settled in San Francisco, where he secured an associate professorship in industrial design at the California College of Arts and Crafts, marveling that "America [is] still the country of unlimited possibility."[55] One of his earliest projects, in 1940, was a poster and exhibition design for the show *Space for Living* at the San Francisco Museum of Art (now the San Francisco Museum of Modern Art), which was organized by Telesis, a group of architects and landscape designers who sought to raise awareness about housing and urban planning in the Bay Area (3.15). Through this project Landor established many important contacts, including architects Erich Mendelsohn and William Wilson Wurster and the museum's director, Grace McCann Morley. He established the firm Walter Landor & Associates with his wife, Jo Landor, in 1941, initially offering graphic-design services but quickly expanding to include packaging, product design, signage, exhibition design, and retail design.

Over the course of his fifty-year career, Landor became one of the leading figures in integrated product marketing, corporate identity, and consumer research. Just one example of a combined graphic- and product-design program is the Arrowhead Spring Water easy-tilting glass bottle, for which Landor designed the bottle's shape and label (3.16). The problem was that a traditional

3.15. Walter Landor. *Space for Living,* 1940. Cat. 160

3.16. Walter Landor. Arrowhead Spring
Water bottle, c. 1953. Glass, metal,
paper, 10¾ x 5 x 8½ in. (27.3 x 12.7 x
21.6 cm). National Museum of American
History, Kenneth E. Behring Center,
Smithsonian Institution

glass bottle filled with water was too heavy to lift and pour, so the Landors created a half-gallon bottle with a rounded edge that could be tilted (Jo Landor
modeled the original bottle in clay).[56] Landor explained how the bottle worked
on both formal and functional levels: "The Arrowhead brand image is no longer
expressed in the trade-mark alone but by the uniqueness of glass shape and
function, facilitating pouring without lifting."[57]

Although Landor enjoyed great success in America and demonstrated a
keen understanding of the American psyche, he preserved some aspects of his
European origins. In many ways he was determined to become American—he
changed his name from Landauer to dissociate himself from his German origins, and he spoke and wrote letters exclusively in English from his arrival in the
United States. While his formal dress, courtly demeanor, and indefinable
European accent created a non-American impression, his phenomenally successful career suggests an astute understanding of the deepest desires of the
American consumer. Perhaps, as Adorno noted, it was Landor's status as an
outsider that gave him a unique perspective on American culture.[58]

Any designer who trained in Europe and immigrated elsewhere would inevitably incorporate European ideas in later work. The architect-designers in this

final group displayed an uncanny aptitude for identifying and catering to American preferences for spaciousness, luxury, and comfort. Although they never renounced their roots, their built work demonstrates how deeply their designs absorbed significant aspects of American and Californian lifestyles. Paul László and Victor Gruen exemplify this third model of émigré adaptation—one that drew heavily on American values and reflected American taste. In László's case, the work resonated with the preference of his Hollywood clientele for opulent modernism and luxurious scale. Gruen, like Landor, was closely attuned to the desires of American consumers in his designs for individual shops, shopping malls, and urban plans.

László was born in Debrecen, Hungary, and briefly studied architecture at the Staatliche Akademie der Bildenden Künste Stuttgart (Stuttgart State Academy of Art and Design) before apprenticing with architect Fritz A. Breuhaus in Cologne.[59] In 1924 he established his own firm in Vienna, which he later moved to Stuttgart. By 1936 László felt the oppression of Nazi Germany and, being half-Jewish, decided to immigrate to the United States.[60] He arrived in New York that year and traveled on to Los Angeles, which he chose both because of Hollywood's allure and because he had read about California in a Hungarian children's book and remembered its promise of opportunity.[61] László instantly connected with California culture and lifestyle, recalling that he had no emotional attachment to Hungary or Austria but "from the first day on [in California], it was a love affair."[62] Early on, many of László's clients were other émigrés from Europe, but his practice soon broadened to include American-born clients, particularly those working in the entertainment industry. Signaling his desire to be seen as American, within six months of arriving in Los Angeles he ceased speaking German or Hungarian, subsequently conducting all spoken and written communication in English.[63] Further reinforcing his American identity, he emphasized in 1985 that his wife and his children were born in America and said, "I hope I am hundred percent American."[64]

László could work in a range of styles to suit his clients' needs. For the showroom of the McCulloch Corporation in Los Angeles, he employed an industrial language of shiny steel fixtures, dynamic lines, and vibrant primary colors (3.17). The disposition of furniture has been compared to the German interior-design strategy of the Wohninsel, or "living island," where furniture is arranged in intimate groups to encourage conversation and social interaction.[65] The chair he designed with double-lobed backrest, steel frame, and wrench-shaped cross brace evokes corporate modernity and efficiency (3.18). For an upholstery textile design, he drew on the biomorphic shapes of Hans Arp and Joán Miró (3.1). In general, generous dimensions and modern elegance characterized László's designs. He explained, "I try to give the modern style an ageless importance, to be a little ahead of my time and yet build a comfortable home."[66] Even the American industrial designer George Nelson remarked that

"Men like László . . . whose personal taste did not include austerity, and whose clients generally refused to accept the glorification of economy, pursued a path whose directions led towards the merger of the qualities of the old and the new."[67] In this sense, his approach resembles Grossman's way of combining Scandinavian and Californian elements in a single unified interior.

Like László, Victor Gruen established his career in Europe and flourished in the United States. Born in Austria, Gruen studied architecture in a technical high school and spent one year at the Vienna Kunstakademie (Academy of Fine Arts). He cited Adolf Loos as a key teacher and influence. He established his own firm in Vienna, mostly working on remodeling projects because of the depressed interwar economy; when the Nazis annexed Austria in 1938, he fled to New York. In his early years there, he worked on designs for buildings at the 1939 New York World's Fair, as well as shops and theater sets. He moved to Los Angeles in 1941 to be closer to his largest client, Grayson department store. The scope and ambition of his projects quickly expanded as he designed larger chain stores, malls, and ultimately entire urban plans.[68]

Gruen rarely drew attention to his European background, although it would have been hard to ignore his thick Viennese accent. He saw his own life as perpetually moving forward, and he acknowledged his success by writing in the notes for his memoir, "Step by step I have been moving throughout my professional activities from architect to environmental architect to finally environmental planner."[69] Gruen rarely spoke of his refugee experience as a hindrance; in fact, according to his own account, he was always "filled with boundless optimism."[70] A biographer wrote of Gruen's belief that "his future lay in America so he settled in to become a part of it as soon as possible."[71] This forward-facing attitude was a trait he shared with Paul László.[72] In December 1941, when applying for American citizenship, Gruen requested to change his name from Gruenbaum. His family has conjectured that the name change originated from fears of anti-Semitism in the United States as the war in Europe progressed and also as an assimilation tactic so that his Jewish and Austrian heritage would not deter potential clients.[73]

While still in New York, Gruen accepted a commission from fellow refugee Michael Klein to design the candy shop Barton's Bonbonniere. In a move that was progressive for its time, Gruen's firm designed not only the shop interior but also the packaging and brand identity for Barton's.[74] In 1948 the *New York Times* reported that Barton's had opened its twenty-first retail store with "the customary magenta, yellow, and gray décor of the Barton chain, in modern style," indicating that the brand identity Gruen had created was consistently applied by the client and contributed to the company's success.[75] Gruen did not design that twenty-first store, however; after he completed the first several shops, Klein fired him and worked with less costly contractors to replicate the design in subsequent stores.[76] However, Klein invited Gruen back to design the company's fiftieth store, in New York City, in 1952 (3.19).[77] The lighting fixture for a store subsequently built in San Francisco shows his concern for functionality as well as his awareness of contemporary style (3.20). The wide uplight casts a glow on a Calder-like mobile of colorful metal disks, while the downlight illuminates the merchandise displays.

A key member of the Gruen office and a fellow émigré was Rudi Baumfeld, who joined Gruen in 1943. Baumfeld and Gruen had been friends in Vienna, and Baumfeld became a partner in the firm, responsible for the architectural design of all projects for the Los Angeles office. In particular he designed several Joseph Magnin stores (see 9.25) and much of the South Coast Plaza shopping mall in Costa Mesa.[78]

Following his move to Los Angeles and the commissions for several Grayson department stores in the 1940s, Gruen received the two most influential commissions of his career: Northland Center, near Detroit, an open-air shopping mall surrounded by a sea of parking; followed by Southdale Center, near Minneapolis, the first enclosed shopping mall, which would be copied in nearly every city in the U.S. and around the world. Gruen envisioned building a full-service city surrounding these cathedrals of consumption, complete with apartment buildings, schools, parks, and community centers, replicating the

3.17. Paul László. Showroom interior, McCulloch Corporation, Los Angeles, c. 1954. Photo by Julius Shulman, 1957

3.18. Paul László. Chair for the McCulloch Corporation showroom, c. 1954. Cat. 163

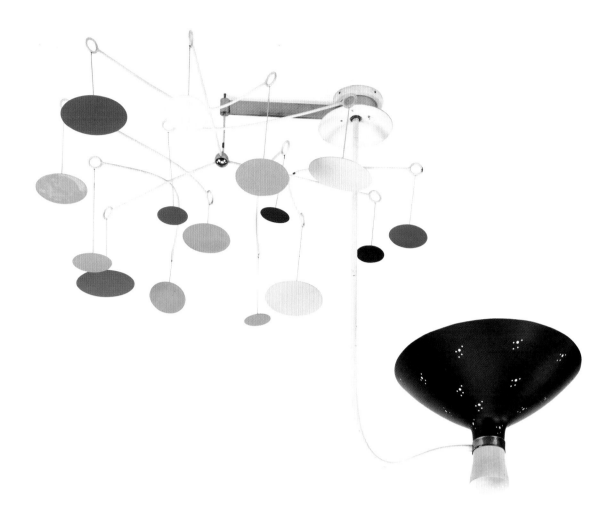

experience of urban life in central Vienna, but those plans were never realized.[79] Later in his career, he became deeply troubled by the impact of cars on the environment and social fabric, spending the bulk of the 1960s and '70s designing urban plans to resuscitate city centers and writing articles with titles such as "Who Is to Save Our Cities?" and "Are Centers Necessary?"

Gruen's genius for designing environments that coaxed money out of consumers' wallets testifies to his shrewd understanding of Americans' commercial desires. He was able to identify and exploit aspects of human nature—possibly due to his status as an outsider. His impassioned declarations of his intent to make constant progress reveal a characteristically American drive for success and recognition. A major factor in both László's and Gruen's success was their marketing genius. Both copiously published their buildings in widely read architecture periodicals, and both were featured in mainstream news outlets (László was in *Time* in 1952, Gruen in *Fortune* in 1962).[80]

Finally, there are some designers who seemed to wholly absorb American culture and become prophets of contemporary taste and style, anticipating fashions and setting trends. One of those prognosticators was Rudi Gernreich, who unveiled one cutting-edge design after another in the postwar period, from unstructured knit bathing suits and sportswear, miniskirts, and vinyl and

3.19. Victor Gruen. Interior of Barton's Bonbonniere, New York, 1952. Photo by Robert Damora, 1952

3.20. Victor Gruen. Lighting fixture from Barton's Bonbonniere, San Francisco, c. 1952. Cat. 118

plastic clothing to the scandalous topless swimsuit.[81] Gernreich hailed from Vienna, arriving in Los Angeles at age sixteen on the same Italian freighter as Gertrud and Otto Natzler, and he quickly established a reputation as a fashion designer catering to the most avant-garde tastes. His form-fitting wool-knit dress from about 1953 (3.21) was revolutionary compared to the structured and tailored garments of the time, and he continued to create radical fashion designs throughout his career.

The phenomenon of designers seeking new lives and new opportunities in the Golden State was not limited to those born in foreign countries. Many designers moved to California from other regions of the United States. In the words of journalist William L. Worden, "These are the individualists, the wooly nonconformists, the seekers after free land or free air or just aloneness."[82] For example, after graduating from Wayne State University in Detroit, designer-makers Jerome and Evelyn Ackerman wanted to start a new life and settled in Los Angeles in 1952 near Evelyn's brother.[83] They established the firm Jenev Design Studio (a combination of their first names), which produced slip-cast ceramics, and later opened ERA Industries, for which they created mosaics, tapestries, carved wood panels, and many other products. Another example is designer Gere Kavanaugh, who, when given the option to join the Saarinen office in New Haven, Connecticut, or the Gruen firm in Los Angeles, chose the latter because she thought that the most exciting design developments were happening in California.[84] And California's strong system of higher education as well as several formidable art schools attracted students and teachers alike, which is why jeweler Arline Fisch moved from Skidmore College in Saratoga Springs, New York, to accept a position teaching art at San Diego State University in 1961.[85] Dozens more examples could be cited to demonstrate how many members of the design community deliberately decided to make a home in California.

Each émigré designer achieved a unique balance between assimilation into American culture and preservation of European cultural and educational values. The figures discussed here had a significant impact not only through their own prolific work but also through teaching and passing on enduring aspects of European education. The acclaimed designer (and leapfrogger between New York and Los Angeles) Alvin Lustig wrote that what made California different was its "freedom from European tradition."[86] Yet despite that freedom from historical styles and from the barriers between disciplines that characterized the European apprenticeship system, the many émigrés who settled in the Golden State infused its design culture with the legacy of Europe.

3.21. Rudi Gernreich. Dress, c. 1953. Cat. 111

NOTES

1 Paul László, "Designing with Spirit," interview by Marlene L. Laskey, 1984–85, Oral
   History Program, University of California,
   Los Angeles, 75–76. He acknowledged
   having joined the club both for recreation
   and to meet potential clients.

2 "Man with Mass," *Designs*, August 1947, 12.

3 Ehrhard Bahr, "California Modern as
   Immigrant Modernism," in *Weimar on the
   Pacific: German Exile Culture in Los
   Angeles and the Crisis of Modernism*
   (Berkeley: University of California Press,
   2007), 148–51.

4 Russell A. Kazal, "Revisiting Assimilation:
   The Rise, Fall, and Reappraisal of a
   Concept in American Ethnic History,"
   American Historical Review 100 (April
   1995): 437–71. This historiography sum-
   marizes research in assimilation studies.
   See 463–65 in particular for explanation
   of the pluralist model.

5 William Jordy, "The Aftermath of the
   Bauhaus in America: Gropius, Mies, and
   Breuer," in *The Intellectual Migration:
   Europe and America, 1930–1960*, ed.
   Donald Fleming and Bernard Bailyn
   (Cambridge, Mass.: Charles Warren
   Center for Studies in American History,
   Harvard University, 1968), 523.

6 For background, see Jarrell C. Jackman
   and Carla M. Borden, eds., *The Muses Flee
   Hitler: Cultural Transfer and Adaptation,
   1930–45* (Washington, D.C.: Smithsonian
   Institution Press, 1983), particularly
   Jackman, "German Émigrés in Southern
   California." See also Anthony Heilbut,
   *Exiled in Paradise: German Refugee Artists
   and Intellectuals in America, from the
   1930s to the Present* (New York: Viking
   Press, 1983); Stephanie Barron with Sabine
   Eckmann, eds., *Exiles + Emigrés: The
   Flight of European Artists from Hitler* (Los
   Angeles: Los Angeles County Museum of
   Art; New York: Abrams, 1997), especially
   233, for Franz Schulze's concept of "the
   reciprocity of the encounter"—the theory
   that émigrés did not simply relocate and
   continue their work on different soil but
   instead found artistic inspiration in their
   new environment; Bahr, *Weimar on the
   Pacific*; and Joseph Horowitz, *Artists in
   Exile: How Refugees from Twentieth-
   Century War and Revolution Transformed
   the American Performing Arts* (New York:

   Harper, 2008), particularly 7–8, explaining
   Horowitz's ideas about "cultural exchange," in
   which he examined adult immigrants from
   non-English-speaking countries who both
   "stayed foreign and became American."

7 I am grateful to Gail Reynolds Natzler for
   confirming the circumstances of the
   Natzlers' immigration.

8 Otto Natzler, interview by Ruth Bowman,
   July 7–14, 1980, Archives of American Art,
   Smithsonian Institution, 37.

9 Marguerite Wildenhain, *The Invisible Core: A
   Potter's Life and Thoughts* (Palo Alto: Pacific
   Books, 1973), 54.

10 Victor Ries, "Religious Artistic Expression in
   Metal Sculpture," interview by Suzanne B.
   Riess, November 7, 1983, in *Renaissance of
   Religious Art and Architecture in the San
   Francisco Bay Area, 1946–1968*, Regional
   Oral History Office, Bancroft Library,
   University of California, Berkeley, 1985,
   499a–e, http://www.lib.berkeley.edu/cgi-
   bin/roho_disclaimer_cgi.pl?target=http://
   digitalassets.lib.berkeley.edu/roho/ucb/text/
   renaissance_v2.pdf.

11 Mann, quoted in Heilbut, *Exiled in Paradise*, 54.

12 See "The Salon in Exile," *Jewish Women and
   Their Salons: The Power of Conversation*, exh.
   cat., ed. Emily D. Bilski and Emily Braun (New
   York: Jewish Museum; New Haven, Conn.:
   Yale University Press, 2005), 138–47; Salka
   Viertel, *The Kindness of Strangers* (New
   York: Holt, Rinehart, and Winston, 1969);
   Katia Mann, *Unwritten Memories* (New York:
   Knopf, 1975); Lawrence Weschler, "Paradise:
   The Southern California Idyll of Hitler's
   Cultural Exiles," in Barron with Eckmann,
   eds., *Exiles + Emigrés*.

13 On Neutra's social world, see Thomas Hines,
   *Richard Neutra and the Search for Modern
   Architecture* (New York: Oxford University
   Press, 1982), 161–91.

14 László, interview, 77–85.

15 Bahr, *Weimar on the Pacific*, 34–35.

16 Marguerite Wildenhain, interview by Hazel
   Bray, March 14, 1982, Archives of American
   Art, Smithsonian Institution, 2; Wildenhain,
   Invisible Core, 20.

17 Wildenhain, interview, 20. This was the standard model for training at the Bauhaus.

18 Marguerite Wildenhain, "Pottery," *Arts and
   Architecture*, March 1947, 46.

19 Wildenhain, quoted in Don Wallance,
   Shaping America's Products (New York:
   Reinhold, 1956), 154.

20 Wildenhain, interview, 14.

21 Barbara Perry, ed., *American Ceramics: The
   Collection of the Everson Museum of Art*
   (New York: Rizzoli, 1989), 192; *Eleventh
   National Ceramic Exhibition* (Syracuse, N.Y.:
   Syracuse Museum of Fine Arts, 1946), 29.
   Wildenhain received a prize of $100 given by
   Richard B. Gump of San Francisco.

22 Wildenhain, quoted in "Pond Farm
   Workshops," *Arts and Architecture*,
   December 1949, 25.

23 *School of the Pond Farm Workshops 1950*
   (brochure), in *Renaissance of Religious Art
   and Architecture in the San Francisco Bay
   Area*, vol. 2, appendix K.

24 *The Letters of Gerhard Marcks and Marguerite
   Wildenhain, 1970–1981: A Mingling of Souls*,
   ed. Ruth R. Kath and Lawrence J. Thornton
   (Ames: Iowa State University Press, 1991), 121.

25 Wildenhain, "Pottery," 46.

26 Marguerite Wildenhain, *Pottery, Form and
   Expression* (Palo Alto: Pacific Books, 1962), 74.

27 Sigrid Weltge-Wortmann, *Women's Work:
   Textile Art from the Bauhaus* (San Francisco:
   Chronicle Books, 1993), 59–61, 172.

28 Lisa Aronson (sister of Trude Guermonprez),
   conversation with author, April 1, 2010.

29 Biographical accounts can be found in Yoshiko
   Uchida, "Trude Guermonprez," *Craft Horizons*,
   March–April 1959, 27–31; Hazel V. Bray and Kay
   Sekimachi Stocksdale, *The Tapestries of Trude
   Guermonprez*, exh. cat. (Oakland: Oakland
   Museum, 1982); Jan Janeiro, "Trude
   Guermonprez: A Quiet Journey," *Surface
   Design Journal*, Fall 1991, 6–8.

30 *School of the Pond Farm Workshops 1950*
   (brochure), n.p.

31 Questionnaire, Trude Guermonprez file,
   Oakland Museum of California Art Library.

32 Albrecht Pohlmann, "Trude Guermonprez:
   'Still Not Old Enough to Avoid Foolishness,'"
   trans. Wilfred Bunge, in *Marguerite
   Wildenhain and the Bauhaus: An Eyewitness
   Anthology*, ed. Dean and Geraldine Schwarz
   (Decorah, Iowa: South Bear Press, 2007),
   367; originally published as Albrecht
   Pohlmann, *Modell, Künstlerin, und 'wahre
   Eva': Das Abenteuereliche Leben der Trude
   Guermonprez* (Halle an der Saale, Germany:
   Verlag Janos Stekovics, 2003), 258–66.

33 Ed Rossbach, "Trude Guermonprez 1910–
   1976," *Craft Horizons*, August 1976, 10.

34 Trude Guermonprez, Southern California
   Handweavers lecture, 1954, folder 1, box 2,
   Trude Guermonprez Papers, Oakland
   Museum of California Art Library.

35 Victor Ries artist file, Oakland Museum of California Art Library.

36 Ries, interview, 533.

37 Ibid., 541.

38 Artist's archive, collection of Victor Ries and Noa Mohlabane.

39 *School of the Pond Farm Workshops 1950* (brochure), n.p.

40 Ries, quoted in "Pond Farm Workshops," *Arts and Architecture*, December 1949, 24.

41 Grossman, quoted in Rose Henderson, "A Swedish Furniture Designer in America," *American Artist*, December 1951, 56. For more on Grossman, see Evan Snyderman and Karin Åberg Wærn, eds., *Greta Magnusson Grossman: A Car and Some Shorts* (Stockholm: Arkitekturmuseet, 2010).

42 "Swedish Modern," *Designs*, January 1947, 9.

43 Employment Data, Greta Magnusson Grossman, Biographical Files (Reference Collection), record series 745, University Archives, University of California, Los Angeles.

44 Ancestry.com, *California Passenger and Crew Lists, 1893–1957* (online database), Provo, Utah: Generations Network, 2008.

45 Grossman, quoted in Henderson, "Swedish Furniture Designer in America," 56.

46 "Some Modern Is Nothing but Unpretentiousness," *House Beautiful*, March 1943, 26.

47 "Rusticity Improved, Comfortable Living on the Well-Furnished Hillside," *Interiors*, February 1950, 69–75.

48 Janet McHendrie, "House with a Nordic [*sic*]," *Los Angeles Times*, March 5, 1950, H4.

49 Otto Natzler, *Gertrud and Otto Natzler: Ceramics* (Los Angeles: Los Angeles County Museum of Art, 1968), 1–31.

50 Ibid., 43, and Otto Natzler, interview, 102.

51 Otto Natzler, interview by Jo Lauria at the Los Angeles County Museum of Art, December 18, 1998; videotape in LACMA's Decorative Arts and Design Department.

52 *Form and Fire: Natzler Ceramics, 1939–1972*, exh. cat. (Washington, D.C.: Renwick Gallery of the National Collection of Fine Arts; Smithsonian Institution Press, 1973), 19.

53 Natzler, *Gertrud and Otto Natzler: Ceramics*, 56; Otto Natzler, interview by Jo Lauria at the Los Angeles County Museum of Art, January 7, 2004; videotape in LACMA's Decorative Arts and Design Department.

54 Susan Landor Keegin (Walter Landor's daughter), email correspondence with author, August 26, 2010.

55 Walter Landor to his parents, December 14, 1939, collection of Susan Landor Keegin.

56 Bernard F. Gallagher, "A Brand Is Built in the Mind: Walter Landor and the Transformation of Industrial Design in the Twentieth Century" (master's thesis, State University of New York College of Oneonta, 2007), p. 37. I am grateful to Susan Landor Keegin for explaining the role of her mother, Jo Landor, in the design process.

57 Walter Landor, "Design Moves Merchandise If It Moves People," *Good Packaging Yearbook*, 1957, 94.

58 I am grateful to Susan Landor Keegin, SB Master, and Ellen Magnin Newman for sharing with me their memories of Walter Landor and for helping me understand his cultural identity.

59 László, interview, viii.

60 Ibid., 67.

61 Ibid., 90.

62 Ibid., 70.

63 Ibid., 175.

64 Ibid., 176.

65 Monica Penick, "A Little Paradise: Paul László and the Modern California House" (lecture, annual meeting of the College Art Association, New York, February 25, 2009).

66 Paul László, August 6, 1952, text written for but not used in the 1952 *Time* article (see note 80), Paul László Collection, Architecture and Design Collection, University Art Museum, University of California, Santa Barbara.

67 George Nelson, introduction to *Paul László: Industrial Designer, Interior Decorator*, n.d. This is one of three volumes that László self-published, each with an introduction by a leading designer; copies on file in the LACMA library.

68 For more on Gruen, see Alex Wall, *Victor Gruen: From Urban Shop to New City* (Barcelona: Actar, 2005); Jeffrey M. Hardwick, *Mall Maker: Victor Gruen, Architect of an American Dream* (Philadelphia: University of Pennsylvania Press, 2004).

69 Victor Gruen Papers, folder 2, box 77, Manuscript Division, Library of Congress, Washington, D.C.

70 Hardwick, *Mall Maker*, 16; Gruen Papers, folder 18, box 20.

71 Unidentified writer, Gruen Papers, folder 2, box 77.

72 László, interview, 19.

73 Gruen Papers, folder 7, box 22; Hardwick, *Mall Maker*, 57.

74 "Recent Work by Gruenbaum, Krummeck & Auer," *Architectural Forum*, September 1941, 191–200.

75 "Candy Shop for Times Square," *New York Times*, November 7, 1948, R4.

76 Gruen Papers, box 77.

77 "Playful Chocolate Shop," *Architectural Forum*, August 1952, 100–103.

78 Rudi Baumfeld file, Gruen Associates, Los Angeles office.

79 "Shopping Centers of Tomorrow," *Arts and Architecture*, January 1954, 12–17; Hardwick, *Mall Maker*, 131–35.

80 "Art: Rich Man's Architect," *Time*, August 18, 1952, 54; W. Guzzardi, "Architect of Environments," *Fortune*, January 1962, 76–80, 134, 136, 138.

81 Arlene Monks, "Latest Style Developments More Than Some Can Bare," *Los Angeles Times*, June 20, 1964, B1; Marshall Burchard, "The Miniskirt Is Here to Stay (Till Spring, Anyway)," *Time*, December 1, 1967, cover and 70–80; Brigitte Felderer et al., *Rudi Gernreich: Fashion Will Go Out of Fashion* (Philadelphia: Institute of Contemporary Art, University of Pennsylvania, 2001).

82 William L. Worden, "The Pacific Coast," *Better Homes and Gardens*, November 1955, 201.

83 Jerome and Evelyn Ackerman, conversation with author, October 28, 2007.

84 Gere Kavanaugh, conversation with author, February 12, 2009.

85 *Elegant Fantasy: The Jewelry of Arline Fisch* (San Diego: San Diego Historical Society; Stuttgart: Arnoldsche, 1999), 118.

86 Alvin Lustig, "California Modern," *Designs*, October 1947, 7–10.

TYPICAL CLASS R'M
ACTIVITY TRAIN'G
FOR RICHARD

4

Open World: California Architects and the Modern Home

NICHOLAS OLSBERG

At dusk on March 10, 1933, during one of the harshest periods of the Great Depression, a great earthquake struck underwater to the west of Long Beach. Among the many casualties—including over a hundred dead—were at least a score of the region's brick-and-mortar schools, in which thousands of children might have perished had the temblor hit a few hours earlier. New rules on school construction—favoring single stories, lightweight construction, and easy egress in an emergency—appeared within months of this nearly catastrophic event. A rapid program of school building followed, to which the economy and speed of

4.1. Richard Neutra. *Typical Classr[oo]m, Activity Train[in]g*, Corona Avenue School, Bell (interior perspective), 1935. Cat. 221

modern techniques and materials were essential. California schoolchildren, in consequence, were among the first to inhabit truly modern buildings as part of their everyday lives. In these low-slung, transparent, lightweight pavilions, free of doorways, vestibules, stairwells, and halls, life flowed easily from classroom to playground, from activity to activity, and between the sheltered and the open worlds.

Scaled down to near-domestic proportions, the schools became models for the light-filled, open-plan California homes that would prove so appealing after World War II. Richard Neutra, who developed the most inventive of them, portrayed his first experimental unit, at the Corona Avenue School in Bell, in drawings that picture a convergence of solitary space and common ground, teacher and child, group and community, indoors and out (4.1). This was a world of discovery tailored to satisfy what his former partner R. M. Schindler called "the urge for growth and extension of our . . . selves."[1] It came by loosening the boundaries—physical, visual, and cultural—between activities. The drawing carries a touching dedication to Neutra's own severely impaired son, Richard, but it was surely also dedicated to a vision of a newly dynamic society that would have the same openness and of the open dwellings that would house it.

In the same year, Neutra applied that same sense of mobility to a prototype for a house in thin-gauge steel, built in the San Fernando Valley for film director Josef von Sternberg (4.2). With spaces molded like a racetrack and set off with a course of water, the house takes its cues both from the sweep and sheen of aircraft and from the satin surfaces of the silver screen. As the dynamic lines of his sketch suggest, Neutra has left behind the static, linear, stacking geometries of early modernism and moved into a language that is fluid, unfixed, and reflective, with shiny steel, light dancing on water, and aerodynamic walls. Although the house itself was still organized into distinct rooms, and the whole complex was surrounded by a wall, Neutra virtually eliminated the boundary between indoor and outdoor space inside the enclosure.

Together these two projects by the figure who became the standard-bearer for West Coast ideas of the modern expressed elements central to the diverse reinventions of the home that California's architects were to make in the twenty-five years to come. Spaces—within the dwelling, outside it, and between the dwelling and its surroundings—would be continuous. Borders and boundaries would be fluid. Each space would adapt to many activities. There would be no ceremonial rooms. Light, motion, and vista would be the principles around which architecture would be planned. And much of the joy of life would come from the joy of moving around the space for living.

Schindler and Neutra had both worked with Frank Lloyd Wright, and even though their own visual languages quickly diverged from his, they shared with Wright—and passed on to the many who in turn trained with them—his fundamental belief that architecture was "a powerful instrument of social progress

Nicholas Olsberg

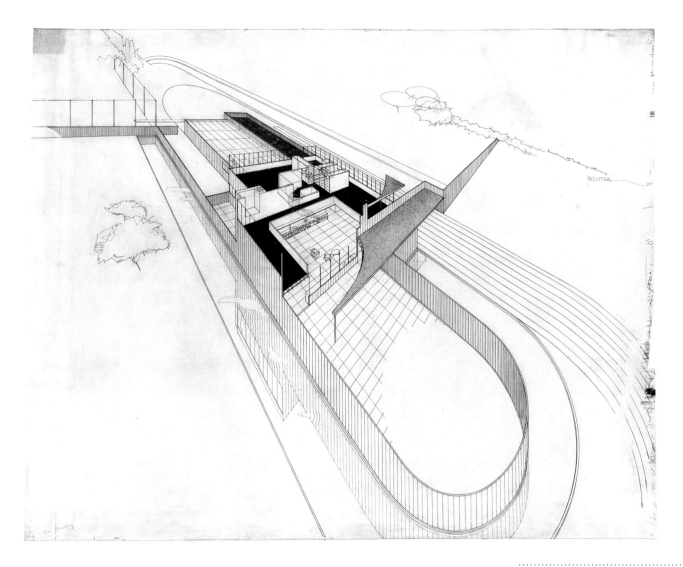

4.2. Richard Neutra. Josef von Sternberg House, Northridge (aerial perspective), 1934–35. Cat. 220

capable of bringing about a better world through radical changes in mankind's habits of living."[2] Wright himself took that idea of architecture as a social agent right into the California home, with a house in Palo Alto built in 1937 for Paul and Jean Hanna. The Hannas were pioneers in the new science of child development, with a "whole philosophy of living." They saw the household as a "small society," in which privacy and community were carefully calibrated, where spaces would flow easily between sanctuaries of solitude and settings for conversation and from indoors to out.[3] A single story and a single volume were obviously essential to achieve this. But at the scale required, any orthodox geometry would have left a dark center and set up fixed axes, vistas, and patterns of movement. Wright therefore turned to the honeycomb, with its hexagons and tetrahedrons, to set the ground rules for a looser plan. Light could now be drawn in from many different points and at many different hours of the day. Shallow shifts in level matched the rise and fall of the site, allowing each space to float out to the terrain and leaving fluid boundaries between inside and out. Movement circled around a skylit central kitchen. No room had a center point, nor was there a sense of front and back to the whole. Exterior walls were light screens of wood and glass. The most splendid space with the widest opening to the world and skies was the children's playroom (4.3). Wright himself delivered

building blocks to furnish it, hoping to spur the young Hannas into imagining a larger world modeled on this open dwelling and its "small society."

From this point on, with his annual visits to the state, a growing number of clients and former apprentices there, and an eventual satellite office in San Francisco, Wright became an increasingly frequent presence in California, while his writings, exhibitions, and widely published new buildings cast an ever longer shadow on the landscape of design. Perhaps Hanna House—like Neutra's von Sternberg residence, William Wilson Wurster's Clark Beach House, and much else from the exploratory period of the mid-1930s—was too caught up in experimenting with a new vocabulary, new materials, and a new system of construction to speak with complete confidence. But it became one of Wright's signature works, and its fundamental ideas—involving, as did those other contemporaneous projects, a liberation from the conventions of scale and enclosure; carrying the same lines and materials from house to terrace; opening everything to movement—were published worldwide as demonstrations of a new spirit of living.

It is no coincidence that, with such examples, California became a proving ground for how to make a new society out of new homes. From the arrival of the transcontinental railroad onward, California's growth had been built on the

4.4. William Wilson Wurster. Clark Beach House, Aptos, 1937. Construction photograph, 1937
The wide-board wood siding and paned windows suggest traditional forms, but Wurster makes us look at them afresh by enlarging scale, using a flat roof, stripping away detail, and emphatically outlining the shapes to draw attention to their simplicity.

promise of a home of one's own; and vast sectors of the state's economy were devoted to delivering that promise. Hence the everyday middle-class house—not the reshaping of city skylines, not the rethinking of social housing, not the reconfiguration of vast urban maps—was the primary field for modern design in California, from the easing of the Depression in the mid-1930s to the end of the state's baby boom in the early 1960s. That focus on the home as the engine of better living had all the hallmarks of a genuine movement, with broadly consistent approaches that could be applied to different scales and budgets. The central concept of loosening the boundaries between spaces and between the functions they served, inside and out, was endlessly adapted to diverse needs, topographies, tastes, and resources. Yet it was expressed not through uniformity but through the extraordinary variety that came from the divergent imaginations and traditions of its protagonists.

As California's postwar world emerged, ideas at play ranged widely. There was the rationalism of Neutra, the idea of harnessing science and industrialization to the arts of living promoted by Charles and Ray Eames, the equally passionate but antimechanistic artisanal aesthetics of Schindler, the structural flamboyance of John Lautner, and the fascination of Harwell Hamilton Harris and Whitney R. Smith with advancing the native Arts and Crafts tradition in architecture and the Japanese wooden house with which they associated it. Add to these the massively influential "soft modernism" of the Bay Area's William Wilson Wurster, whose works had begun to be seen by war's end as an international model for reconstructing the domestic landscape on newly humanist, regionally sympathetic lines. In Wurster's Clark Beach House of 1937, the familiar shapes of California wooden houses are transformed by reducing them to the simplest terms, changing their scales, and rearranging the usual relationship of volumes (4.4). Reconciling modernist sensibilities to familiar materials and the conventions of local construction, Wurster described this approach as "avoiding exotic materials, using indigenous things so that there is no affectation."[4]

From the early 1920s on, as massive population growth stretched its infrastructure to the limits, Southern California increasingly turned to denser housing patterns and especially to what was then called "flats." More than a duplex and less than an apartment building, these were small structures on single lots housing multiple units, each of which was a separate dwelling with its own front door. More compact than the region's characteristic early bungalow courts, they posed the same challenges to finding a balance between privacy and community. Asked to fit four tiny two-bedroom housing units on a single suburban lot south of Carthay Circle in Los Angeles, Gregory Ain took the standard two-story row house of traditional cities and turned it around with his Dunsmuir Flats of 1937 (4.5). The conventional narrow town house faces the street, is dominated by its staircase and its front and back doors, and extends deep into the lot to leave only a pocket backyard. It offers meager light, little space, and less vista, with a lot of tight turns and interrupted movement. Keeping the scale and economy of such standard blue-collar row houses, Ain turned his sideways, stepped them up the lot, and staggered them slightly from left to right, transforming the urban terrace from a row of dark funnels to a suite of pavilions. Flooded with daylight from high clerestory windows on the sheltered and secluded sides, they open to a ribbon of windows in the back (4.6). Private patios flow into a shared landscape of connected gardens, and secluded balconies welcome sunshine and skies.[5]

Published and exhibited worldwide, Dunsmuir Flats was the first in a ten-year sequence of community designs in which Ain progressively developed his ideas into a system of liberated low-cost housing.[6] He made the kitchen part of the social space. He extended everyday living into the garden. He used sliding walls and partitions both to save space and to allow for changing ways of living within the same plan. He built benches, beds, tables, shelves, and closets into the shell, leaving nothing to block light, sight, or movement. He cut construction costs to a minimum through standardization and repetition, but then staggered units on the site to give each the sense of occupying a space of its own. Ain's experiments became a crucial model for progressive approaches to mass housing: it would be efficient, varied, and autonomous but also true to

Nicholas Olsberg

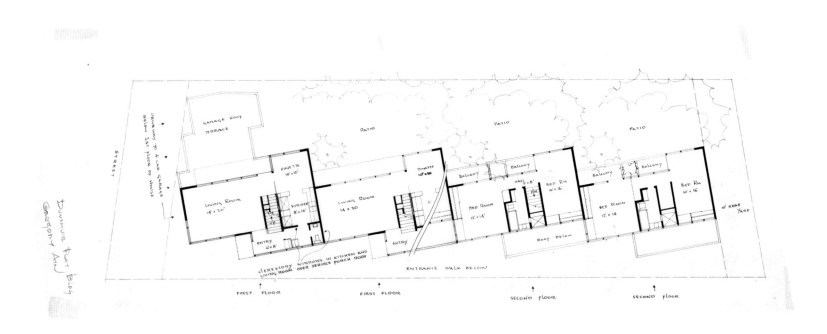

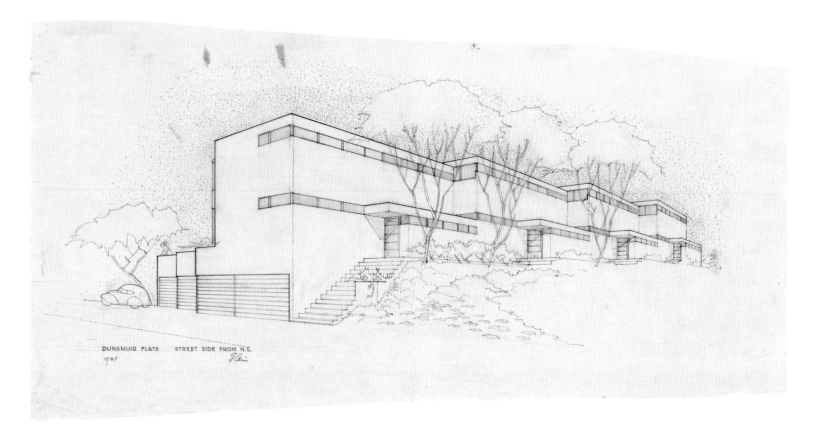

4.5. Gregory Ain. Dunsmuir Flats, Los Angeles (plan), 1937. Cat. 7

4.6. Gregory Ain. Dunsmuir Flats (exterior perspective), 1937. Cat. 6

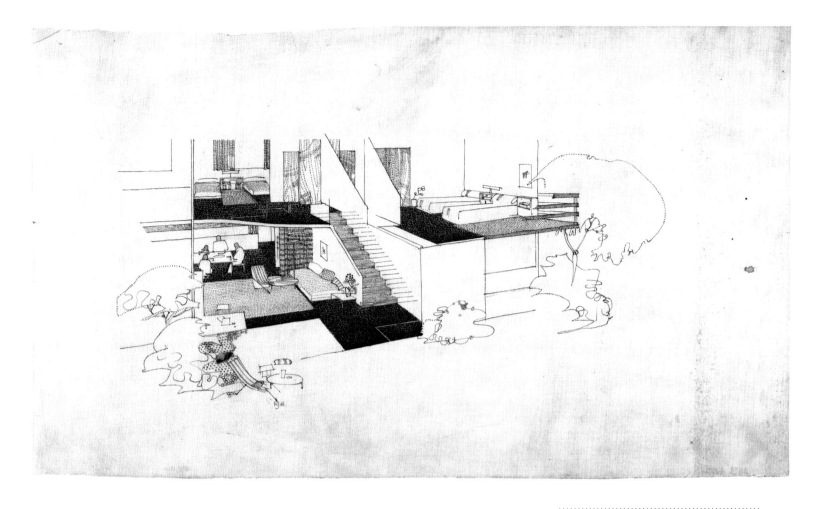

the sociable traditions of the bungalow court, in which boundaries, sight lines, and pathways remained neighborly. The demands and constraints of World War II—along with a new program of public housing—encouraged other explorations of clustered housing that would balance privacy and society, contraction and expansion, vista and shelter, stillness and activity. This balance made it all the more painful that Ain's most ambitious schemes for an open world—multiracial and multiethnic—eventually foundered on the rocks of a closed one: the insistence of lenders on racial and ethnic exclusion.[7]

the sociable traditions of the bungalow court, in which boundaries, sight lines, and pathways remained neighborly. The demands and constraints of World War II—along with a new program of public housing—encouraged other explorations of clustered housing that would balance privacy and society, contraction and expansion, vista and shelter, stillness and activity. This balance made it all the more painful that Ain's most ambitious schemes for an open world—multiracial and multiethnic—eventually foundered on the rocks of a closed one: the insistence of lenders on racial and ethnic exclusion.[7]

With space at a premium and budgets at a minimum, the dialogue inside each unit between private and family space, sitting and working, sleep and play was as critical as the dialogue between inside and out. This is made clear in Neutra's cutaway drawing for defense workers' housing at Channel Heights (1941–42), near the port of Los Angeles in San Pedro (4.8). Here Neutra opened up the movement between internal functions and between indoors and out, built in all the bulkier furniture to save space, designed a readily movable chair that could be used in multiple ways (4.7), and organized the interior around sight lines that allowed children to move freely but still be watched. In Schindler's unbuilt designs of 1943 for an apartment house for T. Falk, units are scrupulously stacked and staggered so that each would turn away from the

4.7. Richard Neutra. Chair from Channel Heights Housing Project, 1941–42. Cat. 224
True to the ideals behind his housing complex, Neutra designed this chair with inexpensive materials that could be used both indoors and out, allowing maximum flexibility. The design frequently appeared in promotional photographs of Neutra's buildings; this example is a rare survival from the architect's own home.

4.8. Richard Neutra. Channel Heights Housing Project, San Pedro (interior perspective), 1941–42. Cat. 223

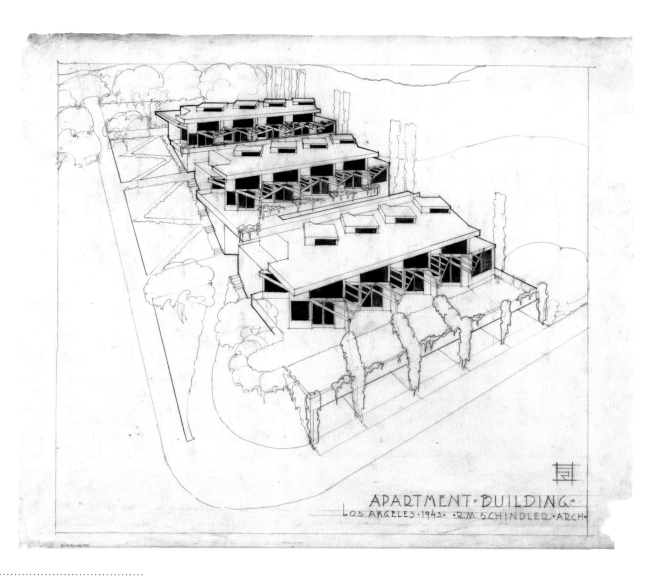

APARTMENT · BUILDING ·
LOS ANGELES · 1943 · R·M·SCHINDLER · ARCH·

4.9. R. M. Schindler. T. Falk Apartments, unrealized (aerial perspective), 1943. Cat. 251

4.10. R. M. Schindler. *Typical Apartment*, T. Falk Apartments, unrealized (interior perspective), 1943. Cat. 252

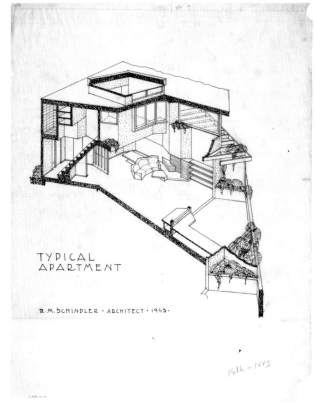

TYPICAL
APARTMENT

R·M·SCHINDLER · ARCHITECT · 1943 ·

Falk – 1943

street to gain a private view of the Silver Lake reservoir and to focus on its own large sheltered terrace (4.9). Sleeping space was perched on a rear mezzanine, and furnishings were built in, so that the space that remained would encourage a conversation between the body, the room around it, and the prospect of the world beyond (4.10). In both schemes—Neutra's for working families in defense and Schindler's for white-collar workers without children[8]—even the tightest quarters are given a sense of openness, ease, and outlook.

These projects—from the open walls of Corona Avenue School to the angled terraces of the Falk Apartments—share a common feature: they focus on daylight. Nothing better caught this determination to revel in the passage of light, to capture it at a height that would suffuse a room, and to dramatize the visitor's progress toward it than Harwell Hamilton Harris's "Sky House" in Berkeley (1939–41) for John Weston Havens Jr.[9] Harris placed this large house, built for a wealthy bachelor and his collection of modern design, at the lower end of the steep site and laid it out on two floors, each resting on a shallow V-shaped hull (4.11). In this way he could raise the living area nearly to the level of the street behind; support open interior spaces without foundation posts; shelter an outdoor room between a hanging garden and the house on the lower level; and provide access along an entry bridge straight to the top floor. There the huge window wall, bathing the living areas in light, comes as an astonishing surprise (see 2.32). Moving through dark redwood to an uninterrupted view across the bay moves us, too, from the tangible solids that connect the house to the hill to the ineffable mists, waters, and horizons that seem to release it from the land. Thus Havens House illustrates an idea key to the California modern house—rejecting the "picture window," or framed view, in favor of a diffuse or transcendental outlook that brings the skies in as much as it leads the eyes out. Nonetheless, the Havens House was still essentially a fixed container with a generous visual boundary. A year later, at the Birtcher House, on a peak overlooking Los Angeles, Harris moved a step further, allowing whole sides of the house to slide away so that the physical boundary between the distant ocean vista and the wide shelter is eliminated altogether (4.12). It is an idea fundamental to the emerging California tradition—what Ray Kappe (who followed Harris's example into the next generation, just as Harris had learned from Wright, Schindler, and Neutra) describes as seeking "the edges, the views, and a feeling of expansiveness."[10]

Neutra's steel house for von Sternberg had marked the beginning of experiments in mass housing that grew out of California's special industries and resources—the cheap lightweight composites, shaped plywood, sheet metal, and shells that served or sheltered the aircraft and film industries, ranging from open-span hangars in concrete to Masonite stage sets. This inquiry intensified with a succession of California housing crises, from the resettlement of Dust Bowl migrants in the 1930s to the massive influx of labor to prewar defense

industries and then to wartime defense plants. It was also fueled by booming postwar businesses, from the manufacture of aircraft and "California casual" clothing to a rapidly growing range of consumer and retail services. The pace at which homes could be delivered and constructed became as important as their cost: the watchwords were "ready-made," "minimum dwelling," "standard-unit system," and "mechanization." The desire to construct a more open world was wedded to the possibility of opening that world more widely. By 1943 Californians were already anticipating a huge influx of workers eager to share in its coming peacetime prosperity and to embrace in a sunlit clime the promise—first made in Roosevelt's second inaugural address and sworn as a pledge to the troops on mobilization—that every American family had a right to a modern, hygienic home, as democracy's "second line of defense."[11]

Translating that expectation into an effort to show what a rationally developed, hygienic, and efficient postwar house might look like, and realizing that no one would want a "modern" house until they could see one, the Los Angeles–based magazine *Arts and Architecture* announced in January 1945 a series of "case study" model homes to be published in the magazine and built as demonstrations of the livability of homes in tune with the scientific age.[12] The program is now best remembered for the alliance with industrial materials

that marked its minimalist projects of the 1950s and early '60s. But it was the first, intensive series of twenty-one prototypes, all designed during the last year of the war and the first two years of peace, that better shows the characteristics of California's postwar exploration of the modern home. Designed by ten architects, ranging from Wurster to Neutra to Eames, they reflected many approaches to a newly open world. They came in steel, wood, or adobe; targeted large suburban lots or blue-collar tracts; were boxed or sprawling, lightweight or substantial.

Thus they announced the special character of at least a decade of postwar experiments on the single-family dwelling for California. It would be witty, improvisational, essentially egalitarian, and immensely varied. It would work at a modest scale in modes that could be built quickly. It would be democratic, suburban rather than metropolitan, against display, and geared as carefully to tract houses as to privileged enclaves. Above all, it would make clear that modernity and democracy arise not from things being the same but from common principles that can be expressed in widely differing ways. Sheer numbers were essential to demonstrate the force of these ideas; and in this, postwar California was perhaps unique. Consider dwellings by postwar modernists elsewhere—even in such expansive environments as Tel Aviv, Rio de Janeiro, or

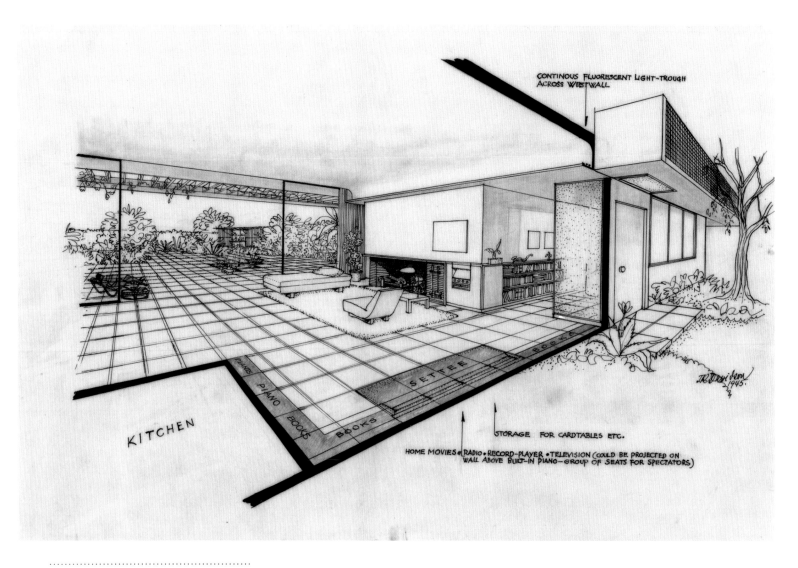

Labels in image:
CONTINOUS FLUORESCENT LIGHT-TROUGH ACROSS WESTWALL
KITCHEN
PIANO · BOOKS
BOOKS
SETTEE · BOOKS
STORAGE FOR CARDTABLES ETC.
HOME MOVIES · RADIO · RECORD-PLAYER · TELEVISION (COULD BE PROJECTED ON WALL ABOVE BUILT-IN PIANO–GROUP OF SEATS FOR SPECTATORS)

4.13. J. R. Davidson. Case Study House #1, unrealized (perspective of living room and terrace), 1945. Cat. 57
For the first published Case Study House, Davidson originally proposed a large open-plan suburban house that could be maintained efficiently without staff. Deciding that the times required models on a smaller budget and scale, Davidson then simplified the project and its systems into an affordable, ready-built model dwelling (Case Study #11). That version, the first of the Case Study Houses to be built and presented to the public, in 1946, attracted more than fifty-five thousand visitors.

4.14. Charles Eames and Ray Eames. Eames House (Case Study House #8), Pacific Palisades, 1945–49. Photo by Julius Shulman, 1949

4.15. John Lautner. Carling House, Hollywood Hills (exterior perspective), 1947. Cat. 166

Algiers—and one can point to a handful of singular constructions for the high bourgeoisie or to a vaguely repetitive sequence of apartment buildings. In postwar California, inventive new single homes would rise in the thousands; in design vocabularies that fit every level of income, need, and aspiration; and at sites of varying scope and pliability, from mountain to desert, city to beach, the "unbuildable" sloping lot to the vast flat tract.

Designs for the first set of case studies began appearing in February 1945, with built examples rising only slowly as materials and labor were gradually released from defense uses. The first published Case Study House, by J. R. Davidson, structured the exterior landscape so that house, terrace, and garden would read as continuous space with a common surface (4.13). Number 8, a studio and home of their own by Charles and Ray Eames, developed as two high, light-filled, open-span containers, made of industrial steel, glass, and curtain wall and resting on the landscape with nearly no mediating boundary. The idea of continuity with the landscape was expressed first through the incorporation of plants into sheltered space, then through reflective surfaces that mirrored the landscape outside, and finally in the echoes sounded in its very structure between the tree trunks on the land and the posts that support the house and studio (4.14).

Nicholas Olsberg

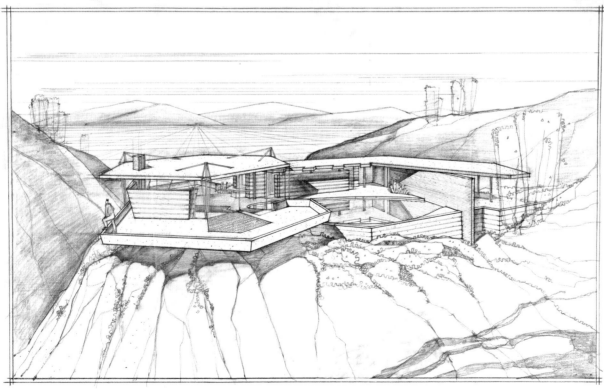

The opposing approaches of these two Case Study projects—one stretches out to the landscape and the other draws the landscape's logic in—were radically brought together by John Lautner in his Carling House (4.15). Lautner was not part of the Case Study program, but—like the Eameses—he was deeply concerned with uncovering standard construction systems that could liberate dwelling space. Designed in 1947 on a small crown lot in the Hollywood Hills, the house was a bachelor dwelling for Foster Carling, a movie composer who worked from home. By suspending the roof on cables from three thin metal pylons, Lautner got rid of bearing walls and posts and allowed for endless variations in the shape of the ceiling and the rooms beneath it. Like Davidson, he reached for continuity between indoors and out. But he was working on a constricted lot that would not allow for similarly extensive terraces, so he took three drastically original steps to achieve fluidity. He placed all work, recreational, and dining activities into a single volume, with slight shifts in level and orientation to mark them out. He pulled a portion of the outside pool inside to the living space. And he pushed another portion of the house out from it—allowing the principal wall of the principal room, with its built-in furniture, to swivel into the open air. By transforming a wall of the house to a wall of the terrace at the turn of a handle, Lautner drew in the landscape and extended toward it in the same machine age gesture.

Thus each of these three houses connects with the outside world in distinct but equally fluent modes. They seem to paint what the landscape designer Garrett Eckbo called a "landscape for living."[13] And—as the images of the Eameses in their house show so well (see 5.21 and 5.37)—they exemplify a newly relaxed and very Californian approach, with a decided lack of interest in such things as picture-hanging walls or furniture that obstructed motion and views, and with a decided love of the low slung, of stools, cushions, benches, and constant movement between indoor and out, recreation and work, standing up and slouching, gatherings and solitude. This was a mode of living that became so well integrated into the social landscape that by 1959, when the photographer Julius Shulman choreographed the Mirman family at play and at rest in their new steel garden pavilion, their clothes, the cushions, and the fruit and pots on the table could all be neatly coordinated (see pp. 2–3).

In his writings and garden plans, Eckbo proposed that the garden itself be seen as a set of living spaces, broadly zoned into functions, like the house, and—as in the Shulman photograph of the Mirman House—shaped, textured, and colored with the same aesthetic and a continuous set of materials, indoors and out. At the same time, he began to conceive the whole of a development as simply a garden on a larger scale—"park-planned" systems in which the landscape of a community was orchestrated into different uses, from recreation to wilderness and private space to community. As is evident in drawings for a cooperative housing development in Ladera Heights, south of San Francisco,

these approaches involved working closely with the architects. The drawing for John Funk and Joseph Allen Stein's model house (4.16) beautifully illustrates Eckbo's concept of dividing the outdoors into a set of connecting outdoor rooms that carried the function of the adjacent inside space—lounging on one side and dining on the other—out of doors. Eckbo's landscape designs for the suburb's master plan (4.17) show how a similar notion would work at subdivision scale: the community's pathways would flow freely from open parkland to a set of recreational facilities at its center. As with Eckbo and Ain's great plan for Reseda, in which each group of houses was to be organized around its own recreational park, the Ladera association failed because of its insistence on permitting a racial and ethnic mix.

At the same time, the interior of the house—physically and visually continuous with its external vistas and connections and lived in as loosely as a garden might be—was becoming no less a landscape than the exterior. As a result, that idea of continuity and flow began to move toward a fusion of house and garden. Whitney R. Smith, in an unbuilt prototype for a house designed in rough timber for the Barr Lumber Company, ran the entire house in a shallow strip along the length of its lot so that it became, in essence, just an inhabited garden wall (4.18). Nothing could better express the variety with which that same fundamental

4.16. Garrett Eckbo, John Funk, and Joseph Allen Stein. House and garden for Ladera Peninsula Housing Association, 1947. Gelatin silver print of a line drawing, sheet: 8½ x 11 in. (21.6 x 27.9 cm). John Funk Collection, Environmental Design Archives, University of California, Berkeley

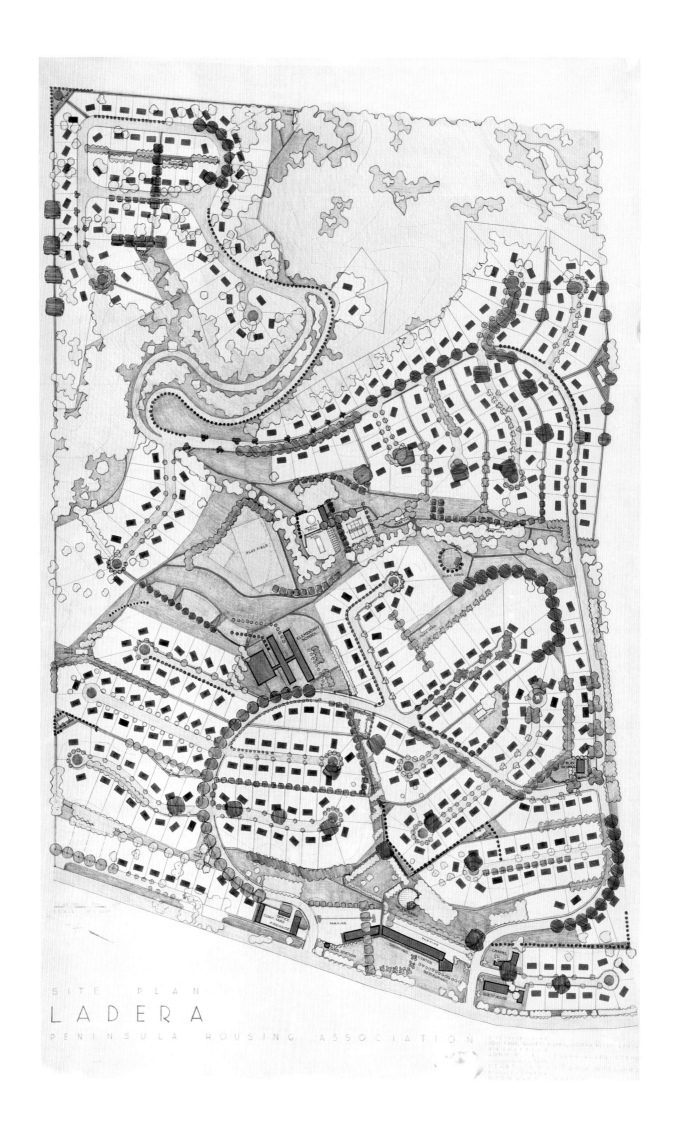

SITE PLAN
LADERA
PENINSULA HOUSING ASSOCIATION

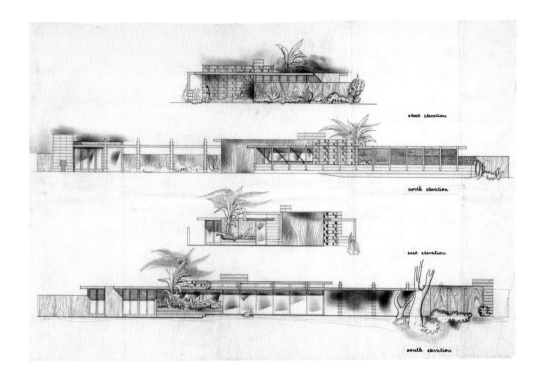

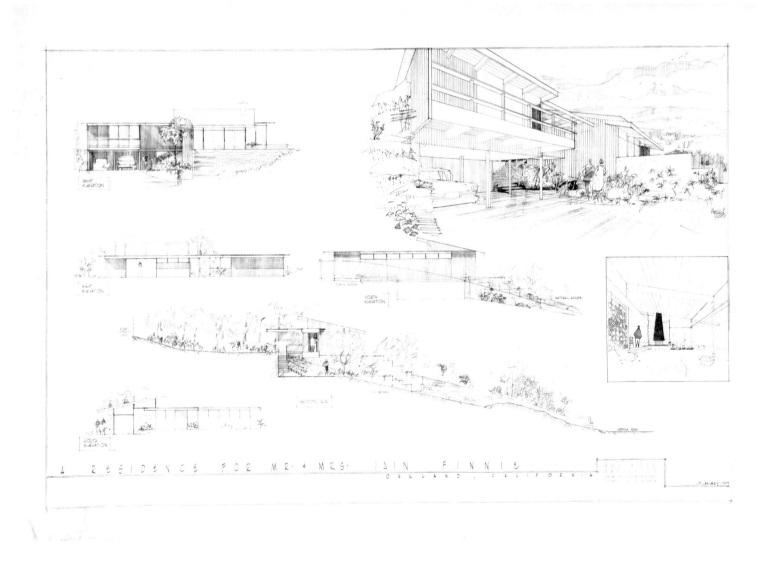

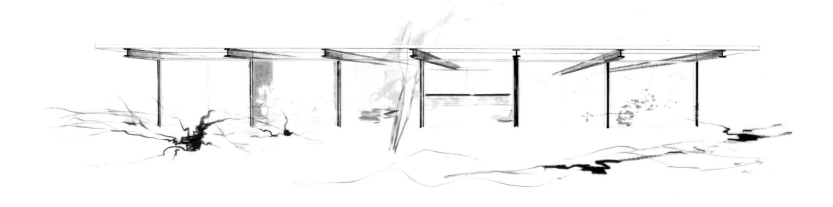

EICHLER HOMES

ARCHITECT
RAPHAEL S. SORIANO, A.I.A.

102/RD/005

Architect: Thornton M. Abell, Los Angeles.

For Open World living at its best...a sunny climate and L·O·F Plate Glass

When you build a new home in a sunkist climate, you want to enjoy true "Open World" living—large glass areas, window walls, sliding glass doors.

For places where heat and glare may be problems, L·O·F makes two special types of plate glass—*Parallel-O-Grey* and L·O·F Heat Absorbing. For exposures where sunlight is no problem, there's *Parallel-O-Plate*. (See diagrams.)

In all cases, you're getting the finest plate glass. *Parallel-O-Plate* and *Parallel-O-Grey* are ground simultaneously on both sides, then polished with jeweler's rouge, to insure maximum freedom from distortion. You'll be living in your new home for years . . . so make sure you get the best plate glass now. Write for our booklet, "Look at Living in the Open World". Send 10¢ to L·O·F, 2253 Libbey·Owens·Ford Building, Toledo 2, Ohio.

Libbey·Owens·Ford
Toledo 2, Ohio

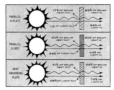

These diagrams illustrate, in simplified form, the difference between the three kinds of L·O·F Plate Glass.

idea about the interpenetration of house and garden could be realized than the contrast between the pastoral compression in this project; the crowded sense of change and movement achieved by Roger Lee in a hillside house for Mr. and Mrs. Iain Finnie in Oakland in 1959 (4.19); and Raphael S. Soriano's conception for Eichler Homes of a simple steel-frame house within a nursery of plants (4.20). Those differences in how to relate nature and structure are vividly expressed by the contrasting approach the three took to the art of drawing itself. Smith borrowed perspectival techniques from his early experiences in drawing film sets to show how the natural forms collapsed into built ones and how the soft edges of one set off the hard lines of the other; Lee incorporated the art traditions of his Chinese American heritage to make a dialogue between architectural hard lines and natural soft ones; Soriano, working in pastels on plastic sheets, seemed to bring to architecture the kind of expressively colorful simplicity that characterized the best of the Blaue Reiter and the Fauves.

By the beginning of the 1950s, California had already assumed its role as the model for future domestic life in America. In August 1949, *Time* magazine presented Neutra on its cover and his housing ideas inside; that November, *Ladies' Home Journal* called the state a "vast incubator of new designs"; and *Holiday* devoted its first issue of the new decade to Southern California as a vision of the future.[14] In the summer of that year, Ain's system-built demonstration house filled the garden of New York's Museum of Modern Art (see 10.7), while thousands of visitors toured the prototype of a precut modern ranch house by Californian Cliff May at the great Chicago home fair of 1950. Back in California, new designs were relentlessly promoted in the weekly "Home" sections of local newspapers, in developers' model homes, and in "demonstration houses" designed to advance new techniques, products, and utilities. California futurism was also marketed very effectively by advertising copy. A Toledo-based company, Libbey-Owens-Ford, sold its Thermopane glass across the nation by matching gloriously staged representations of California's transparent house designs with the idealistic rubric "Open World" (4.21). The campaign clearly resonated with a universalism that stretched through the Cold War culture of the western democracies—from the Museum of Modern Art, with Edward Steichen's great *Family of Man* exhibition of 1955, to Disneyland, with its "Small World" ride in the early 1960s. In the same vein, the designer and entrepreneur Cliff May was particularly careful to offer many slight variations on his basic precut ranch house, tying the "Carefree Californian"—as one of his affordable house models was called—to the interlocking ideas of security, freedom, and individualism.[15] The promotion of Eichler Homes—which (like Cliff May Homes) extended the comforts of a private, leisure-filled, indoor/outdoor lifestyle to a new class through the economies gained by building from a designer's standard kit of parts—brilliantly captured the same open-world ideology, dwelling less on the shape of their designs than on the freedom of

4.20. Raphael S. Soriano for Eichler Homes. Prototype steel house, Palo Alto (elevation), 1955. Cat. 267

4.21. Libbey-Owens-Ford advertisement featuring Thornton Abell house, published in *American Home*, May 1963, p. 103

4.22. Promotional photograph by Ernie Braun for Eichler Homes, c. 1958

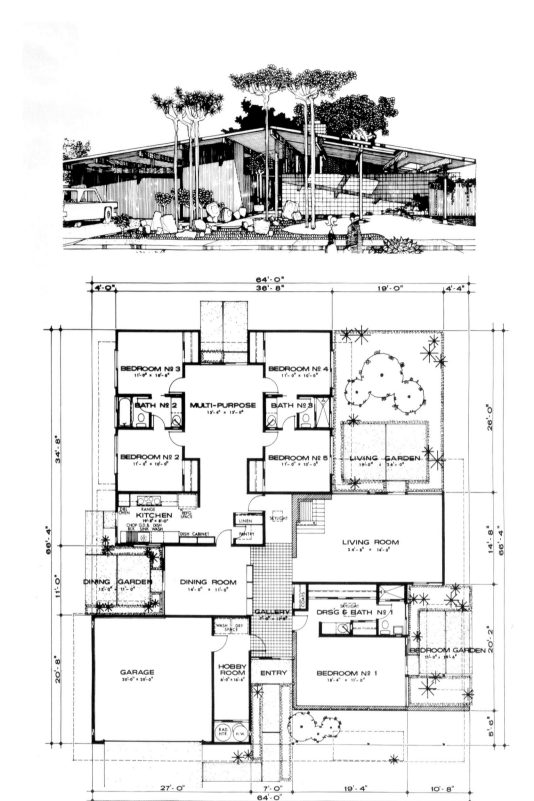

4.23. A. Quincy Jones and Frederick E. Emmons for J. L. Eichler Associates. *Plan 3.5* (exterior perspective and plan), c. 1966. Cat. 143

5 BEDROOMS

3 BATHS

House	2,344 sq. ft.
Garage	424 sq. ft.
Living Garden	494 sq. ft.
Dining Garden	143 sq. ft.
Bedroom Garden	215 sq. ft.
TOTAL	3,620 sq. ft.

PLAN

3.5

DESIGNED BY A. QUINCY JONES AND FREDERICK EMMONS, AIA, FOR J. L. EICHLER ASSOCIATES, INC.

movement they allowed and finally, as desegregation became more acceptable, on the Eichler neighborhood as a model of social and racial camaraderie (4.22).

Experiments in new structure, fabrication, and materials that borrowed from industry never quite worked for mass housing. Faced with the rising costs of steel and concrete, stricter codes, and the increasing resistance of banks and government lenders to innovation, neither Soriano's steel-frame house nor those that A. Quincy Jones and Frederick E. Emmons designed for Eichler in this material moved beyond demonstration stage (see 5.20). As Jones pointed out, conventional dry construction in wood frames and wood panels remained the most practicable, available, and flexible way to develop new ideas for the mass-produced components of a standardized tract house.[16] That was the system adopted by Jones and Emmons in their first designs for Eichler, also in Ladera Heights, and it was the one that persisted. Since Eichler tracts housed families of changing size and means and disparate incomes, plans and profiles were varied to adapt to growing households; there were extensive closets and flexible work zones (4.23).[17] Acknowledging the necessary alliance between these new suburbs and the automobile, Jones and Emmons carefully incorporated carports, assuring rapid, pleasant transitions from family car to family living.

Though it failed as a means of mass housing in prefabrication, the kinds of new materials and technology that the Eameses explored in their Case Study home and studio eventually did take root in custom villas of the late 1950s. When clients could afford experiments in steel and concrete, there emerged such inventive structural poetry as in Lautner's first curved concrete shells, with their transcendental sense of light, vista, and "disappearing space"; or in the reductive structures of Soriano, Donald K. Olsen, Craig Ellwood, and Pierre Koenig.[18] Each of those figures found a different way to make the physical craft of assembling the building so visible that it would open questions on the metaphysical or invisible: how shape and space are made to begin with or how inanimate structures can adopt the vital characteristics of a living form. Thus the architects' exploration of technology and structure began to reflect a similar discourse in abstract art—from how a sculpture could change perceptions of the space around it to how a painted surface could seem to throb. So one begins, as the 1950s ends, to locate in California modern houses the same complex metaphysics evident in many abstract works of art.

Garrett Eckbo enunciated this concept of the abstract in architecture most boldly by asking that gardens be a collage of the inert and the mobile, living plants and pristine plastics, so that they would appear "as artificial abstractions in the natural realm."[19] Unlike Roger Lee or Whitney R. Smith, whose work encouraged a sympathetic conversation between the two languages of building and nature, Eckbo's case for landscape abstraction rests on the idea of treating the natural and the built worlds as a continuum in which both speak the same tongue. His own garden, developed as a futurist projection for the

aluminum manufacturer Alcoa, brings into the natural world the same "abstract" artificial matter used in the built landscape. It is filled with structures in primary colors, reflective surfaces, plastics, and metals (4.24).[20] In a similar spirit, Albert Frey used lightweight materials from the aerospace industry to continually reshape his own first house, originally built in the 1930s on the desert floor. By the mid-1950s it read like a mechanical folly of abstract forms rising in the wild— a house growing like a garden unto itself (4.25). In his house for designer Raymond Loewy (see 5.3), Frey followed a different logic, extending the idea of Eckbo's continuum so that the natural materials of the desert folded into the machine age artifice of the structure.

Pierre Koenig captured Eckbo's idea of maintaining a consistent language between the open and the enclosed by constantly repeating the constructive elements of a design, from the geometry of a joint to the basic building blocks of its structure, in the cornice of a cabinet or in the soffit of a roof. His Case Study House #21 (1958) relies on recurring alternations: of solid and liquid platforms outside, of transparent and solid rectangles in the elevations, and of dark and light squares of cabinetry in the details (see p. 20). Rejecting the dynamism inherent in the material experiments that preceded him, Koenig—like his mentor Soriano—turned the grammar of the machine into a language of

4.24. Garrett Eckbo. Alcoa Forecast Garden, Los Angeles, completed 1959. Photo by Julius Shulman, 1959
The Aluminum Company of America (ALCOA) commissioned Eckbo to create a garden for his own home in Laurel Canyon to promote aluminum as the ideal material for the built landscape. Acclaim from the press and the public was enormous, and the company used images of the garden in its advertising for several years.

4.25. Albert Frey (1903–1998). Frey House, Palm Springs, remodeled 1953. Photo by Julius Shulman, 1956

ROSEN HOUSE
CRAIG ELLWOOD ASSOCIATES

repose, in which the idea of an open world is expressed through the almost sensuous satisfaction that comes from perceiving the unity of things at different scale, to different purpose, on different planes, indoors or out.

This effort to locate the pastoral within the technological also animated Craig Ellwood, a race-car driver, designer, and artist. Unlike Koenig, for whom the house could not exist without the hardscape around it, Ellwood moved back to the beautifully sited but autonomous containers of the Eames home and studio. By standing apart from the landscape, Ellwood's pavilions are essentially self-referential, focusing on the charged sense of structure—inside and out—that governs them. Rather than extend into a larger world, they enlarge and extend the world they construct for themselves, as in the Rosen House, with its perfect rectangular forms, set on a slope, that seem to hover just above the ground (4.26). The same proportions and structure are scrupulously moved inside the house to shape cabinetry, so that an object like the stereo cabinet recalls those geometries but shifts them to another scale (4.27). The result is a feeling of poise or tension in which the scale of the building and its ability to stay grounded both seem to become uncertain.

These are all invitations to explore not just the freedoms, convenience, or luxuriance of an open world but its poetics. Each, like Neutra's experimental

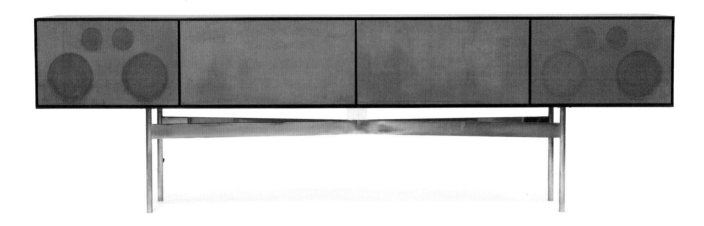

steel house, moves from the three dimensions of architecture into the space-time-motion equation of a fourth. Or, as in Ellwood's Rosen House, suggests the suspended or shifting states of being in the fifth. Those are transformations that the architects of temples and great halls—in a rational quest for perfect proportions or a mystical search for the atmospherics of the sublime—have always tried to achieve. But in California—with what Schindler called the "subtle transparent shades" cast by a unique light and the "unlimited horizons" into which space could be woven[21]—these rather grand matters of awareness were set right into the commonplace. The everyday home thus served as a sort of philosopher's garden, a playground of perception that might awake the same childlike readiness for exploration as Neutra's open classrooms thirty years before, or the same delight in motion as the dancing figure that graces one of the last covers of an Eichler brochure, in which nothing more is needed to describe a modern California home than a woman in joyful movement plus a few well-placed lines to suggest the subtlest sunlit surroundings that can shelter her (4.28).

4.26. Craig Ellwood. Rosen House, Brentwood (presentation drawing), 1961–63. Cat. 86

4.27. Craig Ellwood for Laverne Originals. Stereo cabinet for the Rosen House, 1961–63. Cat. 87

4.28. *Eichler Homes Designed to Make Your Everyday a Holiday!*, sales brochure, c. 1960. Cat. 334

NOTES

1   Rudolph M. Schindler, "Space Architecture," *Dune Forum*, February 1934, 45. For Neutra, see Sylvia Lavin, *Form Follows Libido: Architecture and Richard Neutra in a Psychoanalytic Culture* (Cambridge, Mass.: MIT Press, 2005); Barbara Mac Lamprecht, *Richard Neutra: Complete Works* (Cologne and New York: Taschen, 2000); Thomas S. Hines, *Richard Neutra and the Search for Modern Architecture* (New York: Oxford University Press, 1982).

2   Wright, quoted in Winthrop Sargent, "Frank Lloyd Wright," *Life*, August 12, 1946, 88.

3   Paul R. and Jean S. Hanna, *Frank Lloyd Wright's Hanna House: The Clients' Report*, 3rd ed. (Palo Alto: Hanna House/Stanford University Libraries, 2006), 25.

4   Wurster, quoted in *Sunset Western Ranch Houses* (San Francisco: Lane Publishing, 1946), 67. For Wurster, see Marc Treib, ed., *An Everyday Modernism: The Houses of William Wurster*, exh. cat. (San Francisco: San Francisco Museum of Modern Art; Berkeley: University of California Press, 1995).

5   Esther McCoy, *The Second Generation* (Salt Lake City: Gibbs M. Smith, 1984), 96–98.

6   "Los Angeles: Dunsmuir Flat Building: Stepback Planning Gives Privacy," *Architectural Record*, May 1940, 45–47; Elizabeth Mock, ed., *Built in USA, 1932–1944* (New York: Museum of Modern Art, 1944), 52–53; Anthony Denzer, *Gregory Ain: The Modern Home as Social Commentary* (New York: Rizzoli, 2008).

7   McCoy, *Second Generation*, 118–30; Frank Escher, ed., *John Lautner: Architect* (London and Zurich: Artemis, 1994), 41.

8   Lionel March and Judith Sheine, eds., *R. M. Schindler: Composition and Construction* (London: Academy Editions, 1993), 183.

9   For Harris, see Lisa Germany, *Harwell Hamilton Harris* (Berkeley: University of California Press, 2000).

10 Ray Kappe, quoted on the home page of the Kappe+Du Architects website, http://www.kappedu.com/RayKappe.html.

11 For the "second line of defense," see, for example, wartime issues of *American Home*, which carried this slogan on its masthead. For one Californian example, see Herbert Matter, Charles Eames, and R. Buckminster Fuller, "Prefabricated Housing," *Arts and Architecture*, July 1944.

12 "Announcement: The Case Study House Program," *Arts and Architecture*, January 1945, 37–41. See also Esther McCoy, *Case Study Houses, 1945–1962*, 2nd ed. (Los Angeles: Hennessey and Ingalls, 1977); Elizabeth A. T. Smith et al., *Blueprints for Modern Living: History and Legacy of the Case Study Houses*, exh. cat. (Los Angeles: Museum of Contemporary Art; Cambridge, Mass.: MIT Press, 1989).

13 Garrett Eckbo, *Landscape for Living* (New York: Duell, Sloan and Pearce), 1950. See also Garrett Eckbo, *Art of Home Landscaping* (New York: F. W. Dodge Corporation, 1956); and Mark Treib, *Garrett Eckbo: Modern Landscapes for Living* (Berkeley: University of California Press, 1997).

14 "New Shells," *Time*, August 15, 1949, 58–62; Richard Pratt, "Cream of the Coast," *Ladies' Home Journal*, November 1949, 49; Hamilton Basso, "Los Angeles," *Holiday*, January 1950, 26–47.

15 See Nicholas Olsberg, ed., *Carefree California: Cliff May and the Romance of the Ranch* (forthcoming).

16 A. Quincy Jones and Frederick E. Emmons, "The Ladera Project," *Arts and Architecture*, July 1951, 27–31.

17 Ibid. For Jones, see Cory Buckner, *A. Quincy Jones* (London: Phaidon, 2002).

18 Nicholas Olsberg and Frank Escher, *Between Earth and Heaven: The Architecture of John Lautner* (New York: Rizzoli, 2008); Wolfgang Wagener, *Raphael Soriano* (London: Phaidon, 2002); Neil Jackson, *Pierre Koenig, 1925–2004: Living with Steel* (Hong Kong and Los Angeles: Taschen, 2007); Pierluigi Serraino, *NorCalMod: Icons of Northern California Modernist Architecture* (San Francisco: Chronicle Books, 2006); Esther McCoy, *Craig Ellwood: Architecture* (New York: Walker, 1968); Neil Jackson, *Craig Ellwood* (London: Laurence King, 2002).

19 Quoted from notes in the Eckbo files, Architecture and Design Collection, University Art Museum, University of California, Santa Barbara; see also Treib, *Garrett Eckbo*.

20 For more on the Alcoa Forecast Garden, see Marc Treib, *The Donnell and Eckbo Gardens: Modern Californian Masterworks* (San Francisco: William Stout, 2005).

21 Schindler, "Modern Architecture," in March and Sheine, eds., *R. M. Schindler*, 57.

5

At Home with California Modern, 1945–65

PAT KIRKHAM

The people of America have found a new mode of living, and southern California, the richest community in the world, is fostering the economical, colorful, casual California Way of Life that you may all enjoy.

RICHARD NEUTRA, *THE CALIFORNIAN*, MARCH 1948

This essay focuses on California modern homes, with special reference to interiors and the objects within them. The term "California modern" here refers to Californian versions of postwar modernist design: buildings, interiors, furnishings, domestic appliances, and decorative objects.

5.1. John Lautner. Living area, Malin ("Chemosphere") House, Hollywood Hills, 1960. Photo by Julius Shulman, 1961

The California modern "look" was one of studied informality, sophisticated simplicity, and carefully considered casualness. It was "democratic" in the sense that it could be created by people with relatively little money as well as by the more well-to-do. In 1947 *Everywoman's Magazine*, then one of the most popular women's magazines in the United States, described California modern as "a new, not-too-expensive interior decorating trend"; it also claimed, over-optimistically, that the West Coast was "on its way to becoming for homes, what Paris was for fashion."[1]

Previous depictions of California modern homes have tended to focus somewhat narrowly on informality and on the indoor/outdoor living played out around pools and patios in perennial sunshine, as touted in magazines such as the *Californian* (1946–52). The intent here, however, is to offer a more nuanced picture of living in modern ways in postwar California. Greater informality (see 5.44) did not, in fact, spell the end of formality—not least because certain social conventions, particularly those related to evening entertaining, demanded a degree of formality in interiors, furnishings, and tableware, just as they did in dress (see 5.3, 5.4, and 8.31). Not all domestic activities involved the outdoors, and demarcations between inside and out remained strong. Although indoor/outdoor living, a symbol of affluent living in the 1930s, did become a feature of middle-class life in postwar California, the weather was not always accommodating. The fog and rain endemic to parts of Northern California were not conducive to year-round outdoor living, and Southern California summers could be blisteringly hot (few houses had air conditioning), with fall and winter cool and sometimes wet.[2] The climate disappointed a home-furnishings critic who moved to the Los Angeles area only to find that people did not "engage in the glamorous pastimes shown in Kodachromes and slick fashion magazines" and that it was "generally too cold in the evenings to sit out in the spacious patios."[3] *Sunset*, another lifestyle magazine aimed at western readers, suggested fire pits and fireplaces as means of extending the outdoor season, and the Hawk House company produced a brazier that could also be used for barbecuing—one of the great male rituals of the postwar years (5.2).[4]

Large expanses of glass brought so much light into the postwar home that *Sunset* advised potential home buyers to pay particular attention to the orien-tation of the living room lest too much afternoon sun make life unpleasant, especially in summer.[5] Maria Kipp of Los Angeles (see 8.3), who supplied woven fabrics to leading architects, felt that such large areas of glass needed softening with draperies.[6] As Virginia Stewart noted in 1951, in "What Makes the California Look," an issue of the *Los Angeles Times*'s "Home" magazine: "Like furniture, Southern California fabrics have been influenced by architecture. . . . But architecture's specific influence on fabrics is found in the problems posed by large window areas, and the solutions devised for curtaining them. The close, even texture of the usual machine-woven fabrics was unsatisfactory. So

5.2. R. Coelho-Cordoza for Hawk House. Barbecue-brazier, c. 1948. Cat. 47

5.3. Albert Frey (1903–1998) with Raymond Loewy. Living room and pool area, Loewy House, Palm Springs, 1947. Photo by Peter Stackpole, 1947

designers such as Kipp hand-wove fabrics that were loose and open, of distinctive texture and sometimes translucent. They complemented the airy, open structure they served."[7]

The views that were a feature of California modern living spaces varied considerably, from magnificent mountain or desert panoramas to small patios with workaday wooden fencing, as did views from different rooms in the same house. In John Lautner's Malin ("Chemosphere") House of 1960 (5.1), however, all the main living spaces enjoyed cinematic relationships to the outdoors; their panoramic views resembled those offered by the new widescreen technologies coming out of Hollywood in the 1950s, such as Cinerama, CinemaScope, and VistaVision.[8] A living room with an unusually intimate relationship to the outdoors is found in the house designed by Albert Frey for (and with) industrial designer Raymond Loewy in Palm Springs, in 1947, where the pool meandered indoors (5.3).[9] By entering the living space, albeit for only a few feet, the pool helped break down barriers between inside and out. Another type of open space within a building—the atrium—also brought the outdoors in and became a selling point in houses by Eichler Homes, a leading housing-development company that brought California modern design to suburbia (5.4).

Space may have flowed freely between indoor and outdoor "rooms," but

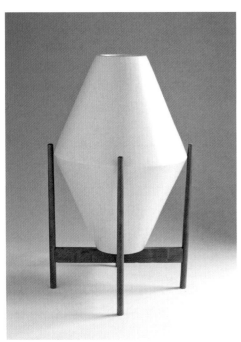

there was seldom a seamless integration of the two. Distinct differences remained in terms of furniture, ground or floor coverings, equipment, and accessories. The thick carpeting and formal furnishings of the living room at the Loewy House, for example, were in strong contrast to the open pool area, with its rattan chairs and patio cushions. The abutment of carpet against a rougher outdoor surface marked the divide, disrupting the integration of indoors and out, as did the safety barrier (see 5.3). Indeed, the interplay between difference and similarity, conventions and their subversion, in these two types of space and furnishings helped make California modern living a visually rich and conceptually intriguing experience. Despite the high-traffic wear and tear caused by indoor/outdoor living, plain carpeting and rugs were surprisingly popular. Often in white or beige and often plush and luxurious, they epitomize the desire for luxury, comfort, and conventional furnishing types within the California modern home.

Planters placed inside and out, such as those designed by La Gardo Tackett, John Follis, and Rex Goode for Architectural Pottery, were advertised as making patios more like outdoor living rooms, but the differences between those two types of spaces were acknowledged by the company's introduction, in 1957, of wooden stands to help integrate the planters "with the softened, elegant, carpeted living-dining-entry room décor" (5.5).[10] Even when the same planters, plants, materials, and furniture were featured on both sides of a glass door, they usually stopped within a few feet into the space or were configured differently (5.7).[11] Architect J. R. Davidson linked inside and out in his unrealized plan for Case Study House #1 (1945) by using tile for the patio, entrance, and living room (see 4.13), but more often any material that was continued from indoors to outside was only one among several. At William Cody's Cannon House in Palm Springs (1961), tile extended to meet concrete, pebbles, pebbled concrete, and grass, and at the Bass House by Buff, Straub & Hensman (1957–58), pebbled concrete and grass joined the quarry tile used to link inside and out (see 5.16).[12]

Despite the intentions of designers and the claims of manufacturers and publicists, very little California modern furniture appears to have been used both inside and out. Outdoor living called for special types of furniture, and California became noted for it. Metal was a popular choice, especially if rust-proof, but metal furniture tended to be uncomfortable unless softened by ample cushions or upholstery, and it also retained heat. One way around these problems was to use the more resilient woven rattan, cord, or sturdy California redwood in conjunction with metal frames. Van Keppel-Green—a company headed by the designers Hendrik Van Keppel and Taylor Green, which became noted for its high-quality outdoor furniture—was one of many companies to use such combinations (5.6).[13] Van Keppel-Green examples aimed at both the indoor and outdoor markets included a line of elegant rattan furniture with black wrought-iron frames, the smooth black metal contrasting nicely with the

THE CALIFORNIAN
Contemporary metal furniture in Museum of Modern Art's "Good Design Exhibit"
(Designer—Milo Baughman)

THE PALISADES
Budget-minded stressed canvas chairs with matching pieces fit kitchens, dens or patios
(Designer—Milo Baughman)

THE AMERICANA
At last...indoor/outdoor metal furniture with a modern and traditional touch
(Designer—Paul Laszlo)

THE GRAND CANYON
The most exciting metal furniture shown today...according to the nation's editors
(Designer—Al Blake)

6 new showrooms

Metal furniture has suddenly become a national "rage" and the excitement is due to style ideas never before attempted in this field.

Today's great demand for Pacific Iron Products proves that there is real profit in offering something daring and unique.

Now to meet the decorator needs we have provided new showrooms for complete service.

SHERMAN KARPEN CO.
520 North Dearborn Street, Chicago, Illinois
MARION HEUER
984 Linden Avenue, Hubbard Woods, Illinois
MAXWELL CO.
North Miami Avenue at 11th Street, Miami, Florida
ARNOLD PANNING
312 North Doheny Drive, Los Angeles, California
ARNOLD PANNING
1122 Sutter Street, San Francisco, California
LEHIGH FURNITURE CORPORATION
16 East 53rd Street, New York City, N. Y.

Pacific Iron Products wants established wholesale showrooms in principal cities to handle professional inquires and decorator trade. Please write attention of Department 1A.

Pacific Iron Products

1150 East Pico Blvd., Los Angeles 21, Calif.

Write for free catalog of all 7 Pacific Iron Products lines.

5.8. Walter Lamb for Brown-Jordan Company. Chaise, c. 1954. Cat. 159 **While living in Hawaii in the 1940s, Lamb first created patio furniture with bronze he allegedly salvaged from sunken navy ships after the attack on Pearl Harbor. When he moved to California in the early 1950s, his designs were licensed and produced by the manufacturer Brown-Jordan.**

5.9. Advertisement for Pacific Iron Products, published in *Interiors*, January 1951, p. 19

light color and rough texture of the rattan. Softer to the body than wood or metal and with a degree of "give," strung cord (usually of sturdy marine cotton) was also used with metal frames for chairs, loungers with ottomans, and recliners (see 6.6).[14] At the more expensive end of the market, Walter Lamb designed an elegant line of patio furniture in cord and "ageless bronze"—furniture that was promised to "last a lifetime" (5.8).[15]

Even though it was clear by the mid- to late 1950s that metal furniture designed for indoor use would not command a huge market, earlier in the decade several metal-furniture companies in California had addressed the issue of upholstery, including Los Angeles–based Pacific Iron Products, which commissioned several local designers (5.9). Although advertised as suitable for

5.10. Charles Eames and Ray Eames and
Eames Office for Herman Miller Furniture
Company. Promotional photograph,
c. 1960. Left: *Aluminum Group* chair and
ottoman, 1958. Right: Lounge chair and
ottoman, 1956

5.11. Danny Ho Fong for Tropi-Cal. *Wave*
chaise, 1966. Cat. 103

5.12. Miller Yee Fong for Tropi-Cal. *Lotus*
chair, 1968. Cat. 104

both indoor and outdoor use, Paul László's *Americana* suite, with its thin metal-rod frames and removable padded cushions, was visually less appropriate for domestic living spaces than for sunrooms and porches. The latter were transitional spaces between indoors and out that tended to disappear as architects and homeowners increasingly favored an immediate shift outside via sliding glass doors. By comparison, Milo Baughman's side chair with metal frame, *The Californian*, was so well upholstered that it is difficult to imagine anyone using it outdoors, whereas *The Palisades*, also by Baughman, with its removable covers and lightweight frame, may well have been used more flexibly. The Eameses also attempted to create indoor/outdoor furniture using aluminum, a material they thought sufficiently durable and stylish to work both inside and out. Their *Aluminum Group* furniture (1958), however, ended up mainly in high-end domestic interiors and offices, partly because some people considered this elegant furniture more appropriate to indoors, but largely because it proved too expensive to use outside; people were simply not prepared to pay as much for outdoor furniture (5.10).[16]

With the postwar emphasis on outdoor living, rattan furniture—so popular for sunrooms and porches in the prewar years—tended to move outdoors. Natural, lightweight, and easily cleaned, it was loaded with exotic associations.

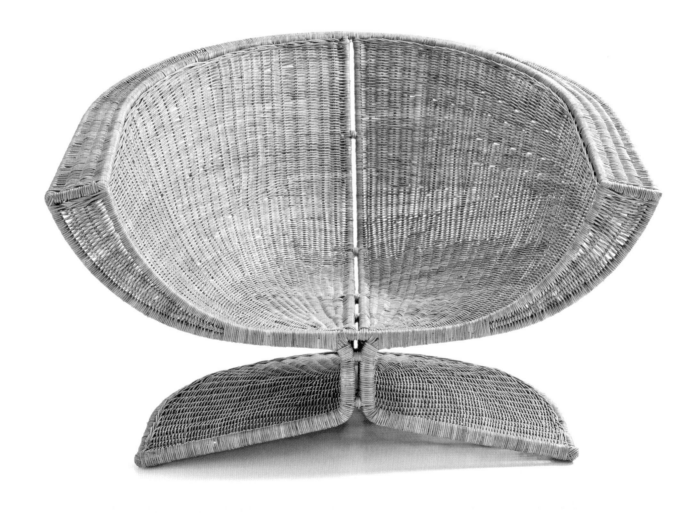

László's 1948 rattan lounge chair for Ficks Reed (headquartered in Cincinnati but with representatives in California) was every bit as stylish, commodious, and comfortable as the one he based it on: a Paul T. Frankl chair produced in the Philippines during the late 1930s (see 2.23). Most outdoor furniture of the postwar period, however, was much smaller and lighter. The best-known California designer working in rattan during those years was Danny Ho Fong, a self-taught immigrant from China who was cofounder of Fong Brothers (renamed Tropi-Cal in 1954). His many designs include a portable metal cabana (1957) with sailcloth curtains and a woven roof of driftwood rattan, which brought style to poolside or beach. By the mid-1960s he was achieving in rattan the organic forms so popular in the 1960s and so often produced in the new plastics of the period. The elegant continuous line of his minimal *Wave* chaise was made possible by using a hidden wrought-iron frame (5.11).[17] His son Miller Yee Fong, trained in architecture at the University of Southern California, continued to create organic forms; his widely published *Lotus* chair was described as a "seductive well of comfort"[18] (5.12). The Fongs worked with fine Indonesian rattan, and the close handweaving, which was done in Hong Kong, was also of high quality.[19]

Despite, and partly because of, all the interest in outdoor living, there remained a desire for enclosure. Some of the long, low interiors by Lautner—whose mentor Frank Lloyd Wright grasped better than most the importance of psychological markers of "home"—were cavelike. The Eameses likened their home to an "old cave," and the sensation of being in the Entenza House next door was compared to "looking out of a broad-mouthed cave."[20] The latter house (designed by Charles Eames and Eero Saarinen) also had a small windowless, soundproof, womblike study, which reinforces the sense that there was a contemporary responsiveness to ideas of enclosure and comfort, as does the popularity of Saarinen's *Womb* chair (1948), so called because of the way it partially enclosed the sitter. Many modernist architects and designers, Saarinen included, dismissed indoor fireplaces as "absurdly romantic," but many California modern homes had them, and with fires lit and drapes drawn, rooms took on a cozier ambience, as at the Entenza House (5.13).[21] When guests were seated around the fireplace, and the curtains were pulled back to reveal the night sky, it felt like a "sheltered camp-fire" (5.14).[22]

The interwar feature of combining living and dining areas to give a greater feeling of spaciousness gained in popularity, not least because postwar houses were generally smaller than prewar ones. "Room dividers" often demarcated space within these combined rooms; some dividers were custom-made, others simply a piece of furniture, a blind, or a piece of fabric (5.16 and 5.17; see also 8.4). Sliding partitions, folding doors, and curtains opened up or closed off spaces in other parts of the house as well: children's bedrooms could be joined to form larger playrooms; kitchens were separated from dining areas, family

Pat Kirkham

rooms, or recreation areas; and studies or guest bedrooms were created within living areas. Closing off spaces with such temporary partitions brought greater privacy but little reduction in noise, a recurrent problem with open-plan homes. The zoning of adult and children's spaces for privacy and peace meant that bedrooms were located at opposite ends of the living space, but supervising children was made easier by placing multipurpose family rooms and children's play spaces within sight of the kitchen, or "work zone" (5.15).

The prewar attention to low maintenance and work efficiency within the home continued. "Built-in" kitchens remained the ideal, with modular floor and wall cupboards and continuous counters—now in durable and colorful plastic laminates. Most appliances were also built-in, although the ever-larger refrigerators were often freestanding.[23] Integral ovens and burners increasingly replaced the stove, with burners often set in separate islands that also housed breakfast bars, where diners perched casually on counter stools for simpler postwar breakfasts of cereal, toast, and fresh orange juice (5.19). In the glamorous kitchen of Pierre Koenig's Stahl House (1959–60), high in the Hollywood Hills, the long row of units brought the sophistication of a living room credenza to the work zone (5.18). Koenig set the kitchen within a pavilion-like structure, with the side nearest the formal dining/living area partly open so the cook

5.13. Charles Eames and Eero Saarinen. Living area, Entenza House (Case Study House #9), Pacific Palisades, 1950. Photo by Julius Shulman, 1950
Both the Entenza House and the Bass House (see 5.16) prominently featured Saarinen's *Womb* chair.

5.14. Conversation and relaxation area, Entenza House. Photo by Julius Shulman, 1950

5.15. Family room/kitchen, promotional photograph for Eichler Homes, c. 1953. Photo by Ernie Braun

5.16. Buff, Straub & Hensman. Living/dining area, Bass House (Case Study House #20), Altadena, 1957–58. Photo by Julius Shulman, 1958

5.17. Greta Magnusson Grossman for Glenn of California. Screen, c. 1952. Cat. 115

5.18. Pierre Koenig. Kitchen, Stahl House (Case Study House #22), Hollywood Hills, 1959–60. Photo by Julius Shulman, 1960

5.19. Vista Furniture Company. Counter stool, c. 1952. Cat. 301
Vista Furniture Company provided modernism to the masses with affordable metal and wood furniture such as this counter stool.

5.20. A. Quincy Jones for Eichler Homes.
Kitchen/dining area, X-100 House,
San Mateo, 1956. Photo by Ernie Braun
**The all-steel X-100 featured an open
plan, floor-to-ceiling windows, and steel
beams, but the high costs of steel prohibited the model from moving beyond
the prototype stage.**

5.21. Charles Eames and Ray Eames.
Conversation/relaxation area, Eames
House (Case Study House #8), Pacific
Palisades, 1945–49. Left to right:
Director Billy Wilder, Audrey Wilder, Ray
Eames, and Charles Eames. Photo by
Paul Fusco, 1961
**This photograph appeared in J. Peter,
"A Visit with Designer Charles Eames,"
Look, June 20, 1961.**

could chat with family and guests—another material expression of the informality of social intercourse. Suburban kitchens could also be glamorous, and the
one in the X-100 House, designed by A. Quincy Jones for Eichler Homes in San
Mateo (1956), showed how sophisticated they might become (5.20). By the
mid-1950s even modest suburban houses had a garbage disposal and dish-
washer,[24] yet despite up-to-date appliances and easy-to-clean surfaces,
housework did not, of course, disappear. This was partly because of raised
expectations of domestic cleanliness and competence[25] and partly because
"outdoor rooms" and the frequent movement of people, food, drinks, toys,
and occasionally furniture between indoors and out required additional work,
a factor recognized in house plans that placed outdoor play areas near bath-
rooms or utility rooms and outdoor barbecues near kitchens.

The *California Manor* line of home furnishings (1947)—which was coordi-
nated in terms of color and pattern but, according to Eugenia Sheppard in
Everywoman's Magazine, "not in too matched a way"[26]—is an early example of
California modern eschewing interior design as a Gesamtkunstwerk, or total
work of art, in favor of a studied informality and mixing as opposed to matching.
This type of informality had its roots in Europe, particularly interiors by the
Austrian architect-designers Adolf Loos and Josef Frank. Frank immigrated to
Sweden in 1933, and the impact of his bold patterns, "mismatched" chairs,
and informal arrangements of furniture can be seen in the Beverly Hills home
that the émigré Swedish designer Greta Magnusson Grossman designed for
herself in 1949 (see 3.13).

More casual living brought dedicated areas for conversation and relaxation.
Starting in the late 1940s, the Barker Brothers department store in downtown
Los Angeles showed custom-designed "conversation groups" as part of room
settings by Grossman, whose design services were available to customers
wanting something similar.[27] Cushions carefully placed on carpeted steps in
one part of the Entenza House living area and built-in seating around the fireplace in another were meant to encourage conversation (see 5.13 and 5.14).[28]
The same purpose was served at the Eames House by an alcove (5.21). At
about the same time that Grossman was custom designing conversation
groups for Barker Brothers, she was also designing sofas for mass production
for the Modern Line company, in Gardena, that could be placed at right angles,
with a corner table between them, to facilitate conversation and relaxation. A
later custom example of a sofa designed to facilitate conversation was A. Quincy
Jones and Frederick E. Emmons's L-shaped unit for the Spencer House in
Beverly Hills (1961–64), complete with integral table (5.22). At its longest, it
measured over ten feet. Two freestanding sofas could also be placed side by
side to achieve this ultra-long, low look. Sofas placed opposite each other
were probably more conducive to social intercourse, but they took up consid-
erable space in what were relatively small houses. At the much larger

Montgomery House in San Diego, the living room featured two curved sofas facing each other, each eight feet long (see 5.41), while the family room featured a huge built-in L-shaped seating unit in white leather.

In addition to a sofa, most conversation ensembles included a large chair that made a bold visual statement in its own right. Among the lounge chairs most frequently used in this manner in top-end California modern interiors was Saarinen's boldly sculptural *Womb* chair (see 5.16).[29] The Eames fiberglass armchair (put into production in 1950; see 6.16) was sometimes used as part of a conversation group, and from 1956, when furniture manufacturers across the United States were addressing consumer demands for greater comfort, the more expensive Eames lounge chair and ottoman, which offered modern form along with the comforts and familiarity of an English gentleman's leather club chair, was also available (see 5.10).[30] The most ubiquitous larger chair was the *Hardoy*, or *Butterfly*, chair (see 5.36). Designed in 1938–39 by three Brazilian modernists, with a leather cover and forms that echoed modern art, the chair was produced in the U.S. by Knoll from 1947 until 1951, when legal action to stop wholesale copying failed. "Rip-offs" flourished; canvas versions sold for about seven dollars in the early 1950s.[31] Their lightweight folding frames and easily cleaned removable covers in bright colors made them extremely popular for outdoor use, but they were also used indoors, especially by younger, less wealthy homemakers.

Coffee and cocktail tables (the terms appear to have been interchangeable) were also a feature of conversation ensembles. Described by Eugenia Sheppard as "the heart, soul and center of a home" and the one piece of furniture on which a housewife might "splurge," coffee tables came in all sizes, shapes, and materials.[32] The one by Milo Baughman shown here, from about 1950, has an integral planter that echoed in miniature the use of planters within the home (5.23). Light and elegant, the table came in solid birch or walnut, with panels of glass and wood, a perforated Masonite lid for the storage compartment, and a lacquered cigarette compartment. As the compartment suggests, designers catered to the prevalence of smoking in the home with fashionable ashtrays and cigarette holders (5.24).

5.22. A. Quincy Jones and Frederick E. Emmons. Sofa and table from the Spencer House, Beverly Hills, 1961–64. Cat. 142

5.23. Milo Baughman for Glenn of California. Cocktail table, c. 1950. Cat. 25

5.24. Michael Morrison for William Haines, Inc. Cigarette holder, 1950s. Cat. 214

5.25. Hudson Roysher. Decanter set, c. 1948. Cat. 246

5.26. Adolph Tischler. *Duo* flatware, c. 1955. Cat. 287
This set was owned by the legendary Los Angeles photographer Julius Shulman.

5.27. Porter Blanchard. Teapot, creamer, and sugar, c. 1965. Cat. 29
The original set came with five pieces, including a coffeepot and tray.

5.28. Frank Irwin for Metlox Manufacturing Company. *California Contempora* covered vegetable dish, beverage server, and juice cup in *Freeform* shape, c. 1955. Cat. 135

Dining implements, whether formal or casual, were also updated. Hudson Roysher's silver-and-cane decanter set gave exotic flair to the cocktail hour (5.25). Adolph Tischler's *Duo* flatware (5.26) and Porter Blanchard's tea and coffee set (5.27) both aspired to luxury but were, in fact, made of inexpensive materials. (Although the handles of the Tischler flatware looked like ebony, they were nylon, and the Blanchard set was produced in a very reflective pewter in order to resemble silver.) For everyday dining, Heath Ceramics produced several lines of dinnerware that was both durable and moderately priced (see 1.13), and Frank Irwin applied the loopy, whimsical *California Contempora* design to Metlox's dinnerware and serving pieces (5.28).

Domestic sound equipment, another "must-have" for the modern home, was usually placed in living areas, following prewar conventions, but television sets, which were new to the home in the 1950s, had no specific room of their own and were located in places as various as the family room, den, study, or living room.[33] Sound equipment and televisions were not generally combined, although by 1962, when television was well established within the American home, Glenn of California produced a cabinet with space for both.[34] From the late 1950s, stereo sound was highly desirable, and stereo equipment, when not built into a "sound wall," was increasingly housed within freestanding cabinets

resembling contemporary furniture. JBL's top-of-the-line *Paragon* stereo speaker system, designed by Arnold Wolf in 1957 (5.29), brought film-industry-quality sound to the family living room. The *Baronet* stereo cabinet (1959) designed by Milo Baughman and Richard Thompson for Glenn of California housed a variety of sound products, from record players and tape recorders to speakers and amplifiers.[35] Homemakers with sufficient money or do-it-yourself skills could, of course, add purpose-built units to hold whatever equipment they wanted wherever they wanted it, including the bedroom. Craig Ellwood brought the elegance of the credenza form so popular with Scandinavian designers to the stereo cabinet he designed for the Rosen House (see 4.27).

Televisions were available in both console and tabletop models throughout the 1950s, but the latter appeared more frequently in lifestyle magazines and model homes, partly because they were more discreet, tucked easily into custom units, and when stood on a long low bench or coffee table, fit in well with the California modern look (5.30). The *Arts of Daily Living* exhibition, which was part of the Los Angeles County Fair in 1954, featured "A Special Room for Television" (5.31) designed by local architect George Wright and furnished by local designer-craftsman Sam Maloof.[36] In order to better integrate the television set, a symbol of modern technology, into this room full of references to

Pat Kirkham

handcraftsmanship and tradition, Maloof created a wooden casing for a standard set from the Pacific Mercury TV Manufacturing Corporation, Van Nuys; it had a special swivel mechanism that allowed the set to be angled so that the room's occupants could choose whether or not to see the screen. Certain products were promoted as suitable for the new pastime of watching television, including an armless upholstered lounge chair by Grossman and an upholstered lounger by Van Keppel-Green.[37] In 1950 *Life* magazine showed film director Billy Wilder testing a low Eames lounge chair with a metal-rod base in which he claimed he could "easily jump around while watching television."[38] Household carts were often used to support console models, and by 1961, two years after the first portable television set was produced in the U.S., James Kelso designed a "transportable" set for the California company Packard-Bell Electronics, which combined the idea of a television and a serving cart (5.32).[39]

Even though Los Angeles was second only to North Carolina as a furniture-making center, Californians did not restrict their consumption to goods designed or made locally.[40] Some prewar design influences—from Arts and Crafts, European modern, and Spanish colonial revival to Asian, Mexican, and Native American traditions—continued, but to a lesser degree. In 1955 the magazine *Living for Young Homemakers* described California modern as "internationally

5.29. Arnold Wolf for JBL. *Paragon* speaker, 1957. Promotional photograph, 1960s. See cat. 315

5.30. Family room, promotional photograph for Eichler Homes, c. 1956. Photo by Ernie Braun

5.31. Designed by George Wright; furnished by Sam Maloof. "A Special Room for Television," *Arts of Daily Living*, Los Angeles County Fair, Pomona, 1954. Photo by Maynard L. Parker, 1954

5.32. James Kelso. Transportable TV set for Packard-Bell Electronics, 1961

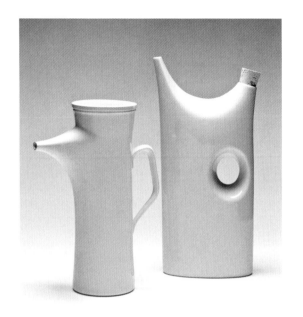

minded," citing inspiration from the Far East, Scandinavia, and Italy,[41] while Mexican influences—including brick floors and colorful pottery and rugs—brought a strong vernacular flavor to California design that was at once foreign and local. The experience of foreign cultures by U.S. military personnel during World War II encouraged a broad mix; so did both the huge rise in tourism after the war—particularly from the late 1950s on, when jet travel brought Europe, Japan, Indonesia, India, Hawaii, and South America within easier reach of middle-class Californians—and the representations of foreign places in Hollywood films such as *House of Bamboo* (1955), *South Pacific* (1958), and *Blue Hawaii* (1961). Objects collected on trips took their place in interiors as souvenirs and cultural capital, along with locally made craft objects. Postwar discourses of cultural pluralism and a "hands-across-the seas" liberal internationalism, what philosopher Horace M. Kallen called "the federation or commonwealth of nationalities," also fed into new ways of thinking about design and modern living.[42]

California's long awareness of its proximity to Asia ensured that the Pacific Rim had a powerful impact on postwar California design. By the early 1950s a strong East-meets-West trend was evident, from tatami mats to low tables and floor cushions.[43] "Hikies," low upholstered beds offering daytime seating, were featured in Raymond Loewy's furniture for Mengel, together with a shoji screen of translucent paper within a latticelike frame, the pattern of which was repeated in the chair backs.[44] A shoji screen and a low "sukiyaki table" were also included in a line designed by Peter Rooke-Ley for California Contemporary, as part of the "Pacifica" marketing initiative that promoted Pacific Rim–influenced furnishings and accessories made across the U.S.[45] Japanese-inspired design graced the table through such forms as La Gardo Tackett's coffeepot for Schmid Kreglinger, which was manufactured in Japan (where Tackett lived for two years), and a condiment bottle by Kenji Fujita (5.33).[46]

The multicultural mélange at a Japanese tea ceremony held at the Eames House in 1951 illustrates the embrace of things Japanese after World War II within an ethos of cultural pluralism that incorporated both people and material culture (5.35).[47] Guests included Japanese film star Yoshiko (Shirley) Yamaguchi; her husband, Japanese American artist-designer Isamu Noguchi, whose glass-topped coffee tables featured in many California modern homes; U.S. character actor Ford Rainey; international star Charlie Chaplin, whose "One World" politics were almost as famous at that point as his comic performances; and British bohemian poet Iris Tree. Starring alongside them, and happily intermingling with each other, were handmade Japanese ceramics and small low tables, influenced by Japanese examples, that had recently been mass-produced to designs by the Eameses. The ritual was performed by Sōsei Matsumoto, who opened a school that year to teach the tea ceremony in Los Angeles.[48] Japanese domestic rituals, however, were formal, whereas low furniture and floor seating were markers of the casual and informal in California.

Like rattan, bamboo was a natural material that went well with the light, airy aspects of California modern. From Indonesia, the Philippines, and the Pacific Islands came bamboo blinds and drapes, place mats in various natural fibers, hemp and sisal rugs, grass cloth for wall coverings, grass squares made into matting, and other inexpensive items that added exotic touches while marking interiors as modern. The craze for things Pacific in general and Hawaiian in particular, though less evident in home furnishings than in souvenirs and clothing, ranged from boldly patterned and brightly colored fabrics in tropical designs to "surfboard" tables (5.34). From the mid- to late 1950s, South Asian items from carved wooden screens to textiles also found their way into California modern homes, with some merging into more "hippy-style" interiors by the mid-1960s.

Postwar "Scandinavian modern" furniture—with its emphasis on elegance of form, high-quality natural materials (especially wood), and superb craftsmanship—also had a huge impact on the California modern home. Furniture by Alvar Aalto—the Finnish modernist architect-designer who eschewed machine age modernism because he felt that hard, cold metal surfaces were not sufficiently in tune with "the human point of view"—had become available in California in the late 1930s when Elizabeth Church (wife of landscape architect Thomas Church) became the first distributor of Aalto furniture on the West Coast, at the Cargoes store in San Francisco.[49] Aalto's plywood furniture, including amply upholstered armchairs, graced many California modern homes in the postwar period, especially the first decade after the war (5.36).[50] The leading emporia of modern design in California, such as Frank Brothers in Long Beach and Carroll Sagar in Los Angeles, vigorously promoted Scandinavian modern design. In addition to advertising such imports almost monthly in *Arts and Architecture*, Edward Frank (co-owner and artistic director of Frank Brothers) traveled to Scandinavia, selecting products and working with companies to modify designs to better suit his clientele.[51] By the mid- to late 1950s, a panoply of Scandinavian design, mainly furniture, was available to Californians, and Scandinavian designers such as Bruno Mathsson, Folke Ohlsson, Hans

5.33. Left: La Gardo Tackett for Schmid Kreglinger. *Forma* coffeepot, c. 1959. Cat. 283. Right: Kenji Fujita. Condiment bottle, c. 1960. Cat. 109

5.34. Charles Eames and Ray Eames and Eames Office for Herman Miller. *ETR* (elliptical table rod base), 1951. Cat. 79

5.35. Tea ceremony at the Eames House. Left to right: Sōsei Matsumoto, Yoshiko (Shirley) Yamaguchi, Charlie Chaplin, and Iris Tree. Photo by Charles Eames, 1951

5.36. Richard Neutra. Living room, Bailey House (Case Study House #20), Pacific Palisades, 1947–48. Photo by Julius Shulman, 1948

The living room featured an Alvar Aalto armchair and George Nelson's slat bench for Herman Miller. The *Butterfly* chair, originally designed by Antonio Bonet, Jorge Ferrari-Hardoy, and Juan Kurchan, sat on the patio.

Olsen, and Hans Wegner became known by name. Ohlsson left Sweden in 1953 to establish a branch in San Francisco of the Swedish company Dux, which imported "distinguished designs handcrafted to famous perfection."[52]

Given the Scandinavian emphasis on craftsmanship, it is perhaps not surprising that two of the California furniture makers most strongly influenced by Scandinavian precedent were designer-craftsmen. John Kapel's large handmade armchair from about 1958 (see p. 23) has a close affinity to chairs by Danish designer Finn Juhl, whom Kapel got to know while on an extended visit to Copenhagen.[53] Kapel designed and created prototypes for companies such as Glenn of California, a small but high-profile firm that produced machinemade furniture with hand finishing. There his experience in George Nelson's industrial-design office stood him in good stead. He also continued to make custom pieces by hand, as did Sam Maloof, who focused on this type of work. Scandinavian influence was also evident in lower price ranges, as in the knockdown chair with webbing upholstery by CalFab, which closely followed a 1941 design for Knoll by the U.S.-based Danish designer Jens Risom.[54] Indeed, such was the craze for things Scandinavian that in 1958 Packard-Bell produced a hi-fi set in "modern walnut form" that was named *Scandia*: Scandinavian modern had become part and parcel of California modern.[55]

Within the Eames House, objects from different cultures, past and present, coexisted, de- and recontextualizing one another while decorating and personalizing a space constructed from prefabricated, standardized parts (5.37).[56] At a time when there was greater focus on standardized production than ever before, the Eameses' approach to interior decoration involved integrating handicrafts into groupings of disparate objects from a variety of places and times—some made by hand, some by machine, some natural, some "found," some bought. The Eameses were not alone in favoring what the British architect-designers Peter and Alison Smithson called an aesthetic of "extra-cultural surprise"—namely, the deliberate juxtaposing of objects of different materials, colors, ages, object types, sizes, and so on.[57] Contemporary sources (particularly furnishing catalogues, lifestyle magazines, and photographs) show a range of handmade objects—including Native American kachinas, Japanese kites, Pre-Columbian artifacts, and Chinese masks (see, for example, the low handmade chairs from India on which Ray and Charles Eames sit in 5.37)—alongside natural and "found" objects such as driftwood, tumbleweeds, starfish, pebbles, and contemporary art and crafts. In many California modern homes, such objects helped personalize and humanize both standardized and mass-produced structures and the standardized or mass-produced furniture and textiles within them.[58] The small (550 square feet) Santa Barbara home of furniture designer Paul Tuttle featured a fascinating mix, from his own furniture designs to Japanese tatami mats and paper lampshades, antique Japanese stencils, models of vintage cars, a lamp made from a ship's lantern, and a contemporary wood sculpture by Dutch émigré Jan de Swart, who was noted for working by hand with power tools (5.38).[59]

Some designers and architects such as Richard Neutra continued to protest when clients wanted to include older furnishings and personal items in the houses he designed for them, but others saw homemakers as active agents in the creation of their own living environments. San Francisco–based color and interior-design consultant Everett Brown suggested color as a cheap do-it-yourself way to add "excitement and high style."[60] Homeowners looking to adorn their walls could buy a "portable mural" like Elizabeth McCord's *Big Pink* (5.39) through the Los Angeles Art Association, which advertised the paintings in its May 1951 exhibition as "designed especially for mid-century architecture."[61] The Eameses argued that those who inhabited spaces, including standardized mass-produced homes, should use "the accessories of his or her own life" to transform them into personal statements.[62] Lifestyle magazines recounted how California couples, and the occasional single person, did just that, from refurbishing family furniture to making new furniture and wall decoration.[63] Women had long created soft furnishings such as pillows and curtains, but during the postwar years, when do-it-yourself was the fastest-growing leisure activity in the U.S., large numbers of men became involved with home

improvement, including making furniture, from benchlike sofas and book-shelves to dining and coffee tables.[64] Some furniture projects appear to have been undertaken jointly, usually with men making and women finishing. Both men and women assembled knockdown chairs such as those from CalFab or the wood-and-steel-frame chair designed and manufactured by Maurice Martiné, which was available with the customer's choice of a cord or wooden dowel seat (5.40). It was praised for the fact that it could be easily assembled by an unskilled person using only a screwdriver.[65]

Living in a modern way in postwar California was often compared to living in paradise, but it was not without its problems. John Entenza, the force behind the Case Study House Program, lived in his own Case Study House for only five years. His leaving partly involved a falling-out with his neighbors and close friends the Eameses, but it was also due to his discovery that his dream house did not suit his needs after all. According to architecture and design critic Esther McCoy, who knew Entenza well, the house, with its large living area, was "off the mark for a bachelor who hated big parties. . . . Nor was he keen on sunlight, yet light flooded into every room."[66] What she called the "goldfish bowl" effect of the huge expanses of glass in the living area disturbed the daughter of the couple who bought the house from Entenza. After recalling feeling exposed in a "glass box," she stated: "The house was creepy for a kid, with all those huge glass windows. . . . I never liked being home alone, even in high school."[67]

Racism also made a mockery of the concept of California as paradise. Eichler Homes was one of the few housing-development companies that sold houses to anyone who could afford them, regardless of color or creed—unusual at a time when housing covenants preventing sales to nonwhites and Jews were still common—but the relatively high cost of its desirable suburban California modern houses placed a de facto restriction on access, while broader cultural and social factors also kept the suburbs predominantly white.[68] Some owners of Eichler Homes objected when the first Asian American family moved into an estate in the early 1950s, and 1955 brought uglier objections when inhabitants of another, more expensive development objected to a black family moving in:

5.37. Charles Eames and Ray Eames. Living room, Eames House. Photo by Julius Shulman, 1958

5.38. Paul Tuttle. Living room, Tuttle House, Santa Barbara, published in *House Beautiful*, July 1965, p. 64

5.39. Elizabeth McCord. *Big Pink*, 1951. Cat. 212

one man posted a sign warning potential customers and Realtors that "Eichler Homes Sells to Negroes."[69] Although the local television station noted a turnabout in attitudes within the year, by 1960 sales to African Americans and Asian Americans still accounted for only about 4 percent of Eichler's total sales.[70]

Nonetheless, California modern did occasionally cross the color bar. In 1960 *Ebony*, a magazine established to celebrate African American life and achievements, featured the Montgomery House (1960), in San Diego (5.41). One of the largest, most luxurious examples of California modern design, it was home to Mr. and Mrs. Alpha Montgomery, both successful African American lawyers, and their son. At 5,600 square feet and a cost of $87,500 (most California modern houses were between eight hundred and two thousand square feet and cost eight thousand to twenty thousand dollars), this was as luxurious as anything in a "white" lifestyle magazine, from the swimming pool and views over San Diego to the European convertible in the drive.[71]

After the "making do" and recycling of the wartime years, the seemingly never-ending supply of new goods was a welcome aspect of the postwar modern lifestyle for most people. *Sunset*, however, noted that some consumers complained to the magazine about kitchens with too many appliances and gadgets that would "go on the blink" or "rapidly become obsolete."[72] Many designers, particularly industrial designers, were deeply mindful of such issues. The social responsibility embedded within European modernism, though often said to have disappeared from American versions of it, was sustained by numerous California designers, including most of the designer-craftsmen. The Eameses, after becoming more aware of the polluting effects of many products and worried by the extent of contemporary consumption, went so far as to suggest that the main question facing designers would soon be "*should* rather than *how* we do it."[73]

Cold War fears about the possibility of nuclear attack gave new meaning to the idea of home as shelter as the government pressed citizens to build, stock, and furnish fallout shelters. Relatively few were built, because of cost and lack of conviction about their efficacy, but wealthy California had more than its fair share, with Hollywood celebrities Pat Boone, Groucho Marx, and Dinah Shore among those who installed elaborate shelters.[74] As early as 1950 Paul László had conceived of *Atomville, U.S.A.*—an underground city that promised both California modern design and safety from atom bombs (5.42).[75] László extended his architectural practice to include bomb shelters, designing one with an elevator as well as its own generator and geiger counter. The most luxurious of all underground sanctuaries was the one that wealthy Hollywood contractor and playboy Hal Hayes created for his own home, which was to be accessed via the swimming pool (Hayes believed that the pool would serve as a decontamination space)—a novel use for such a familiar symbol of the California good life (5.43).[76]

At the same time, as the peace movement grew apace in California, the now-familiar peace sign appeared on furnishings such as small tables designed by Howard McNab and Don Savage for Peter Pepper Products of California in the early 1960s. So, too, did petals—symbolic of "flower power" and of the counterculture movement that flourished in the U.S., and California in particular, between about the late 1950s and the mid-1970s.[77] By the early to mid-1960s, many aspects of California modern living, particularly the strong focus on consumption and material possessions, were being challenged by those seeking alternative modes of living. Nonetheless, the emphasis on casualness, informality, and indoor/outdoor living, together with a strong appreciation of nature, organic materials, and handicrafts, fed into alternative notions about new ways of living. But how that all unfolded within the California counterculture is another story.

HILLTOP LIVING

San Diego family has modern home overlooking the city

IN THE sun-tanned hills of California, casual living is the unchallenged way of life. And probably nobody has found their place in that sun more casually than the Alpha L. Montgomerys of San Diego, whose startlingly designed $87,500 home perches on a 3½ acre plot atop one of the city's Emerald Hills.

Built on a 5,600-square foot concrete slab, the home is in the architectural style of a Roman town house with three patios, three major hallways, and all rooms having access to the atrium—or central patio. For inside entertainment, the Montgomerys have room-to-room high fidelity and TV, and a stereophonic sound-wired family room. When they go outdoors, there is a swimming pool and a panoramic view that includes not only the home of San Diego's Mayor Charles Dale on the next hill, but also the Pacific Ocean, and the borders of nearby Mexico.

....
5.40. Maurice Martiné. Left: Chair, 1948. Cat. 203. Right: Maurice Martiné. Chair, 1948. Cat. 202

Customers could choose between wooden dowels or cords for the seat and back of the Martiné chairs. The cords were presumably more comfortable, but they stretched out of shape; cushions could be used to protect the body from direct contact with the dowels.

....
5.41. Living room, Montgomery House, San Diego, 1960

Paul László, A.S.I.D.

....

5.42. Paul László. Project for *Atomville, U.S.A.*, 1950. Cat. 162
Atomville was a proposed community of subterranean homes that would protect citizens from nuclear attack while providing all the modern conveniences, including ample light wells, a range of modern appliances, and individual helicopter landing strips.

....

5.43. Hal Hayes (1911–1993). Proposed bomb shelter, Hollywood, published in *Popular Mechanics*, August 1953, p. 109

NOTES

I am grateful to Wendy Kaplan and Bobbye Tigerman for involving me in this exciting project. Thanks also to Staci Steinberger, Kate Fox, Liz St. George, and Craig Lee for research assistance; to Amy Ogata for sharing her copies of *Living for Young Homemakers*; and to Sarah Lichtman for discussions about bomb shelters.

1   Eugenia Sheppard, "California Modern: A New, Not-Too-Expensive Interior Decorating Trend," *Everywoman's Magazine*, September 1947, 23.

2   "Design on the West Coast" (special issue), *Industrial Design* 4 (October 1957): 50–51.

3   Ibid., 57. Even Architectural Pottery's planters shattered if not protected from freezing weather (Architectural Pottery, artist-in-residence program, vol. 1, retail price list, n.d., copy stamped "Dec 11 1953," folder 23, box 4, Max and Rita Lawrence Architectural Pottery Records [Collection 1587], Department of Special Collections, Charles E. Young Research Library, University of California, Los Angeles).

4   "A Critical Look at the Changing Western House," *Sunset*, May 1956, 74; and "An Outdoor Thanksgiving . . . ," *Los Angeles Examiner*, "Southland Living" magazine, November 23, 1952. The date for the product is taken from a Hawk Barbecue-Brazier brochure, 1948, LACMA's Decorative Arts and Design Department research files.

5   "Critical Look at the Changing Western House," 75.

6   Marlyn Renee Musicant, "Maria Kipp: Modern Hand-Woven Textiles" (master's thesis, Bard Graduate Center, 2002), 71.

7   Virginia Stewart, "The Looms of Los Angeles," in "What Makes the California Look," *Los Angeles Times*, "Home" magazine, October 21, 1951, 8.

8   See www.widescreenmuseum.com.

9   For the Loewy House, see Michael Stern and Alan Hess, *Julius Shulman: Palm Springs*, exh. cat. (Palm Springs: Palm Springs Art Museum; New York: Rizzoli, 2008), 51–53, 56–58; "A House to Swim In," *Life*, March 24, 1947, 113–17; and "They're Swimming in the Parlor," *Californian*, June 1947, 46–47.

10 See Virginia Stewart, "New Shapes for the Patio," *Los Angeles Times*, June 10, 1956, 53; and Architectural Pottery news release, July 1957, folder 4, box 9, Max and Rita Lawrence Architectural Pottery Records.

11 Stern and Hess, *Julius Shulman*, 97. For contrasts between inside and out at the Edris and Bailey Houses, see ibid., 91, and Esther McCoy, *Case Study Houses, 1945–1962*, 2nd ed. (Los Angeles: Hennessey and Ingalls, 1977), 48, respectively. For the Opdahl and Robertson Houses, see Herbert Weisskamp, *Beautiful Homes and Gardens in California* (New York: Abrams, 1964), 160–62 and 163–65, respectively.

12 For the Cannon House, see Stern and Hess, *Julius Shulman*, 124–27. For the Bass House, see "Case Study House 20: By Buff, Straub and Hensman, Architects, in Association with Saul Bass," *Arts and Architecture*, November 1958, 18–20, 31.

13 Van Keppel-Green sold a wide range of furniture and furnishings other than its own designs and offered an interior-design service. It is often cited in *Arts and Architecture* as responsible for furnishing some Case Study Houses. See also www.vankeppelgreen.com.

14 Laura Tanner, "Outdoor Furniture That Can Stay Out," *House Beautiful*, May 1950, 160–61. See also Jo Lauria and Suzanne Baizerman, *California Design: The Legacy of West Coast Craft and Style* (San Francisco: Chronicle Books, 2005), 31–38. Greta Magnusson Grossman's cord lounger for Modern Color Inc. (1950) was another top-end cord product.

15 Lauria and Baizerman, *California Design*, 34–35. The quotations come from, respectively, a Brown-Jordan advertisement published in the *Los Angeles Times*, July 5, 1953, B4; and *Walter Lamb: Bronze Furniture* (Pasadena: Brown-Jordan Co., 1954), n.p. The often-repeated story of Lamb's war salvaging is summarized in Jeffrey Head, "Walter Lamb," in the brochure for the antique show *Los Angeles Modernism*, 2009.

16 Pat Kirkham, *Charles and Ray Eames: Designers of the Twentieth Century* (Cambridge, Mass.: MIT Press, 1995), 248–49.

17 For Fong, the cabana, and the chair, see Lauria and Baizerman, *California Design*, 30–33; and Virginia Stewart, "Design for '54. Furniture. The Problem: How to Better Co-ordinate Designer and Manufacturer," *Los Angeles Times*, October 25, 1953, J12.

18 "California Design X," *Los Angeles Times*, March 31, 1968, A14.

19 Company advertisement, *Living for Young Homemakers*, October 1952, 56.

20 For Lautner, see Nicholas Olsberg, ed., *Between Earth and Heaven: The Architecture of John Lautner* (New York: Rizzoli, 2008), especially 18–30, 116–20, 145, 176–77, 194–95, 200–216. For the Eames House, see Kirkham, *Charles and Ray Eames*, 119. For the Entenza House, see Olga Gueft, "The Castle-Cabana of John Entenza: Eames and Saarinen Design a Machine for Expansive Living," *Interiors*, December 1950, 92.

21 For Eero Saarinen and "absurdly romantic," see Ray Eames to author, 1983, quoted in Kirkham, *Charles and Ray Eames*, 119.

22 Gueft, "Castle-Cabana of John Entenza," 95.

23 "Critical Look at the Changing Western House," 78.

24 Ibid.

25 For raised expectations regarding housework, see Ruth Schwartz Cowan, *More Work for Mother: The Ironies of Household Technology from the Open Hearth to the Microwave* (New York: Basic Books, 1983).

26 Sheppard, "California Modern," 23. For studied informality, see Pat Kirkham, "New Environments for Modern Living: 'At home' with the Eameses," in Penny Sparke, ed., *Designing the Modern Interior: From the Victorians to Today* (Oxford and New York: Berg, 2009).

27 "For Sale: Custom Design. Greta Magnussen [sic] Grossman, Los Angeles," *Interiors*, September 1947, 98.

28 Gueft, "Castle-Cabana of John Entenza," 92.

29 It was used in the Eames House from about 1949 to 1957, in the Bass House from 1958, and in the more humble Urritias House in the early 1950s. "Living in Los Angeles," *Living for Young Homemakers*, June 1952, 87.

30 Pat Kirkham, "The Evolution of the Eames Lounge Chair and Ottoman," in *The Eames Lounge Chair: An Icon of Modern Design*, exh. cat., ed. David Hanks (Grand Rapids, Mich.: Grand Rapids Art Museum; London: Merrell, 2006), 42–63.

31 Designed by Antonio Bonet, Jorge Ferrari-Hardoy, and Juan Kurchan. See www.knoll.com. For advertisements of "knock-offs," see *Living for Young Homemakers*, March 1952, 28, 30.

32 Sheppard, "California Modern," 23. Some coffee tables—such as Richard Neutra's "Camel" table, c. 1940 (see 6.11), and Gene Tepper's *Versitable*, 1953 (see 6.10)—could be raised up for dining, but when they were used near sofa-style seating, as so many were, they were at the wrong height. The *California Manor* line also included a combination coffee/dining table.

33 See Lynn Spigel, *Make Room for TV: Television and the Family Ideal in Postwar America*

(Chicago: University of Chicago Press, 1992); and Cecelia Tichi, *Electronic Hearth: Creating an American Television Culture* (New York: Oxford University Press, 1991).

34 "Looking and Listening," *House and Garden*, October 1962, 220.

35 The sound-system center by Best Associates, shown at the 1957 *California Design* show, had space for a radio, tape recorder, two stereo amplifier speakers, and a Garrard three-speed record deck. For Baughman and Thompson, see *Interiors*, August 1959, 111.

36 "The Arts of Daily Living Exhibition," *House Beautiful*, October 1954, 173 and 245.

37 Both items of furniture were launched in 1954. Stewart, "Design for '54," J12–13.

38 Wilder, quoted in Kirkham, "Evolution of the Eames Lounge Chair and Ottoman," 53.

39 This model was displayed in *California Design 7* (1961), entry 601. Lauria and Baizerman, *California Design*, 25. Portable televisions were already being imported from Japan, and in 1962 Sony's "micro-tv" was advertised as suitable for "picnicking on the patio"—a thoroughly Californian activity (*House and Garden*, October 1962, 234).

40 "Design on the West Coast," 44–46, 50–51.

41 "California Designers Present," *Living for Young Homemakers*, December 1955, 88–89.

42 See Horace M. Kallen, *Cultural Pluralism and the American Idea: An Essay in Social Philosophy* (Philadelphia: University of Pennsylvania Press, 1956).

43 Marilyn Hoffman, "East Meets West under One Roof in Present Trend toward Oriental Décor," *Christian Science Monitor*, April 29, 1953, 10.

44 Ibid. See also Mengel advertisement for the *Prismata* group (*Living for Young Homemakers*, September 1953, 10–11).

45 "Pacifica: Furniture and Accessories," *Arts and Architecture*, June 1952, 20–23, and *House and Garden*, April 1953, 98–154.

46 Advertisement for Seibu department store, *Los Angeles Times*, September 11, 1962. The advertisement erred in stating that the line was designed by "Japan's talented Kenji Fujita." Though of Japanese ancestry, Fujita was born in the United States.

47 See B. L. C. Mori, "The Tea Ceremony: A Transformed Japanese Ritual," *Gender and Society* 5, no. 1 (1991): 86–97; Kirkham, *Charles and Ray Eames*, 143–99; and Kirkham, "New Environments for Modern Living," 178.

48 For Sōsei Matsumoto, see www.discovernikkei.org/en/interviews/profiles/113/.

49 For Aalto and the "human point of view," see Kirkham, *Charles and Ray Eames*, 204; for Aalto furniture sold in California, see Marc Treib, ed., *Thomas Church, Landscape Architect: Designing a Modern California Landscape* (San Francisco: William Stout, 2003), 40, 70.

50 For example, Case Study Houses #16 (1946–47) and #20 (1947–48); see Elizabeth A. T. Smith et al., *Blueprints for Modern Living: History and Legacy of the Case Study Houses*, exh. cat. (Los Angeles: Museum of Contemporary Art; Cambridge, Mass.: MIT Press, 1989), 39 and 44–45.

51 Ron Frank, conversation with Wendy Kaplan and Bobbye Tigerman, July 26, 2007. Ron Frank was Edward Frank's nephew and business partner.

52 Quoted in *Arts and Architecture*, April 1960, 13, and May 1960, 6. The company relocated to Burlingame in 1959.

53 The information about Kapel and Denmark comes from John Kapel, conversation with Wendy Kaplan, June 26, 2010.

54 For CalFab in homes, see "Living in Los Angeles," 81. For a chair with cord, see *Living for Young Homemakers*, December 1952, 14, and July 1952, 16. With ash frames and webbing, the kits cost $17.95.

55 Shown in *California Design 4*, 1958; it cost $295.

56 See Kirkham, "New Environments for Modern Living," 171–82; and Pat Kirkham, "Humanizing Modernism: The Crafts, 'Functioning Decoration' and the Eameses," *Journal of Design History* 11, no. 1 (1998): 15–29.

57 Kirkham, *Charles and Ray Eames*, 190.

58 Kirkham, "Humanizing Modernism," 15–29.

59 "Young Man on a Mountain: Paul Tuttle, Furniture Designer," *House Beautiful*, July 1965, 63–64.

60 For Neutra, see "New Shells," *Time*, August 15, 1949, 58–62. For the Eameses and for Brown, see Evan Frances, "If I Could Tell a Woman One Thing about Furnishing a Home . . . ," *Family Circle*, March 1958, 27–31; and Kirkham, "New Environments for Modern Living," 172–82.

61 "Six Portable Murals," exhibition announcement, Long Beach Museum of Art object file. The exhibition also included paintings by Elise, Lorser Feitelson, and Knud Merrild.

62 Frances, "If I Could Tell a Woman One Thing," 27.

63 See "Living in Los Angeles," 77 and 81.

64 See Steven M. Gelber, *Hobbies: Leisure and the Culture of Work in America* (New York: Columbia University Press, 1999); and Kathryn Grover, ed., *Hard at Play: Leisure in America, 1840–1940* (Amherst: University of Massachusetts Press, 1992).

65 "Chairs by Maurice Martiné," *Arts and Architecture*, December 1948, 28; and George Nelson, ed., *Chairs* (1953; repr., New York: Acanthus Press, 1994), 114.

66 Esther McCoy, "Remembering John Entenza," in *Arts and Architecture: The Entenza Years*, ed. Barbara Goldstein (Santa Monica: Hennessey and Ingalls, 1998), 13.

67 Linda Cervon, email correspondence with author, September–October 2002.

68 *Race and Housing: An Interview with Edward P. Eichler, President, Eichler Homes, Inc.* (Santa Barbara: Fund for the Republic, 1964), 19.

69 Ibid., 10.

70 Ibid., 19–20.

71 "Hilltop Living: San Diego Family Has Modern Home Overlooking the City," *Ebony*, February 1960, 37–38 and 40–42. The average sizes and costs of the California modern house are based on a survey of homes referred to in *Living for Young Homemakers*, *Sunset*, and *Arts and Architecture*.

72 "Critical Look at the Changing Western House," 78–79.

73 Ray Eames to author, 1987, quoted in Kirkham, *Charles and Ray Eames*, 379.

74 "Survival: Are Shelters the Answer?," *Newsweek*, November 6, 1961, 19, cited in Kenneth D. Rose, *One Nation Underground: The Fallout Shelter in American Culture* (New York: New York University Press, 2001), 189. For shelters and the Cold War, see Sarah A. Lichtman, "Do-It-Yourself Security," *Journal of Design History* 19, no. 1 (2006): 39–55.

75 For László, see "Subterranean Atomic Suburbia," *Interiors*, February 1953, 70; "Atomic Hideouts," *Popular Mechanics*, March 1958, 148; and Carson Kerr, "At Home, 2004 A.D.," *Popular Mechanics*, October 1954, 154–56, 266, 268.

76 "House for the Atomic Age," *Popular Mechanics*, August 1953, 108–11.

77 For table with petal decoration, see *Interiors*, August 1961, 96; and for both tables, see Howard McNab and Don Savage, "Occasional 'Peace' Table" (lot 440) and "Occasional 'Flower' Table" (lot 441), *Los Angeles Modern Auctions, October 14, 2007* (Sherman Oaks: Modern Auctions, 2007), 211. The resin tops were manufactured by Frank Rohloff.

5.44. Joseph Zukin of California. Playsuit, c. 1945. Cat. 144

6

War and Peace: Unexpected Dividends

BILL STERN

World War II made California a primary center of the nation's war-related economy, producing such essential goods as steel, tires, vehicles, aircraft, ships, and electronics. The result was an unprecedented influx of new residents: between 1941 and 1945 the state's population grew from 7,237,000 to 9,344,000, a staggering 29 percent increase.[1] Another two million people would arrive between 1946 and 1952, mainly ex-servicemen and their families plus those drawn to California by entrepreneurial opportunities and jobs in revitalized civilian industries. These pervasive

6.1. Muriel Coleman (1917–2003) for California Contemporary. Room divider, c. 1952. Iron and redwood. From *House and Garden*, April 1952, p. 98

changes paid unexpected dividends in terms of modern design in postwar California. Even before the war ended, many leaders in the design community recognized that some effects of the war would persist in peacetime. When he announced the Case Study House Program in the January 1945 issue of *Arts and Architecture*, editor John Entenza wrote, "The house[s] . . . will be conceived within the spirit of our time, using as far as is practicable, many war-born techniques and materials best suited to the expression of man's life in the modern world."[2]

Throughout the war the design of commercial consumer products in the United States had been on hiatus. The co-opting of essential materials by the military (or their unavailability due to rationing and the lack of imports)[3] stymied the development of new products and the redesign of existing ones. Between 1940 and 1945 most of California's makers of domestic products curtailed what had been increasingly imaginative efforts and retreated to well-accepted conservative models. In dinnerware, for example, the cutting-edge designs of the 1930s gave way to traditional floral patterns intended to replace those that could no longer be imported, resulting in such derivative patterns as Vernon Kilns' *Chintz* and *May Flower* from 1942.[4]

For a few years in the late 1940s many of the companies that had continued to make consumer goods during the war, as well as those that resumed production soon after, still used prewar streamlined styling. A pair of circular candleholders composed of war-surplus Micarta[5] disks with spun-aluminum fittings produced about 1948 by the Aero Art division of Los Angeles's Franz Industries could easily be mistaken for a 1930s product (6.2). At about the same time, plastic disk-shaped pitchers with Moderne decorations—whose flat sides, a holdover from the 1930s, made them ideal for confined spaces like refrigerators—were being produced by Los Angeles's Burroughs Manufacturing Corporation (6.3).

As the American consumer economy revived after the war, so did product design. Even though the end of the war prompted optimism,[6] the immediate postwar years were a time of limited options for design and production. Luxury materials—and some staples as well—were still not available, and it would be some time before they would return to houseware stores and furniture departments. It was in that frugal postwar climate that legions of newcomers to California—a large percentage of them young families—went about furnishing their new homes. Describing the nature of these enlightened consumers, David Halberstam wrote about the wartime and postwar years, "There had been a great influx of new industry to Southern California (mostly in the scientific and defense fields) and this had brought a wave of migrants different from those of the past, younger and better educated."[7] In addition to individuals in the arts and in education, these were the kind of forward-thinking newcomers who would commission homes in Los Angeles by modern architects including Richard Neutra and John Lautner. Those with fewer financial resources could choose, for example, one of the eight models designed by architects A. Quincy

Jones and Whitney R. Smith for the nonprofit Mutual Housing Association (now Crestwood Hills) development in Brentwood.[8] Elsewhere in California, a single developer, Joseph Eichler, built more than eleven thousand modern houses in both Southern and Northern California, about five thousand of them designed by Jones and his partner, Frederick E. Emmons.[9] And the market for suitable home furnishings grew apace.

After the war ended and military procurement had ceased, but before supplies of raw materials became generally available again, a number of California designers found imaginative reuses for surplus war materials. In Sausalito, Luther Conover turned surplus rebar—iron rods for reinforcing concrete, which had been used for almost half a century but always kept out of sight—into fully visible frames for furniture (6.4).

Others employed industrial materials that had been commonly used during the war. In the Bay Area, Muriel Coleman designed furniture for her family's company, the San Leandro–based California Contemporary.[10] Coleman, a painter with a Master of Fine Arts degree from Columbia University, used rebar for large shelf units that could double as sturdy room dividers (6.1). With their redwood shelves in a contrasting lighter color and their completely exposed construction, these units brought a distinctively modern look to the interiors of new homes, while Coleman's line of indoor/outdoor furnishings with steel-bar legs and frames did the same for patios. At the same time, in Southern California, the company Van Keppel-Green was experimenting with panels of expanded metal that had been perforated and pulled to create gridlike openings,[11] and Coleman and Vista Furniture were using the same material for chair backs and desks (6.5).

Exposed materials such as rebar embodied two principal tenets of modern design: eschewing unnecessary decoration by enlisting the structural elements of an object to provide visual interest and attempting to make products as affordable as possible. The goal was to encourage what was unabashedly dubbed "good design" and promoted by progressive museums throughout the country, most notably the Walker Art Center, with its *Everyday Art Quarterly* and eponymous gallery, and the Museum of Modern Art (MoMA), with its *Good Design* exhibitions held annually between 1950 and 1955.

A vigorous competition developed among California's designers and manufacturers to attract a share of the state's (and the nation's) newly burgeoning consumer market. Because it would be several years before imports from America's traditional trading partners, notably Britain and Germany, rebounded and new design competitors, like Italy, developed a strong export market, California designers and producers enjoyed a commercial advantage in the feverish competition for West Coast consumers. Proximity favored local manufacturers because many of the materials needed for production had been stockpiled or were being made in-state, and retail prices on the West Coast were free of

6.2. Franz Industries. Candleholders, Aero Art Product, c. 1948. Cat. 107

6.3. Clarence M. Burroughs for Burroughs Manufacturing Corporation. Pitcher, c. 1948. Cat. 34

6.4. Luther Conover. Chair, c. 1950. Cat. 48

VAN KEPPEL-GREEN

MODERN
FURNITURE

BEVERLY HILLS, CALIFORNIA

VKG

cross-country shipping charges. (In national advertisements by East Coast producers, "Prices slightly higher in the West" was a common small-print advisory.)

Nonetheless, California's undercapitalized start-up companies couldn't afford the greatest expense associated with mass production: "tooling," the manufacturing of the machines and dies needed to make the basic elements of a product. The successful manufacturer of a chair, for instance, could eventually make a profit by amortizing the tooling cost over thousands of chairs; but if the first chair off the line cost $500,000 and then each subsequent one cost $11, the initial investment was obviously beyond the means of California's small companies.[12] As a result, the production of chairs and tables, storage units and bed frames, lamps and candleholders often relied on available—as opposed to molded or die-cut—stocks of metal. Those inexpensive, mainly war-surplus rods and strips had to be individually cut and bent:[13] the rods and tubes often into a hairpin shape that maximized the strength of metal legs.[14] The use of exposed metal, whether as solid rods or hollow tubes or flat strips, became one of the defining features of California furniture and accessories in the years after the war. Although this was clearly an expression of the modernist spirit of the time, it was also a practical response to the economic situation. Well into the 1950s, much of California's commercial furniture shared a fundamental characteristic

with objects being made by the designer-craftsmen then working in clay or plastic or metal: small-batch production.

One of the state's enduring characteristics—its openness to new designs, new materials, and new technologies—gave it a commercial edge during this postwar period of nationwide economic expansion. The sudden growth in California's commercial design market spurred many entrepreneurial designers and designer-craftsmen to start their own production enterprises. Some—like the furniture designer Hendrik Van Keppel, a Californian who came to Los Angeles from San Francisco in 1937, and Bakersfield-born Barbara Willis, who started her own company making slip-cast pottery in Los Angeles's Fairfax District in 1943—continued the simple rectilinear forms that characterized Bauhaus and International Style–influenced modern design in the 1930s. About 1939 Van Keppel introduced an innovative chair of cotton cord and enamel-coated steel that, because of wartime materials restrictions, was not widely available until the late 1940s (6.6). Such furnishings of steel frames with cotton or vinyl strapping became emblems of mid-century modern design. Because her raw materials weren't rationed, Willis began producing commercial ceramics in 1943 (6.7), and she continued until imports and the new popularity of plastics undercut the market for American-made ceramics in the 1950s.[15]

6.5. Van Keppel-Green. Sales catalogue, 1957. Cat. 352
The cover highlights details of Van Keppel-Green's characteristic use of all-weather materials: architectural glass, expanded metal, marine cord, and rattan.

6.6. Hendrik Van Keppel, Van Keppel-Green. Lounge chair and ottoman, designed c. 1939; this example made c. 1959. Cat. 298

The modest size of so many California companies making household products was a function of the state's unique circumstances: most of them were created by new arrivals or young local entrepreneurs, and the California market was quite small compared to that in the Midwest and East.[16] Many of those new companies were, initially at least, sole proprietorships owned by an individual designer-craftsman or a couple—among them were Van Keppel-Green (Hendrik Van Keppel and Taylor Green), ERA Industries (Jerome and Evelyn Ackerman), Heath Ceramics (Edith and Brian Heath), and Luther Conover, who began making his first furniture with the help of high school students. Other small businesses included Barbara Willis's Terrene Pottery, which had no more than fifteen employees at the apogee of its production; despite the small size, Willis has calculated that in the course of ten years the company produced more than 250,000 ceramic pieces.[17] The prominent furniture company Brown-Saltman had perhaps thirty employees, and Architectural Pottery, about fifty.[18] All of them were small businesses by national standards.[19]

In about 1950 the Claremont-based studio potter Rupert Deese became a small-shop producer of utilitarian stoneware products: a line of carafes, cocktail pitchers (see p. 6), mugs, and ashtrays, which were the mainstay of any number of ceramic producers at that time. Deese's stoneware was press-molded or slip cast in molds, but with their elegant glazes the pieces retain the look usually associated with hand-thrown wares. Other studio potters had brief encounters with commercial production. Among them, the renowned ceramist Otto Natzler worked with a producer to make slip-cast bowls covered with his trademark glazes for a company called the Guild in about 1945 (6.8). In about 1953, while producing her one-of-a-kind lusterware vessels in her Ojai studio, the usually hands-on Beatrice Wood created an extensive slip-cast ceramic dinnerware service for Knox China.[20]

California's distance from the furniture manufacturers in Michigan, New York, North Carolina, and elsewhere in the East and Midwest helped many small design and manufacturing companies to flourish, however briefly. Innovative small-shop producers of furniture and housewares included Maurice Martiné, who designed a versatile wooden chair frame that could have either a wood dowel or a cord seating surface and that was designed to be sold flat-packed and assembled by the owner (see 5.40); Ralph O. Smith Manufacturing Company, which had a staff of two or three employees who produced lamps designed by Greta Magnusson Grossman (see p. 7) and Olga Lee in Burbank; and Barney M. Reid, who printed his designs on textiles in San Diego (see 8.9). As Don Wallance noted in *Shaping America's Products* (1956), "The small firm is flexible in operation and can therefore produce specialized, advanced or even experimental products which originally would not have mass acceptance."[21] For example, in 1957 designer John Caldwell, while still a student at Pasadena City College, took a shoebox containing a chair model made of electrician's

wire and upholstery thread to Bob Brown at Brown-Jordan, a Pasadena manufacturer of metal outdoor furniture. By the next afternoon a prototype of the chair had been constructed out of scrap aluminum tubing, and the *Mai Tai* line of outdoor furniture, made with aluminum tubing and extruded vinyl (a war-developed product), went into production that same year (6.9).[22]

This was a time when the limited space available to young homemakers prompted a fad for convertible furniture: for example, a bookshelf that could be reconfigured as a dining table, and the *Versitable*, designed by Gene Tepper (6.10 and see cat. 284), which could be used as either a dining table or a coffee table (or stowed away).[23] Even architect Richard Neutra had earlier contributed to this appealing but impractical exercise by making what has become known as the "Camel" table (when partially lowered it looks like a kneeling dromedary) for his own home (6.11), as well as several others he designed in the 1940s and '50s.

Renowned designers Charles and Ray Eames transformed the furniture industry by developing new manufacturing techniques and applications for new materials.[24] In the summer of 1941 the couple moved to Los Angeles, committed to developing a way to mass-produce molded-plywood chairs with compound curves. Such chairs would provide better, body-contoured support, eliminating the need for heavy, costly padding and springs. This was not an

6.7. Barbara Willis for Barbara Willis Pottery. Pillow vases, c. 1945. Cat. 312

6.8. Otto Natzler for Guild. Bowls, c. 1945. Cat. 217
Otto Natzler served on the home front during World War II, where a dental technician taught him how to cast plaster, a skill Natzler later developed in an aircraft production job. After the war, he used the skill to produce this short-lived line of slip-cast ceramic housewares.

6.9. John Caldwell (b. 1938) for Brown-Jordan. *Mai Tai* chair, 1957. Aluminum and vinyl, 40¾ x 33½ x 27⅜ in. (103.5 x 85.1 x 69.5 cm). Collection of Andy Hackman

6.10. Gene Tepper for Tepper-Meyer Associates. *Versitable*, 1953. Steel and Formica, 29½ x 60 x 29¾ in. (74.9 x 152.4 x 75.6 cm). Collection of Gene Tepper. See cat. 284

academic exercise—it addressed the need for high-quality low-cost furniture for modern living. As Charles declared: "The concept was to do a piece of furniture which had a certain minimum of means, but a cushion chair, austere only in that it would be of a hard substance, which would be really comfortable. . . . It must be, we decided, a chair which was the product of mass production, and mass production would not have anything but a positive influence on it."[25]

The previous year Charles Eames and Eero Saarinen, who were both trained as architects and taught at the Cranbrook Academy of Art in Michigan, had collaborated on furniture designs to address this problem. About the same time, Eames met his future wife and partner, Ray Kaiser, who had studied painting with Hans Hofmann in New York. In 1940 MoMA announced a competition for young designers, in which the winning entries would be put into production by manufacturers. Eames and Saarinen entered designs for several pieces of furniture (Ray worked on the presentation drawings), and they won first prize for living room furniture in what came to be known as the Organic Design competition.[26] They worked with the manufacturers Heywood-Wakefield and Haskelite to make chair shells out of a single piece of plywood, but because the technology did not exist to mass-produce the designs, very few were actually made (6.12).

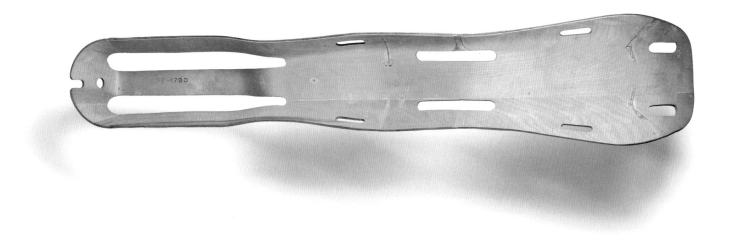

In 1941, working in their Neutra-designed apartment in Westwood, Charles and Ray continued to experiment with plywood-chair manufacture. Soon after war was declared, their friend Dr. Wendell Scott suggested that they apply their work to making splints for wounded servicemen and -women.[27] The Eameses proposed to the U.S. Navy that molded-plywood splints would be more lightweight and effective than the metal ones then in use. They received a contract, and production began in 1943. With access to the latest materials and techniques—including new, more water-resistant synthetic glues that yielded much stronger plywood—the Eameses were able to mass-produce the first molded-plywood product with compound curves (6.13).[28] Using the same technique, they also designed a body litter, but this did not go into production (6.14).

After the war they returned to their original goal of mass-producing molded-plywood furniture. Having established the Molded Plywood Division of Evans Products Company in 1943, they then produced a small batch of children's furniture (including a plywood elephant toy; see p. 5) and a larger run of molded-plywood chairs such as the *DCW* (dining chair wood) (6.15). This line featured rubber shock mounts that absorbed vibrations and distributed stress— a novel way to join seats and backs to frames and one that served the goal of creating a very comfortable chair without the need for upholstery.[29] MoMA

6.11. Richard Neutra. "Camel" table (prototype) for the Richard Neutra VDL Research House, Silver Lake, 1932; table designed and made c. 1940. Cat. 222

6.12. Charles Eames and Eero Saarinen, Heywood-Wakefield, and the Haskelite Manufacturing Corporation. Chair, 1940. Cat. 71
This chair was displayed in MoMA's *Organic Design in Home Furnishings* exhibition in 1941.

6.13. Charles Eames and Ray Eames for Molded Plywood Division, Evans Products Company. Leg splint, designed c. 1941–42; manufactured 1942–45. Cat. 72

curator Eliot Noyes noted that this technique "has long been a standard practice in automobiles and aircraft, but this is the first time that it has been used on chairs."[30] In the late 1940s Herman Miller, a Michigan-based furniture manufacturer that had marketed and distributed the plywood furniture since 1946, began to manufacture the furniture in its own plant using Eames-designed equipment that had been shipped from Venice, California. That the Eameses not only designed the furniture but also invented the process to mass-produce it and created the necessary tooling is central to understanding their work. But Charles and Ray had even greater ambitions, as they wrote: to "do something where the act of mass-production made the chair *better*."[31]

The next breakthrough for low-cost mass-produced furniture was also a result of wartime material innovations. During the war fiberglass had been used primarily for nose cones and radar domes, but the Eameses would find a commercial application for this new material, spurred by MoMA's 1948 International Competition for Low-Cost Furniture Design. According to MoMA director René d'Harnoncourt, the goal of the competition was to address the "need for adaptable furniture for small apartments and houses, well-designed yet moderate in price, comfortable but not bulky, and easily moved, stored and cared for; in other words, mass-produced furniture that is planned and executed to fit the needs of modern living, production, and merchandising."[32]

The Eameses returned to the idea of a chair with arms and body made of one continuous shell, a design that would require fewer individual parts and production steps and hence have a lower cost. They developed several forms in metal that were submitted to the MoMA competition, winning second prize in the seating-unit division. But because the stamping proved cumbersome and expensive, and the result was heavy and cold to the touch, they turned to John Wills, a noted fabricator of car bodies, to model the chair in fiberglass. With a model in hand, the Eameses then turned to the aerospace company Zenith Plastics in Gardena to develop a way to mass-produce molded-fiberglass shells. As MoMA curator Edgar Kaufmann Jr. wrote: "This molded fibre [*sic*] glass chair is in many respects an astonishing fulfillment of the ideas developed by Charles Eames and his occasional associate Eero Saarinen in 1940 when similar designs of theirs won first prize in The Museum of Modern Art's *Organic Design* competition. . . . Now it has been possible to find a plastic substance and a molding process which allow this kind of shape to be produced economically. . . . Never before used in furniture, this airplane plastic is virtually indestructible and withstands stains and mars."[33] The plastic chair proved to be one of the most successful ever produced, and by 1966 Herman Miller announced that more than two million had been sold (6.16).[34]

The Eameses' successful experimentation with fiberglass is one critically important manifestation of how the enormous resources poured into the development of new materials and techniques during the war had a great

impact on postwar design and manufacturing. The new popularity of surfboards and California's existing small-scale automobile manufacturing also
transformed fiberglass from a specialized military material into a basic ingredi-
ent of domestic American life.

For decades after surfboards were introduced into California from Hawaii
in the nineteenth century, they were individually made solid wood behemoths
whose weight, in the range of one hundred to two hundred pounds, dramatically restricted their use. In the 1930s some surfers began experimenting with
ways to reduce the weight of surfboards. But whether the boards were hollow
or made of lighter wood, like balsa, they shared the same problem: water would
penetrate and weigh them down. One of the first, if not *the* first, fiberglass-
covered waterproof surfboards was made in Southern California by Preston
"Pete" Peterson in 1946.[35] Fiberglass was not yet available on the retail market,
and Peterson, like other surfers who covered boards with fiberglass to seal
them, got the material from friends or family members who worked for aircraft
manufacturers. In Peterson's case, it was W. Brandt Goldsworthy, who in the
early years of the war had pioneered fiberglass-reinforced tools and molded-
fiberglass ammunition chutes at the Douglas Aircraft Company in El Segundo.[36]

It was the introduction of polyurethane foam boards covered with fiberglass and resin in the mid-1950s that made light surfboards practical. But even
so, well into the decade surfing remained a pastime limited to the few, since
boards still had to be either hand shaped by individual surfers or made to
order. That changed after Hobart "Hobie" Alter and Gordon "Grubby" Clark
started making boards out of polyurethane foam wrapped in fiberglass and
resin at Hobie's Surf Shop in Dana Point in 1954; in 1956 Dave Sweet produced
"the first commercially offered polyurethane foam surfboard" in Santa Monica.[37]
Readily available thirty-pound boards would eventually turn this once regional
all-male sport into a national, and international, pastime open to all.[38]

In addition to increasing the market for surfboards, the new materials gave
shapers of surfboards the possibility of devising sophisticated designs previously
impossible to execute. This is well illustrated by the complex design of a board
that Alter made for Chuck Quinn in 1961 (6.17).[39] After cutting the polyurethane
foam blank with arcs of red-hot piano wire, then gluing the pieces of foam and
redwood stringer (needed for strengthening as well as ornamenting the board),
Alter encased the assembled board in a seamless waterproof carapace of fiberglass and resin.[40] Neither this board nor the millions that followed could have
been made without fiberglass and polyurethane and the resin that melded them.

The huge popularity of *Gidget* attests to the rapid proliferation of this
essential Californian (and Hawaiian) phenomenon. The story of a teenage girl in
Los Angeles who, with her polyurethane-and-fiberglass-wrapped balsa board,
broke into the all-male surfing clique, it went from a book (1957) to a movie
(1959) and finally to a television series (1965–66).[41] In the wake of *Gidget* came

6.14. Charles Eames and Ray Eames for
Molded Plywood Division, Evans Products
Company. Body litter (prototype), 1943.
Cat. 73. Photo by Eames Office, 1943

6.15. Charles Eames and Ray Eames for
Molded Plywood Division, Evans
Products Company and Herman Miller
Furniture Company. *DCW* (dining chair
wood), 1946–49. Cat. 75

6.16. Charles Eames and Ray Eames for
Herman Miller Furniture Company.
LAR (low lounge chair), 1948–50; this
example made c. 1951. Cat. 77

6.17. Hobart "Hobie" Alter. Surfboard for
Chuck Quinn, 1961. Cat. 9

6.18. La Gardo Tackett for Architectural
Pottery. Garden sculpture, c. 1955.
Cat. 281
**These examples were installed at the
Los Angeles home of Max and Rita
Lawrence, the founders (with John
Follis) of Architectural Pottery. The
design was modular: each column consisted of several stacked elements, so
buyers could create their own combinations. Company catalogues promoted
their potential uses as screens, pipe
concealers, and fountains.**

the Beach Boys' hit albums *Surfin' Safari* (1962), *Surfin' USA* (1963), and *Surfer Girl* (1963) and the films *Beach Blanket Bingo* (1965) and *The Endless Summer* (nationally released in 1966). California beach culture went national. In June 1965, *Time* magazine reported: "Last week, from Maine to Miami, beaches with a rolling surf were bristling with the sleek Fiberglas slabs. . . . On Long Island, where 40 surfboards were sold in 1960, 4,000 have been snapped up this year, with the season just under way. . . . Even landlocked youths strap their boards on top of their cars [and] take off on long surfing safaris. . . . Before long, Eastern surfers may well outnumber those in the West."[42]

In 1961, while walking on the beach near Oxnard with his wife, Rita, Max Lawrence, the entrepreneur who had cofounded Architectural Pottery in Los Angeles in 1950 with his wife and the designer John Follis, saw a young man carrying a sixteen-foot paddleboard made of fiberglass and urethane foam. Max Lawrence recognized that, with this long board, the surfer Bill Flannigan (who had made the board himself) had solved the problem of reinforcing fiber-glass, which would permit the fabrication of sizable fiberglass products like furniture and planters.[43]

Architectural Pottery produced large-scale modern ceramics—mainly planters and large ashtrays for public spaces (6.18). In time the Lawrences recognized the limitations that clay imposed on their products. The weight of the objects, the crating and shipping costs, and manufacturing problems as well as limited durability frustrated their desire to provide their corporate customers with planters and group seating on a scale appropriate for public facilities, including shopping centers and airports. Having adapted reinforced fiberglass to commercial products for outdoor and indoor use, the Lawrences engaged several of Architectural Pottery's designers to create products for an offshoot company, Architectural Fiberglass (established 1961)—among them, John Follis, Marilyn Kay Austin, Elsie Crawford, and Douglas Deeds, who became the company's design director.[44]

Being a synthetic material, fiberglass-reinforced plastic was subjected to a great deal of public scorn.[45] But as demonstrated by the Architectural Fiberglass designs, many of which were included in the *California Design* exhibitions of the 1960s and '70s, this material did not limit the originality or gracefulness of products made with it. Among them is a Douglas Deeds bench that uses a structurally robust form to generate a piece of light yet durable outdoor furniture (6.19). It is one of three Deeds benches that were exhibited in the *California Design 9* show at the Pasadena Art Museum in 1965. The California-designed and -made products by Architectural Fiberglass were so durable and so well designed that nearly half a century later they still look contemporary in use at the University of California, Los Angeles; the Brand Library in Glendale; the Mormon Temple in Los Angeles; and many other locations.

Some designers made the tactile fibers of fiberglass a design element. In

Los Angeles, Mitchell Bobrick used sheets of raw fiberglass to diffuse the light from his floor and desk lamps, its coarse weave evoking the then-popular look of handwoven Polynesian textiles (6.20). Others found inspiration in the visually appealing properties of synthetic materials, manipulating various resins in both handcrafted works and commercial designs. In Big Sur and Berkeley during the 1950s, the Paris-educated designer Zahara Schatz evoked the biomorphic abstractions of Joán Miró and Alexander Calder by suspending colored wires in the clear acrylic of her handmade lamp bases (see 7.16). During his long career as a commercial designer, Charles Hollis Jones has favored the use of the expensive transparent material Lucite, beginning with his furniture and accessory lines for Hudson Rissman, a Los Angeles showroom, in 1963 (6.21).

While the designs of the Eameses, Bobrick, and Schatz brought new materials into the home, other innovators applied these technologies to automobile design. In a state often criticized for its reliance on cars, the dependence went beyond convenient transportation: automotive production played a central role in the region's economy. As early as the 1920s, Ford and Willys-Overland produced cars in Los Angeles, which by 1957 ranked "second only to Detroit as a national center of automobile assembly, with an annual capacity of 650,000 cars."[46] The Art Center School in Los Angeles provided the industry with designers, playing such a significant role that *Industrial Design* estimated in 1967 that "more than half of all of the Detroit automakers' designers are graduates of this one school."[47] With one of the country's earliest industrial-design departments (founded in 1932), Art Center made "transportation design" an official major in 1948, headed by former Buick and Cadillac designer George Jergenson. That same year, the Pasadena-born Art Center graduate Strother MacMinn joined the faculty. MacMinn, who had worked with Henry Dreyfuss on the Convair (Consolidated Vultee Aircraft) car (see 1.12), taught at Art Center for forty-six years, greatly influencing the next generation of automotive designers.[48]

In addition to attracting the major automobile companies, California was distinguished by the number of small producers of cars operating there. These producers, as well as automobile customizers, owed much of their success to a wealthy clientele in the movie industry.[49] Film stars of the period tended to flaunt their individuality through the cars they drove, which provided a reliable market for customizers like Howard "Dutch" Darrin, an American who had personalized luxury cars in Paris before moving to Hollywood in 1937. He customized Packards and other cars for local celebrities—including Clark Gable, Rosalind Russell, and Al Jolson—but the war economy (and, no doubt, public relations concerns about indulging in luxuries during wartime) curtailed such extravagances. Once the war was over, California's custom car culture reemerged in a less grandiose mode, invigorated by the introduction of car bodies made of fiberglass. Dutch Darrin was among the first California designers to begin fashioning car bodies of this unglamorous material in the late 1940s.

The high point of California's small-scale production of automobiles was undoubtedly the 1952 Glasspar G2, designed by Bill Tritt (6.22). Even though only about a hundred examples were made, it was the first production-line car with a fiberglass body, and it attracted national press attention. A headline in *Life* magazine announced: "Plastic Bodies for Autos: Rustproof, Dentproof, Synthetic Shells Go on Market in California."[50] As was the case with other California designers of fiberglass products, Tritt had first encountered the new material during the war. Using technology learned while working at Douglas Aircraft, he created the first fiberglass masts and spars for sailboats before turning his attention to cars.[51]

For a brief moment, another California-designed fiberglass-bodied car seemed poised to star on the national stage. In 1961 the declining automobile company Studebaker-Packard hired Raymond Loewy to execute the design of a car that a new company president had sketched out. Because Loewy owned a home in Palm Springs, he specified that the design work be done with his own team there in order to be free from the constraints of Detroit.[52] His *Avanti*, which means "forward" in Italian, was introduced at the 1962 New York Motor Show (6.23). *Time* magazine described the car as "finless, aerodynamically clean, and fast," and its grille-less front still seems futuristic.[53] However, the

6.19. Douglas Deeds for Architectural Fiberglass. Bench, c. 1962. From *Architectural Fiberglass: Benches* brochure, c. 1965. See cat. 58

6.20. Mitchell Bobrick for Controlight Company. *Controlight* lamp and bookshelf, c. 1949. Cat. 30

6.21. Charles Hollis Jones (b. 1945) for Hudson Rissman. Table, c. 1963. Manufactured by Joe Roide Enterprises. Lucite and chromed brass, 20 x 20 in. (50.8 x 50.8 cm). Collection of Charles Hollis Jones

6.22. Bill Tritt (b. 1917) for Glasspar Company. Glasspar G2 automobile, 1952. Fiberglass body. Promotional photograph, 1950s

6.23. Raymond Loewy for Studebaker Corporation. *Avanti* automobile, designed 1961, manufactured 1963–64. Image from company brochure, 1962. See cat. 179

6.24. H. Koch & Sons Company. Suitcase, c. 1950. Cat. 155

6.25. Henry Dreyfuss and James M. Conner for Polaroid Corporation. *The Swinger* camera, 1965. Cat. 70

company's production facilities couldn't adapt to working with fiberglass fast enough to keep up with demand, and within two years Studebaker (as the company was then named) stopped making automobiles.

By the time the Glasspar went into production, the San Francisco luggage manufacturer H. Koch & Sons Company had developed fiberglass–polyester resin carrying cases (6.24). Their lightness, strength, and durability made them especially well suited for airplane travel and for military purposes. The luggage was used by the air force during the Korean War, as were the molded-fiberglass domes for airplanes also produced by the company.[54] Koch, which moved to Corte Madera in 1951, was emblematic of the boom in products made for industry and for institutional use by airlines, construction companies, and restaurants that paralleled the growth in design for retail consumption in postwar California. So it is hardly surprising that the state would attract talented commercial designers from other parts of the country.

Before moving to Pasadena in 1944, Brooklyn-born Henry Dreyfuss was already renowned for several nationally recognized products, including the Big Ben alarm clock (first designed about 1935) and the locomotive of New York Central Railroad's 20th Century Limited (1938). Even after relocating, Dreyfuss kept his main office in New York, managing the distance through daily airmail reports and frequent visits. From his West Coast office, Dreyfuss and his staff produced notable designs for several major clients nationwide, among them the Lockheed Corporation, Deere and Company (also known as John Deere), and the Polaroid Corporation. In 1960 Edwin Land, whose revolutionary Polaroid camera had debuted in 1948, asked Dreyfuss to design a new Polaroid camera. The ergonomic design of Dreyfuss's inexpensive, easy-to-use *Swinger* (1965) gave it "an undeniably pop-art appearance" (6.25).[55] The substantial hand grip, which also accommodated the simple-to-load roll of film, made it easy to hold the camera steady.[56]

Dreyfuss and Loewy both achieved a well-earned measure of public acclaim, but that recognition is unusual in industrial design; designers' names are rarely known to the general public, even when their products have become part of everyday life. For example, Henry C. Keck, who had trained in industrial design at the California Institute of Technology on the GI Bill, was responsible for two familiar American objects, both of which were commercially practical and completely modern. For half a century his unfaceted and unornamented glass-and-chromed-steel sugar shakers have graced the tabletops of American restaurants so unobtrusively that they seem to have always been there (6.26). Keck, who designed them for the Dripcut Starline Corporation of Santa Barbara, in about 1957, estimated that more than thirty-five million were sold in the first fifty years of production—perhaps because they are more durable and far easier to keep clean than their predecessors.[57] Equally familiar is the Roadside barricade light that Keck designed in about 1963 (6.27). As originally executed—

6.26. Henry C. Keck for Dripcut Starline Corporation. Salt, pepper, and sugar shakers, c. 1955–57. Cat. 148

6.27. Henry C. Keck for Electronic Engineering Company of California. Roadside barricade light, c. 1963. Cat. 149

The Roadside barricade light, exhibited in *California Design 9* (1965), was one of the industrial-design objects described by the catalogue as illustrating the "growing role of the State as a manufacturing center."

6.28. Heinz Haber for Walt Disney Productions. "Atomic Genie," illustration from *The Walt Disney Story of Our Friend the Atom* (New York: Simon and Schuster, 1956), p. 105

6.29. Packard-Bell promotional display (detail), 1954. Collection of Daniel Ostroff

a pure, unornamented circle and an equally pure, unornamented rectangle—it is the epitome of modernist reduction.[58] Anyone who has traveled in the United States has probably seen examples of this California design in use at roadside and building construction sites.

The influence of World War II on materials was a practical matter of availability, functionality, and economy. But wartime developments and the Cold War that followed it also had an impact on decorative imagery. Postwar modern decoration often reflects the influence of contemporary fine artists—including Alexander Calder, Salvador Dalí, Paul Klee, and Joán Miró—but more discomfiting imagery was inspired by rockets and nuclear fission. As Jane Pavitt points out in *Fear and Fashion in the Cold War*, "In one of the strange contradictions of the Cold War world, the atomic bomb was assimilated into everyday culture as a jaunty symbol of modernity."[59]

In an effort to reassure Americans that the nuclear age did not mean that the end was near and that, as historian Spencer Weart has observed, "atomic utopia could become a reality in their lifetimes,"[60] President Dwight D. Eisenhower announced the Atoms for Peace Program in 1953. It supplied optimistic information about nuclear energy to schools as well as equipment for using radiation in hospitals and research institutions in the U.S. and in other countries. This propaganda effort was aided by the 1955 "Atoms for Peace" U.S. postage stamp, which depicted the Earth as the nucleus of an atom, and *Our Friend the Atom* (1957), a Disney film in which Walt Disney himself tells us that "the atom is our future." Both the film, which was shown in school auditoriums and science classes as well as on the *Disneyland* television show, and the book (published the year before) present a benign view of atomic power.

As the nation's center of aeronautics development, California companies often used atomic and rocket imagery to extol their achievements. It appeared in logos, including that of Packard-Bell, maker of consumer radios and military electronics (6.29 and 6.32), and in promotional products, including the enameled-copper dishes designed by Alexander for Convair (6.31). Atomic imagery can even be discerned in the design of the 1961 Hobie Alter surfboard discussed earlier (see 6.17). And it was California that produced one of the nation's most widely distributed examples of this imagery on a consumer product, Franciscan's popular *Starburst* dinner pattern (6.30), which found its way onto thousands of American dinner tables beginning in 1954.[61]

Eventually the widely reported proliferation of atom- and hydrogen-bomb tests and the spiraling production of nuclear weapons would dampen public opinion, which had been ambivalent at best. Even in *Our Friend the Atom*, which depicts atomic power as a human-controlled force to be channeled for social good, Disney compares it to Aladdin's genie—a powerful force that could grant all earthly wishes but was potentially dangerous if released unwittingly (6.28). As the public turned against the atom, its burst of graphic stardom rapidly waned.

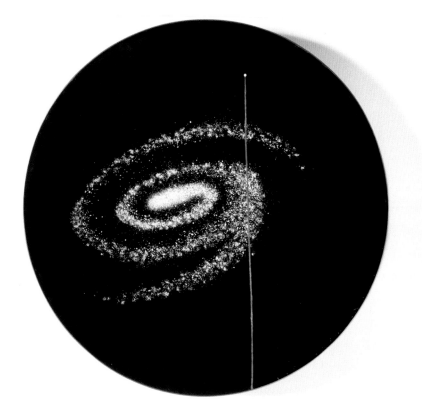

6.30. George James, form, and Mary C. Brown, decoration, for Gladding McBean & Co., Franciscan Division. *Starburst* platter in *Eclipse* shape, 1953. Cat. 136

6.31. Alexander for Convair Division of General Dynamics. Plate, c. 1960. Cat. 8 The plate depicts a rocket speeding through a starry sky. The aspirations of the period are clearly expressed in the verso inscription: "The Heavens Are Not Too High "

The war and its aftermath did bring unforeseen dividends to California, but nonetheless the state remained what it had been, though perhaps more intensely so: a destination for the talented and the ambitious; a petri dish of lifestyle experiments; and above all, a wellspring of innovation. However, the fertile climate for innovative materials and innovative designs in California cooled as imports from recovering industries in Europe and Japan resumed, aided in part by a United States foreign policy that actively encouraged the rebuilding of the war-ravaged economies of Germany, Japan, and Italy. America's recent enemies were now allies against a new foe: the Soviet Union and its expanding Communist sphere of influence. The war had barely ended when the United States government began overseeing the reconstruction of the Japanese ceramic industry,[62] and soon thereafter the U.S. instituted much broader programs—notably, the Marshall Plan, the Truman Doctrine, and favorable tariffs—to further its geopolitical goals. As a result of these efforts, renewed imports would soon end California's brief period of necessity-driven creativity and with it the distinctive period in American design whose distinguishing features we call "Mid-Century Modern."

California was (and arguably still is) "America's own New World."[63] Half a century after California's post–World War II boom waned, the state's enduring design contributions are still very much with us. As this essay is being written, Eames chairs fill the windows of Design Within Reach stores; white cylindrical planters inspired by Architectural Pottery adorn office buildings, banks, gas stations, and private homes; hundreds of thousands of foam and fiberglass surfboards are being sold each year; and Henry Keck's Roadside barricade light blinks at us from thousands of construction sites across the country.

6.32. Packard-Bell. Radio, c. 1947. Cat. 229

NOTES

I am grateful to Wendy Kaplan, Bobbye Tigerman, and Staci Steinberger for their valuable contributions to this essay. And to Daniel Ostroff, Dr. Geoffrey Hacker, Andy Hackman, Gerard O'Brien, and Chris Menrad for their research assistance.

1   California Department of Finance, "Population of California and the United States," http://www.dof.ca.gov/HTML/FS_DATA/stat-abs/documents/B1.pdf.

2   John Entenza, "The Case Study House Program," *Arts and Architecture*, January 1945, 39.

3   Metal for civilian use was in such short supply during World War II that "Oscars were made of painted plaster for three years." Academy of Motion Picture Arts and Sciences website, http://www.oscars.org/awards/academyawards/about/awards/oscar.html. Aluminum, previously used in many household goods, was reserved for the production of aircraft. Copper, needed for wiring and shell casings, was so scarce that the 1943 U.S. penny was made of zinc-coated steel.

4   "American Dishes: Home Product Fills Gap Made by War and Boycott," *Life*, September 9, 1940, 76.

5   Micarta, a trade name for linen impregnated with resin, had been developed by Westinghouse for use as insulation board in the early twentieth century. During the war, Micarta was valued as an electrical insulator.

6   June Axinn and Herman Levin, "Postwar Air of Social Optimism," in *Social Welfare: A History of the American Response to Need* (New York: Harper and Row, 1975), 234.

7   David Halberstam, *The Powers That Be* (New York: Alfred A. Knopf, 1979), 274.

8   Cory Buckner, *A. Quincy Jones* (London: Phaidon, 2002), 88–90.

9   The number of Eichler Homes comes from Paul Adamson and Marty Arbunich, *Eichler: Modernism Rebuilds the American Dream* (Salt Lake City: Gibbs Smith, 2001), 22 and 119.

10 California Contemporary was established in about 1950 by Coleman's family (see company catalog, c. 1952, Museum of California Design, Los Angeles); their other company, Fabricated Metals, made iron farm equipment.

11 Expanded metal is made by cutting slits in sheets of soft steel and stretching the sheets until a mesh of diamond-shaped openings appears (see *Municipal Journal and Engineer* 30 [May 3, 1911]: 647). Although it has long been used as lath in plaster walls, expanded metal was used during World War II to reinforce concrete walls.

12 Industrial designer Gene Tepper, conversation with author, August 23, 2010.

13 Ibid.

14 Michael Morrison, conversation with author, December 2, 2010.

15 "The break-even point cannot be met . . . in today's market subjected to the impact of imports and other domestic products such as plastics." Douglas Bothwell, sales manager, Vernon Kilns, to Mrs. Florence B. Miller, the Dinnerware Store, Tallahassee, Florida, January 17, 1958, regarding the closing of Vernon Kilns, one of California's largest producers of pottery dinnerware. Letter in the collection of the Museum of California Design, Los Angeles.

16 In 1950 the combined population of New York City (7,891,957) and Chicago (3,620,962) was greater than that of the entire state of California (10,586,223). For the New York and Chicago populations, see http://www.census.gov/population/www/documentation/twps0027/tab18.txt; for the California population, see www.census.gov/dmd/www/resapport/states/california.pdf.

17 Barbara Willis, conversation with author, June 15, 2000.

18 The figures for Brown-Saltman are from John Caldwell (who designed for the company), conversation with author, June 3, 2010. The figures for Architectural Pottery are from Bill Hertel (an executive with the firm), phone conversation with author, June 24, 2010.

19 Current U.S. government standards for "Furniture and Related Product Manufacturing" define a small business as having up to five hundred employees. See *U.S. Small Business Administration Table of Small Business Size Standards Matched to North American Industry Classification System Codes*, http://www.sba.gov/contractingopportunities/officials/size/table/index.html.

20 Wood's pieces are shown in a catalogue (collection of Barbara Willis) from about 1948 for Knox China, in Laguna Beach—an offshoot of Dick Knox Displays, which represented designer-craftsmen, mainly ceramists.

21 Don Wallance, *Shaping America's Products* (New York: Reinhold, 1956), 81.

22 Caldwell, conversation with author, June 3, 2010.

23 Hendrik Van Keppel and Taylor Green designed a convertible wood bookshelf/table for the company Brown-Saltman. The *Versitable* was exhibited in the 1953 *Good Design* exhibition at MoMA. When the exhibition was first shown at Chicago's Merchandise Mart—the show's cosponsor—the Versitable was voted the "favorite 'Good Design' item" by retail store buyers. *Retailing Daily*, December 1, 1953, 12, collection of Gene Tepper.

24 My deepest thanks to Daniel Ostroff for sharing with me many archival sources about Charles and Ray Eames and for shaping the narrative in the following paragraphs. This information has been drawn from the many sources cited, as well as from Pat Kirkham, *Charles and Ray Eames: Designers of the Twentieth Century* (Cambridge, Mass.: MIT Press, 1995); and Eames Demetrios, *An Eames Primer* (New York: Universe, 2001).

25 Charles Eames, quoted in Digby Diehl, *Supertalk* (New York: Doubleday, 1974), 41.

26 Eliot Noyes, *Organic Design in Home Furnishings* (New York: Museum of Modern Art, 1941); and Kirkham, *Charles and Ray Eames*, 211.

27 Demetrios, *Eames Primer*, 42–43.

28 Kirkham, *Charles and Ray Eames*, 212.

29 "Charles Eames' Forward-Looking Furniture," *Magazine of Art* 39 (May 1946): 179–81.

30 Eliot Noyes, "Charles Eames," *Arts and Architecture*, September 1946, 44.

31 Ray Eames, interview by Ralph Caplan, February 24, 1981, Herman Miller Archives.

32 D'Harnoncourt, quoted in "[Blank] Participates in International Furniture Competition Organized by Museum of Modern Art," template for press release, August 8, 1947.

33 *Prize Designs for Modern Furniture from the International Competition for Low-Cost Furniture Design* (New York: Museum of Modern Art, 1950), 19–20.

34 Herman Miller promotional brochure, 1966, collection of Daniel Ostroff.

35 Ben Marcus, *The Surfboard: Art, Style, Stoke* (Minneapolis: Voyager Press/MBI Publishing Co., 2007), 83.

36 Goldsworthy was the plastics process engineer at Douglas Aircraft Co., 1942–44; see James P. Harrington, *Who's Who in Plastics and Polymers* (Lancaster, Penn.: Technomic Publishing, 2000), 197; and "Brandt Goldsworthy: Composites Visionary," *High-Performance Composites*, May 2003, http://www.compositesworld.com/articles/brandt-goldsworthy-composites-visionary.

37 Mark Fragale, "Dave Sweet—First in Foam," *Longboard Magazine*, September–October 2000.

38 Corky Carroll, in Michael Scott Moore, *Sweetness and Blood: How Surfing Spread from Hawaii and California to the Rest of the World* (New York: Rodale, 2010), 20.

39 The twenty-seven-year-old Quinn was an avid participant in the surf scene in his native California during the transition to foam surfboards in the 1950s.

40 The unconventional design surprised Quinn, who didn't know what the board was going to look like. "I was amazed! I'd never seen anything like it." Phone conversation with author, June 11, 2010. Due to the time and difficulty entailed in their production, Alter apparently made only five or six more of these boards.

41 Moore, *Sweetness and Blood*, 28–29.

42 "Surfing: Go East, Golden Boy," *Time*, June 25, 1965, 62.

43 Damon Lawrence (son of Max Lawrence), conversation with author, July 14, 2010, and email message, July 22, 2010.

44 Barry Rosengrant (former president of Architectural Fiberglass), email message to author, December 2, 2010.

45 Daniel Spurr, *Heart of Glass: Fiberglass Boats and the Men Who Made Them* (Camden, Maine: International Marine; New York: McGraw-Hill, 1999), 8–9. In *The American Design Adventure* (Cambridge, Mass.: MIT Press, 1988), 156, Arthur J. Pulos cites the public's "lingering doubts about anything called plastic." The public perception of resin, whether fiberglass-reinforced or not, was that it was plastic: for example, the Eames "fiberglass" chair has always been called "Molded Plastic Chair" by the Eames Office and its producer, Herman Miller. "Fiberglass chair" and "plastic chair" are used interchangeably in John Neuhart, Marilyn Neuhart, and Ray Eames, *Eames Design: The Work of the Office of Charles and Ray Eames* (New York: Abrams, 1989), 141.

46 Kevin Starr, *Material Dreams: Southern California through the 1920s* (New York: Oxford University Press, 1990), 94; Kevin Starr, *Golden Dreams: California in an Age of Abundance, 1950–1963* (New York: Oxford University Press, 2009), 218.

47 "Professionalism on the Campus," *Industrial Design*, June 1967, 58.

48 Thomas E. Stimson, Jr., "Designs for Tomorrow," *Popular Mechanics*, January 1952, 193–97, 398–99; Robert Dirig and Jay Sanders, "Wheels in Motion: A Look at Art Center's Transportation Design Department," http://blogs.artcenter.edu/dottedline/2010/10/14/transportationhistory. I am grateful to Staci Steinberger for providing the research about Art Center's Transportation Design Department.

49 Carroll M. Gantz, *Design Chronicles: Significant Mass-Produced Designs of the 20th Century* (Atglen, Penn.: Schiffer, 2005), posted by the author on the Auburn University website, http://www.industrialdesignhistory.com/node/453.

50 "Plastic Bodies for Autos: Rustproof, Dentproof, Synthetic Shells Go on Market in California," *Life*, February 25, 1952, 99.

51 Spurr, *Heart of Glass*, 76.

52 John Hull, *Avanti: The Complete Story* (Hudson, Wis.: Iconografix, 2008), 12.

53 "Autos: Avanti, Studebaker!" *Time*, April 13, 1962, 89.

54 "About H. Koch and Sons," http://www.hkoch.com/company.cfm; *P-G-E* [Pacific Gas and Electric Company] Progress 33 (July 1956): 8, collection of Steve Cabella. Thanks to Steve Cabella for sharing his research files on Koch.

55 Russell Flinchum, *Henry Dreyfuss, Industrial Designer: The Man in the Brown Suit* (New York: Rizzoli, 1997), 190.

56 Ibid.

57 Henry Keck, email message to author, June 27, 2010.

58 Keck's client, Los Angeles–based Electronic Engineering of California, asked him for a warning light that was "more durable, less subject to abuse and more attractive" than what was on the market, yet with a low production cost. Keck added his own principle: "Just what you had to have with no extraneous embellishment." Henry C. Keck, conversation with author, August 18, 2010.

59 Jane Pavitt, *Fear and Fashion in the Cold War* (London: V&A Publishing; New York: Abrams, 2008), 8.

60 Spencer Weart, *Nuclear Fear: A History of Images* (Cambridge, Mass.: Harvard University Press, 1988), 163.

61 The elliptical shape of the form, called *Eclipse*, also makes reference to atomic orbits; it was designed by George James, design director of Franciscan Pottery, which at the time was one of the nation's largest dinnerware producers. According to James Elliot-Bishop, author of two books about Gladding McBean, the popularity and fifteen-year run (1954–69) of *Starburst* was due to its appeal to "the hopes and aspirations of a generation looking to the future and not at the past" (email message to author, November 24, 2010).

62 Talbert M. Brewer (Recruitment Officer, Special Recruitment Section, Division of Departmental Personnel, U.S. Department of State) to Homer Laughlin, American Domestic Pottery Manufacturing Co., March 19, 1946: "We are seeking your assistance in the selection of two Ceramic Engineers to serve as advisors to the Chief of the Economic and Scientific Section of the Military Government and Control Activities in Japan regarding technical problems of the Japanese Ceramic Industry." Photocopy, Museum of California Design, Los Angeles.

63 James J. Rawls, "California: A Place, a People, a Dream," in *California Dreams and Realities*, ed. Sonia Maasik and Jack Solomon (Boston: Bedford; New York: St. Martin's, 1999), 9.

7

Serious Business: The "Designer-Craftsman" in Postwar California

GLENN ADAMSON

In the spring of 1957 a group of craftsmen stood before a thirteen-foot-tall bronze vase, trying to decide what to make of it (7.2). They had just arrived in San Francisco from the First Annual Conference of American Craftsmen, held at Asilomar in Monterey, to view the exhibition *Designer Craftsmen of the West* at the M. H. de Young Museum. The previous days had been spent in passionate discussion about the role of the artisan in modern life. With few exceptions, the 450 conference attendees had reached a consensus. Craft, they thought, was best positioned as an

7.1. Sam Maloof. Executive office chair, c. 1962. Walnut and leather. From *California Design 8* (Pasadena: Pasadena Art Museum, 1962), p. 27

individualist counterpart to industry. It should be the human face of modernism, simple and direct in its aesthetics and offering a functional enrichment to daily life. The de Young show, too, was premised on these principles. Its jury had issued a statement reading, in part: "The first prerequisite of a craftsman's product is that it should be well made, well executed, that it not make a fetish of crudeness nor a virtue of sloppiness. . . . The jury looked for creativeness, not novelty."[1]

In the monumental bronze vessel, however, the visitors were faced with quite another idea of what craft might look like—an idea from another time and place. Made in the late 1870s at a Paris foundry to the designs of Symbolist artist Gustave Doré, who had devised an undulating swirl of exquisitely sculpted, fantastical figures, it was an extraordinary feat of workmanship.[2] The editors of the magazine *Craft Horizons* recalled the scene:

> *Of all the sights in and about the De Young, most startling to many was the 12-foot-tall, grotesquely, magnificently, amazingly configurated bronze vase that sits to the left in front of the entrance. A maze of frantically active cupids, satyrs and maidens, it stands a resplendent monument to ornamental uselessness—a pot that yearned to be a sculpture, a sculpture that tried to be a pot. . . . There it stood, in all its craftsmanship, a hilarious, mocking altar vessel to esthetic dictatorship—a symbol for artists of all time.*[3]

This encounter between modernists and the nineteenth century might seem a curious introduction to craft in postwar California, a place where just about everyone was eagerly looking to the future. Yet the response of the Asilomar delegation to the Doré vase—the craftsmen's combination of confusion and fascination—gets right to the heart of what was happening out West in 1957.

One of the few people who had had a bad time at Asilomar was Peter Voulkos, the de facto leader of the ceramic avant-garde that had just begun to rear its head in Los Angeles. After listening to one too many discussions of craft's relations with industry, he had snapped: "This brings to mind why I try to avoid most organizations. You start getting all kinds of rules and regulations. The only reason I do what I do is that I like to do it."[4] The fact was that Voulkos's own ceramics (7.3) and those by several of his students at the Otis Art Institute, such as Paul Soldner, John Mason (7.4), and Henry Takemoto, were heading exactly in the direction of Doré's seemingly incoherent vase: this giant "pot that yearned to be a sculpture, a sculpture that tried to be a pot." Over the next decade, a similarly defiant, nonutilitarian artistic impulse would come to seem California's primary contribution to the American craft movement. Expressionism and Funk, created in the hothouse environments of the state's university system, would soon sweep across the country and through all the crafts media.

In 1957, though, few saw that coming. California had been chosen as the site for the first national craft conference for various reasons. The good weather was doubtless a factor, as were the facilities at Asilomar's scenic conference

center. But the chief consideration was that the state was the national model for "designer-craftsmen" production—that is, activity that sought to bridge the gap between the studio and the factory. This had little to do with the position that Voulkos was staking out—or indeed with any potential exchange between the crafts and fine art, itself a rather marginal activity on the West Coast in the 1950s. It was, rather, a matter of California's expansive economy related to domestic products. Nowhere else in the United States were there so many artisans working cooperatively with industry or successfully operating small-batch production businesses. The dramatic increase of California's population led to a postwar building boom, which in turn afforded innumerable architectural commissions to craftspeople—many in ecclesiastical contexts, where handmade artifacts were considered most appropriate. The well-funded state education system provided a framework for established craftspeople to teach, and for students to learn, that was more extensive than in any other state. Michael Higgins, a Chicago-based glass artist, drily remarked at Asilomar: "If we go on like this we're all going to be up to our ears in crafts-people—in fact, I notice the people in California growing broader shoulders so they can stand on each other's."[5]

Little surprise, then, that many of the top designer-craftsmen in each key craft discipline were tied to California. The weaver Dorothy Wright Liebes had relocated to New York in 1948, but by that time she had already inspired many weavers in San Francisco, encouraging them not only to incorporate metallics and vividly colored synthetic threads in their work but also to design fabric lengths as samples for industry[6] (see 8.2). Liebes had also organized the decorative arts section at the 1939 Golden Gate International Exposition in San Francisco, creating arrangements of Scandinavian and American design and craft in relaxed modernist interiors. In Alta Loma there was Sam Maloof, who by dint of hard work and intuitive design skill was competing with small-batch industrial production on something close to level terms (7.5). His hand-carved walnut dining chairs were not vastly more expensive than the manufactured wooden chairs shown alongside them in the *California Design* exhibitions.[7]

In San Francisco, there was Margaret De Patta, a jeweler with impeccable modernist credentials thanks to her training with the Bauhaus Constructivist László Moholy-Nagy at the Institute of Design in Chicago. The leader of a circle of innovative metalsmiths, De Patta was best known for her one-off pieces featuring dynamic compositions and asymmetrical stone settings, but she also designed silver jewelry for production (7.6 and 7.7). And then there was Edith Heath, America's most successful small-scale ceramic entrepreneur.[8] After her move to San Francisco in 1941, Heath began concentrating on ceramics, studying glaze chemistry and developing techniques like jiggering that aided in the production of long runs of more or less identical dinnerware forms. Within a decade Heath Ceramics was operating out of a large factory in Sausalito and selling in retail outlets nationwide. Like De Patta, Heath had trained in Chicago

7.2. Gustave Doré (France, 1832–1883). *The Vintage Vase (Poème de la Vigne)*, 1877–78. Bronze, 156 x 82 x 82 in. (396.2 x 208.3 x 208.3 cm). Fine Arts Museums of San Francisco, Gift of M. H. de Young

7.3. Peter Voulkos. *Standing Jar*, c. 1954–56. Cat. 302

7.4. John Mason (b. 1927). *Spear Form*, 1963. Stoneware, 59½ x 24 x 10 in. (151.1 x 61 x 25.4 cm). LACMA. Smits Ceramics Purchase Fund

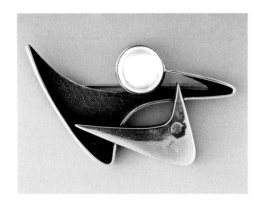

in a modernist climate fostered by Moholy-Nagy; also like De Patta, she was occasionally chastised by her peers for the use of mass-production techniques.[9] Frances Wright, one of the principals at the American Craft Council's New York shop America House (and, as it happens, the daughter of architect Frank Lloyd Wright), told Heath that in adopting machinery she was "selling out. . . . Now you're going to be making things for the mass market, and it won't be the same thing."[10] Yet Heath ensured that her work retained a strong craft aesthetic through her use of custom-made glazes and clays (7.8).

What these leading figures had in common with thousands of other California designer-craftsmen was their flexible attitude to production. Even Maloof, often held up as an example of craft purity due to his folksy charm and idyllic home and workshop, relied on a team of assistants and collaborators (not least his wife, Freda, who functioned as his business manager). He adeptly promoted his work through media outlets, museum exhibitions, and high-profile commissions.[11] Like the "silversmiths to the stars" working in Los Angeles, such as Philip Paval and Allan Adler, Maloof won the patronage of local celebrities and wealthy executives.[12] One of the most surprising of postwar craft objects, from California or anywhere else, is surely a Maloof office chair complete with orange leather upholstery. This odd collision between the pastoral and the

corporate was included in the 1962 installment of the *California Design* exhibition series, its unexpectedness underscored in a catalogue photograph taken en plein air (7.1). The image seems almost as strange today as Doré's gargantuan vase did in 1957. But when it was new, this chair—and the hybrid of rustic craftsmanship and routine professional life that it represents—evidently seemed entirely "natural."

What lay behind the success of California's designer-craftsman movement, and its eventual collapse in the face of a new, fine art–oriented approach? To answer this question, we need to look not only at the state's infrastructure of craft organizations, exhibitions, and universities but also at the broader context of production. What this investigation shows is that the impurity of California's craft economy was also the secret of its success. On all sides, professional craft practice in the state was sustained by precisely the elements that it superficially opposed: mass production, hobbyism, and to some extent, even media-driven suburban homogeneity. There were many ways of working in the expansive and open environment of postwar California. But the model we might initially imagine as typical—the lone craftsperson working in a studio—was, if not exactly rare, then relatively ineffective. Craft was most vibrant when it engaged with adjacent areas of production.

"Experimentation Gives Vitality": Ways of Working in 1950s California

Even as the nation's elite craftspeople were deliberating at Asilomar, the editors at the magazine *Industrial Design* were pondering a difficult question of their own. They were puzzled by a seemingly paradoxical fact about California: despite the fact that industry was expanding more quickly there than anywhere else on earth, there were few opportunities for professional industrial designers. Why was this? As the magazine reported in its October 1957 issue, there were several contributing factors. First, much of the state's large-scale manufacturing base was composed of "branch factories" of corporations that were based elsewhere, like the Detroit carmakers. The products might be made in California, but the actual designing was still happening back East. Second, the specialist technical firms that made up much of the state's economy, such as defense contractors, had little use for aesthetic styling. And third, the velocity of California's expansion made it easy for manufacturers to rush products to market: "A haven for renowned artists, architects and artisans is dotted with the monstrosities of too much, shot through with the errors of too fast."[13]

Yet *Industrial Design* argued that there was another, more positive reason for the lack of opportunities for full-time designers: grassroots entrepreneurship. Manufacturing in Los Angeles, according to the article, was done mostly in workshops of fewer than fifty people, too small to afford the services of a freelance designer:

> But more often than in any other city, one encounters the manufacturer who started his business in his own garage, invented a fairly unusual product (often a household gimmick or cheaper fabrication method) and built his business up to a comfortable level for his personal needs. As a type, he's habitually more dependent on his own wits than on the bright ideas of specialists, and has so much vitality that he often rolls up his sleeves and plunges not only into engineering, but into design development as well.[14]

The picture painted here is one of scrappy, multitasking self-starters, innovating their way into collective prosperity. *Industrial Design*'s correspondents did not have craft in mind, exactly. They were thinking of light industry—fields like electronics, appliances, contract furniture (made in limited mass production for schools, offices, and such), and transport. But this world of small, agile manufacturers was the context that fostered craft activity in California; and in turn, small-scale craft activity was often seen to be exemplary of California's entrepreneurial spirit. Even Alvin Lustig, whose interests lay primarily in graphics and architecture, praised the state's ceramics and textiles: "Although they are usually produced by individuals or small concerns, they have made a distinct mark and often represent California at its best. These smaller industries reflect a care for craftsmanship and design quality that is rarely seen in the more ambitious manufacturing."[15]

7.9. Bob Stocksdale. Bowl, 1958. Cat. 276

It may seem odd to refer to ceramics and textiles as "smaller industries," but this was true in a real sense in postwar California. Like other small-shop entrepreneurs, craftspeople often built their own equipment. Weavers' looms, potters' kilns, and silversmiths' benches and stakes all had to be made by hand. Edith Heath's husband, Brian, constantly developed "contraptions" for use in their small-scale ceramic factory, including clay mixers and a tile extruder built using rollers from a washing machine.[16] Byron Wilson did the same at the California College of Arts and Crafts (CCAC; now the California College of the Arts), where he began teaching in 1956, building an entire metal foundry mostly with scavenged materials. This can-do aesthetic is also reflected in his jewelry, which anticipates the found-object aesthetic of a decade later.[17]

Some craftspeople were able to develop a sideline in selling tools of their own design or manufacture. The wood turner Bob Stocksdale (7.9), who had created his own specialized gouge for making bowls in the 1940s, went on to develop a version with Jerry Glaser, a hobbyist turner and aerospace engineer, that became a standard tool in the craft.[18] F. Carlton Ball—remembered today not only for his straightforwardly earthy ceramics (7.10) but also for his teaching at CCAC, Mills College, and elsewhere—was a pioneer in constructing high-fire stoneware kilns and also improved wheels for throwing. Trained at the University of Southern California (USC) under Glen Lukens, who had usually hand built his wares from slabs, Ball had used an unsatisfactory treadle wheel early in his career. After he had the opportunity to work with a superior kick-powered model while demonstrating at the 1939 World's Fair in New York, he was deter-mined to develop his own version. He succeeded while teaching at Mills, at first working with the college's carpenter, then selling the wheels through the San Francisco Potters Association. Eventually the design was copied and put into production by the Western Ceramic Supply Company, itself a small entrepre-neurial firm in San Francisco.[19] Materials suppliers, which included not only Western but also S. Paul Ward and Westwood Ceramics (both in Los Angeles), are an underrated factor in the vibrancy of California's ceramic history. They could well be said to share some credit for the gorgeous pots that were thrown by Gertrud Natzler and then glazed by her husband, Otto, which were fittingly advertised with the ringing slogan "Experimentation gives vitality"[20] (7.11 and 7.12).

These instances of self-reliance—tool making, kiln building, glaze mixing, and the like—were all part of the designer-craftsman ideal, which was to apply technical and aesthetic lessons learned in the studio to the factory setting. To some degree, this was a self-justifying rhetoric.[21] It arose not because of any demonstrable need on the part of industry but rather because craftspeople wanted to create a pretext for their own work. Nonetheless, the idea had a good modernist pedigree. Its trajectory can be traced from late-nineteenth-century German design reform through the formation of the Bauhaus and thence to California via immigrants like Marguerite and Frans Wildenhain and

7.10. F. Carlton Ball. Vase, c. 1966. Cat. 15

7.11. Gertrud and Otto Natzler working in their studio at the Brandeis Camp Institute in Simi Valley, 1950s

7.12. Gertrud Natzler and Otto Natzler. Bowl, 1958. Cat. 216

7.13. Glen Lukens. Bowl, c. 1940. Cat. 182

Trude Guermonprez (see Bobbye Tigerman, "Fusing Old and New," in this volume). There were also influences from the East Coast. In 1953 the American Craftsmen's Educational Council (based in New York), under the leadership of Aileen Osborn Webb, sponsored a major exhibition at the Brooklyn Museum entitled *Designer Craftsmen U.S.A. 1953*. After a stop at the Art Institute of Chicago, it toured to the San Francisco Museum of Art (now the San Francisco Museum of Modern Art), where it was on view from June to August 1954—a few months before the first *California Design* show was held in Pasadena.[22] So the "designer-craftsman" idea was hardly a California invention. Nonetheless, it could be said to have been perfected in the state. As in some European countries like Italy and Denmark, the prevalence of small-scale industry opened up opportunities for craftspeople to work directly with mass production, to get involved (as designer Gene Tepper recently put it) "in some kind of volume business."[23]

The designer-craftsman idea found fertile intellectual ground in California, too. Glen Lukens, who had pioneered both jewelry and ceramics education at USC before the war, was a committed modernist and very sympathetic to the qualities of industrial design (7.13). Though he did not work as a design consultant himself, he saw an affinity between manually and mechanically produced objects: "Hand crafts must live not only with modern design, but with that

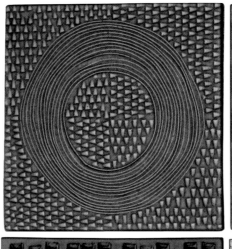

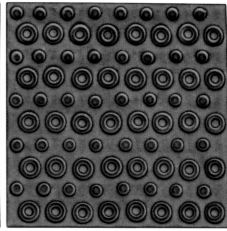

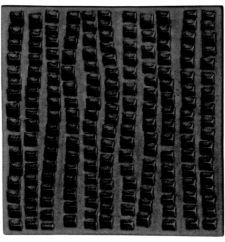

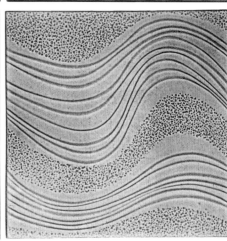

particular brand of design that comes from a machine."[24] He also argued that craftspeople existed on a continuum with mass production, not in opposition to it: "The only vital difference between the home industry potter producing 50 pieces a week and the factory turning out 10,000 pieces is the manner in which the articles are merchandised."[25] At Asilomar, the wood turner and sculptor James Prestini, whose work had attracted attention from the Museum of Modern Art (MoMA) and other East Coast institutions in the 1930s, echoed Lukens's sentiments in blunter language: "I'd rather make bowls for 10,000 people than for ten."[26] It was a sentiment spurned by Voulkos but actively embraced by most potters in California, including Laura Andreson, the founder of the ceramics department at the University of California, Los Angeles (UCLA). In addition to her teaching there, which continued an amazing thirty-six years, she produced large quantities of modestly scaled functional ware, making a particular specialty of brightly colored glazes (7.14) and, later in her career, hand-thrown porcelain.

The 1950s saw craftspeople in California not only producing serially in this way but also successfully forging links with industry—a goal that mostly eluded their colleagues in other parts of the country. Harrison McIntosh, for example, executed tableware for the Metlox Manufacturing Company (as did his studio partner, Rupert Deese) and architectural tiles for the Interpace Corporation.

McIntosh's tiles lack the nuance of his exquisite handmade pots (see p. 13), but their surface textures and impressed decoration bespeak years of experience with clay (7.15). Susan Peterson, the mainstay at USC after Lukens's retirement, not only designed for industry but also developed her own clay bodies and glazes for commercial use.[27] In furniture, there were makers like Frank Rohloff and John Kapel, both of whom alternated between one-of-a-kind pieces and design prototypes. Rohloff distinguished himself through the incorporation of plastic elements into his studio pieces; Kapel had worked in the New York office of industrial designer George Nelson for a few years prior to his arrival in California in 1955. He contributed designs to such companies as Glenn of California but also executed beautifully modulated chairs reminiscent of Sam Maloof's work (see p. 23). In textiles, Ida Grae, Trude Guermonprez (see 3.6 and 8.5), Maria Kipp (see 8.3), Lea Miller, and Mary Walker Phillips—along with numerous hobbyist weavers—followed Dorothy Wright Liebes's lead in creating sample lengths that could then be put into production on power looms. High hopes for large paychecks from eastern mills were not realized, but these weavers were nonetheless successful in supplementing their teaching and studio practice with design consultancy work.[28] Another example of the back-and-forth between craft studios and industry can be found in the work of Zahara

7.14. Laura Andreson. Bowl, 1940. Cat. 11

7.15. Harrison McIntosh for Interpace Corporation, Franciscan Division. Architectural tiles, c. 1964–66. Stoneware, each: 12 x 12 x ½ in. (30.5 x 30.5 x 1.3 cm). Collection of the designer, Harrison McIntosh

7.16. Zahara Schatz. Lamp, c. 1949. Cat. 248

7.17. Allan Adler. *Teardrop* coffeepot, teapot, creamer, and sugar, c. 1957. Cat. 3

7.18. Glen Lukens. *Autumn Rose* charger, c. 1955. Cat. 183

7.19. Ruth Radakovich. Top: Brooch, 1958. Cat. 236. Bottom: Svetozar Radakovich. Brooch, 1963. Cat. 237

7.20. Malcolm Leland. Prototypes of modules, c. 1952. Cat. 171

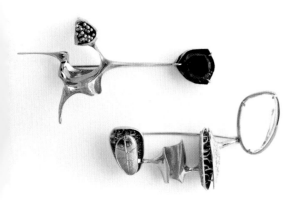

Schatz. She adopted plastic, a material more readily associated with industry, as her principle medium, developing techniques for heat-forming acrylic embedded with graphic patterns in metal wire (7.16). One of her lamps was designed for mass production and displayed in the Low-Cost Lighting Competition held at MoMA in 1951; her handmade lamps as well as her jewelry in plastic were featured in the Walker Art Center's design magazine *Everyday Art Quarterly*.[29]

Beyond such instances of external collaboration with manufacturers, there were craft entrepreneurs who built their own small factory firms. Heath Ceramics was the most prominent of these, but there was also Allan Adler, a silversmith who parlayed a wartime defense contract into a large-scale shop (7.17). At the height of his career, Adler operated three separate stores in Los Angeles and a fourth in San Francisco, all the while selling through department stores across the United States—enough to keep as many as twenty workers busy in his shop on the Sunset Strip. Like Heath, Adler employed machinery when expedient, often devising new tools to fit a particular job.[30] Even in the field of glass—the least developed of the craft media in the 1950s—there were examples of successful manufacturing. Lukens was again the pioneer, creating simple but effective dishes inspired by the desert landscape that were made through "slumping" (casting in an open-topped mold) (7.18). This same technique—initially inspired by an ashtray made at home by an amateur—was employed by Wilbur George and Carl Ryan of Monrovia. Operating under the name Mandala Productions, the partners sold architectural and decorative glass through venues like Gump's department store in San Francisco. With six employees working under them, they viewed themselves as operating "a studio industry: somewhere between mass production and the hobbyist who makes one piece at a time."[31]

When California's craftspeople were not investing in depth, they expanded in breadth instead. Multidisciplinarity was the order of the day, particularly in the rapidly proliferating educational institutions, where limited facilities and staff required instructors to master many media. Flexibility was also important for those producing architectural commissions, an area identified by the potter, weaver, and designer Bernard Kester as "the best opportunity for crafts today."[32] The San Diego–based couple Svetozar (Toza) and Ruth Radakovich worked in wood, stained glass, cast bronze, and forged iron, all at architectural scale—and this in addition to their work in fine jewelry (7.19). Dextra Frankel, a prime mover in Southern California's craft organizations, worked alongside her husband, Charles, in making metalwork (cast, etched, enameled, and patinated) and clay reliefs for building projects, while Malcolm Leland produced architectural sculptures in cast aluminum and bronze, concrete, and earthenware (7.20). Bob Trout, known for his studio lathe turnings, also did large-scale projects in wood and metal.[33]

For all of these craftspeople, architectural work presented an ideal opportunity to operate at a quasi-industrial scale without losing the expressive control of an individual studio. As Victor Ries, a Bay Area metalsmith who produced many ecclesiastical commissions, proudly noted of his own studio practice, "The scale of work is from half an inch to thirty-five feet"[34] (see 3.7 and 3.8). Then there was the multitalented design duo Evelyn and Jerome Ackerman, who moved from Detroit to Los Angeles in 1952. The Ackermans lived the designer-craftsman ethos to its fullest extent. Operating under the name ERA Industries, the couple worked in a bewildering range of media: woven and hooked tapestries and rugs, carved wood panels, enamels, aluminum sculptures for architectural settings, cabinet hardware, and mosaic plaques and tables (though they desisted with the latter once hobbyists began copying their work) (7.21). Sometimes they realized designs themselves—Evelyn Ackerman was active in the studio as a weaver and carver—but they were more than willing to turn to fabricators, too. Along with many other California craftspeople, they found suburbia to be a ready market for their work. As the developer Joseph Eichler said to them: "I'll be building enough homes that if you sell a pot to everybody who buys one, you'll be okay."[35]

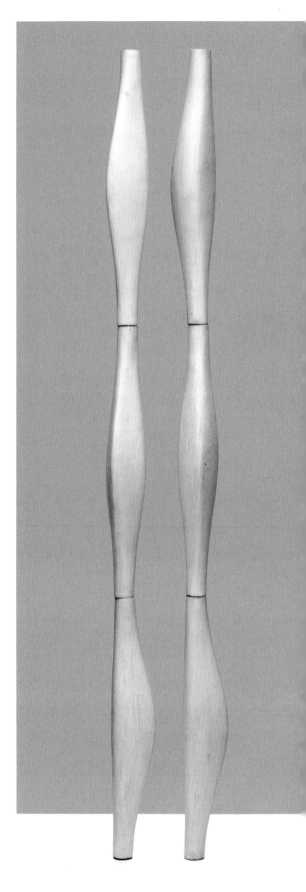

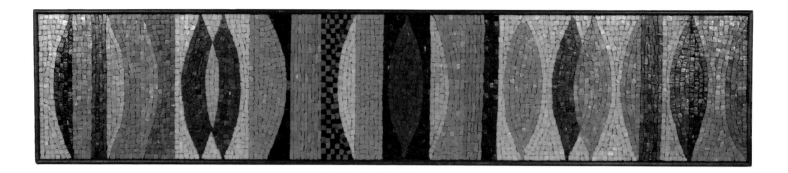

Making Distinctions: The *California Design* Exhibitions, 1954–68

Institutionally speaking, the biggest boost to the "designer-craftsman" model of production was provided by the *California Design* exhibitions at the Pasadena Art Museum. Based directly on the *Good Design* shows that MoMA organized with the Merchandise Mart in Chicago (1950–55), these exhibitions initially made no clear distinction between objects made by hand and those produced industrially. As should now be clear, it would have been quite difficult to draw that line, given the eclectic production strategies prevalent in California; but Clifford Nelson, director of the first seven installments (held annually from 1954 to 1961), certainly had no interest in doing so. He held no particular brief for individualism—the primary ethical principle of the East Coast craft establishment—and took a dim view of "arty" conceits, austerely noting that "design is not the aloof doodlings of an artistically inclined individual but rather the logical, factual procedure by which an idea finds its way across the drafting table and into the production shop."[36]

Much like his counterpart Edgar Kaufmann Jr. at MoMA, Nelson operated according to a commercially oriented ethos of design reform. Both had the stated goal of improving taste: the taste of producers and the public alike. Nelson wrote, "It is through taste and thoughtful purchasing that the discerning consumer can guide the manufacturer in the development of better products,"[37] and in a way he himself acted as a "thoughtful purchaser" when putting together the *California Design* shows. Working without a jury, he made selections himself, mostly by trawling through the Los Angeles Furniture Mart (a smaller local version of the one in Chicago) and picking out what he considered to be the cream of the crop. As a result, his choices were very much guided by, and influential on, the local housewares industry. (With very few exceptions, only objects made in Los Angeles County were included in the first seven *California Design* exhibitions, because the series received funding from the County Board of Supervisors.)

Nelson made no distinction when it came to scale of production. Each of the catalogues produced under his auspices cautioned prospective consumers: "Many of the items are handmade and often cannot be duplicated exactly. Generally this is the case when the designer is also shown to be the manufacturer,"

but that was his only concession to making a clear division between studio and factory.[38] Nor was this design-craft alliance to be troubled by any implication of fine art status. Given the vigorous struggles over this issue in the following decades, Nelson's policy seems to have been remarkably uncontroversial; a fact sheet that was circulated with the 1956 exhibition (which traveled to San Diego, Colorado Springs [7.22], and the Walker Art Center in Minneapolis) tersely noted: "All items on display are in some form of production. If they are not produced in mass quantity they are available on order from either the craftsman or his representatives. This requirement thus eliminates any fine arts as such."[39] So much for that: these were exhibitions about production, not expression.

Yet Nelson's modernism was not in any sense doctrinaire. From the beginning, his *California Design* exhibitions had a high craft quotient. This was the result of his close contact with two Los Angeles organizations—the Design Division of the American Ceramic Society and the Southern California Handweavers Guild. (This helps explain the fact that the city's ceramists and weavers were better represented in the shows than its silversmiths.) Both of these organizations crossed over the somewhat indistinct boundary between professional and hobbyist activity, and even before 1954 the two groups had

7.21. Evelyn Ackerman and Jerome Ackerman for ERA Industries. *Ellipses* mosaic, c. 1958. Cat. 1

7.22. *California Design 2*, installation at the Colorado Springs Fine Art Center, April 29–May 26, 1956
In the early years of the *California Design* **exhibitions, selections from the shows went on tour. The traveling version of** *California Design 2* **was seen at the Fine Arts Gallery of San Diego and the Walker Art Center, Minneapolis, as well as in Colorado Springs.**

Overleaf 7.23. "Parker Pattern and Foundry Company electric compact wagon loaded with and surrounded by pots from California craftsmen." From *California Design 8* (Pasadena: Pasadena Art Museum, 1962), pp. 34–35

Parker Pattern and Foundry Company electric compact wagon loaded with and surrounded by pots from California craftsmen.

Frank Matranga's stoneware garden pot
34 in. high
Kayla Selzer's stoneware, "Man Image."

Helen Watson's coil stoneware pot with
striped decoration 24x22 in.

F. Carlton Ball's brown and white stoneware
vase, 4 ft. 9 in.
Bernard Kester's eight-sided brown and
white stoneware footed bowl.

Charlotte G. Arnold's pinchpot stoneware
bottle, green glaze, 26 in. high.

Paul S. Berube's stoneware candelabra.

Helen Watson's red stoneware vase of
strip construction.

Louis H. McLean's grey and beige clay wine jug (on truck floor).

Thomas Ferreira's 23 in. high vase of unglazed stoneware with thorny texture.

Sheldon Kaganoff's 3 ft. floor pot of red stoneware.

Bernard Kester's brown stoneware footed planter.

Rhoda Lopez's flask, 19 in. high, of teadust glaze stoneware.

Philip Barkdull's covered stoneware jar with loop lid handle.

Steve Salisian, Jr.'s coil stoneware pot.

Laura F. Andreson's vase of mesquite ash glazed porcelain.

Clifford Stewart's low footed stoneware planter, 17 in. wide.

Bertil Vallin's figure vase of red stoneware, 11 in. high.

Loet Vanderveen's hanging planter of rough texture stoneware.

staged an annual joint exhibition of pots and weavings at the Pasadena Art Museum.[40] The inclusion of craft material in the *California Design* exhibitions, some of it by amateurs, distinguished them from their precedents at MoMA, where handmade objects were welcome only if they embodied a purist, undecorated aesthetic—for example, James Prestini's bowls.[41] One spokesman described the objects in the *California Design* exhibitions as "inventive yet conciliatory," which may sound like faint praise but was actually an attempt to grasp the specific contributions of small-scale, flexible production to the modernist project.[42] Nelson expressed it better in 1958, writing in that year's catalogue that the "designer craftsman . . . offers a warmth and personal involvement in his product which larger manufacturers are unable to match." Even though he immediately proceeded to offer a rather unconvincing functionalist argument—"the individual craftsman may change and evolve his product at will," he wrote, "thus marking the way for the more slowly progressing industrial field"—Nelson clearly saw craft as playing an aesthetic role within the "soft" modernism of California.[43]

When the irrepressible Eudorah M. Moore took the reins of the *California Design* series in 1962, she immediately recognized the cracks that were growing in the seamless "designer-craftsman" continuum. It is probable that few observers noticed this, however, as there were other, more pronounced changes. First and foremost, the exhibition was now to be a triennial rather than an annual, and it would include products made throughout the entire state. This new time frame would allow for a much larger show and, crucially, an ambitious illustrated catalogue.[44] The organizational support for the crafts component of the project also shifted. A jury was instituted in order to ensure breadth of expertise, and for *California Design 8* (1962) the Southern California Designer-Craftsmen (SCDC) was a cosponsor.[45] In fact, membership in the organization was a prerequisite for entry in either of the two craft categories— "objects of accessory dimension, such as pots, weavings, etc., and objects of architectural scale and application."[46] More important in the long run, arguably, was an additional division of the exhibitors into "manufacturers" and "designer-craftsmen." It was now possible to discern a divergence between these two groups, though Moore also took pains to demonstrate the connections between them (7.23). Among her innovations was to include prototypes within the exhibition: handcrafted objects that played a direct role in mass production.[47] As Moore noted, prototypes had a particular public appeal, and they might also exert pressure on manufacturers who had yet to commit to a cutting-edge design. She spoke of "exposing the works of designers to the public before submitting them to the dilutions and compromises sometimes thought necessary by manufacturers."[48]

Despite such maneuvers, *California Design 8* was the first in the series to be cleanly divided into manufactured and handmade sections, and in retrospect

7.24. Peter Voulkos. *5000 Feet*, 1958. Cat. 303

Glenn Adamson

this can be viewed as a sign of changing times. Both the shared modernist aesthetic and the free-form production milieu of the 1950s had begun to fragment. Partly this was a result of academicism. A full generation had now gone through the new university programs, and they had a more experimental orientation than those who had preceded them. In weaving, for example, there was a gradual shift away from the weaving of sample yardage and toward making sculptural forms, often with off-loom techniques. Kester observed in 1965: "The designer-craftsman is not in competition with the designer for industry. These are two fields parallel in operation, and motivated to different goals. The hand craftsman in design thus can focus on a different thing . . . self-contained ideas exemplified in wall hangings, tapestries without the tradition of pictorial content, and 'weavings.'"[49]

The changes were most dramatic in ceramics. A portent of things to come was Voulkos's refusal to submit work to *California Design 8*, despite a direct invitation from Moore.[50] It is not surprising that Voulkos no longer felt he had a place within the largely commercial exhibition, despite the fact that his work had been included in the series previously. In the five years since his off-message participation at Asilomar, he had shown his work at MoMA (admittedly, in a small members' gallery and without much in the way of critical response), and he had been feted as the leader of an entirely new, boldly sculptural approach to clay—and, by implication, to craft at large (7.24).[51] Robert Arneson, then an adherent of Voulkos's expressionist style, inadvertently created the symbolic object of this rupture while horsing around in a demonstration booth at the California State Fair in 1961. After throwing a beer bottle form in clay and capping it—a willfully nonfunctionalist declaration—he emblazoned the object with the slogan "no deposit, no return" (7.25). The incident caused a personal furor with his colleague at Mills College, the formalist potter Antonio Prieto (7.26), but it also became emblematic of a generational clash within the California craft scene.[52]

The expanded geographical scope of the *California Design* series also had the effect of exposing differences among the state's craftspeople. From 1962 onward, the exhibition was open to makers and designers from the entire state. Though the public statements associated with the shows continued to speak of a shared aesthetic, the sheer size of California led to atomization, with many different craft organizations active and not necessarily in direct contact with one another. As jeweler Arline Fisch noted, "It's hard to have a movement when you're a thousand miles long"[53] (7.27). She—together with Toza and Ruth Radakovich, Ellamarie and Jackson Woolley (7.28 and 7.29), and (for the short time of his residence in California) the designer Harry Bertoia (7.31)—was among the luminaries of San Diego's craft group, the Allied Craftsmen, which began exhibiting in 1947. Despite, or perhaps because of, the relative isolation of San Diego, the city developed a vibrant craft scene, with particular strengths

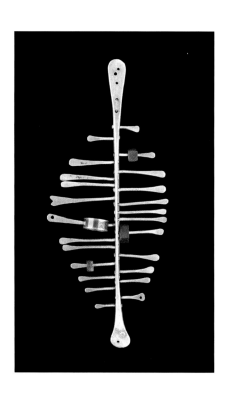

in architectural crafts and enameling.[54] San Diego State University boasted an unusually ambitious furniture program, headed from 1948 by the multitalented John Dirks—who had trained as a potter at USC with Lukens—and subsequently by Larry Hunter and Jack Rogers Hopkins, who would become the primary exponents of "fantasy furniture" in the state in the late 1960s. Unlike most of the "designer-craftsmen" organizations founded in America during the postwar years, the Allied Craftsmen is still active today.

The Bay Area, too, had a distinctive profile. By 1965 it had become a hotbed of avant-garde ceramics, partly thanks to Voulkos's arrival at the Berkeley campus in 1959. The husband-and-wife fiber artists Ed Rossbach and Katherine Westphal, teaching at UC Berkeley and UC Davis, respectively, were among the first American craftspeople in any medium to experiment with found objects and Pop art imagery. Rossbach's experiments with plastic bags, cut-up commercial textiles (see 8.7), and other "poor" materials have affinities with contemporary work by Robert Rauschenberg. Rossbach and Westphal also traveled widely, incorporating a diverse range of non-western textile traditions into their work (see 8.8). To be sure, Northern California still had its share of modernists exploring the formal possibilities of their materials and processes, such as the master enamelist June Schwarcz (7.32) and the husband-and-wife

7.30. Peter Macchiarini. Teapot, sugar, creamer, and tray, 1950s. Cat. 198
Even though Macchiarini was adamantly opposed to subjecting artistic expression to the dictates of industrial production, criticizing his contemporaries when they attempted to mass-produce their work, he did conduct one experiment with multiples. This is one of three very similar tea services he made in the 1950s.

7.31. Harry Bertoia. Pin, 1943–50. Cat. 26

7.32. June Schwarcz. Bowl, 1964. Cat. 254

7.33. Left: Peter Macchiarini. Pin/pendant, 1950. Cat. 197. Right: Peter Macchiarini. Brooch, late 1930s. Cat. 196

team of wood turner Bob Stocksdale and weaver Kay Sekimachi (see 8.4). Bay Area craft activity was well organized through groups such as the Designer-Craftsmen of California (not to be confused with the Southern California Designer-Craftsmen), founded in 1955, and the Metal Arts Guild, founded in 1951, which included De Patta, Peter Macchiarini (7.30 and 7.33), Merry Renk, Florence Resnikoff, and Bob Winston, among others.[55] These makers did not have the antagonism to the "designer-craftsman" ideal that Voulkos or Rossbach did, but some—notably Macchiarini—adopted a more expressive idiom in the 1960s and began to sell their work within the emerging countercultural craft marketplace that was cohering in the Bay Area. Similarly, the furniture maker Arthur Espenet Carpenter, a seemingly pragmatic man who had taken the unusual decision to "drop out" of urban life in the 1950s and build his own studio in remote Bolinas, was starting to attract the attention of younger makers (7.34). He referred to them as "hippy dippy types" but would eventually train a whole generation of woodworkers through the Baulines Craft Guild (founded 1972).[56]

San Francisco's craft community was also becoming more ethnically diverse than it had been in the previous decade. The Chinese American enamelist and potter Jade Snow Wong—prominent not only for her work but also for her widely read memoir, *Fifth Chinese Daughter* (1950)—was a frequent

Glenn Adamson

exhibitor in the city (7.35). African American craftspeople, including longtime residents like the silversmith Harry S. Richardson, were sufficiently numerous in the Bay Area to have their own exhibition at Mills College, curated by the print-maker, metalsmith, and textile artist Evangeline Montgomery.[57] Even though the Northern California craft scene was hardly a model of diversity (to this day, no urban craft community in America has achieved that distinction), the bur-geoning counterculture was making it easier for craftspeople from all backgrounds to participate.

By 1968 the end of the designer-craftsman era in California had become evi-dent to anyone paying attention. This was primarily a generational, not a geographical, divide. *California Design 10*, held that year, marked a dramatic embrace of the new Funk spirit in craft, most notably a dose of aggressively experimental work in ceramics. Even though Voulkos was still conspicuously absent (as was Arneson), the exhibition included work by Ralph Bacerra, Michael Frimkess, Jerry Rothman, and other ceramists exploring new terrain: kitsch imagery, crass humor, and sexually suggestive forms reminiscent of Surrealism. More traditional forms by Andreson, McIntosh, and the Natzlers were still present, but they were surrounded by a legion of more challenging pots (7.36). The later *California Design* shows (the series continued until 1976) were also notable for metalwork and glass, including large-scale "body jew-elry" by Arline Fisch and Funk objects by Marvin Lipofsky and Robert C. Fritz, instructors at CCAC and San Jose State University, respectively.[58]

For better or worse, the designer-craftsman had been replaced by the artist-craftsman. Many factors were involved in bringing about this change. Some were felt more strongly in California than elsewhere, such as the ever-increasing dominance of art school culture in the crafts (the state had more academic institutions with craft departments than any other, and its avant-garde was effectively subsidized through teaching salaries) and the influence of the coun-terculture, which began early in the Bay Area and continued to flourish there into the 1970s. Other reasons for the fine art turn in the crafts were national, and even international, in scale. As the craft movement matured, its constituent organizations became steadily more interlinked and adventurous. *Craft Horizons* editor Rose Slivka, though based in New York, enthusiastically adopted the California clay movement as emblematic of a broader shift in American craft.[59] Gallerists across the country, notably Lee Nordness and Garth Clark (both in New York) and Helen Drutt (in Philadelphia), showed craft objects in ambitious art gallery settings; California had equivalent galleries operated by Margery Anneberg and Ruth Braunstein in San Francisco, while Edith Wyle in Los Angeles operated an offbeat café-cum-craft gallery called the Egg and the Eye.[60]

As always, Eudorah M. Moore had an inventive response. She was entranced by the individualism, expressiveness, and freedom that fine art–oriented studio

7.34. Arthur Espenet Carpenter. *Rib* chair, 1968. Cat. 38

7.35. Jade Snow Wong. Ice bucket, 1952. Cat. 316

7.36. "Pots on steps . . ." From *California Design 10* (Pasadena: Pasadena Art Museum, 1968), p. 101

work afforded to makers, but her projects (unlike those of East Coast curators) tended to be explicitly oriented to issues of lifestyle—a topic that had been at the heart of California modernism since its inception but was now becoming a considerably more divisive and even political issue. A left-leaning ethical stance was increasingly detectable in Moore's California-wide craft survey in 1968, further installments of the *California Design* series in 1971 and 1976, a project on the turn-of-the-century California Arts and Crafts movement in 1974, and above all the evocative photographic survey book *Craftsman Lifestyle: The Gentle Revolution*, published in 1977 (7.37). These projects showed how the counterculture could become an unlikely breeding ground for successful craft and design business ventures, from handbuilt homes and hot tubs to record-album covers. In effect, the *California Design* series had come full circle. Having started as a statement about modern living and the seamless integration of craft and design, the exhibitions had passed through an "arty" patch that would no doubt have tried Clifford Nelson's patience and arrived at a statement about a new lifestyle-driven economy in which craft and design—though now quite distinct—each had a role to play.

What then was the legacy of the 1950s "designer-craftsman" movement? In an immediate sense, one can say that it formed a solid foundation for the increasingly adventurous experiments to come. Throughout the fragmented, anxious 1970s; the market-driven 1980s and 1990s; and the current postdisciplinary climate for craft, the educational and marketplace structures fostered during the confident years immediately after World War II have been of inestimable continuing importance. University programs active in the 1930s and '40s still employ and train many of the leading figures in the field, and California still enjoys a quantity and quality of exhibition spaces uncommon elsewhere in America. More important, perhaps, a half century after the designer-craftsmen of California were at their apex, their pragmatism continues to exert a strong appeal. Many observers now feel that the studio craft movement has begun an irreversible decline and that the craft community can thrive only by integrating itself fully into the adjacent terrains of design and art practice.[61] From this point of view, the permissiveness of West Coast craft in the 1950s and the assumption that makers could move fluidly among different productive spheres are deeply attractive. Makers then were not forced to label themselves or take sides. They were happy to see themselves as leading double and even triple lives. The same was true of the things they made, which might be objects of aesthetic value, inspirational prototypes for mass production, and symbols of a progressive lifestyle all at once. The story of postwar California may not provide all the answers for today's makers, but it does offer an important lesson: under the right circumstances, craft can be a powerful force for innovation.

7.37. J. B. Blunk studio (top) and house (bottom), 1959. Photos, c. 1976. Top from Olivia H. Emery, *Craftsman Lifestyle: The Gentle Revolution* (Pasadena: California Design Publications, 1977), p. 176 **Blunk, based in remote Inverness, north of the Bay Area, was one of the most inventive artist-craftsmen to emerge in California during the 1960s. His hand-built house was emblematic of the alliance between craft and a new countercultural lifestyle.**

NOTES

1 Quoted in Dan Defenbacher, review of *Designer Craftsmen of the West*, *Craft Horizons* 17 (July–August 1957): 37.

2 The vase, entitled *Poème de la Vigne*, which was cast in 1877-78 by the Thiébaut Brothers foundry, still stands in Golden Gate Park. It was originally intended for the 1878 Universal Exposition in Paris but was not ready on time, so it was first shown at the 1882 Paris Salon and then at the 1893 World's Columbian Exposition in Chicago, where it was purchased by Michel H. de Young. "From Orphanage to Honor: The Doré Vase, 'Poem of the Vine,' " *World's Fair* 3, no. 2 (1983), charon.sfsu.edu/DORE/DoreVase.html.

3 "Asilomar: An On the Scene Report," *Craft Horizons* 17 (July–August 1957): 30.

4 "Asilomar: First Annual Conference of American Craftsmen," unpublished proceedings, June 1957, American Craft Council Archive, 142.

5 Higgins, quoted in "Asilomar: An On the Scene Report," 28.

6 Dorothy Bryan, "Northern California," *Handweaver and Craftsman* 11 (Spring 1960): 49–50. Bryan noted that the situation in 1960 was "dull by comparison" to the decade just after the war: "No one, today, produces on the scale of Mrs. Liebes."

7 In a price list included in the second *California Design* exhibition catalogue, Maloof's chairs were recorded as selling for $130, while prices for mass-produced walnut chairs were in the range of $50.

8 Amos Klausner, *Heath Ceramics: The Complexity of Simplicity* (San Francisco: Chronicle Books, 2006), 29.

9 Peter Macchiarini recalled a disagreement with De Patta as part of a broader conflict within the Metal Arts Guild: "A few of them were mass-producing with rubber molds what was ostensibly hand-crafted. I said to them, if you want to put your mass-produced work on the same shelf with the individually crafted ones, you should mark your pieces as such. But they didn't agree to that. DePatta [*sic*] died in 1964, and it all ended. I admired her work enormously, regardless of what she thought of my ideas." Quoted in Ginger Moro, "The Outsider Turns Inward," *Echoes* 8 (Winter 1999): 57.

10 It should be noted, however, that Wright may also have recommended Heath's work to her father; see Klausner, *Heath Ceramics*, 27. See also Edith Heath, "Tableware and Tile for the World, Heath Ceramics, 1944–1994," interview by Rosalie Ross, 1990–92, 1994, Regional Oral History Office, Bancroft Library, University of California, Berkeley.

11 Edward S. Cooke, Jr., "The Long Shadow of William Morris: Paradigmatic Problems of Twentieth-Century American Furniture," *American Furniture 2003* (Milwaukee: Chipstone Foundation; Lebanon, N.H.: University Press of New England, 2003).

12 Jeremy Adamson, *The Furniture of Sam Maloof* (Washington, D.C.: Smithsonian American Art Museum; New York: W. W. Norton, 2001), chap. 2.

13 "The West Coast: A Designer's View," *Industrial Design* 10 (October 1957): 45.

14 Ibid., 47. The article went on to note that, conversely, the professional designers who did work in California often had to get their hands dirty. A profile of Bob Mason and Bill Cameron of Industrial Design Consultants, based in Los Angeles, described their tactic of saving "time and a client's money by reversing the usual design procedure. Frequently it's faster to don a welder's helmet and fabricate a part in the client's shop. They then check it out later with engineering drawings." As Mason succinctly put it, "Designing while making saves time and money" (ibid., 65).

15 Alvin Lustig, "California Modern," *Designs* 1 (October 1947): 10.

16 Klausner, *Heath Ceramics*, 27.

17 Toni Lesser Wolf, "Byron Wilson: The Gadget Man," *Metalsmith*, Winter 1992, 35.

18 Howard Lewin, "A Revolution in Turning Technology," *Fine Woodworking*, http://www.finewoodworking.com/pages/w00132.asp.

19 Hazel V. Bray, *The Potter's Art in California, 1885-1955*, exh. cat. (Oakland: Oakland Museum, 1980), 58; F. Carlton Ball, "Autobiographical Notes, Part 2," *Ceramics Monthly*, April 1981, 32.

20 *Original Ceramics: Gertrud and Otto Natzler* (pamphlet) (Los Angeles: Dalzell Hatfield Galleries, c. 1941).

21 Important statements of the designer-craftsman ideal are Don Wallance, *Shaping America's Products* (New York: Reinhold, 1956); and Rose Slivka, "U.S. Crafts in This Industrial Society," *Craft Horizons* 19 (March–April 1959): 8–21.

22 Californians were heavily represented in the Brooklyn exhibition, making up about 20 percent (39 out of 203) of the craftspeople included. Among them were Laura Andreson, Arthur Espenet Carpenter, Margaret De Patta, Albert King, Lea Miller, Gertrud and Otto Natzler, Antonio Prieto, Merry Renk, Kay Sekimachi, Bob Stocksdale, Marguerite and Frans Wildenhain, and Beatrice Wood. American Craftsmen's Educational Council, *Designer Craftsmen U.S.A. 1953* (Brooklyn: Brooklyn Museum, 1953).

23 Gene Tepper, personal communication with author, March 22, 2009.

24 Glen Lukens, "The New Hand Craftsman," *California Arts and Architecture*, December 1934, 13.

25 Glen Lukens, "Potters of West Develop New Art," *Los Angeles Times*, August 24, 1941.

26 Prestini, quoted in "Asilomar: An On the Scene Report," 20.

27 *Craftsmen of the Southwest* (New York: American Craftsmen's Council, 1956), 101. Other instances of potters designing for industry include work by a group including Henry Takemoto for Gladding McBean (a connection made by Millard Sheets, who was on Gladding McBean's board of directors), and David Cressey's Pro Artisan line for Architectural Pottery. Bernard Kester, personal communication with author, April 16, 1999.

28 See Bryan, "Northern California," 50. Looking back, Ed Rossbach reflected ruefully on the over-optimism of Californian weavers, most of whom obviously lacked Dorothy Wright Liebes's superb entrepreneurial skills: "We had vague undefined feelings that what we were weaving would possibly influence taste and the design of textiles that 'industry' was power weaving. Merely by making the textiles, and occasionally exhibiting them, we were exerting an influence on industry. I don't know how we acquired this feeling." Ed Rossbach, "Fiber in the Forties," *American Craft* 42 (October–November 1982): 15–19.

29 Schatz was born in Israel (then Ottoman Palestine), where her father, Boris Schatz, was the founder of Bezalel, the leading art school. She moved to New York City in 1937 and then to California the following year. See Marbeth Schon, *Modernist Jewelry, 1930-1960* (Atglen, Penn.: Schiffer, 2004), 205; and Margaret Anderson, "An Artist Works in Plastic," *Craft Horizons* 12 (July–August 1952): 8–12.

30 Janice Penney Lovoos, "Allan Adler: A Top Name in Silver Connotes Versatility," *Craft Horizons* 14 (November–December 1954): 19–22; Alvin Pine and Rebecca Adler, "Master Metalsmith: Alan [*sic*] Adler," *Metalsmith*, Fall 1985, 21–25.

31 Douglas Hope, "Artists Double as Businessmen," *San Gabriel Valley Daily Tribune*, January 9, 1962, box 3, California Design Archive, Oakland Museum of California.

32 "The New American Craftsman—First Generation," *Craft Horizons* 26 (June 1966): 17.

33 On Trout's studio work, see Edward S. Cooke, Jr., et al., *Wood Turning in North America since 1930* (New Haven, Conn.: Yale University Art Gallery; Philadelphia: Wood Turning Center, 2003).

34 Ries, quoted in *Craftsmen of the Southwest*, 238.

35 Joyce Lovelace, "Mid-Century Modernists," *American Craft*, June–July 2009, 32–39. The Ackermans were the subject of recent exhibitions at the Mingei International Museum, San Diego (2009), and the Craft and Folk Art Museum, Los Angeles (2011).

36 Clifford Nelson, foreword to *California Design 2* (Pasadena: California Design Publications, 1956).

37 Clifford Nelson, foreword to *California Design 5* (Pasadena: California Design Publications, 1959).

38 This integrative approach was carried into a film that accompanied *California Design 2* in 1956, which featured designers and craftspeople in an alternating stream, without any clear demarcation between the two.

39 "Fact Sheet," 1956, box 2, California Design Archive.

40 Bernard Kester, personal communication with author, April 16, 1999. The Southern California Handweavers Guild was founded in 1946, principally as an amateur group, and published a newsletter called the *Tie Up*. Andrew J. Howie, "Southern California," *Handweaver and Craftsman* 11 (Spring 1960): 50–51.

41 Edgar Kaufmann Jr. was a particular supporter of Prestini's work, acquiring many pieces for the MoMA collection and contributing to a beautifully produced book, *Prestini's Art in Wood* (New York: Pantheon Books, 1950).

42 Armin Kietzmann, "Pacific Design: Inventive Yet Conciliatory," reprinted as an undated press release by the Pasadena Art Museum, *San Diego Union*, February 12, 1956, box 2, California Design Archive.

43 Clifford Nelson, foreword to *California Design 4* (Pasadena: California Design Publications, 1958).

44 Though *California Design 6* was accompanied by an illustrated catalogue, thanks to subsidies provided by local manufacturers, it was not as substantial as the hardcover books produced from 1962 on under Moore's leadership.

45 The SCDC profited from active participation by leading craftspeople such as Laura Andreson, F. Carlton Ball, Dextra Frankel, Vivika Heino, Bernard Kester, and Robert Trout. The organization had been active in staging exhibitions since 1958, when it cosponsored the show *Craftsmanship* at the Los Angeles County Museum. A successor exhibition was held in 1960, and another show of the group's members was staged at Otis Art Institute in 1965.

46 Eudorah Moore to Gifford Phillips, November 13, 1961, box 3, California Design Archive.

47 An announcement sent to prospective *California Design 8* exhibitors noted: "We especially invite designers to submit prototypes not yet in production. Protection . . . will be afforded by copyright of the catalog." Untitled announcement, June 8, 1961, box 3, California Design Archive.

48 Eudorah Moore, "The Designer Is Knocking: Are You Listening?," script for a talk, 1969, box 35, California Design Archive.

49 Bernard Kester, "Textiles," in *Filmstrip Notes*, c. 1965, box 8, California Design Archive. See also Glenn Adamson, "The Fiber Game," *Textile* 5 (Summer 2007): 154–76.

50 Eudorah Moore, personal communication with author, April 2, 1999.

51 For more on Voulkos and his colleagues at Otis, see Garth Clark, "Otis and Berkeley," in Jo Lauria, ed., *Color and Fire* (Los Angeles: Los Angeles County Museum of Art, 2000).

52 For the story behind the work's creation and the falling-out it caused between Arneson and Prieto, see Robert Arneson, interview by Madie Smith, August 14–15, 1981, Archives of American Art, Smithsonian Institution.

53 Arline Fisch, personal communication with author, April 14, 2010.

54 Dave Hampton, "Collaboration: Arts and Architecture in Mid Century San Diego," unpublished article, 2007. The Allied Craftsmen were founded as a spin-off of an all-media arts group called the Allied Artists Council. Their history is related by enamelist and AC member Phyllis Wallen in "Allied Craftsmen Remembered," http://www.objectsusa.com/localscene4.htm. My thanks to Dave Hampton for sharing his research and insights on postwar San Diego and its craftspeople.

55 The founding credo of the Designer-Craftsmen of California describes its typical member as a professional craftsman "who designs and executes his own work, who may also teach, and/or designs for industry and whose craft is an integral part of his life." My thanks to Steve Cabella for access to this and other archival documents relating to the group.

56 Glenn Adamson, "California Dreaming," *Furniture Studio 1: The Heart of the Functional Arts* (Free Union, Va.: Furniture Society, 1999).

57 Evangeline Montgomery, *California Black Craftsmen* (Oakland: Mills College Art Gallery, 1970).

58 Reviewer Helen Giambruni noted with approval its forays into what she called the "new and challenging," in contrast to what she saw as the "overrefinement" of earlier installments in the series. She attributed the new attitude "to a more progressive jury for crafts"—namely, Bernard Kester, Paul Mills, and Frank Laury. "California Design X," *Craft Horizons* 28 (March–April 1968): 11, 54–56.

59 Rose Slivka, "The New Ceramic Presence," *Craft Horizons* 21 (July–August 1961): 30–37.

60 See Margery Anneberg, "Anneberg Gallery, 1966–1981, and Craft and Folk Art in the San Francisco Bay Area," interview by Suzanne B. Riess, 1995, Regional Oral History Office, Bancroft Library, University of California, Berkeley; and Ruth Braunstein, "SFMOMA 75th Anniversary: Ruth Braunstein," interview by Jess Rigelhaupt, 2007, Regional Oral History Office. The Egg and the Eye was relaunched as the Craft and Folk Art Museum in 1973, and Anneberg opened the San Francisco Craft and Folk Art Museum in 1983 as a successor to her gallery.

61 See, for example, Garth Clark, "How Envy Killed the Crafts" (2008), in *The Craft Reader*, ed. Glenn Adamson (Oxford and New York: Berg, 2010).

8

Distinctly Californian: Modernism in Textiles and Fashion

MELISSA LEVENTON

Modern fashion and textile design blossomed in California during the interwar and postwar periods. Fueled by the state's surging population, relaxed lifestyle, and the decreased influence of Paris fashion, the California sportswear industry grew from modest beginnings in 1930 into a mass-market fashion leader in men's wear and a strong player in women's wear. The housing boom; a growing community of designer-craftsmen and the schools to train them; and modernist philosophies imported from Germany, Austria, and Scandinavia via émigré designers and

8.1. This photograph of Dorothy Wright Liebes in her San Francisco studio appeared on the cover of *Life* magazine in January 1947.

architects combined to make this also a tremendously fruitful period in textile design. California's distance from the design and manufacturing hubs of New York and Chicago, especially in the 1930s, encouraged the development of distinctive local styles, but its landscape-linked palette, the seductive appeal of its casual lifestyle, and its glamorous association with Hollywood made "The California Look" attractive to consumers across the country.

California Modern Textiles

What makes a fabric modern? Essentially that it is created in terms of today, with materials of today, within a whole set of conditioning factors. Chief of these are function, architecture, and related textures.[1]

Dorothy Wright Liebes, 1939

Modernism in American textiles began to develop well before 1930. During the 1920s both industry and the public regarded art as the means to high-quality design in fashion, furnishings, and decorative textiles; this period saw gifted artists, many trained as painters, designing handmade and manufactured textiles that reflected aesthetic preoccupations ranging from European modernism, to indigenous textiles from the Americas, Africa, and the Pacific Rim, to American life itself.[2] Surface design was a primary concern of 1920s textiles, but toward the end of the decade, aesthetic preferences shifted away from elaborate surfaces to abstract imagery, and designers began to focus increasingly on texture and structure. Additionally, Bauhaus ideas about the primacy of the building as a focus of creative output helped shift the source of inspiration for many designers from art to architecture.[3] The new textiles were intended to be simultaneously beautiful, functional, and economical, as befitted a world hit hard by the Depression. As Mary Schoeser has noted, this new modern aesthetic was especially suited to "rugmaking, weaving, and hand-screenprinting,"[4] and these were just the kinds of textiles that Californians were designing and making. The emphasis on architecture and design for industry, the demand fostered by California's spectacular population growth and building boom, and the need for the softness and warmth of textiles to mitigate the severity of modernist wood, glass, and steel encouraged many textile designers to concentrate on making useful, rather than purely decorative, textiles for the home—upholstery, drapery, and table fabrics instead of wall hangings. Designers even envisioned textiles that in themselves might have seemed more decorative than functional, such as room dividers and patio hangings, as having a purpose that related specifically to the local climate and the flexible spaces of modern California architecture.

Dorothy Wright Liebes was by far the best known of the substantial number of handweavers working in California during the modernist period (8.1). Indeed,

8.2. Dorothy Wright Liebes. *Chinese Ribbon* textile (detail), 1940. Cat. 178

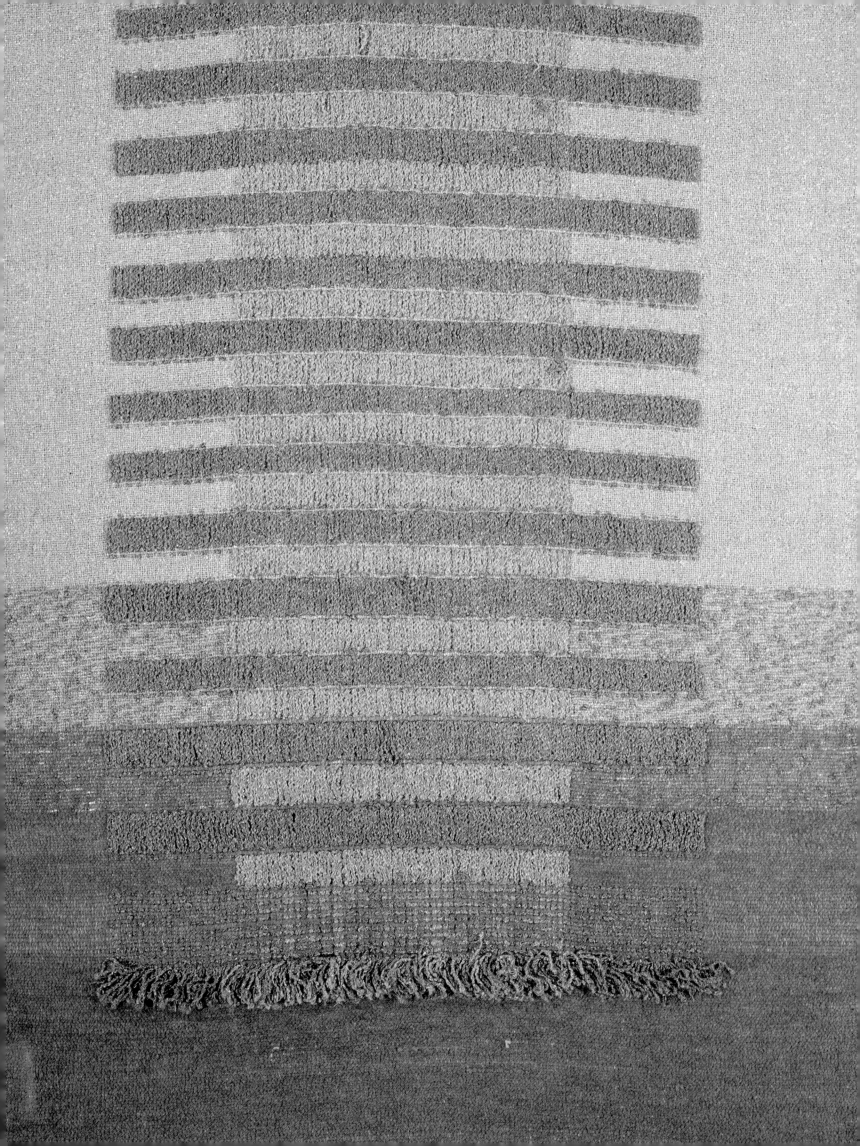

in the 1940s and 1950s Liebes was arguably the most influential textile designer in the United States. The Santa Rosa–born Liebes trained as a painter, then studied weaving at the University of California, Berkeley, and with the noted handweaver Paul Rodier in Paris. She opened a studio in San Francisco in 1930, where she designed and wove textiles for interior designers and architects such as Gardner Dailey, Timothy Pflueger, and Frank Lloyd Wright. Within a decade Liebes had received major commissions for public buildings in addition to steady work designing and weaving a wide variety of furnishing textiles for private homes.[5]

Even in a community of handweavers emphasizing modern aesthetics, Liebes's textiles stood out for their unusual materials—among them, wood, ribbons, tape measures, cellophane, and metallic yarns—and their often jolting color combinations: vibratingly intense blues and greens; hot yellows with reds, oranges, and gold; brown and black punched up with turquoise and chartreuse. To Liebes, color was a "magic elixir,"[6] one she used freely and confidently (8.2). All these elements combined to create what she originally called "the California Look" and that subsequently became known as "the Liebes Look."[7]

Liebes's custom work, coupled with her charm, seemingly boundless energy, and a shrewd head for business, raised her profile in design circles, but her greater importance lies in her work with industry as a designer, consultant, and spokeswoman. Liebes's belief that ordinary people should be able to afford good design led her in 1940 to begin to design and consult for large-scale fabric manufacturers, to whom she provided handwoven prototypes of textiles to be mass produced. Her goal was to design a power-loomed fabric that would preserve the handwoven feel of her custom textiles, making the mass-market product seem as much like the custom-made as possible and offering the public "better and better for less and less."[8] Her range was enormous; at the height of her popularity, Liebes textiles found their way into fashion as well as virtually every aspect of architectural and industrial design. Her resounding success made her a household name, enabled her to forge ties between major manufacturers like DuPont and the architecture and interior-design industries, and allowed her to become an especially effective promoter of design for industry.[9]

The German-born designer-weaver Maria Kipp, one year Liebes's junior, was one of the first of the émigrés to influence modern American textile design. Kipp had trained as a painter, textile designer, and weaver before immigrating to Los Angeles in 1924; she soon opened a studio that specialized in handwoven textiles for interior designers and architects such as fellow émigrés R. M. Schindler, Paul T. Frankl, and Richard Neutra.[10] Her output included textiles for upholstery, drapes and casements, and even lampshades. Kipp also designed and wove textiles for various public buildings, and she was one of two Californians who supplied handwoven textiles for the superliner SS *United*

8.3. Maria Kipp. Textile, c. 1938. Cat. 153

States (Liebes was the other).[11] Kipp's and Liebes's textiles share many characteristics of texture, open-weave structure, dimensionality, and abstract imagery, but Kipp's palette was far quieter (8.3). Unlike Liebes, but in common with many others, Kipp chose to remain primarily a small-batch handcraft producer for the entirety of her long career.

Trude Guermonprez, who studied with Bauhaus-trained Benita Otte and worked with Anni Albers at Black Mountain College, connects California modern textiles directly both to the Bauhaus and to Scandinavian modernism. She was also important both as a designer and as a teacher at California College of Arts and Crafts (now California College of the Arts).[12] There she trained some of the first generation of California fiber artists, including Kay Sekimachi, who was inspired to become a weaver by Guermonprez's thorough, Bauhaus-style teaching.[13] Guermonprez's advice to "let the warp come through"[14] and her experiments with painted warps can be seen in Sekimachi's fondness for warp ikat, which she used in a sophisticated, semitransparent linen room divider patterned in dark and light chevrons (8.4). Guermonprez's textiles are firmly rooted in a love of technical exploration and in Bauhaus philosophy and aesthetics, but after her move to California they began a slow shift toward a more representational style. *Calico Cat* (8.5), in which the figure is at once abstract and discernible, is an early example, one that inspired a related work by Sekimachi (8.6). A decade later, several important commissions for textiles for synagogues in California and Ohio (see 3.6) showed Guermonprez exploring contrast through a brighter, California-inspired palette and the incorporation of recognizable letters and symbols.[15]

Guermonprez was one of a group of influential teachers at California colleges in the 1950s, 1960s, and beyond, including Ed Rossbach at University of California, Berkeley; Mary Jane Leland at Long Beach State College; Bernard Kester at University of California, Los Angeles; and, beginning in 1966, Katherine Westphal at University of California, Davis. All of them served as bridges from mid-century modernism, with its philosophy of textiles in service to architecture and industry, to the nonfunctional fiber art movement that defined the post-1965 period. Both Rossbach and Leland studied under the Finnish émigré textile designer Marianne Strengell at Cranbrook Academy of Art, where students were taught to weave utilitarian yet attractive textured textiles in three-yard exhibition lengths. Rossbach absorbed the lessons of the textile program at Cranbrook but later said that they stifled his creative impulses. He found more scope in the Decorative Art Department at the University of California, Berkeley, where he began to teach weaving in 1950. The department's approach to weaving was based on study of techniques found in the university's holdings of anthropological textiles, and these new influences plus Rossbach's own inclinations helped propel him toward the wall hangings and vessels that characterize his mature work.[16]

8.4. Kay Sekimachi. Room divider, 1960. Cat. 256

8.5. Trude Guermonprez. *Calico Cat* textile, 1953. Cat. 119

8.6. Kay Sekimachi. *Reflection #2* textile, 1959. Cat. 255

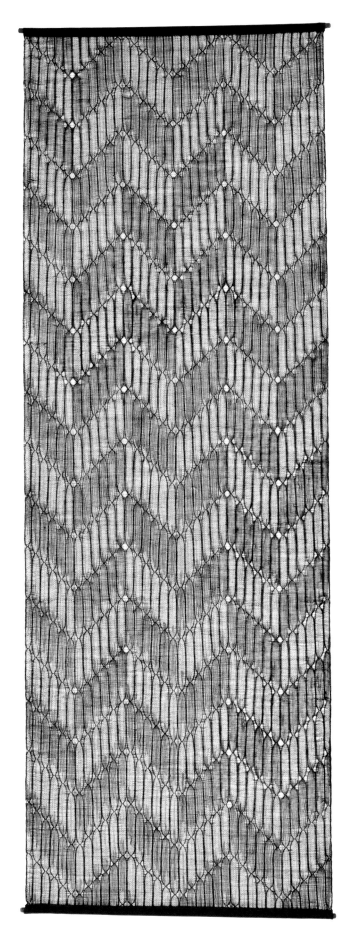

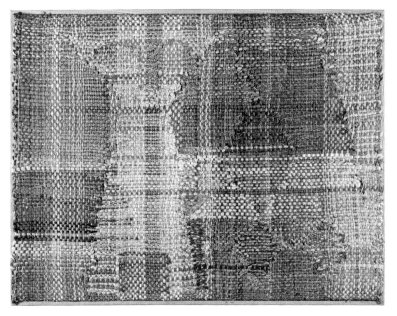

Rossbach's *Reconstituted Commercial Textile* (8.7) is a transitional piece, its foundation a modern striped cloth that Rossbach bleached, cut up, encased in plastic tubing, and rewove to reorient the stripes. It is both modern design and fiber art, and conceptually, it suggests the systematic destruction of modernist design and its transformation into something new. Early in his career Rossbach had rejected the idea of focusing on design for industry, feeling he was temperamentally unsuited to it, but his wife, Katherine Westphal, designed commercial printed textiles during the 1950s, and Rossbach enjoyed contributing to her efforts.[17] Westphal used her own wildly varied cotton batiste design samples in her transition to fiber art in the early 1960s. Realizing she could "sew these all together and do things that are like paintings on them!"[18] she cut them up and reorganized them into a series of pieced quilts that featured dense, painterly collages of images (8.8). Westphal intended her quilts to be functional but noted that not one of them had ever been used. Instead, they were exhibited— this one at the Milan Triennale, others at various exhibitions in the U.S.[19]

Printed textiles were widespread, and hand-screenprinting was a popular and practical printing technique among California designers, especially from the late 1930s on. Screenprinting was relatively fast, it was easily adaptable to serial production, the entry costs were low, and it was economical to print relatively

short runs, which was ideal for small-scale manufacturing and for designers who wished to print their own work.[20] It also got a boost from the decline of roller printing during World War II, when many manufacturers contributed their copper rollers to be melted down for the war effort. Although there was little or no commercial fabric-weaving industry in California during this period, there were companies devoted to textile printing—small manufacturers, some designer owned, and this was precisely where the innovation in print design was centered.[21] Barney M. Reid, for instance, who worked in a variety of media, started a textile-printing business when he first came to California about 1950 (8.9).[22] Many others, however, worked with manufacturers who were based elsewhere.

Modern screenprinted furnishing textiles are often—though not always—abstract in design, and many have a lightness and sense of whimsy that their geometric woven counterparts may lack, perhaps because the prints often include curved lines as well as straight ones (8.10). In modern handwovens, texture and technique were key components; modern screenprints might use textured fabric but frequently relied primarily on carefully balanced color, contrast, and pattern to create dimensionality and movement. Brightness was usually used sparingly, even in the raucous 1960s, when colors brightened noticeably. The patterns that dance across screenprints drew on a number of sources, which designer Alvin Lustig cited as modern technology and engineering, modern paintings, and the "crisp geometry" of modern architecture.[23] Textile patterns that were not abstract often show their California origins through their imagery, as in Elza Sunderland's designs inspired by Mexican pottery and Mesoamerican ceramics (8.12). The Bay Area designer Lanette Scheeline's *Egyptian Garden* uses the style of ancient Egyptian tomb paintings, with their flat perspective and walking figures in profile, to depict a garden in the California suburbs populated with characters dressed in casual California sportswear (8.11). Unlike the designer-craftsmen who were professional handweavers, a number of those making screenprints designed but did not print their textiles; many, like Lustig, had primary careers in other design fields, particularly graphic and industrial design and architecture. Graphic design and printed-textile design, of course, require similar skills, and since modern textiles were philosophically aligned with architecture, it is not surprising that the architect and furniture designer Paul László, for example, designed his own textiles to ensure that his vision of a unified modern environment was applied throughout (see 3.17 and 3.18).

Exhibitions were an important way for textile designers to publicize their work, and the 1939 Golden Gate International Exposition (GGIE), held in San Francisco and visited by more than ten million people, was an excellent showcase. Dorothy Wright Liebes was director of the entire decorative arts section, and the textile category alone included pieces by more than 110 artist-craftspeople from eleven countries, some 15 or 20 percent of whom were from

8.9. Barney M. Reid for Reidart. *Geodetic* textile, c. 1951. Cat. 238

8.10. Bernard Kester for Crawford & Stoughton. *Strand* textile, c. 1962. Cat. 151

8.11. Lanette Scheeline. *Egyptian Garden* textile, c. 1939. Cat. 249

8.12. Elza Sunderland. *Mexican Pottery* textile design, 1939. Cat. 278

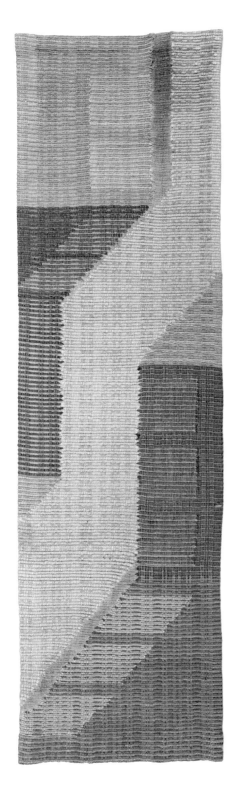

California. Most of the work, such as Lydia Van Gelder's *Houses on a Street* (8.13), was made specifically for the exposition and was available for purchase.[24]

Museums and competitions were another promotional vehicle, one that may have helped connect designers with manufacturers and exhibition opportunities. Ray Eames, for example, submitted *Cross Patch* (8.14) and *Sea Things*, two of a handful of textiles she had designed in about 1945, to the 1947 competition for modern textile designs at the Museum of Modern Art (MoMA). Even though the charmingly naive *Cross Patch* did not win, Schiffer Prints produced it as part of its *Stimulus Collection*, and in 1950 it was chosen for the first of MoMA's widely disseminated *Good Design* exhibitions. California-designed textiles were regularly included in the *Good Design* shows, many produced by textile manufacturers based in the East. Olga Lee—who designed furnishings and interiors in partnership with her furniture-designer husband, Milo Baughman, in Los Angeles and worked with New York printer L. Anton Maix—had several textiles included in the 1953 show (8.15).

Designers who worked with East Coast manufacturers like Schiffer and Maix or Laverne Originals and textile giant Cohama, as Lustig did, gained the advantage of national distribution, but local promotion was also important. Like the *Good Design* shows, the *California Design* exhibitions in Pasadena sought to showcase the best in modern design for the home. Starting in 1962, the textile submissions were both juried and invited, and they ran the gamut from place mats to rugs. While handwoven yardage continued to be displayed, nonfunctional tapestries and other wall hangings were prominent as well.

Like artist-craftspeople in other media, designers of modern textiles, particularly handweavers, emerged from service to architecture and industry in the 1960s and set off in new directions. Whereas designers of the 1920s had regarded art as a path to high-quality textile design, creators of fiber art in the 1960s and beyond regarded their own work as Art with a capital A. Fiber artists focused on aesthetics and content, and they often repurposed utilitarian objects, such as quilts and baskets, as wall hangings and sculptural vessels. They also experimented with a raft of disused techniques—collage and piecing, embroidery, painting, resist-dyeing, tapestry, and off-loom weaving, to name only a few. The shift from designer-craftsman to artist-craftsman took place statewide, but Northern California became a particularly important center for fiber art, in no small part because of the rise of the counterculture, with its do-it-yourself ethos, and because of artists and teachers like Guermonprez, Rossbach, and Westphal, whose work had already made the transition from modernism to fiber art. Guermonprez, originally a Bauhaus disciple who was committed to design for industry, ended her career weaving "surprising and wonderful"[25] expressive wall hangings that sported swaths of text as well as images. Her journey from one to the other symbolizes the seismic shift in California textiles.

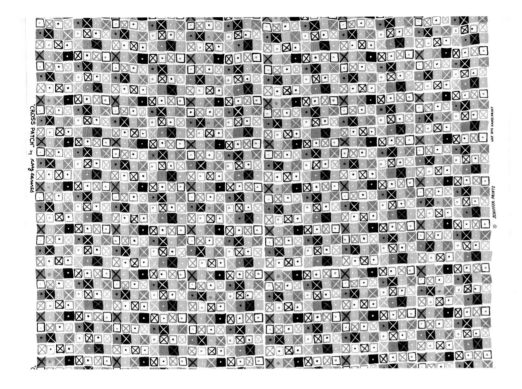

8.13. Lydia Van Gelder. *Houses on a Street* textile, 1939. Cat. 296
Van Gelder wove this piece from commercial cotton mop yarn in response to a specific request from the exhibition organizers for a heavily textured textile in natural colors, specifically yellows, chartreuse, or blue-greens.

8.14. Ray Eames for Schiffer Prints. *Cross Patch* textile, c. 1945. Cat. 84

8.15. Olga Lee for L. Anton Maix Fabrics. *Elements* textile, c. 1952. Cat. 168

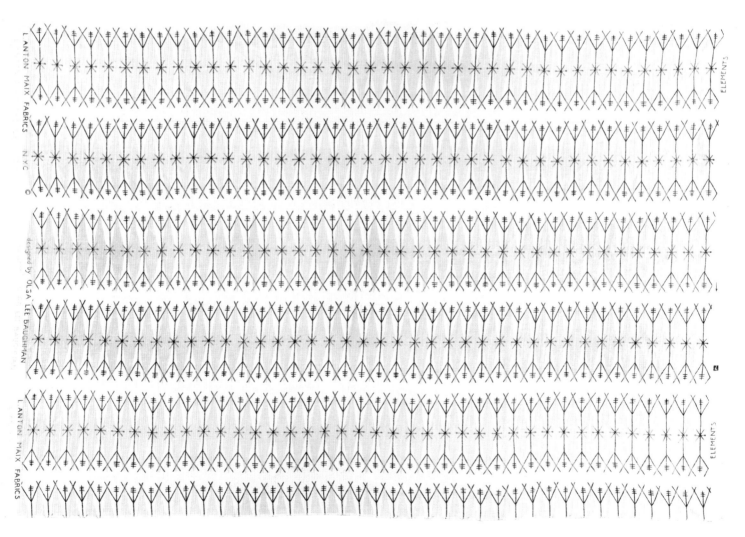

California Modern Fashion

Modern California fashion design abounded with garments that were specifically suited to an everyday, if idealized, California way of life—bathing suits, playsuits, hostess pajamas, cabana suits, and western wear. These assumed a relaxed, outdoorsy, and leisure-filled existence for a wearer immersed in the state's casual socializing, athletic culture, and the indoor/outdoor living enabled by modern architecture and Southern California's climate (8.16). Modern fashion also reflected the state's rugged western image, influences from Asia and Mexico, and the importance of its movie industry as an economic engine and shaper of culture. Fashion sportswear was neither new nor unique to California, but it had usually been portrayed in the fashion press as upper-class clothing. California sportswear, by contrast, promised accessibility to everyone.

In 1930 American fashion was just beginning to feel the effects of the Depression, which substantially decreased the number of garments imported from France and increased reliance on homegrown design.[26] The New York fashion industry was the primary beneficiary, but California benefited, too. The small ready-to-wear fashion industries in Los Angeles and San Francisco developed rapidly in the ensuing twenty years as reduced foreign competition allied with tremendous demographic growth and increasing marketing savvy. By the end of the decade California had become the second most important American producer of women's wear overall and the most important producer of sportswear. It also churned out significant amounts of men's sportswear, and both its men's wear and women's wear were concentrated in the high and middle ranges of the market, where design, not price, was a key selling factor.[27] Moreover, high quality and innovative design were determined to be far more important to the industry in California than in New York, in part because a significant number of West Coast manufacturers either were headed by designers or had a designer and a manufacturer in partnership.[28]

Elegant San Francisco and casual Los Angeles each had its own design identity, although a full range of women's wear, from sportswear to formal suits and evening clothes, coats, and even furs, was designed and manufactured in both cities. One of San Francisco's most significant manufacturers was undoubtedly Levi Strauss & Co. In 1930 it was still primarily a regional purveyor of work wear, but during this period it became a national powerhouse of leisure wear for both sexes (8.17). It was L.A., however, that became the primary locus for sportswear for both men and women; beginning in the 1930s, sportswear was considered to be the quintessential California contribution to fashion. It was also in the 1930s that designers and manufacturers began to conceive of and promote their fashions as distinctively Californian, translating the state's unique geography and desirable lifestyle into specific garment types, imagery, and color. In promotional materials, color was usually linked to the local landscape, in all its variations. That allowed for an enormous range of hues to be associated with California, from chartreuse to old rose to Chinese red, electric blue, gray, golden tan, dusty brown, mesquite green, and of course "the yellow of the California sun, in all its warmth and glow."[29] Sportswear designed elsewhere was colorful, too, but color undoubtedly became synonymous with California in the public mind.[30]

California sportswear focused on garments that suited its climate and lifestyle, particularly playsuits, pants, and bathing suits. Casual separates, although not unique to California, became characteristic of its sportswear. The typical outfit started with a playsuit or bathing suit and added a skirt, trousers, or a jacket in matching or coordinating colors. Some had many more pieces: Cole of California's winter 1942 line included a "Swim-Play Ensemble" that had a poncho-cape blouse, street-length skirt, short playskirt, and bathing suit, while a competitor advertised a seven-piece play ensemble.[31] The outfit's flexibility would allow the wearer to experience the full range of California activities as she went from pool to patio to supermarket to barbecue, simply by adding or subtracting a piece or two. The backyard barbecue print on DeDe Johnson's yellow cotton playsuit and skirt from the late 1950s (8.18) would likely have reinforced those positive lifestyle connotations since "barbecues mean good food and gaiety . . . blue jeans and cotton dresses, laughter and a blithe, carefree spirit."[32]

Linked to the popularity of casual separates was the growing acceptance of trousers—and by extension, shorts—as appropriate attire for women. Hollywood, which costumed actresses like the sporty Katharine Hepburn in trousers, is often credited for their increasing acceptance nationwide, and it likely did hasten the trend, but trousers had been slowly evolving into women's wear for use in sports like cycling and for leisure wear like lounging pajamas. California hostess pajamas, unlike the formal, luxurious versions designed in Paris or New York, are usually casual and comfortable and often executed in ordinary materials, as is Addie Masters's mannish version with short sleeves and full trousers of rayon striped in hot sunset colors (8.19). The trade magazine *California Stylist* suggested that the increasing casualness of women's dress was the reason men were dressing more casually, too, since women insisted that their husbands "have some smart sportswear for informal gatherings. Barbecues have done a lot for this. Plenty of hostesses have said over the phone, 'Just wear your slacks, and tell the boys not to dress up.' So your man's closet has a real, genuine, new section and it's going to stay there and grow."[33]

For men, "not dressing up" meant sports jackets, colorful sports shirts, casual slacks and shorts, and western wear; bathing suits and related garments were also part of modern men's leisure wear. There was, in fact, tremendous growth in the use of leisure wear by men across the country, not all of it due to their wives. Men, too, needed and wanted comfortable, casual clothes for their increasing hours of leisure, and California style was as desirable to them as to women, if not more so.[34] Western leisure wear was marketed especially heavily

8.20. *California Men's Stylist*, July 1945
This two-page spread illustrates three pillars of California men's style: sport shirts, western wear, and casual suits.

8.21. Point of sale advertisement for Levi Strauss & Co., *Lady Levi's*, mid-1950s
As the advertisement shows, *Lady Levi's* were marketed as leisure wear at home.

8.22. Levi Strauss & Co. Jeans (1934) and *Rodeo* shirt (late 1930s) from the *Lady Levi's* line. Cats. 174 and 175
The jeans were purchased by Harriet Atwood at Best & Co. in New York in 1934 to wear at the Soda Springs dude ranch in Arizona.

to men, perhaps because its manly associations with the romantic yet rugged figure of the cowboy made it more culturally acceptable (8.20). Western leisure wear for both sexes used elements associated with the clothes worn by stage and screen cowboys, such as shaped or contrasting yokes on shirts and jackets, flapped pockets, piping, fringe trim, Wild West ranch imagery, and, of course, blue jeans.

The transformation of these sturdy work pants into leisure wear began with Levi Strauss, which added "glamor, sex, the western theme"[35] to jeans and was quickly seized upon by others. In the 1930s Levi's began to link its jeans specifically with cowboys in its advertising and manufactured its first lines of western leisure wear for both sexes. In 1934 the company specifically targeted women with its *Lady Levi's* line of jeans, which it touted as both stylish and tailored specifically to fit women's figures (8.21). Levi's suggested that women wear them for urban and suburban activities like "walking, motoring, or just loafing." They also included them in their *Dude Ranch Duds* line, which aimed to capitalize on the craze for dude ranch vacations offering riding, hiking, and camping in the company of cowboy guides.[36] Naturally, jeans were prescribed wear for both "dudes" and "dudines." To go with them, Levi's offered a glamorous line of western-styled *Rodeo* shirts of rayon satin in colors like gold, royal blue, purple, and winter rose (8.22). The company promoted its leisure clothes at expositions like the GGIE, where its mechanical rodeo populated with moving, singing puppets dressed in Levi's jeans, rodeo shirts, and cowboy hats was the hit of Vacationland. At the time of the fair, the company's distribution, with the exception of one or two New York outlets, was restricted to eleven western states, so the GGIE may have been the first in-person exposure to California western style for many Americans.

California women's fashion made its strongest mark in swimwear. Two of that industry's three giants, Cole of California and Catalina, were located in Southern California (Jantzen, the third, was in Portland, Oregon), along with many of their smaller competitors, such as Rose Marie Reid and Mary Ann DeWeese, the former in-house designer at Catalina. Cole's effort to meld high fashion and bathing suits coupled with the emergence of new elastic materials such as Lastex (introduced in 1931) opened the door to significant changes in swimwear design. Lastex, a weavable, knittable yarn with a rubber core, spawned a flood of new stretchable fabrics like Matletex, developed by Margit Fellegi, who became Cole's swimwear designer in 1936 (8.24). The process, which shirred cotton onto elastic yarn, enabled her to design form-fitting suits from any fashionable fabric she chose. Thirties swimsuit styles also became progressively barer, culminating in the first two-piece suits for women at mid-decade, and finally, widespread acceptance of men publicly doffing their tops and bathing in trunks only, a trend that had been promoted by Hollywood. The glamour of swimwear was greatly enhanced by Hollywood, which fell in love

early with bathing beauties and which, by the 1930s, was promoting its actors and films in fan and fashion magazines with pictures of lithe Hollywood stars sunning themselves at the pool and the beach (8.23).[37]

The lack of elastics during World War II forced design adaptations in swimwear. Fellegi's *Swoon Suit* (8.25) had attractively ruched shorts fitted to the body with lacing up the sides in place of elastic and could be augmented with a matching skirt to become a playsuit. It proved hugely popular, and Fellegi dressed it up in a variety of colors and fabrics—including, in 1944, red, gold, aqua, and white, the colors of the parachutes that Cole was also manufacturing (8.26).[38] The *Swoon Suit*'s success notwithstanding, swimsuit designers welcomed the return of elastic after the war. Matletex reappeared, and suits in newer elasticized satins, nylons, and polyesters were offered by virtually every bathing-suit designer. The bright Lastex-and-rayon hand-printed *California Lobster* suits designed by DeWeese in 1949 are from Catalina's *Sweethearts in Swim Suits* line, which clearly linked men's and women's leisure activities and styles (8.27).

By the 1950s a more curvaceous female body had emerged as the fashionable ideal, and swimsuits became more heavily constructed, architectural, and dresslike. New synthetics, such as Spandex (invented in 1959), and firm, fusible materials used for suits' inner corsetry allowed women's swimsuited bodies to be

Melissa Leventon

molded to shape, with prominent, carefully cantilevered breasts over slender waists and curvy hips (8.28). Not all designers followed this style, however, especially the iconoclastic Rudi Gernreich, who preferred to work in elasticized wool and whose 1952 braless knitted maillot covered an unfettered body (8.29).

Swimwear was also an important market for California hand-screenprinted textiles. Companies like California Hand Prints supplied fabrics to Catalina in the 1950s, and Elza Sunderland (Elza of Hollywood) designed and hand-printed exclusive textiles for both Cole and Catalina beginning in the late 1930s; she later supplied Rose Marie Reid and Mary Ann DeWeese. Elza's synthetic and natural printed fabrics were also used for sportswear and home furnishings by designers and retailers nationwide who emphasized her California-style imagery and use of color. "*Color*fornia by Elza of Hollywood . . . Splash prints in the tints of the California sun . . . The clear singing blues, greens, yellows of a sunny California day" ran one typical ad.[39]

The California sportswear market that was established in the 1930s continued to grow steadily, even during World War II. Wartime increased the population of Los Angeles and increased the production of sportswear, despite shortages of materials, government restrictions, and the conversion of some factories to defense production. Ready-to-wear designers and movie costumers stoutly

8.23. Nickolas Muray (1892–1965). Douglas Fairbanks Jr. and Joan Crawford on the beach in Santa Monica, 1929. This sensuous photograph ran in the October 1929 issue of *Vanity Fair*.

8.24. Margit Fellegi for Cole of California. Woman's swimsuit, 1936. Cat. 90

8.25. Margit Fellegi for Cole of California. *Swoon Suit* woman's swimsuit, 1942. Cat. 91

8.26. Cole of California. Advertisement for a *Swoon Suit*, c. 1944

8.27. Mary Ann DeWeese for Catalina Sportswear. Woman's two-piece swimsuit, man's swim trunks, and man's shirt in *California Lobster* pattern from the *Sweethearts in Swim Suits* collection, 1949. Cat. 66

8.28. Rose Marie Reid (1906–1978). Woman's swimsuit, c. 1963. Spandex, center-back length: 15¼ in. (38.7 cm). LACMA, Gift of Esther Ginsberg and Linda Davis in honor of Lesli Baker-Gee

8.29. Jimmy Mitchell, Rudi Gernreich's first fitting model, in Gernreich's shapely but unconstructed wool-knit maillot, 1952

assured the public that they were more than ready to meet the restrictions imposed by Limitation Order 85, the materials-rationing guidelines issued by the government in March 1942. L-85 curbed civilian use of natural fibers, nylon, leather, and rubber; regulated the amount of fabric that could be used for each type of garment; and, to reduce overall clothing consumption, prohibited designers from introducing extreme style changes. Orry-Kelly, chief costume designer at Warner Brothers, said, "We accept the rules as a challenge, and I predict that we in the studios will set an example of adherence to rules without the slightest loss of loveliness in design."[40]

The California designer who probably benefited most from wartime restrictions was Gilbert Adrian, whose suits from the 1940s demonstrate his skill at sharp cutting, precise tailoring, and adept deployment of decorative elements like stripes (8.30). Adrian, MGM's chief costume designer from 1928 to 1941, used his Hollywood renown to propel the couture and wholesale ready-to-wear business he opened in 1942. His favored silhouette was broad shouldered—the prevailing fashionable line—and slim hipped, which fitted perfectly with government guidelines; his very successful fall 1942 line was presented as his *L-85 Collection.* Although Adrian was not particularly known for sportswear, his work contains important elements of California modernism. His daytime clothes are "uncluttered and free from self-consciousness,"[41] and his sense of humor gave his work a lightness and casualness that was very Californian and rare in high fashion. His color sense was almost as bold as Liebes's, and he was fond of using nubby textures and modern abstract handwoven textiles, although his often came from New York designer Pola Stout. Adrian was also interested in new materials and processes, and he enjoyed incorporating movie and other popular culture references into his clothes—as in a 1950 collection entitled *The Atomic 50s*, which featured clothes trimmed with mushroom-cloud-like fabric poufs and projecting flounces (8.31).

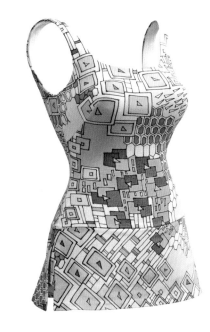

Adrian was the first of California's fashion designers to gain widespread recognition from the national media. In wartime and postwar coverage of the best of American fashion by magazines like *Vogue*, *Harper's Bazaar*, and *Life*, he was often the only Californian included. After Adrian retired in 1952, his place in the national spotlight was soon taken by Rudi Gernreich. Gernreich grew up in Vienna, where modern architecture and the Wiener Werkstätte formed some of his seminal aesthetic influences;[42] at the age of sixteen, in 1938, he fled Austria and settled in Los Angeles. Gernreich's taste for European modernism made him one of the most avant-garde fashion designers of mid-century. Sportswear was his forte; he favored simple, straight lines (unusually fashion forward in the early 1950s, but right on the mark for the 1960s) and pure, bright, sometimes clashing colors (see 3.21) often set in stark contrast to a Wiener Werkstätte–style background of black and/or white, or deployed in a checkerboard motif.[43] The fashion establishment thought of his work, perhaps a little nervously, as "free-wheeling experimental designs in off-beat colors,"[44] but Gernreich transformed casual California style into high fashion so success-fully that he became, in December 1967, only the sixth fashion designer in *Time* magazine's forty-four-year history to grace its cover.

In fashion, especially, the idea of California and all that the name conjured was a selling point; according to a survey published by *Women's Wear Daily* in 1946, buyers associated "California" with original styling and prestige.[45] Manufacturers took care to put "Made in California" on their labels, and a rash of companies included "California" in their names to capitalize on these seduc-tive associations. California fashion designers and manufacturers did, however, suffer from their distance from the major midwestern and East Coast markets; shipping goods east was slow and expensive, and many out-of-town wholesale and retail buyers simply were not willing to make the long trek west. Trade associations in both Northern and Southern California helped by organizing members' participation in trade fairs around the country, as well as by staging fashion shows, merchandise tie-ins, and other buying events in California, sometimes providing sponsorship for out-of-town buyers.[46] The L.A. association also published two magazines, *California Stylist* and *California Men's Stylist*, which were indefatigable industry boosters (8.32). Designers, too, formed

Page 254 8.30. Gilbert Adrian. Woman's two-piece suit, 1946–48. Cat. 4 **This suit postdates the war, but its lines and materials hardly differ from those of Adrian's wartime suits.**

Page 255 8.31. Gilbert Adrian. Two-piece dress from *The Atomic 50s* collection, 1950. Cat. 5

8.32. *California Stylist*, December 1954, cover

8.33. Man's swim trunks and shirt (cabana set), c. 1963. Cat. 293 **This is similar to the cabana sets that were worn in films of the period.**

associations, such as the Affiliated Fashionists, founded in 1936 by Mabs Barnes, Addie Masters, Louella Ballerino, and five other women, to reach out to buyers locally and around the country. Individual designers and manufacturers also wooed eastern and midwestern markets by persuading retailers to set up California-theme boutiques in their stores, sponsoring their buying visits, and entertaining them lavishly.[47]

Hollywood was key to L.A.'s fashion identity, and manufacturers were well aware of the promotional power of its glamour; as *California Stylist* acknowledged, "Motion pictures are the greatest single means of publicity for fashion that has ever existed."[48] Its designers were promoted by the studios as celebrities, and the press regularly solicited their opinions on coming fashions. Hollywood, however, was more a popularizer than a trendsetter. Its designers strove to create contemporary clothes, neither too far ahead nor too far behind the mode, that Americans could see on their favorite stars and imagine themselves wearing. Both sexes wore California sportswear onscreen, often regardless of where the film was set,[49] and fan magazines frequently ran photographs of them wearing it offscreen as well, swimwear especially. Beaches and pools were favorite film settings, from Mack Sennett's bathing beauties to the Esther Williams aquatic spectacles of the 1940s to the *Beach Blanket* flicks of the early 1960s, in which the nice girls often wore maillots and "the good guys wore puffy boxers in plain colors and cabana sets"[50] (8.33). Stars were used for direct promotion—as with Cole's line of bathing suits, designed by Fellegi, that Esther Williams endorsed beginning in 1948 (8.34 and 8.35)—and frequently appeared modeling clothes of all kinds in fashion magazines. Costume designers also functioned as promoters: Catalina, whose labels read "Styled for the Stars of Hollywood," hired Orry-Kelly during the 1930s to create a line of swimsuits, and in 1942 the company announced that a phalanx of Hollywood designers, including Howard Greer and Walter Plunkett, would collaborate with then in-house designer Mary Ann DeWeese on its spring line.[51]

Throughout this period, fashion and textile designers regularly took style elements from film costume,[52] and women could shop from the ready-to-wear lines created by Hollywood designers like Greer and Adrian. In the 1930s women could also purchase adaptations that were licensed from the studios by manufacturers, who arranged for the clothes to be made and in stores coincident with each movie's release and provided promotional materials as well. The Modern Merchandising Bureau, founded in 1930 by New Yorker Bernard Waldman, retailed many of its clothes through its Cinema Shop boutiques within stores like Macy's, which carried mid-range to expensive clothes.[53] Hollywood Cinema Fashions, sponsored by *Photoplay* magazine and sold at boutiques within stores from Cleveland, Ohio, to Cedar Rapids, Iowa, was a less expensive line (8.36); and Studio Styles specifically licensed Warner Brothers' designs.[54] These clothes were adaptations, not copies, as is made clear in

Hollywood: Style Center of the World (1940), a promotional film that told of a farm girl who visits her local Cinema Shop and buys a suit that is "styled the same" as an Adrian suit worn by Joan Crawford in *Susan and God* (1940). The film shows both the original, worn by Crawford, and the copy, and their similarities and differences are plain. But the attraction of Hollywood clothes is also clear, as the announcer intones, "Today, the girl from the country is just as modern, and dresses just as smartly, as her big-city sister."

Hollywood fashion promotions, most effective during the studio-system years, fragmented in the 1950s, though individual stars still influenced the clothing choices of moviegoers, as James Dean and Marlon Brando did with a generation of jeans-wearing teenagers. Faster, cheaper travel and improved communication made regional differences less pronounced but also increased the reach of California fashion across the country, ensuring that it remained a leader in sportswear design and manufacture, particularly for men.

By 1965 California modern abstract, textured textiles and innovative, casual sportswear had clearly gone from modest beginnings in 1930 to being major contributors to mainstream design in America. There are many reasons: the state's oft-invoked superior climate and varied terrain nurtured the creation of

distinctive imagery, colors, and garments, while the promotional power of the movies coupled with the pleasures of the relaxed California lifestyle made them enticing. The influx of European émigrés like Trude Guermonprez, Maria Kipp, and Paul László brought expertise and modernist ideology that inspired others, while the concomitant decline of Europe as a design source offered unprecedented opportunities for Americans. The willingness of designers—including Dorothy Wright Liebes, Margit Fellegi, Alvin Lustig, and Rudi Gernreich—to partner with industry made good design available to the mass market, while a number of small-batch studio producers supplied the bespoke market. California's surging population kept demand for modern textiles and fashion humming through World War II, and in the postwar period California also became an important center for training designers of modern textiles. In its postwar maturity, California produced some of the best modern American fashion and textiles, and by the end of the 1950s, its style had become fully integrated into the American design mainstream.

8.34. Margit Fellegi for Cole of California. Woman's swimsuit, 1950–51. Cat. 94
The suit was probably made as promotion for Esther Williams's 1952 movie *Million Dollar Mermaid*.

8.35. Cole of California. Advertisement for the Esther Williams line from *California Stylist*, January 1949, p. 3

8.36. Hollywood Cinema Fashions advertisement, *Photoplay* magazine, January 1935
This ad by a Schenectady, New York, retailer for *Photoplay*'s Hollywood-costume-based clothing line shows a close resemblance between the screen version as depicted in the display photograph and the fashion version mounted on the form nearby. The ad invited readers to visit the store, "where the thrill of selecting Hollywood Cinema Fashions awaits you."

8.37. Nathan Turk. Woman's shirt and trousers, 1950s. Cat. 288

NOTES

1   *Decorative Arts: Official Catalog, Department of Fine Arts, Division of Decorative Arts, Golden Gate International Exposition, San Francisco, 1939*, exh. cat. (San Francisco: San Francisco Bay Exposition Company; H. S. Crocker, Schwabacher-Frey Co., 1939), 93.

2   Mary Schoeser, "Textiles: Surface, Structure, and Serial Production," in *Craft in the Machine Age, 1920–45: The History of Twentieth-Century American Craft*, ed. Janet Kardon (New York: American Craft Museum; Abrams, 1995), 113.

3   Ibid., 114.

4   Ibid.

5   Nell Znemierowski, *Dorothy Liebes: Retrospective Exhibition* (New York: Museum of Contemporary Crafts, 1970), 34. Liebes's major commissions during her time in California (she moved to New York in 1948) included textiles for the St. Francis Hotel, Yerba Buena Club, and Stock Exchange Club in San Francisco; the Ahwahnee Hotel in Yosemite; and the Royal Hawaiian Hotel in Honolulu. See also Alexandra Griffith Winton, "Color and Personality: Dorothy Liebes and American Design," *Archives of American Art Journal* 48 (Spring 2009): 8–9.

6   Liebes, quoted in Winton, "Liebes and American Design," 9.

7   Relman Morin, "Dorothy Liebes," *House Beautiful*, October 1966, 218. Morin was Liebes's husband, a fact not disclosed to the magazine's readers.

8   Elizabeth McCausland, "Dorothy Liebes: Designer for Mass Production," *Magazine of Art*, April 1947, 132. See also Morin, "Dorothy Liebes," 218. Liebes's industrial clients in the 1940s included Goodall Fabrics of Sanford, Maine, and the Dobeckmun Co., which manufactured the Lurex metallic yarns she favored. In the 1950s she went on to consult with DuPont and the rug manufacturer Bigelow-Sanford. Liebes moved her design studio from California to New York in 1948, and she eventually gave up custom work to concentrate solely on industrial consulting and design for mass production.

9   Winton, "Liebes and American Design," 6, 8. See also Regina Lee Blaszczyk, "Designing Synthetics, Promoting Brands: Dorothy Liebes, DuPont Fibres and Post-war American Interiors," *Journal of Design History* 21, no. 1 (2008): 75.

10 Mary Schoeser and Whitney Blausen, "'Wellpaying Self Support': Women Textile Designers in the USA," in *Women Designers in the USA, 1900–2000: Diversity and Difference*, ed. Pat Kirkham (New York: Bard Graduate Center for Studies in the Decorative Arts; New Haven, Conn.: Yale University Press, 2000), 150–51. For in-depth information on Kipp's history, see Marilyn R. Musicant, "Maria Kipp: Autobiography of a Hand Weaver," *Studies in the Decorative Arts* 8, no. 1 (Fall–Winter 2000–2001): 92–107.

11 Schoeser and Blausen, "Women Textile Designers," 153. The textiles were synthetic because all the interior decoration on the boat was required to be nonflammable.

12 See Bobbye Tigerman, "Fusing Old and New," in this volume, for a more in-depth discussion of Trude Guermonprez's background.

13 Kay Sekimachi, in *CCAC: An Oral History (1930–1960)*, 1997, DVD on file in the California College of the Arts library.

14 Guermonprez, quoted in Signe Mayfield, "Kay Sekimachi: Threads of Memory," in Yoshiko Wada et al., *Kay Sekimachi* (Bristol, England: Telos Press, 2003), 12.

15 Hazel V. Bray and Kay Sekimachi Stocksdale, *The Tapestries of Trude Guermonprez*, exh. cat. (Oakland: Oakland Museum, 1982), 9–10.

16 Ann Pollard Rowe, Rebecca A. T. Stevens, and Jane Fassett Brite, *Ed Rossbach: Forty Years of Exploration and Innovation in Fiber Art* (Washington, D.C.: Textile Museum; Asheville, N.C.: Lark Books, 1990), 46–51.

17 Ed Rossbach, interview by Harriet Nathan, *Charles Edmund Rossbach: Artist, Mentor, Professor, Writer* (Berkeley: University of California Press, 1983), 69, 83.

18 Katherine Westphal, interview by Harriet Nathan, *Katherine Westphal: Artist and Professor* (Berkeley: University of California Press, 1984), 19–21.

19 Ibid., 21–22.

20 Schoeser, "Textiles: Surface, Structure, and Serial Production," 121.

21 Charles S. Goodman, *Location of Fashion Industries* (Ann Arbor: University of Michigan Press, 1948), 65. Goodman's analysis was geared to cotton textiles produced for the fashion industry, but it is also applicable to the furnishing-textile industry. He also noted that a lone rayon-knitting plant opened in Pomona in 1947.

22 For Barney Reid's biography, see http://objectsusa.com/images/Gallery/FiberItems/barney-reid-fabric-placemats.htm.

23 Alvin Lustig, "Modern Printed Fabrics," *Design*, July 1952, 27–30, quoted in Lesley Jackson, *Twentieth-Century Pattern Design: Textile and Wallpaper Pioneers* (New York: Princeton Architectural Press, 2002), 109.

24 Fashion also had a small presence at the GGIE, with examples chosen by *Vogue* magazine editor in chief Edna Woolman Chase. Chase, in her catalogue essay, praised the creativity and originality of California designers inspired by film stars and year-round sports, but her choice of participants included only one from California. All the others were from New York. See *Decorative Arts: Official Catalog*, 42–43.

25 Rossbach, interview, 57. Rossbach admitted that he and Guermonprez did not have compatible views of textiles, but he was nonetheless taken with the work she produced at the end of her life.

26 *Women's Wear Daily*, September 16, 1931, cited in Betty Kirke, *Madeleine Vionnet* (San Francisco: Chronicle Books, 1998), 133. According to the same article, business for French couture in America peaked in 1927; by 1931 it had fallen 70 percent.

27 Goodman, *Location of Fashion Industries*, 27–28.

28 Ibid., 35–36.

29 Irene, *California Stylist*, January 1939, 21.

30 Goodman, *Location of Fashion Industries*, 28–29.

31 "Proven Styles," *California Stylist*, March 1941, 10–16; and Sylva Weaver, "Highlight Bright Color," *California Stylist*, November 1942, 29. The seven pieces were a printed playsuit accompanied by a matching turban, a street-length skirt, a jacket, slacks, an evening skirt, and an evening bra top in plain fabric. This was virtually an entire wardrobe.

32 "Barbecues for California Living," *California Stylist*, March 1949, 112.

33 Dick Terkel, "Who Started This Revolution?," *California Stylist*, August 1941, 30.

34 See William R. Scott, "California Casual: Lifestyle Marketing and Men's Leisurewear 1930–1960," in Regina Lee Blaszczyk, *Producing Fashion: Commerce, Culture, and Consumers* (Philadelphia: University of Pennsylvania Press, 2008), for an in-depth discussion of the tremendous increase in the men's leisure-wear industry during this period.

35 Walter Haas Sr., interview by Harriet Nathan, *Levi Strauss: Tailors to the World* (Berkeley: University of California Press, 1976), 17.

36 Levi's was not, of course, the only manufacturer making clothes that catered to the popularity of dude ranches; not only other jeans manufacturers but also other sportswear manufacturers also offered clothes designed specifically to withstand the rigors of a dude ranch vacation. See, for example, the Jean Carroll dude ranch outfit on the cover of *California Stylist*, January 1941.

37 See Richard Martin and Harold Koda, *Splash: A History of Swimwear* (New York: Rizzoli, 1990).

38 *Los Angeles Times*, November 11, 1944, A5.

39 Undated advertisement reproduced in Edward Maeder, *That California Look: Textile Designs by Elza of Hollywood, 1937–1955* (Los Angeles: Los Angeles County Museum of Art, 1986).

40 *California Stylist*, July 1942, 44–45, 98.

41 *Los Angeles Times*, August 16, 1949, A9, quoted in Christian Esquevin, *Adrian: Silver Screen to Custom Label* (New York: Monacelli Press, 2008), 167. The original article, written by Fay Hammond, quotes Adrian saying this at the presentation of his fall 1949 collection.

42 Layne Neilson, "Rudi Gernreich: That Mad Viennese from California," in Brigitte Felderer et al., *Rudi Gernreich: Fashion Will Go Out of Fashion* (Philadelphia: Institute of Contemporary Art, University of Pennsylvania, 2001), 32.

43 Ibid., 32–36.

44 "American Collections: Our Own Fashion Creators Launch New Ideas for Fall," *New York Times*, July 12, 1956.

45 *Women's Wear Daily*, August 20, 1946, 2–76, quoted in Goodman, *Location of Fashion Industries*, 80.

46 Scott, "California Casual," 170. The Men's Wear Manufacturers staged a men's fashion show in Palm Springs in spring 1942—the first ever such show, according to Scott, which enabled the men's sportswear industry in L.A. to make significant inroads into the national market.

47 *California Stylist*, August 1946, 146. An article described the entertainment in store for "a trainload of buyers from New York City" who were arriving that September; it included a fashion show and water ballet staged by Fred Cole, a dinner and fashion show presented by the Affiliated Fashionists, and a brunch hosted by Hollywood milliner Kenneth Hopkins at the Beverly Wilshire hotel, with "Goldwyn girls" modeling.

48 *California Stylist*, April 1939, 4.

49 Patricia Campbell Warner, "The Americanization of Fashion: Sportswear, the Movies, and the 1930s," in *Twentieth-Century American Fashion*, ed. Linda Welters and Patricia A. Cunningham (Oxford and New York: Berg, 2005), 90. For instance, as Warner noted, the chorus girls and the leading ladies Ruby Keeler and Ginger Rogers wear playsuits as rehearsal clothes in *Forty-second Street* (1933), which is set on Broadway.

50 Martin and Koda, *Splash*, 113.

51 *California Stylist*, January 1942, 83.

52 *California Stylist*, January 1949, 81, 164. Cohama and Ameritex fabrics created fabric collections designed after Walter Plunkett's costumes in *Little Women* (1949) as tie-ins to the movie and then provided their fabrics to thirteen designers for use in contemporary fashions.

53 *Modern Screen* (May 1934) and *Fortune* (January 1937), cited in Sarah Berry, *Screen Style: Fashion and Femininity in 1930s Hollywood* (Minneapolis: University of Minnesota Press, 2000), 17. Prices for Cinema Shop clothes were in the $15–$40 range, or about $200–$600 in today's dollars.

54 Ibid., 17–22.

SOUTHERN PACIFIC'S NEW

Daylight

LOS ANGELES - SAN FRANCISCO

9

Developing a Language of Vision: Graphic Design in California

JEREMY AYNSLEY

Graphic designers made a major contribution to defining "living in a modern way" in mid-twentieth-century California. They manifested the styles and principles that characterized California design in easily accessible visual forms: book covers and magazines, posters and advertisements, and film title sequences, as well as exhibition and architectural graphics. The state's adventurous experiments in graphic design were recognized by mid-century. Writing in a 1953 article, "Printing on the West Coast," in the magazine *American Artist*, Eugene M. Ettenberg suggested:

9.1. Southern Pacific Company. *Southern Pacific's New Daylight*, c. 1937. Cat. 269

Σlise

BY MERLE ARMITAGE
AN ARTICLE BY LOUIS DANZ AND A
PORTRAIT BY BEATRICE WOOD

Σ. Weyhe New York

Experimental designers in the West have won over such adherents of traditional conservatism as the producers of insurance policies and annual reports of utilities and aircraft companies, fields of design that in the East are inbred and more or less frozen into set typographic patterns. Letterheads, everyday business forms, cookbooks, menus, publications and newspapers such as the trail-blazing Los Angeles Times *are representative of the unhackneyed approaches we admire from afar.*[1]

Clearly, California and the West were on the cultural map of graphic design in ways that could not have been predicted twenty years earlier.

As many have noted, the 1930s in California were years of only partial realization of modernism, and in this, graphic design was no exception.[2] Pockets of activity by indigenous Californians and designers newly arrived from other parts of the United States, as well as by significant émigrés from Europe, contributed to the incremental establishment of modern graphic design. For example, the circle around Jake Zeitlin—publishers, book designers, poets, and graphic artists retrospectively described as "LA's early Moderns"—was important for the emerging scene.[3] Zeitlin, a poet who arrived in Los Angeles from Texas in 1925, opened his first shop (designed by Lloyd Wright, son of the world-renowned architect) in 1928, where he exhibited work by local printmakers, photographers, and painters. Avant-garde eastern bookstores, such as the E. Weyhe shop in New York, provided a model for Zeitlin. He was the first to show the Californian graphic artist Paul Landacre and other local modern printmakers and photographers, and his program of exhibitions, readings, and book launches would shape a nucleus of avant-garde activity in Los Angeles.[4]

In 1929 Zeitlin set up his own press, publishing the experimental art and literature of his circle in innovative forms now considered to be some of the first modern book designs produced in California. He employed various modes of illustration, all presented in imaginative bindings, in what can be loosely deemed Moderne style. One of his earliest books, *The Aristocracy of Art* (1929), brought together the talents of designer Grace Marion Brown, typographer Grant Dahlstrom, and author and arts impresario Merle Armitage (cat. 51). Partly inspired by this project, Armitage began to design his own books, featuring work by many of his friends, including photographer Edward Weston, artist Rockwell Kent, and Elise, a comedic actress and painter whom Armitage married in 1934 (9.2).

In a state that was expanding so rapidly, many manufacturing and commercial interests propelled modern graphic design, not least to trumpet California's agricultural productivity as the nation's larder. California as a tourist destination, facilitated by expanded transportation networks, was another important theme for graphic designers.[5] Posters were the most visually arresting form of promotion, although as the period progressed, they met competition from

CATALINA Now see Santa Catalina the Scenic Riviera of the U.S.A. . . . .yet only a short delightful voyage from Los Angeles

radio advertising and roadside billboards. In Los Angeles, the advertising agency Foster & Kleiser had pioneered the use of modern graphics on billboards, starting in 1901. By the 1930s, posters were at a renewed height of popularity, refreshed by Art Deco and Moderne styles that featured abstract or figurative designs in strikingly exuberant colors.[6] It was natural that prominent companies and organizations would turn to them to announce their goods or services and to enhance California's image. For instance, to promote the island resort of Catalina, owned by Chicago millionaire William Wrigley Jr., Otis Shepard, who had been art director at Foster & Kleiser between 1923 and 1929, produced a poster with a full-color pictorial rendition of the inviting landscape in an unusual horizontal format (9.3). He combined references to luxuriant vegetation and mission-style architecture with suggestions of modern convenience for the contemporary traveler. Shepard extended his influence beyond the poster, also designing staff uniforms and boat interiors for Wrigley—an early example of modern marketing and the creation of a corporate identity by integrating all aspects of design.[7]

Many posters were adapted as press advertisements in consumer periodicals with a West Coast focus, such as *Touring Topics*, aimed at the motoring public, and *Sunset*. The latter was a magazine founded in 1898, initially to promote the Southern Pacific railroad.[8] Under a new owner, in 1929 the magazine

9.2. Merle Armitage for E. Weyhe. *Elise*, 1934. Cat. 12

9.3. Otis Shepard for Wrigley Company. *Catalina*, 1938. Cat. 260

9.4. The outdoor dining area of architect Cliff May's home (Cliff May House #3, Brentwood, 1939; remodeled late 1940s) on the cover of *Sunset*, March 1950. Photo by Julius Shulman, 1949. Cat. 350

turned to advocating the California way of living. With the advent of color photography, the magazine's covers and feature articles depicted actual modern interiors and gardens of middle-class Californians, with their promise of a casual outdoor lifestyle (9.4).[9] In many respects, the ideal of Californian ease and informality, made accessible through the printed page, superseded the 1920s cult of the Mediterranean in the international imagination.

In their associations with the exotic, labels for display on the sides of citrus crates were one unexpected area for aesthetic innovation in packaging design, once mass transportation of produce became possible after the railroad linked Southern California to the rest of the country, starting in the 1870s. Imagery on the first labels suggests California as both natural garden and cultivated orchard. Various allegorical allusions prevailed, including the Tropical Queen, the Indian Belle, and the eroticized female figure of La Paloma.[10] One surprising twist in the labels' designs came in the 1930s, when companies adopted the newly fashionable Art Deco style, ridding the labels of their historicism by adding a repertoire of chevrons, zigzags, circles, and targets (9.5). Introduced by designers who had received training in the new commercial art schools, rather than in the more traditional fine arts, these vibrant graphic images connected company trademarks to a forward-looking aesthetic and subliminally linked the state with modernity.[11]

Jeremy Aynsley

Modernity and California also became conjoined in promotions of the state's tourism. This was clearly evident in Southern Pacific's campaign for the *Daylight*, a coastal express connecting San Francisco and Los Angeles, which was promoted as "the most beautiful train in the world" when it was introduced in 1937.[12] The *Daylight* made it possible to travel in a day, by luxury rail, between California's two major cities. With its evocation of speed and streamlined travel, the anonymously designed poster for the *Daylight* (9.1) inevitably invites comparison with the famous *Nord Express* poster (1927) by French designer A. M. Cassandre, who visited the Chouinard Art Institute in 1935.[13] In a sophisticated example of modern branding, Southern Pacific repeated these graphic renditions of the train's distinctive look in all the promotional material, assuring travelers that each train in the expanding line could be identified "instantly by their bright red-and-orange color." These colors had been deliberately selected to be as "vivid as the California sun," associating the technological wonder with its attractive natural surroundings (9.6).[14]

By the late 1930s, word had spread to California about the new movement in European design and the experimental ideas of the first generation of "new typographers" through channels such as avant-garde magazines, the writings of typographer Jan Tschichold, and books by the Bauhaus.[15] The latter, a series published between 1925 and 1930, introduced the aesthetic foundations of modernism. Modernist graphic design, or the "new vision," as it became known, was comprehensively defined in the writings of László Moholy-Nagy and György Kepes.[16] In the late 1930s these two designers moved from Europe to Chicago, where they adapted their ideas about modern visual communication in the context of the Chicago School of Design, initially known as the New Bauhaus. Advocates of the new vision embraced photography as the most technically advanced illustrative medium. They combined sans serif typefaces with photomontage in compositions informed by Constructivism and, later, Surrealism. Crucially, they promoted this new "language of vision" as suited to industrial and commercial as well as artistic contexts.[17]

Though clearly not every initiative depended on the arrival of émigré designers or personal contact with them, one important direct link between Europe and California was made when the Swiss graphic designer and photographer Herbert Matter settled in Los Angeles in 1943. Having already established a reputation for the large-format photomontage travel posters he had designed in Zurich, Matter worked for art director Alexey Brodovitch on *Harper's Bazaar* and *Vogue* magazines in New York before designing the Swiss national pavilion for the 1939 New York World's Fair.[18] Although Matter lived in Los Angeles for only three years, his aesthetic approach contributed significantly to the first full flourishing of California graphic design. In addition to contributing many covers and layouts for the magazine *Arts and Architecture* (9.7), he worked in the Eames office until 1946, where he applied his innovative

9.5. Dario De Julio for McDermont Fruit Company. *Red Circle* orange-crate label, c. 1938. Cat. 333

approach to publication and exhibition design. Matter interpreted the new design, such as the Eames chairs seen in 9.7, through his characteristic play with scale, form, and technique; using photomontage, he revealed the technical innovation of the chair's bent-plywood structure.

In contrast to New York and Chicago, where designers worked primarily within established professional boundaries, a distinctive feature of California in the 1940s was that graphic, furniture, interior, and architectural designers could collaborate without the restrictions of precedent or rigid demarcations. Such an environment encouraged experimental, interdisciplinary ventures, and as graphic designer Allen Porter described it, "a freedom to innovate without the baggage of the East."[19]

Graphic design was particularly crucial in shaping an identity for companies associated with the new design. One deceptively simple medium for this was stationery, in the form of letterheads and business cards. As a young designer, Alvin Lustig cut his teeth on such commissions (9.8). Originally from Denver, Lustig opened his first design studio in Los Angeles in 1936. Combining type and symbols in inventive ways for both individual clients and local companies, Lustig soon became recognized as a "brilliant" designer.[20] Sam Hunter asserted in *Art Digest*, "In the market place Lustig has done nothing less than

arts & architecture

PRICE FIFTY CENTS

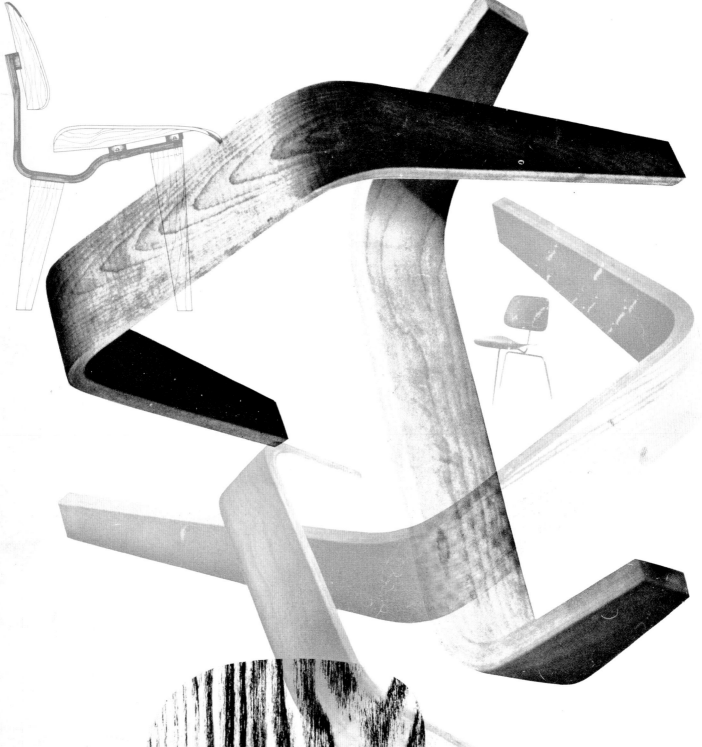

SEPTEMBER 1946

sheela's ▶◀

youthful fashion-wise styles

mademoiselle shoes by carlisle

325 NORTH BEVERLY DRIVE   BEVERLY HILLS   CALIFORNIA   CRESTVIEW 18681

an inspired job of adapting the vocabulary of modernism to the exigencies of mass visual media."[21] Many of Lustig's designs reflected his deep interest in modern art, especially biomorphic Surrealism, through which he developed an individual style: refined, elegant, and when necessary, fashionable. Having studied at Art Center School in Los Angeles, Lustig went on to teach master classes there and was renowned as an inspiring teacher (9.9). Like one of his most important influences, Jan Tschichold, Lustig wrote many essays that explained his approach to design. In "Personal Notes on Design," for instance, he described his commitment to finding a new visual language: "I think we can safely say that in all the arts, the last fifty years have been characterized by analysis and experiment. Every field of plastic expression has shown among its more vital minds a feverish concern for the new, the never-done-before, the furiously non-traditional."[22]

An informal gathering known as the Design Group grew from Lustig's classes, where students discussed his belief that modern graphic design should engage with contemporary culture and be informed by references to modern art, literature, and music (see 1.15). Importantly for the future of California design, he encouraged a multidisciplinary approach, and his own office took on commissions for exhibition, product, and interior design (see endsheets and 1.17), along with graphic design. An early landmark for Lustig was his collaboration with publisher Ward Ritchie on the book *The Ghost in the Underblows* (1940), part of a long poem by Alfred Young Fisher (9.10). Lustig employed the constituents of typography—letterforms and compositor's decorations—to produce illustrations for each of the ten chapters of the book.[23] He used "printer's flowers" (decorative motifs traditionally used for border decorations), printed in strong red and black, to create full-page images in experimental layouts that invited comparison with El Lissitzky and other Soviet designers of the 1920s. Lustig's designs for the New Classics series of paperbacks, started during World War II by the Manhattan-based publisher New Directions, were unusual for their abstraction (see 1.16). In his first designs for them he avoided conventional pictorial interpretations and instead devised covers in which color and abstract motifs established an identity for the individual book as well as for the series—earning him the accolade "father of the modern paperback."[24]

San Francisco had been an important center for newspaper, magazine, and book publishing since the late nineteenth century, as well as home to several private presses. However, it was not until the San Francisco–born designer Jack Werner Stauffacher set up shop that book design in the city took on a thoroughly modern appearance. Not interested in designing within the inherited conventions of America's Arts and Crafts printing, nor solely within the bounds of classical "good" typography as championed by distinguished university presses, Stauffacher linked design for the page with modernism.[25] He collaborated with his brother, the filmmaker Frank Stauffacher, on a project for the Art

9.8. Alvin Lustig. Letterhead for Sheela's, 1947. Cat. 186

9.9. Alvin Lustig teaching at Art Center School, Los Angeles, 1948

THE GHOST IN THE UNDERBLOWS

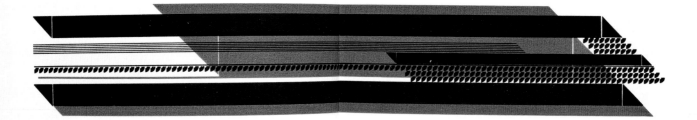

BY ALFRED YOUNG FISHER
EDITED WITH AN INTRODUCTION BY
LAWRENCE CLARK POWELL · DESIGNED BY
ALVIN LUSTIG AND PRINTED BY THE
WARD RITCHIE PRESS AT LOS ANGELES
CALIFORNIA · NINETEEN HUNDRED AND FORTY

9.10. Alvin Lustig for Ward Ritchie Press. *The Ghost in the Underblows*, 1940. Cat. 192

9.11. Jack Werner Stauffacher for San Francisco Museum of Art. *Art in Cinema*, 1947. Cat. 274

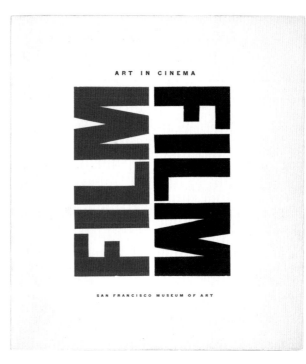

in Cinema Society at the San Francisco Museum of Art (now the San Francisco Museum of Modern Art) in 1947, introducing the work of European avant-garde filmmakers. Jack Stauffacher's design for the book *Art in Cinema* was in keeping with its subject (9.11). Aware of new publications coming from cultural institutions in Europe and elsewhere in America, Stauffacher used a striking square format, pared-down typography, asymmetrical placement of photographic illustrations, active use of space, and bold type in primary red ink.

As demonstrations for his students, Stauffacher often produced experiments that consisted mainly of repeated letterforms and words.[26] In 1963, for example, he began a series of prints called Shifting and Inking, which paralleled contemporary interests in concrete poetry. One print from the series (see p. 346) announced his departure from Carnegie Institute of Technology in Pittsburgh and his return to San Francisco, where he took up the position of typographic director at Stanford University Press; three years later he left Stanford and resurrected Greenwood Press, a small publishing house specializing in experimental book designs and prints, which he had originally founded in 1936.[27]

California gained one of its clearest identities in design through the creative synergy between graphic design and architecture. In February 1942, under editor and publisher John Entenza (who had purchased it in 1938), the magazine *California Arts and Architecture* began its transformation into the single most important publication for the dissemination of modern California architecture and design.[28] Starting with this issue, Alvin Lustig presented a complete redesign of the magazine, including the layout, masthead, and logotype. This development was especially impressive at a time when the war meant that art magazines in other parts of the world were confronting unusual challenges or ceasing publication entirely. In the February 1944 issue, *California* was dropped from the title, and the magazine became the thoroughly modern *arts & architecture*. The cover design of each issue was entrusted to a different designer within Entenza's circle, including Ray Eames (newly returned to California in 1941) and, as previously mentioned, Herbert Matter. Other regular contributors of covers were the designers Charles Kratka, John Follis, and Frederick A. Usher Jr. (see 10.3 and 10.4). Their designs announced that the magazine was self-aware, confident, and able to stand up to the best of international publication design. At once a style manual and a serious exploration of the new design culture, particularly in California, *Arts and Architecture* epitomized modern design, not only with its content but also through its graphics.

Covers displayed an abundant repertoire of the latest graphic trends: photomontage, biomorphic motifs, plans, and diagrams. The issues published during and right after the war stressed the future role of urban planning and science in building a new world, with some covers conveying profound anxiety about the nuclear age (9.12). Others offered vibrantly inventive abstract designs, metaphors of modern architecture played out through graphic design.

The central focus, however, was the modern house and its interior, most prominently the Case Study House Program (see Nicholas Olsberg, "Open World: California Architects and the Modern Home," in this volume). Entenza and the magazine's layout designers commissioned professional product and architectural photography from Julius Shulman, Harry Baskerville, and Ralph Samuels. Their images were integrated into elegant visual essays, accompanied by reproductions of architectural plans, sketches and models of buildings, and details of ceramics, furniture, jewelry, and other accoutrements destined for the modern household (9.13). Largely through *Arts and Architecture*, mid-century modern graphic design achieved its distinctive California variant, looser and more informal than the modernism of an earlier generation. The style shared the fluidity of line found within contemporary sculptural ceramics and furniture design, and a strong correspondence developed between the magazine and the sales catalogues for many modern L.A. design companies, including Victor Gruen Associates, Van Keppel-Green, and Glenn of California (see 6.5 and 10.10).

Entenza avoided advertisements that were not in sympathy with the overall integrity of the magazine's design, and therefore advertising was overseen in-house by "Murray, Dymock, and Carson" ("Murray" was Entenza himself, "Dymock" was Robert Cron, and "Carson," Ralph Carson).[29] The close connection between advertisement and editorial is seen in Louis Danziger's 1949 advertisement for General Lighting Company, in Los Angeles (9.14 and see cat. 54). For this photographic set, a bench was arranged with two lamps set against a grille divider, in front of the steel-frame windows of the still-to-be completed Eames Case Study House #8, itself an *Arts and Architecture* initiative, all conveying a sense of experimental design activity.[30]

One of the first-generation California graphic designers, Louis Danziger (a New Yorker by birth) studied at the Art Center School under Alvin Lustig and, in 1948, at the New School, in New York, under Alexey Brodovitch. The next year Danziger returned to Los Angeles, where he established his career as a freelance designer and consultant. In 1955 he taught at the Chouinard Art Institute and then from 1956 at the Art Center School.[31] Danziger combined teaching with running a small studio, where he attracted clients that in other cities might have gone to larger, more established agencies. Like many of his contemporaries, he particularly flourished in the environment of entrepreneurship and creative energy that Los Angeles offered. Danziger developed a client base that grew from small beginnings to embrace national companies, and his clients included the Dreyfus Company, Clinton Laboratories, Container Corporation of America, and Gelvatex Coatings Corporation. He was drawn to the challenge of manifesting intangible qualities through visual metaphor, which he combined with the clever copy that was becoming increasingly popular in modern advertising at the time. He applied this approach in his work as consultant designer for the Los Angeles County Museum of Art between 1958 and

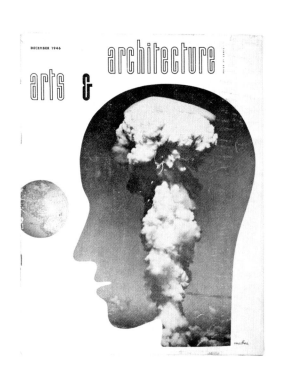

9.12. Herbert Matter. *Arts and Architecture*, December 1946, cover. Cat. 211

9.13. Alvin Lustig. Interior layout for *California Arts and Architecture*, February 1942

defense housing NEW CONSTRUCTION TECHNIQUES

DEFENSE HOUSING PROJECT
Long Beach, California

FEDERAL WORKS AGENCY:
Brig.-Gen. Philip B. Fleming, Administrator
Baird Snyder III, Assistant Administrator
Rufe D. Newman, Jr., Chief of Construction
  Division
Pierce Williams, Director West Coast Area,
  Defense Housing Construction Division

ARCHITECTURE
Eugene Weston, Jr., Architect
Walter L. Reichardt, Associate Architect
Geraldine Knight Scott, Consulting Landscape
  Architect

ENGINEERING
Harold A. Barnett, Civil Engineer
Harry M. Gailey, Mechanical and Electrical
  Engineer
R. Howard Annin, Consulting Structural
  Engineer

CONSTRUCTION
Zoss Construction Company, General
  Contractor

1980, designing catalogues and posters that helped establish an international reputation for the museum in terms of its graphic design (9.15).

With California's growing reputation as a center for design came the formation of several organizations to foster and professionalize graphic design. These organizations and publications also introduced a wider public to the philosophical principles and practical importance of modern graphic design. The Art Directors Club of Los Angeles (ADLA), modeled on the New York precedent started in 1920, was founded in 1941; one of its initial activities was the launch of a poster contest to assist with the war effort.[32] The purpose of the club was to promote a fruitful collaboration between design, clients, and the public through publication and exhibition, as well as to give awards for best practice. Its mouthpiece, *Western Advertising*, was a portfolio of advertising art that was published in San Francisco and featured annual selections of the best advertising, art direction, and publication design produced in "the eleven western states."[33]

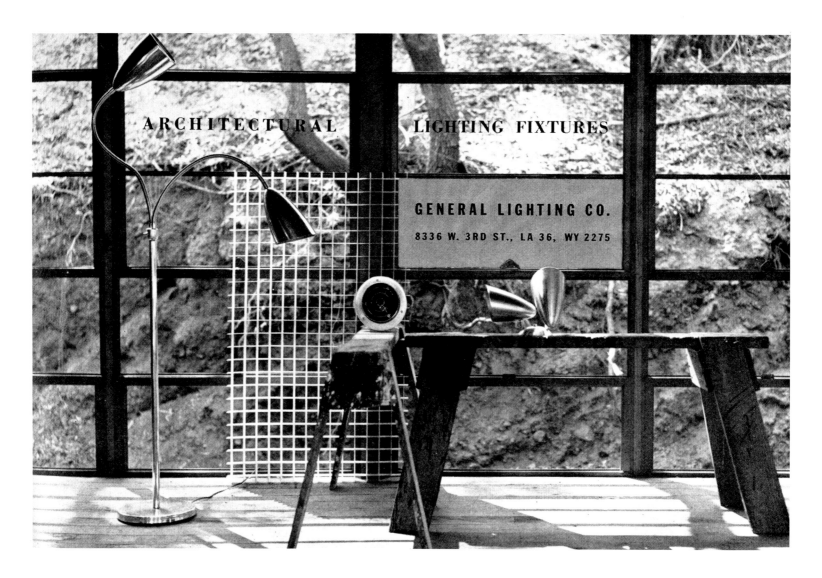

A short-lived group called the Society of Contemporary Designers was established in Los Angeles in 1949. The members of this loose affiliation of modern designers included such prominent figures as Saul Bass, Louis Danziger, and Alvin Lustig. It was unusual in bringing together graphic, product, and exhibition designers, not just from California, who shared ideas and jointly exhibited work. Another group, Los Angeles Advertising Women (LAAW), was formed in the late 1940s to "help women achieve the recognition they so richly deserve" and to capitalize on their advances in the field: "Now women occupy positions of top rank in every branch of advertising" (9.16).[34] An important channel for the professional recognition of graphic design on the West Coast was the launch, in August 1959, of the highly successful *Journal of Commercial Art*, known from the start for the distinctive "ca" logo on its covers and later renamed *Communication Arts*. Based in Palo Alto, it was the result of collaboration between Richard S. Coyne; his wife, Jean A. Coyne; and Bob Blanchard, who, with backgrounds in marketing and advertising, decided to publish a monthly magazine in recognition of the shift in graphic design toward the more inclusive corporate-image programs that were being pioneered in California by Saul Bass, Walter Landor, and others.[35]

A central preoccupation for many designers at this time was to achieve the

spontaneity and directness found in children's art. No other designer or design group in California epitomized this preoccupation with childhood more than Charles and Ray Eames and the team of designers who congregated in their Venice Beach office, collaborating on their many interdisciplinary projects. In terms of graphic design, the Eames office worked in many innovative ways, creating photographic designs for print, film, and exhibitions that would have a profound impact. The Eameses took inspiration from eclectic visual references, gathered by dedicated and imaginative research. For instance, Deborah Sussman, a designer in the office for many years, recalls being sent to Mexico to photograph previously overlooked examples of folk culture for the Eameses' 1957 film *Day of the Dead*.[36] The Eameses also championed constructive play, as in the *House of Cards* of 1952 (9.17). Ostensibly a children's toy, the cards carried images of "patterns" and "pictures" that were photographs from the Eameses' collections of toys, folk art, textile fragments, and natural *objets trouvés*—or, as they put it, "familiar and nostalgic objects from the animal, vegetable, and mineral kingdoms."[37]

The principle of formal and associative juxtaposition that informed the Eameses' visual communication, often through collage and montage, paralleled the "functioning decoration" they used to animate interiors.[38] The two approaches were most effectively synthesized in exhibition designs. In 1961 the

9.14. Louis Danziger. Advertisement for General Lighting Company, 1949. Photo by Marvin Rand, 1949. From *Arts and Architecture*, August 1949, p. 9. See cat. 54

9.15. Louis Danziger for Los Angeles County Museum of Art. *New York School: The First Generation*, 1965. Cat. 53

9.16. Louis Danziger for Los Angeles Advertising Women. *Fourth Annual: Frances Holmes Achievement Award*, 1949. Cat. 52

spring issue 1953

EVERYDAY ART

published by the american crayon company

Eameses developed the design concept of *Mathematica: A World of Numbers . . . and Beyond*, their first exhibition design; a gallery by that name, sponsored by IBM, opened the next year at the California Museum of Science and Industry in downtown Los Angeles (9.19). For it they created a multimedia environment that incorporated film, three-dimensional typography, blown-up photography, and models. It was a logical summation of the designers' commitment to interpreting science through art and testimony to Ray Eames's opinion that there should be no distinction "between education and fun or play."[39] As Charles commented, "In doing an exhibition, as in Mathematica, one deliberately tries to let the fun out of the bag. The catch is that it can't be any old fun but it must be a very special brand."[40]

The relationship between art, design, and science in children's education was also a central focus of *Everyday Art*, the house journal of the American Crayon Company (9.18 and see cat. 98). Designed and art directed from Los Angeles for many years by Frederick A. Usher Jr., this quarterly took full advantage of the talented circle around *Arts and Architecture*, and it became an active force in promoting modernist approaches through art education in schools and colleges.[41] A parallel ambition, also partly dependent on graphic designers, was to produce well-illustrated books that would encourage visual and verbal literacy in children. Among the imaginative, reasonably priced picture books of the period was the award-winning *Baboushka and the Three Kings* (9.20), written by Ruth Robbins and with illustrations by Nicolas Sidjakov, a Paris-trained illustrator and designer born in Riga, Latvia, who had moved to San Francisco in 1956.[42]

One of the most important graphic designers of this generation was Saul Bass; a New Yorker by birth and training, he came to Los Angeles in 1946 and founded Saul Bass and Associates. Bass was a protagonist in the transformation of graphic design from a print-based discipline to one that fully embraced film. An important pioneer of visual communication, he altered the way that movie titles were understood by developing the first visual-identity programs for motion pictures—a crucial chapter in Hollywood history. Bass's career encompassed many landmark film designs; among the first was the revolutionary *The Man with the Golden Arm* (1955), director-producer Otto Preminger's film about drug addiction. To give the title sequence meaning beyond just identifying the cast and crew, Bass introduced a psychological element in the graphic emblem of a jagged arm, symbolic of the lead character's addiction (9.21). The syncopation of text and image to the music of composer Elmer Bernstein produced a tense first sequence. Bass stated, "The intent of this opening was to create a mood—spare, gaunt, with a driving intensity."[43]

Bass wanted to avoid the usual poster that promoted a film with purple prose accompanied by photographs of the leading actors, but because some theater owners protested, a version with pictures of the stars Frank Sinatra and Kim Novak was made. Nevertheless, the graphic emblem of the jagged arm

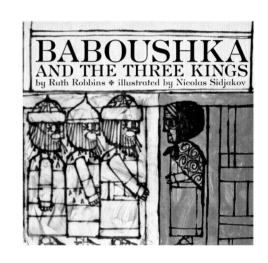

9.17. Charles Eames and Ray Eames for Tigrett Enterprises. *House of Cards*, 1952. Cat. 80

9.18. John Follis and Rex Goode. *Everyday Art*, Spring 1953

9.19. Charles Eames and Ray Eames. The entrance to *Mathematica: A World of Numbers . . . and Beyond*, California Museum of Science and Industry, Los Angeles, 1961—the designers' first multimedia exhibition

9.20. Nicolas Sidjakov for Parnassus Press. *Baboushka and the Three Kings*, 1960. Cat. 261

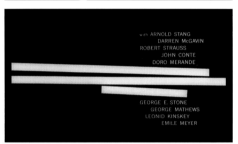

9.21. Saul Bass for Carlyle Productions. *The Man with the Golden Arm* title sequence, 1955. Cat. 22

9.22. Saul Bass for Carlyle Productions. *The Man with the Golden Arm* poster, 1955. Cat. 23

became the icon of the film, used on other posters (9.22) as well as on the album cover, in newspaper ads, and on stationery produced at the time of the film's release (see cat. 24).[44] Bass also turned his hand to other album-cover designs, most notably for Capitol Records. For *Frank Sinatra Conducts Tone Poems of Color* (1956), the first record produced in the newly opened Capitol Records Tower in Hollywood, Bass used his understanding of modern abstract art to establish equivalence between visual and musical harmony (9.23).

Capitol, which had been established in 1942, was the first major West Coast label to compete with RCA-Victor, Columbia, and Decca, all based in New York. To provide striking cover art for the company's five hundred annual releases, Capitol's art director, Marvin Schwartz, cultivated not only renowned graphic designers like Bass but also photographers and illustrators, and he became an important source of work for many, most notably William Claxton and Robert Guidi (9.24). In the case of some classical music and jazz covers, modern art in the form of lively animated figures, mood photography, and Color Field abstraction was featured along with experimental typography. The album covers were designed to capture a mood, to work as display in the stores, and to encourage the browser to buy, often before hearing the full recording.[45]

Graphic design played a part in promoting sales by creating an atmosphere of modernity as well as through new sales techniques. The two were successfully combined in the case of the Joseph Magnin department store. In the early 1950s the store was still in the shadow of its better-known but staid competitor, I. Magnin. Joseph Magnin's son Cyril, together with Cyril's daughter Ellen, transformed its flagship store in downtown San Francisco and expanded the chain to over twenty locations across California.[46] Most significantly for the future reputation of the company, the San Francisco–trained designer Marget Larsen became art director and introduced many innovations. The company logo became *JM*: this use of simple initials reflected the trend toward abbreviation in corporate identities. Leading figures were brought in to design individual stores. For the Century City branch in Los Angeles, for example, Gruen Associates designers Rudi Baumfeld and Marion Sampler combined abstract sculptural motifs and three-dimensional lettering to make a bold statement for the store's frontage, expanding the possibilities of contemporary architectural graphics (9.25). Their approach encompassed innovative window displays, points of purchase, and shop interiors to create a modern, totally designed experience.[47] As a graphic novelty for Magnin, Larsen initiated Christmas gift boxes designed with a different motif every year, such as architecture, alphabet blocks, or musical instruments. These boxes were so alluring (almost as coveted as the goods they contained) that the customer was motivated to purchase more Magnin clothing and accessories just to obtain the complete set. So successful was the strategy that after Larsen left the company, in 1964, the practice continued under her successor, Joe Hong[48] (9.26 and see cat. 133).

Jeremy Aynsley

FRANK SINATRA · ELEANOR PARKER · KIM NOVAK

THE MAN WITH THE GOLDEN ARM

A FILM BY OTTO PREMINGER

With Arnold Stang, Darren McGavin, Robert Strauss, John Conte, Doro Merande, George E. Stone, George Mathews, Leonid Kinskey, Emile Meyer, Shorty Rogers, Shelly Manne,
Screenplay by Walter Newman & Lewis Meltzer, From the novel by Nelson Algren, Music by Elmer Bernstein, Produced & Directed by Otto Preminger, Released by United Artists

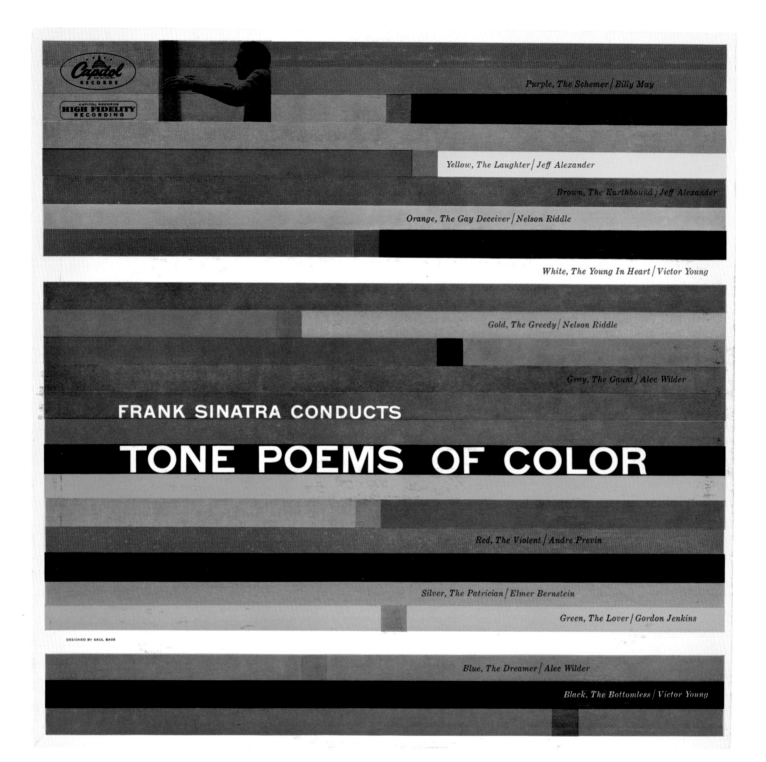

Purple, The Schemer / Billy May

Yellow, The Laughter / Jeff Alexander

Brown, The Earthbound / Jeff Alexander

Orange, The Gay Deceiver / Nelson Riddle

White, The Young In Heart / Victor Young

Gold, The Greedy / Nelson Riddle

Gray, The Gaunt / Alec Wilder

FRANK SINATRA CONDUCTS

TONE POEMS OF COLOR

Red, The Violent / André Previn

Silver, The Patrician / Elmer Bernstein

Green, The Lover / Gordon Jenkins

Blue, The Dreamer / Alec Wilder

Black, The Bottomless / Victor Young

9.23. Saul Bass for Capitol Records. *Frank Sinatra Conducts Tone Poems of Color*, 1956. Cat. 19

9.24. Clockwise from top left: Robert Guidi and Tri-Arts for Contemporary Records. *Lighthouse at Laguna*, 1955. Cat. 121. William Claxton and Pauline Annon for World Pacific Records. *Jazz Canto Vol. 1*, 1958. Cat. 44. William Claxton for Pacific Jazz Records. *Bud Shank and Three Trombones*, 1954. Cat. 45. Betty Brader for Fantasy. *Cal Tjader Quintet*, 1956. Cat. 31

Another San Francisco figure to change the retail landscape was Walter Landor—in his case, attending to identities for grocery companies, major corporations, and eventually multinational brands. In 1957 Landor pronounced, "Design moves merchandise if it moves people."[49] A year later, he wrote in a similarly forceful way under the heading "Why East Comes West for Design": "Dynamic new marketing concepts are becoming more associated with the West Coast. Design particularly thrives in the unique mental climate of the West."[50] The son of a Bauhaus-trained architect, the German émigré Landor (born Walter Landauer) moved to San Francisco after a short stay in New York working on the British pavilion at the 1939 World's Fair. One of the first California commissions he undertook was for the San Francisco Museum of Art, *Space for Living* (1940), for which he oversaw the exhibition design as well as the poster design (see 3.15). He changed his name from Landauer and founded Walter Landor & Associates in 1941. An interdisciplinary industrial, graphic, and packaging design group, his company would become a world leader in introducing many new approaches that would become accepted practice in years to come. To remain at the forefront of the corporate-image business—or "company personality," as he preferred to call it—he offered both graphic and product design (see 3.16), as well as employing retail psychologists and motivational researchers to advise on consumer behavior, as part of the standard services offered to clients.[51]

Landor recognized the importance of a distinctive location for his design studio. His first was a nine-thousand-square-foot building on the Embarcadero, adjacent to San Francisco's World Trade Center; then, in 1964, he moved his office to the ferryboat *Klamath*, docked at a local pier. Landor showed particular talent in developing identities for food and drink companies that grew in scope from individual products to establishing the house style for an entire line. He updated the services that his studio offered to help companies meet modern consumers' needs for brand reliability, and he found ways to embody this need in product lines that could be readily identified in part because of innovative solutions to packaging developed with his company's product designers. This was at a time when such approaches were coming under critical scrutiny by Vance Packard, whose book *The Hidden Persuaders* (1957) proved to be an influential exposé of advertising techniques.[52] Landor summed up his approach with catchwords such as "informative labeling," "specialized appeal," "power to attract," "putting the consumer in the picture," and "whimsy is a humanizing factor."[53] Unlike Packard, he saw the motivational research used by modern advertisers in a positive light, for what it offered the consumer and the client. And he kept design firmly at the center, declaring: "Motivating the consumer is not done by accident. In today's food store when product differences are actually becoming smaller and smaller, the consumer must become persuaded by design" (9.27).[54]

By the early 1960s it was clear that graphic designers had contributed a great deal to the consumer dreams of a modern California lifestyle. The years that followed, with the civil rights movement, the Watts Riots, anti–Vietnam War protests, and the rise of the counterculture—too complex to investigate here—were to present a fundamental challenge to this vision. One poignant example of a time when graphic design punctured the optimism serves to conclude this essay. Corita Kent, a Catholic sister of the Immaculate Heart Community in Los Angeles, was a gifted graphic artist. As head of the art department at her convent, Sister Corita developed a strongly individual style of making screenprints to produce graphic statements that were direct comments on the visual language of commerce.[55] In part a protest against the Los Angeles Catholic Church's resistance to reform, and in part an expression of concern about larger human injustice, Sister Corita's work took on a visual directness admired by the Los Angeles design community. She juxtaposed signs from advertising with texts that subverted its commercial language. In *Enriched Bread* (1965), she combined an everyday product from the supermarket shelf with a text by the French-Algerian writer Albert Camus to encourage reflection on how the word *wonder* could be appropriated to sell such a quotidian product (9.28).

The critical reflection on word and image manifest in Sister Corita's prints was a harbinger of changing times, when many of the principles of the new vision would be challenged by a new generation with different cultural priorities. Nonetheless, the engagement of modern graphic designers with "living in a modern way"; their sense of optimism, innovation, and experimentation; and their firmly held belief that design could make a new and better world were the lasting legacies of California graphic design between 1930 and 1965.

9.25. Rudi Baumfeld (1903–1988) and Marion Sampler for Gruen Associates. Design for Joseph Magnin department store, Century City, c. 1967

9.26. Joe Hong for Joseph Magnin. *Renaissance* series gift boxes, 1966. See cat. 133

9.27. Walter Landor (second from left) and other members of the design team reviewing decanter designs for Old Fitzgerald Whiskey in the studios of Walter Landor & Associates, San Francisco, c. 1960

NOTES

I would like to thank Wendy Kaplan, Staci Steinberger, and Bobbye Tigerman for their many perceptive comments and suggestions. Victoria Dailey, Lou Danziger, SB Master, Louise Sandhaus, and Steve Turner offered many invaluable insights.

1   Eugene M. Ettenberg, "Printing on the West Coast," *American Artist* 177 (December 1953): 3.

2   Mike Davis, *City of Quartz: Excavating the Future of Los Angeles* (London: Verso, 1988), chap. 1, 17–97; and Stephanie Barron, ed., *Made in California: Art, Image, and Identity, 1900–2000*, exh. cat. (Los Angeles: Los Angeles County Museum of Art; Berkeley: University of California Press, 2000).

3   Victoria Dailey, Natalie W. Shivers, and Michael Dawson, *LA's Early Moderns: Art, Architecture, Photography* (Los Angeles: Balcony Press, 2003).

4   Victoria Dailey, *From Z to A: Jake Zeitlin, Merle Armitage and Los Angeles' Early Moderns* (Los Angeles: UCLA Library, 2006), 46; and Roy R. Behrens, "On Merle Armitage: The Impresario of Book Design," in *Graphic Design History*, ed. Steven Heller and Georgette Ballance (New York: Allworth Press, 2001), 81–86.

5   Jim Heimann, ed. *California Here I Come: Vintage California Graphics* (Cologne: Taschen, 2002); and Mark Resnick and R. Roger Remington, *The American Image: U.S. Posters from the Nineteenth to Twenty-first Century*, exh. cat. (Rochester, N.Y.: RIT Cary Graphic Arts Press, 2006).

6   Steven Heller and Louise Fili, *Streamline: American Art Deco Graphic Design* (San Francisco: Chronicle Books, 1995).

7   Mark Gladstone, "Old Poster Revives Interest in Artist," *Los Angeles Times*, September 6, 1981.

8   Hsiao-Yun Chu, "Seeing in a Modern Way: The Modernist Leanings of *Sunset* Magazine, 1940–1965" (lecture, annual meeting of the College Art Association, New York, February 2009).

9   For the impact of color on advertising and the introduction of psychological persuasion, see Roland Marchand, *Advertising the American Dream: Making Way for Modernity, 1920–1940* (Berkeley: University of California Press, 1985); and Michelle H. Bogart, *Artists, Advertising and the Borders of Art* (Chicago: University of Chicago Press, 1995).

10 Henry Knight, "Savage Desert, American Garden: Citrus Labels and the Selling of California, 1877–1929," *U.S. Studies Online: The BAAS Postgraduate Journal* 12 (Spring 2008): http://www.baas.ac.uk.

11 Gordon McLelland and Jay T. Last, *California Orange Box Labels: An Illustrated History* (Beverly Hills: Hillcrest Press, 1985).

12 Text from *Southern Pacific Presents Daylight*, 1937, leaflet in the Victoria Dailey and Steve Turner Collection, Los Angeles.

13 I am grateful to Steve Turner for drawing my attention to Cassandre's Los Angeles visit, which is mentioned in Carla Binder, ed., *Joseph Binder: An Artist and a Lifestyle* (Vienna: Anton Schroll, 1976), 53. The exhibition *Posters by Cassandre* was shown at the Museum of Modern Art, New York, January 14–February 16, 1936.

14 Southern Pacific, *Southern Pacific Presents "Daylight,"* c. 1937, and *Three Daylights Daily*, c. 1941, brochures in the Victoria Dailey and Steve Turner Collection, Los Angeles.

15 Jan Tschichold, *The New Typography: A Handbook for Modern Designers* (1928), trans. Ruari McLean (Berkeley: University of California Press, 1995); and Ute Brüning, ed., *Das A und O des Bauhauses*, exh. cat. (Berlin and Leipzig: Bauhaus Archiv, 1995).

16 László Moholy-Nagy, *The New Vision: From Material to Architecture* (New York: Wittenborn, Schultz, 1947); and György Kepes, *The Language of Vision* (Chicago: Paul Theobald, 1944).

17 For an example of the later application of the phrase "language of vision" in a California context, see Charles Eames, "Language of Vision: The Nuts and Bolts," *Bulletin of the American Academy of Arts*, October 1974, 13–25.

18 Jeffrey Head, *Herbert Matter: Modernist Photography and Graphic Design* (Stanford: Stanford Universities Library, 2005).

19 Allen Porter, *Los Angeles: Modernism and the Creative Fervor of the 50s–60s*, DVD of a presentation at the Third Annual Meeting of Chicago Bauhaus and Beyond, held at the Chicago Architecture Foundation on February 11, 2007 (Chicago: CBB, 2007).

20 Ward Ritchie, *A Tale of Two Books* (Los Angeles: Book Collectors of Los Angeles, c. 1985), 26.

21 Sam Hunter, "An Interior View," *Art Digest*, December 15, 1952, 23.

22 Alvin Lustig, "Personal Notes on Design," *AIGA Journal* 3, no. 4 (n.d.): 16–19, reprinted in *The Collected Writings of Alvin Lustig*, ed. Holland R. Melson, Jr. (New Haven, Conn.: Holland R. Melson, 1958), 38–51.

23 For an account of this book, see Ritchie, *Tale of Two Books*, 26.

24 "Pioneers: Alvin Lustig," *Communication Arts* 41 (March–April 1999): 188.

25 Jack Werner Stauffacher, conversation with author and SB Master, April 14, 2010. The designer's dislike of the original linocut cover commissioned by the San Francisco Museum of Art from Bezalel Schatz prompted him to rebind one hundred copies for his friends with his own typographic design on the cover (see 9.11).

26 Chuck Byrne, "Jack Stauffacher, Printer &c.," *Emigré* 45 (Winter 1998): 16–59.

27 Jack Werner Stauffacher, *A Typographic Journey: The History of the Greenwood Press and Bibliography, 1934–2000* (San Francisco: Book Club of California, 1999), 18.

28 Barbara Goldstein, ed., essay by Esther McCoy, *Arts and Architecture: The Entenza Years* (Santa Monica: Hennessey and Ingalls, 1998); and Elizabeth A. T. Smith et al., *Blueprints for Modern Living: History and Legacy of the Case Study Houses*, exh. cat. (Los Angeles: Museum of Contemporary Art; Cambridge, Mass.: MIT Press, 1989).

29 Louis Danziger, conversation with author, Wendy Kaplan, and Staci Steinberger, August 27 and 30, 2009.

30 Ibid.

31 William B. McDonald, "Louis Danziger," *Graphis* 70 (1957): 148–53; and Marvin Rubin, "Louis Danziger," *Graphis* 191 (1978): 266–73.

32 Dale Jones, "Los Angeles Art Directors Club and Aircraft War Council Co-sponsor a Poster Contest," *Western Advertising*, July 5, 1942, 59.

33 *Western Advertising*, August 1951, frontispiece. *Western Advertising* began publication in 1919.

34 Text from the announcement *Los Angeles Advertising Women's "Fourth Annual"* (Los Angeles: LAAW, 1950), designed by Louis Danziger; see 9.16. Danziger archive, folder 13, box 3, Graphic Design Archive, Rochester Institute of Technology.

35 Patrick Coyne, "*Communication Arts* at 40," *Communication Arts*, March–April 1999, 60–76. The magazine did not cover only California designers, but it did frequently feature them.

36 Deborah Sussman, conversation with author and Staci Steinberger, April 20, 2010.

37 Charles and Ray Eames, quoted in Eames Demetrios, *An Eames Primer* (London: Thames and Hudson, 2001), 229.

38 The term was the Eameses'. For an extended discussion of "functioning decoration," see Pat Kirkham, *Charles and Ray Eames: Designers of the Twentieth Century* (Cambridge, Mass.: MIT Press, 1995), 143–200.

39 Ray Eames, quoted in Demetrios, *Eames Primer*, 185.

40 Charles Eames, "Language of Vision," quoted in Kirkham, *Charles and Ray Eames*, 297.

41 *Everyday Art* was founded in 1922. See "A Program in Print: The American Crayon Company," *Print* 1 (October 1955): 34–45.

42 "Nicolas Sidjakov," *Journal of Commercial Art* 3 (June 1962): 32–35.

43 Bass, quoted in Pat Kirkham, *Saul Bass: A Life in Design and Film* (London: Laurence King, 2011), 118.

44 For film title sequences by Saul Bass, see Emily King, "Taking Credit: Saul Bass, Otto Preminger and Alfred Hitchcock," in *Design and Popular Entertainment*, ed. Christopher Frayling and Emily King (Manchester, England: Manchester University Press, 2009), 123–41.

45 Ted Poyser, "Capitol Album Covers," *Journal of Commercial Art* 2 (September 1960): 42–48; and Dave Hickey, "Cool on Cool: William Claxton and the Way the Music Looked," in Elizabeth Armstrong et al., *Birth of the Cool: California Art, Design, and Culture at Midcentury*, exh. cat. (Newport Beach: Orange County Museum of Art; Munich: Prestel, 2008), 133–50.

46 Ellen Magnin Newman and Walter Newman, conversation with author and SB Master, April 14, 2010.

47 "Marion Sampler," *CA Magazine: Journal of Communication Arts* 9, no. 2 (1967): 70–76.

48 Robert Brewster Freeman, "Marget Larsen," *Communication Arts* 30 (March–April 1988): 87–102.

49 Walter Landor, "Design Moves Merchandise If It Moves People," *Good Packaging Yearbook*, 1957, 83.

50 Walter Landor, "Why East Comes West for Design," *Good Packaging Yearbook*, 1958, n.p.

51 Bernard F. Gallagher, "A Brand Is Built in the Mind: Walter Landor and the Transformation of Industrial Design in the Twentieth Century" (master's thesis, State University of New York College at Oneonta, 2007).

52 Vance Packard, *The Hidden Persuaders* (New York: D. McKay Co., 1957).

53 These terms were used by Landor in "Design Moves Merchandise."

54 Ibid., 83.

55 For Sister Corita Kent, see Julie Ault, *Come Alive: The Spirited Art of Sister Corita* (London: Four Corners Books, 2006); and Lorraine Wild, "Sister Corita: The Juiciest Tomato," posted January 9, 2007, http://observatory.designobserver.com/entry.html?entry=5097.

9.28. Sister Corita Kent, *Enriched Bread*, 1965. Cat. 150

10

"It Has to Be Sold":
The Dissemination of California Design, 1945–65

WENDY KAPLAN AND STACI STEINBERGER

Julius Shulman asserted that "good design is seldom accepted. It has to be sold."[1] He was referring to his own role in staging architectural photography for the press (10.1), but the statement could be equally applied to exhibitions, stores, advertising, and publications, which were the principal agents in disseminating modern California design.

The pent-up demand for new products was enormous, fueled by the lifting of restrictions on domestic consumption after 1945. Even more significant, a prosperous postwar

10.1. Richard Neutra. Kaufmann House, Palm Springs, 1946. Photo by Julius Shulman, 1947
Shulman's extensively published photograph catapulted the Kaufmann House into the canon of California architecture. Featured in an April 11, 1949, *Life* magazine article, "Glamourized Houses," the twilight image obscured Neutra's focus on the relationship of the house to the desert landscape in favor of dramatic lighting.

America required the promotion of a consumer culture. Exhibitions teamed up with magazines: Millard Sheets's *The Arts of Daily Living* exhibition at the Los Angeles County Fair was cosponsored by *House Beautiful*. Magazines formed alliances with building and furniture companies: *Arts and Architecture*'s Case Study House Program was supported with materials donated by the housing industry; its furnishings were provided by local retailers. And none of the many museum shows devoted to "good design" would have been possible without the enthusiastic (albeit self-interested) participation of stores and merchandise marts.

All these collaborations attest to a period of creative experimentation and fluid boundaries between art and commerce, together with a belief in the integration and equality of all forms of artistic expression. And as recent scholarship has demonstrated, the resulting consumer wonderland also played a central role in the Cold War.[2] American furnishings, appliances, and model homes were shown abroad to demonstrate the superiority of capitalism and the American Way of Life; at home, such domestic bounty served as a bulwark against the fear of communism and nuclear war. Since an idealized California, where prosperity and leisure were available to all, had become emblematic of the American dream, its products became an integral part of Cold War ideology.

Selling California products cannot be separated from selling the idea of California itself (10.2). In 1962 a special issue of *Life* magazine was devoted to "The Call of California: Its Splendor, Its Excitement. Why People Go, Go and Go There"—one of thousands of similarly titled articles published in the two decades after the war.[3] Coverage from general news and lifestyle magazines was significant, as were issues dedicated to California in specialty journals such as *Craft Horizons* (September–October 1956) and *Industrial Design* (October 1957). The incessant promotion of the state in the country's popular shelter magazines (among them *House and Garden*, *Interiors*, and *House Beautiful*), however, was most responsible for national recognition for its architects, designers, and manufacturers. These publications often included a section listing the names and locations of everyone whose work was illustrated, which must have greatly increased commissions and sales.

The California marketed in these pages was modern. A *House and Garden* article, which demonstrates that by 1947 every trope was firmly in place, announced that "California is in the vanguard" because of its rejection of tradition, embrace of vibrant color, adoption of casual indoor/outdoor living (made possible by the spectacular climate), and passion for individual expression.[4] *House Beautiful* highlighted California indoor/outdoor furniture, "since new architecture scarcely distinguishes between our lives in the open and under shelter."[5]

In *What Is Modern Design?* (1950), Museum of Modern Art (MoMA) curator Edgar Kaufmann Jr. declared: "Modern Design for the home is more appropriately used to create an atmosphere of 'the good life' than of 'a brave new world.'"[6] This was a new strand of modernism, which historian Beatriz Colomina

10.2. Edward McKnight Kauffer. *American Airlines to California*, c. 1947. Cat. 146

Part of a campaign for American Airlines, this travel poster is the embodiment of the California lifestyle, with the Pacific Ocean, a beautiful girl in a bathing suit, and a beach ball standing in for the sun.

notes emerged after, and in response to, World War II, when "expertly designed images of domestic bliss were launched to the entire world as part of a carefully orchestrated [Cold War] propaganda campaign." As part of this phenomenon, "The figure of the architect changed from the heroic one of the modern movement—serious, masculine, austere, formally dressed, earnest, in public—to the domesticated agent of the postwar years: happy, pleasure seeking, sensual, casually dressed, relaxed, at home."[7] Since California architects and designers had never adhered to the monolithic, stern, moralizing modernism of the International Style (with the possible exception of Richard Neutra, the only Californian to be included in MoMA's eponymous 1932 catalogue), publications presented their work as the perfect embodiment of this new approach.

Even in the 1920s and '30s, California was characterized by a more humanistic modernism, fully embracing comfort and leisure, responding directly to the environment. This distinctly Californian style became renowned throughout the United States and Europe through the pages of *Arts and Architecture* (10.3 and 10.4). The presentation of editor and publisher John Entenza's message owed a great deal to the articles by critic Esther McCoy and the images by commercial photographer Julius Shulman. A transplant from New York, McCoy became the preeminent interpreter of what she called "one of the great proving grounds" of modern architecture.[8] In 1962 she wrote the first book on the Case Study Houses, articulating their importance even before the program was completed. Historians David Gebhard and Robert Winter would later credit almost all of "our present awareness of Southern California architectural heritage" to McCoy's many books and articles; they constituted a "one-woman crusade" to document mid-century innovators as well as to rescue the reputations of California Arts and Crafts movement architects who had fallen from favor.[9] Shulman's meticulously composed shots, as deliberately lit as a movie set, showed architecture at its most glamorous. His iconic image of Case Study House #22 captured the dramatic setting of Pierre Koenig's glass-and-steel cantilever, posing two young women totally at ease above the vertiginous panorama of Los Angeles[10] (10.5).

California modern had many strands, however, and the prefabrication techniques and industrial materials of *Arts and Architecture*'s Case Study Houses were too rigidly orthodox for *House Beautiful*'s editor Elizabeth Gordon, whose hero was the champion of organic architecture, Frank Lloyd Wright. In a direct challenge to Entenza, she initiated the Pace Setter House Program in 1946, which was national in scope but embraced the work of more regionally oriented California architects such as Harwell Hamilton Harris and Cliff May and landscape architect Thomas Dolliver Church.[11] The publication of these "soft" modern designs in a mainstream shelter magazine introduced a wide audience to modern architecture and encouraged some developers to incorporate its vocabulary of open plans and glass walls, advertising such features to distinguish their tract homes from the hundreds of more conservative options (10.6).

Overleaf

10.3. *Arts and Architecture* covers, clockwise from top left: Charles Kratka, September 1952. Cat. 156. Charles Kratka, January 1957. Cat. 158. Herbert Matter, April 1945. Cat. 208. Ray Eames, May 1943. Cat. 83

10.4. John Follis and James Reed. *Arts and Architecture* cover, September 1953. Cat. 101

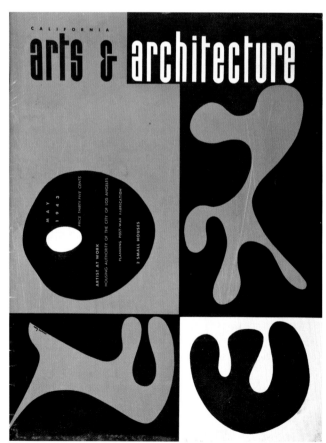

SEPTEMBER 1953

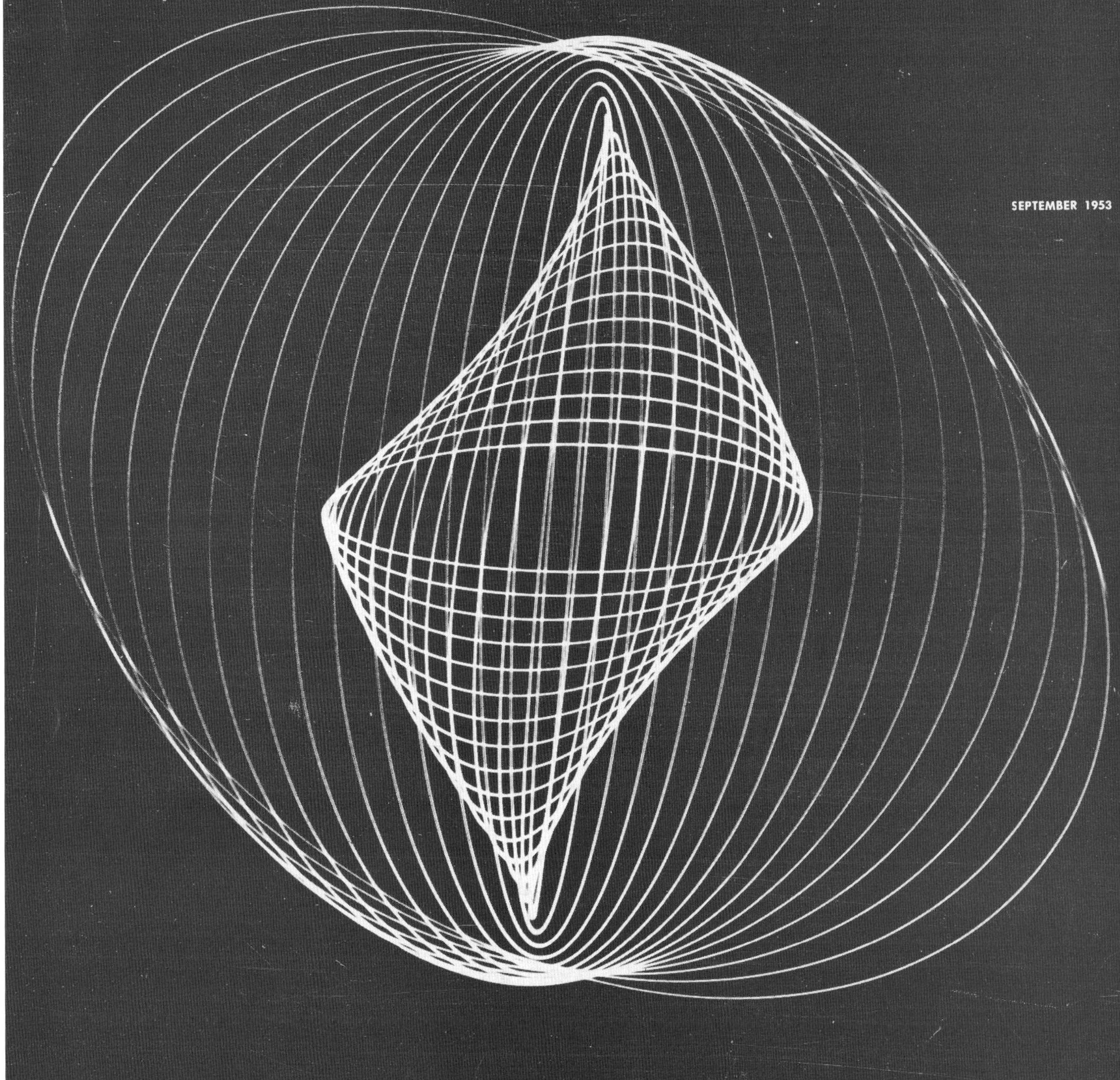

PRICE 50 CENTS

arts & architecture

REED & FOLLIS

Furnishing modern interiors was equally important. As mentioned earlier, *House Beautiful* cosponsored the 1954 *Arts of Daily Living* exhibition at the Los Angeles County Fair, dedicating an entire issue to the twenty-two rooms installed there "to show how the arts may be used in the home and how the home can help you make an art out of living."[12] Some of the rooms were by Californians (see 5.31), but the exhibition included installations by architects and designers from many regions. The fact that *House Beautiful* chose the county fair as the venue to display these rooms demonstrates how central California was to the national conversation about "modern American ways of living."[13]

Since the mid-nineteenth century, raising the standards of commercial production had been part of the mission of art museums, a goal embraced by the new museums of modern art established in the late 1920s and 1930s, and with particular fervor by MoMA. With exhibitions such as *Organic Design* (1941; see 6.12), *Low Cost Furniture* (1948), and the *House in the Garden* series (1949–54), MoMA demonstrated its deep commitment to improving contemporary design and architecture as well as its willingness to partner with stores, company showrooms, and magazines. (Gregory Ain's house for MoMA of 1950 [10.7] was a collaboration with *Woman's Home Companion*.) These programs served as a model for California museums and focused national attention on the California designers included in them, especially with the *Good Design* series spearheaded by Edgar Kaufmann Jr.

Beginning in 1950, Kaufmann and other jurors for the *Good Design* exhibitions selected a few hundred objects for display at the Chicago Merchandise Mart, out of the many thousands submitted. (The competition was not limited to American design, but the objects did have to be available for purchase in the United States.) In November 1950 a smaller group went on view at MoMA, the first of the annual winter design shows that would take place there until 1955, always in collaboration with the Merchandise Mart (10.8). Other museums, notably the Walker Art Center in Minneapolis and the Albright Art Gallery in Buffalo, had similar programs, but MoMA's was the most influential. Kaufmann stated, "*Good Design* serves the public as a buying guide," and as the leading arbiter of modern taste at mid century, the museum was in an unparalleled position to do this.[14]

Californians could learn about *Good Design* through magazines such as *Interiors* and *Arts and Architecture*, but they also had the opportunity to see the work for themselves when selections from the exhibitions were displayed at the Long Beach Municipal Art Center in 1953 and 1954. The *Los Angeles Times* published articles about the shows, focusing on the many California designers who had received MoMA's endorsement; the articles illustrate, for example, an Olga Lee lamp and textile (10.9 and see 8.15) and Gene Tepper's *Versitable* (see 6.10 and cat. 284).[15] Objects vetted by the museum could proudly display the Good Design logo, and MoMA's imprimatur was a major selling point for local

10.5. Pierre Koenig. Stahl House (Case Study House #22), Hollywood Hills, 1959–60. Photo by Julius Shulman, 1960

Sunset Hills

THE FUTURE **CITY** LAKEWOOD AS NEW AS TOMORROW

"BUILT TO ORDER" your HOME the way YOU want it...

Valley Park
MUTUAL HOMES

in fabulous VALLEYWOOD

BY THE BUILDERS OF
LAKEWOOD PARK

manufacturers. The cover of the Glenn of California catalogue proclaims that the Greta Magnusson Grossman chair illustrated there was a winner of the Good Design award, "Keynoting the design superiority of GLENN furniture" (10.10).

The Golden State's boosters, however, wanted an exhibition of their very own. The press release announcing the "First All-California Good Design Exhibition" declared it would be "on a par with those of the Merchandise Mart in Chicago and the Museum of Modern Art in New York" (10.11).[16] The *California Design* exhibition opened in November 1954 at the Pasadena Art Museum and continued to be held for more than twenty years (see Glenn Adamson, "Serious Business: The 'Designer-Craftsman' in Postwar California," in this volume). From the first, the goal, as expressed by the museum's director, Joseph Fulton, was "to encourage designers, manufacturers and retailers to produce better goods by creating a larger demand for them" and to demonstrate "what is going on in the West."[17]

Both the MoMA and Pasadena series celebrated an alliance between art and commerce—there was no apology for displaying household objects in an art museum. The mandate to elevate taste was broad; a museum audience could receive enlightenment from a painting by Picasso, a salt cellar by Cellini, or a planter by Architectural Pottery. The boundaries between high and low art were not fixed at mid-century, and most art museums (especially those dedicated to modern art) shared the populist conviction that the art found in everyday life had a legitimate place in their galleries. Such objects were not displayed with quite the same reverence, however; in general, they were neither ensconced in cases nor placed on platforms. And though not for sale in the exhibitions themselves, they were clearly identified as available for purchase. (All the *California Design* catalogues listed the names of the craftspeople and manufacturers and their locations; the later ones gave their addresses as well.)

A few months after the first *California Design* show opened, Long Beach's Municipal Art Gallery collaborated with San Francisco's de Young Museum to present *California Designed*, which journalist and publicist Elaine K. Sewell described as "a well-rounded example of California's contribution to good design in the home furnishing field."[18] A second *California Designed* was organized with the Oakland Museum the following year; both were curated by Samuel W. Heavenrich, director of the Municipal Art Gallery. Like the *California Design* series, the exhibitions freely mixed handcrafted pieces with those intended for mass production and received funding from the Los Angeles County Board of Supervisors so they could tour to other parts of the country.

Even before the explosion of exhibitions dedicated to California's domestic products, the San Francisco Museum of Art (SFMA, now the San Francisco Museum of Modern Art) had already begun to organize exhibitions that would promote this work. The museum's first director, Grace McCann Morley, was a champion of the avant-garde and of making it fully accessible to museum

10.6. Brochures, clockwise from top left: Barker Brothers. *Sunset Hills*, 1950s. Cat. 326. *Lakewood: The Future City, as New as Tomorrow*, c. 1950. Cat. 345. *Valley Park Mutual Homes in Fabulous Valleywood*, 1950s. Cat. 351. Wallach Builders, *Built to Order*, 1950s. Cat. 353

10.7. Gregory Ain for the Museum of Modern Art. *The Museum of Modern Art—Woman's Home Companion Exhibition House*, 1950. Cat. 324

10.8. Charles Eames and Ray Eames. Installation view of *Good Design* at the Museum of Modern Art, 1950
Charles and Ray Eames designed the first *Good Design* exhibition, both at the Chicago Merchandise Mart and at MoMA.

10.9. Olga Lee for Ralph O. Smith Manufacturing Company. Lamp, c. 1952. Cat. 169

10.10. Glenn of California. Sales catalogue, c. 1952. Cat. 335

good design POINTS TO **glenn**
OF CALIFORNIA
130 North First Avenue — Arcadia

✳ GLENN CHAIR—
Winner, GOOD DESIGN AWARD, Museum of Modern Art
Keynoting the design superiority of GLENN furniture.

audiences. Committed to the widest possible definition of modern art, she asserted, "We believe it very valuable for people to realize that the principles of art which they revere in a painting or sculpture with a famous name are also exemplified in good things of everyday use."[19] In keeping with that philosophy, in 1949 SFMA presented a series of exhibitions in the museum's new decorative arts galleries: *Design in the Kitchen*, *Design in the Dining Room*, *Design in the Living Room*, and *Design in the Patio* (10.12). As with *California Design*, the exhibition catalogues informed the museum visitor where the objects could be purchased.

Since the work was borrowed mostly from local stores such as Amberg-Hirth, the Pacific Shop, and Cargoes Inc. or directly from local designers, most of it had been made by Northern Californians, but the selection was not restricted to the region. Designers such as New York–based George Nelson and Finnish architect Alvar Aalto (whose work was sold in San Francisco stores) were represented, as were some Los Angeles craftspeople. Allan Adler noted on his price list to the museum that he sold his silver at "Gump's, Moderntrend in San Rafael, or Fraser's in Berkeley."[20] The catalogues acknowledged the collaboration with Bay Area stores as integral to the museum's mission of promoting modern design, which was part of its larger mandate to serve as an arena "in which all creative expressions of contemporary art are presented."[21]

These exhibitions were followed by many others, such as *The Pacific Coast Decorative Arts Competition* (1949 and 1951). In 1951 SFMA expanded its outreach even further, becoming the first museum in the country to produce television programs: *Art in Your Life* (1951–53) and *Discovery* (1953–54). Organized and hosted by SFMA curator Allon Schoener, these twice-monthly live broadcasts covered national and international painting and sculpture, but many were also devoted to design and decorative art, taking advantage of California talent. Edith Heath was the guest for "Modern Pottery"; Charles Eames presented "The Story of the Eames Chair"; Luther Conover was featured in "Furniture for Modern Living." The television programs were not overtly promoting sales but did result in increased exposure for California designers and, therefore, potential clients for their furnishings and architecture. A letter that Schoener wrote to Conover confirmed this: "Soon after your appearance on our television program you informed me that there was an increase in your business."[22]

While SFMA's commitment to outreach was extraordinary, many other California museums organized exhibitions about modern California design—the de Young, the Oakland Museum, and the Los Angeles County Museum (now the Los Angeles County Museum of Art) among them. And the annual state and county fairs continued to have art sections, displaying what were usually called

"Arts and Crafts" with a focus on handmade objects. The Los Angeles County Fair followed *The Arts of Daily Living* with one more exhibition consisting of room assemblages: *The Arts in Western Living* in 1955 (10.13). Unlike its predecessor, this exhibition focused on Southern California architecture and furnishings, "all tak[ing] into account the preferred way of life particular to this region" and responding to "an informality possible only in a region where traditions are not hidebound."[23] The catalogue emphasized that all the rooms (including a desert lanai and a beach living room) resulted from close collaborations among all the arts, concluding with a small essay devoted to "The 'Designer-Craftsman.'"[24]

Nothing demonstrates better how the unique qualities of California's products were presented to the world than the *California Design* exhibitions, especially after Eudorah M. Moore took over as director in 1961. For the 1962 exhibition she dramatically changed not only the content of the show but also how it was marketed. Instead of an annual that would tour to various locations around the country, the show became a triennial, with resources redirected toward a greatly expanded range of objects, a far more competitive selection process, and the production of a substantial, nationally distributed catalogue.[25]

The scale of promotion for the series was unprecedented. National coverage for the 1962 exhibition was limited (local reporting was, as ever, extensive), but two years before the 1965 exhibition Moore made a trip to New York to generate publicity, "realizing the importance of personal contact with all publications instead of relying on the dubious success of application by letter."[26] This and other efforts paid off, garnering hundreds of pages of editorial and feature stories from major newspapers across the United States, all the prominent shelter magazines, and international coverage by *Domus* in Italy and *MD Magazine* in Germany.[27]

The range of Moore's activities exemplifies the combination of education and commerce that characterized the dissemination of California design. For the exhibitions in 1962, 1965, and 1968, she produced filmstrips with interpretive brochures "made at the request and with the advice of the Los Angeles School District's Art Department, and now in use in every high school and junior college in that district."[28] Her distribution of the catalogues to professional organizations and museums as well as to department stores substantially raised the profile of the exhibitions.[29] And she worked tirelessly with Macy's in New York and Carson Pirie Scott in Chicago to set up special promotions in their stores drawn from her shows. In 1965 Carson Pirie Scott planned an elaborate display, called "Color from California," and initiated a $1,000 annual award specifically "to further California good design for manufacture"[30] (10.14).

Like the Los Angeles County Fair exhibitions and those at SFMA, the emphasis of *California Design* after Moore became director was not only on what to buy but also on how to live. Objects were selected to "illustrate the informality and freedom from restriction for which California is well known."[31]

Moore declared in a letter that the theme of the 1965 show would be "California Design for a Way of Life."[32] The strategy for shooting the objects for the catalogues reflects this attitude. Moore accompanied the photographer to beaches, deserts, and forests across California and placed furniture, ceramics, and industrial design in these spectacular landscapes (see 7.1). Lifestyle and product were inextricably linked because "the California way of life creates needs with which its designers must comply, for unique implements of living for fun or for function"[33] (10.15).

Moore's activities in the 1960s echoed an earlier trend of coordinated California promotion. In the 1940s, manufacturers and retailers' associations had unified their efforts to market the allure of Western living to an Eastern audience, encouraging department stores to open "California shops" that sold the state's apparel and decor. War shortages and dwindling imports elevated the demand as "everyone with shop shelves to fill raced West to corral, encourage, finance talent."[34] Groups like the Apparel Creators of California and the Furniture Guild of California made strategic efforts to attract clientele; the former opened a hospitality center to accommodate buyers in downtown Los Angeles in 1944; beginning in 1952, the latter developed a "California Corridor" at the Chicago Merchandise Mart.[35]

Within the state, retailing visionaries sold the idea of modern California alongside more tangible products. Oakland-based retailer Harry Jackson, who had spent time in East Asia before and during the war, saw the West Coast's connection with the Pacific as its route to "simplicity, utility, and comfort."[36] His idea of "Pacifica" began in the early 1950s as a promotion at Jacksons, the Bay Area furniture chain he had inherited, but it became something much larger when he convinced the manufacturers of the California Home Fashion Group to develop specific lines around the concept (10.16). The furniture and textiles marketed under the Pacifica name were aesthetically linked only by the "new mood" of casual flexible living—"a native design that has been adjusted to contemporary living needs."[37] Traditional Asian styles were not directly copied; rather, designers used materials like rattan and boldly patterned textiles, and manufacturers added forms inspired by the Far East, such as movable screens and floor mats. Just as Easterners turned to California as an emblem of the carefree life, so California companies used the allure of a distant Pacific paradise to sell the casual style they had been developing. With Jackson as impresario (aided by former *House and Garden* editor Henry Humphrey), Pacifica designs filled the pages of popular shelter magazines in 1952 (*House and Garden* devoted its April issue to the trend), and there was even a Pacifica exhibition at the de Young Museum.[38]

Decades before Jackson began promoting pan-Pacific culture, Abraham Livingston Gump turned his San Francisco store into a treasure trove of exotic art and furnishings. In the 1940s and '50s his son Richard began his own

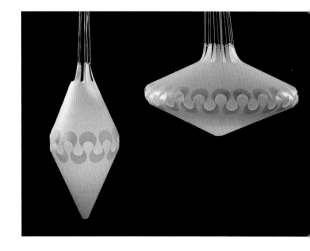

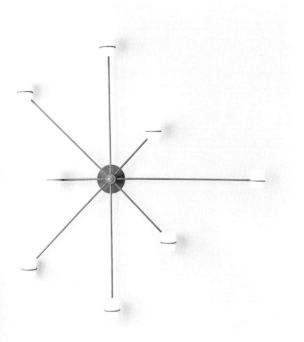

10.16. Display of Pacifica products at Jacksons in Oakland, 1952

10.17. Bruce Hill for Peter Pepper Products. *Starburst* candelabrum, c. 1953. Cat. 132

10.18. Merry Renk. *Folded* hairband, 1954. Cat. 240

mission to elevate the taste of his consumers. The new Gump's gave "shelf room to a $12.50 piece of California pottery . . . alongside a $1,800 piece of Ming Dynasty porcelain," demonstrating the philosophy behind its proprietor's 1951 book, *Good Taste Costs No More*.[39] Through its "Discovery Shop," Gump's became a patron of modern craft, retailing the work of little-known artisans (Bob Stocksdale was one of many to get his start there) and eventually distributing them through a wholesale business.[40] For Edith Heath, the shop played a seminal role; the success of her 1944 custom line made in the Gump's workshop (and the frustration of fulfilling such a large order by hand) was the impetus for founding her acclaimed company, where the pottery would be made in molds.[41]

Other San Francisco shops, notably Amberg-Hirth, promoted the state's designer-craftsmen. Begun in the early 1930s by artists Ernest Amberg and Hugo Hirth, the small shop represented West Coast craftspeople, including San Francisco jeweler Margaret De Patta and leading Los Angeles ceramists Laura Andreson, Glen Lukens, and Gertrud and Otto Natzler.[42] In the 1950s De Patta sold her work through Nanny's Design in Jewelry, the leading emporium for modern jewelry, which also carried works by Bob Winston (see cat. 314) and Merry Renk (10.18).[43] On Sutter Street, the Pacific Shop (associated with the

Wendy Kaplan and Staci Steinberger

larger Robert M. Kasper shop) offered Heath Ceramics along with work by other small California companies, including Peter Pepper Products (10.17) and Hawk House.[44] Agnes Brandenstein's Cargoes Inc. carried both local and international designs—for example, exhibiting in 1941 the landscape work of Thomas Dolliver Church and the furniture of Alvar Aalto.[45]

Southern Californians seeking the Scandinavian designs so resonant with California modern could find them at Barker Brothers in Los Angeles or Frank Brothers in Long Beach.[46] Two decades after Kem Weber had fought for a modern shop there, Barker Brothers proudly advertised a new "Block-long Modern Shop," dedicating its fifth floor to the style.[47] In contrast, Frank Brothers (and especially co-owner Edward Frank) embraced modern design as its sole mission in 1938, playing a central role in the tightly knit Los Angeles–area design community (10.19). "One of the largest all-modern stores in the country" by 1948, the store offered contemporary designs at all price points (10.20).[48] Edward Frank, who argued that consumers were ready for modern design (if only they could see it), lectured and wrote extensively about the subject, becoming one of its most vocal advocates. The store launched many Eames designs (10.21) and promoted other progressive furniture companies such as Glenn of California, which was founded by two former Frank Brothers

10.19. Carlos Diniz for Killingsworth, Brady & Smith. Frank Brothers Furniture, Long Beach (exterior perspective), 1963. Cat. 67

10.20. Advertisement for Frank Brothers furniture store, *Arts and Architecture*, November 1949

employees.[49] In the 1960s Edward and his nephew Ron would further blur the lines between culture and commerce by mounting their own design exhibitions (including *Selections from California Design 10* in 1968). As Long Beach reporter Shirley Ray observed at the Frank Brothers' Danish design exhibition in 1961, these shows made modern design even more accessible, and "as a result, the furniture that was displayed on pedestals in the New York Metropolitan Museum one year ago [in *Arts of Denmark*] will soon be found in living rooms throughout Southern California."[50]

The Frank Brothers' aesthetic reached an even larger audience through the store's involvement in the Case Study Houses. Beginning with Case Study House #2 (1945–47) by Sumner Spaulding and John Rex, the store furnished many of the houses, an association they proudly announced in their monthly advertisements in *Arts and Architecture*. Usually, these carefully composed furnishing schemes did not belong to the homeowners; they served only as props for the photo shoots, as did the products of other companies whose designs appear in images of the Case Study Houses.[51]

The wide distribution of these staged images, especially those by Julius Shulman, did much to reinforce the exaggerated impression that California was, as many writers asserted, "a state where modern interiors are the norm."[52]

FRANK BROS. *feature prominent contemporary interior design—including the work of such prominent designers as (from top left to right): Eames, Saarinen, Robsjohn-Gibbings, Nelson, Martine, Testa, Grossman, Noguchi, Van Keppel, and Green.*

2400 AMERICAN AVENUE • LONG BEACH • CALIFORNIA • PHONE LONG BEACH 4-8137

Frank Bros.

Shulman would often select the furnishings for his shoots from local stores, repeating objects like Van Keppel-Green's metal-and-cord chaise so often that, from the magazines, they seemed an essential part of every California home (see 10.1 and 10.5). Esther McCoy satirized this practice in the *New Yorker*; in her fictionalized critique, a baffled homeowner curiously examines "the low metal frames . . . strung with white cord" that have replaced her own furniture for the architectural photoshoot of her "Important House."[53] In addition, many architects bemoaned, as Richard Neutra did, the "architectural schizophrenia" with which clients furnished their homes when left to their own devices; publicity shoots gave these architects the opportunity to fulfill their own ambitions for the space.[54] Impressed by Van Keppel-Green's pure geometric forms, Pierre Koenig worked closely with the store to select all the pieces that appear in Shulman's photographs of Case Study House #22.[55]

The company was founded in 1939 to manufacture Hendrik Van Keppel and Taylor Green's designs; the partners established a Beverly Hills showroom in 1948. Soon the showroom expanded into a popular design store, offering not only their own furniture but also works by similar-minded designers and craftsmen, from De Patta jewelry to Tupperware[56] (10.22; see 6.5 and 6.6). Though still a minority taste, by the late 1940s the market for modern design in Southern California had grown large enough to support several shops, notably California Contempora and Kneedler-Fauchere in Los Angeles and Armin Richter in La Jolla.

The fashion industry took advantage of the increasing interest in experimental design to add cachet to its own business. In 1947 Cyril Magnin, head of the trendsetting clothing store Joseph Magnin, affirmed, "I have always believed in good design. I believe it pays," and he argued that well-designed advertising would tell customers "that we *know* fashion."[57] Over the next twenty years, Magnin expanded to over thirty locations, most of them designed by Victor Gruen Associates under the direction of partner Rudi Baumfeld. Gruen's team, which included graphic designer Marion Sampler and young designers Gere Kavanaugh and Frank Gehry, developed the interior of each store to suggest shops on a busy street, incorporating dramatic signage and wall graphics, fashionable furniture, and even handcrafted sculpture by artists such as Ruth Asawa and Claire Falkenstein.[58]

Baumfeld's interiors, along with the packages and advertisements art-directed by Marget Larsen, emphasized the bold patterns and colors of Joseph Magnin's clothing (see 9.26). Magnin's buyers deliberately chose intense hues, in sharp contrast to the classic black favored in New York.[59] Color, in fact, became part of the state's unofficial brand, a visual signifier of the "California" that many companies added to their names (Cole of California, Glenn of California, and others). As editor Conrad Brown wrote in his introduction to *Craft Horizons'* special issue on California, "Bright colors seem brighter and warm colors warmer in that brilliant saturation of sunlight that Californians . . . have so much right to

boast about."[60] The strategy spanned decades of boosterism. In the 1930s the California Pottery Guild (an association of companies producing solid-color dinnerware) had proclaimed "California Color Captures Customers."[61] Three decades later, *California Design 8* devoted a whole section to bright orange objects, arguing that the "native color" of sunshine and oranges was a natural design tool[62] (10.23).

A pinnacle of this sun-drenched optimism, Disneyland, opened in 1955. Visitors entered through Disney's nostalgic vision of Main Street USA, after which they could journey to the fantastical (but as yet unfinished) Tomorrowland. Two years later, the MIT-designed Monsanto Home of the Future was erected, and the millions who walked through the modular fiberglass prototype marveled at the limitless range of forms they would be able to purchase in a plastic future[63] (10.24). Thanks to the wildly popular *Disneyland* television program, children (and likely adults) across the nation saw the Anaheim theme park as the state's essential destination, the culmination of its golden promise.[64] Disney's next television venture, the *Mickey Mouse Club*, introduced the country to another symbol of American aspiration, Mattel's Barbie, first advertised on the program in 1959.[65] A dramatic break from traditional baby dolls, the "Teenage Fashion Model" first arrived in a chic swimsuit (see p. 24). Her elaborate costumes

10.21. Charles Eames and Ray Eames for Herman Miller. *ESU* (Eames storage unit), c. 1949. Cat. 78
Frank Brothers was an early retailer of the Eames storage unit.

10.22. Advertisement for Van Keppel-Green shop, *Arts and Architecture*, May 1956

10.23. Grouping from "California Design in Native Color Orange," in *California Design 8* (Pasadena: Pasadena Art Museum, 1962), p. 22
Designers included here are Wes Williams (wall hanging and stool), Van Keppel-Green (library table), Selje and Bond for Peter Pepper Products (clock), John Follis for Architectural Pottery (urns), and Gere Kavanaugh (wallpaper).

10.24. Monsanto Chemical Company. *The Future Won't Wait*, 1960. Cat. 337
San Diego designer Vincent Bonini was hired to redecorate the Home of the Future at Disneyland only three years after it opened. The brochure states that he updated the design "to conform to the flowing curves of the house's plastic shell," anticipating that such trends would become standard "as houses emerge from the conventional cube."

allowed young girls to act out their own dreams of a California future. Naturally, this fantasy included a comfortable but modern "Dream House"—a cardboard ranch complete with an Architectural Pottery–like planter and Scandinavian-inspired furnishings (10.25).

Commercials by Carson/Roberts, a prominent Los Angeles advertising firm, presented Barbie as a human celebrity, a conceit Art Buchwald satirized in a series of newspaper columns. He saw Barbie's constant need to add accessories (ever more clothing, shoes, and cars) as an example of rampant consumerism, but his was a minority viewpoint.[66] The doll's legions of fans saw these props as central to their play scenarios and even made requests beyond the company's offerings. In 1961 Mattel introduced Ken (cat. 125) in response to hundreds of letters pleading for a boyfriend for Barbie.[67] Toys like Barbie allowed the baby boomer generation to experiment with adult roles but also exposed them to adult preoccupations. Designers created playthings that aimed to domesticate real-world problems and encourage children to seek solutions. Architect Sewall Smith invoked the ultimate fear of their era—nuclear annihilation—in a board game called *Boom! Or Golden Age!* (10.26). Unlike Disney's embrace of "Our Friend the Atom" (see 6.28), the game captured not only the optimism but also the dread of its era, challenging players to achieve unity between nations before the bomb was dropped. Inspired by Smith's pledge to donate the profits to real peacekeeping agencies, Eleanor Roosevelt praised the game in her nationally syndicated newspaper column, noting, "If it will help peace, I am sure we will all play it every day of the week."[68]

In contrast, many designers believed that more abstract toys, which gave children the license to invent their own worlds, were best suited for spreading progressive ideals.[69] Charles and Ray Eames were advocates for the power of play; as Charles asserted, "Toys and games are the preludes to serious ideas."[70] Their designs for children, such as the *House of Cards* (see 9.17) and the *Hang-It-All* (10.27), used bold graphics and open-ended directives as frameworks for self-directed play. (The *Hang-It-All* was advertised as simply "For Children to Hang Things On.") A *Progressive Architecture* article from 1966 argues that the point of modern toys was not "whether she will grow up to like 'modern' architecture, but whether she will be pleased by matters of form, relationship, integrity." Among the many examples illustrated were Gere Kavanaugh's wooden blocks, whose geometric buildings and cylindrical flowers would give children free range as city planners[71] (10.28).

The enormous influence that the Case Study Houses had in Europe as well as South America has been well documented by architectural critic Reyner Banham. In one telling anecdote, he recounts, "In many offices that I used to visit in the London of the middle fifties, pages from *Arts and Architecture* were often pinned up on the corkboard above the designers' work stations, and the products of this inspiration could be clearly seen on the drafting boards below."

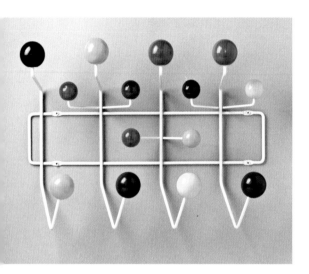

Banham also wrote of first seeing the Eameses' molded-plywood chairs in *Arts and Architecture* in 1949: "Here were designed objects that clearly subscribed to the moral imperatives and material mythologies of the modern movement, yet looked nothing like the International Style furniture."[72] The prominent writers and architects Peter and Alison Smithson became Britain's biggest champions of the Eameses' house (Case Study House #8) as well as their furniture, embracing the relaxed, informal modernism that had so appealed to Banham.

Less known is the impact of California designers other than Charles and Ray Eames, who were not the only designers to achieve recognition outside the United States, although they were certainly the most influential. Craftspeople and designers showed their work at international expositions; for example, in addition to the Eameses' fiberglass chairs, Bob Stocksdale's wood bowls (see 7.9) were exhibited at the Brussels Expo in 1958 (the first world's fair of the postwar period); and Ruth Asawa's sculpture was acclaimed in the Art of the Pacific Coast section at the third São Paulo Bienal, in 1955 (10.29, center). California designers were chosen for Europe's leading design fair, the Triennale in Milan: in 1964 both Katherine Westphal and Ed Rossbach displayed their textiles there, and Hobie Surfboards was awarded a gold medal.[73]

Periodicals and books, however, were the main source of dissemination. American shelter magazines were read in Europe, and California designers were frequently discussed in the most highly regarded compendia of international design, such as *Domus*, *Graphis*, and *Idea*. In the 1950s the designer Roberto Aloi compiled the series *Esempi di arredamento moderno di tutto il mondo* (Examples of international modern interior decoration), with volumes focusing on different forms, including seating furniture, tables, light fixtures, and interiors. Greta Magnusson Grossman, Paul László, Maurice Martiné, Richard Neutra, Bob Stocksdale, Van Keppel-Green, and of course, the ubiquitous Eameses were among the California designers well represented there.[74]

Symbolizing the good life in America, California design became an important agent in Cold War propaganda. To a Europe ravaged by war, America—and California in particular—seemed like a miraculous land of plenty, and the United States government did everything it could to reinforce this impression. Many of the exhibitions circulated by the Marshall Plan (and after 1953, by the United States Information Agency) focused on modern consumer goods. The exhibition *Design for Use, USA*, which toured Europe between 1951 and 1953, exemplifies this effort to demonstrate that the economic renewal of Europe would come from adopting the American model. Organized by *Good Design* impresario Edgar Kaufmann Jr. at MoMA, the exhibition included many California designers and craftspeople: Allan Adler, F. Carlton Ball, the Eameses, Greta Magnusson Grossman, Edith Heath, the Natzlers, La Gardo Tackett, and Van Keppel-Green.[75] Historian Greg Castillo has written about the ideology underlying such exhibitions, in which the "soft power" of the modern appliances, furnishings, and model

Wendy Kaplan and Staci Steinberger

homes would convince people to follow the path of capitalist democracy.[76]

The Eameses helped reinforce this portrayal of the bounty available to any American with their multiscreen presentation *Glimpses of the USA*, shown to millions of people at the *American National Exhibition* in Moscow (1959). However, it was another Californian, Richard Nixon, whose encounter with Nikita Khrushchev at the opening of the exhibition demonstrates the ultimate "soft power" confrontation. In what became known as the "kitchen debate," Nixon attempted to prove the inferiority of communism by showing Khrushchev the shining new appliances in the model house on display. He said: "I want to show you this kitchen. It is like those of our houses in California."[77] That the kitchen was actually made by a firm in Florida attests to the common conflation of American material abundance with the Golden State.

The California presented to the world through publications, exhibitions, and stores was an idealized view, carefully cultivated by the designers, critics, curators, and retailers who promoted California products as entrées into a carefree, comfortable future. Modern living, as they described it, was for everyone—a vision belied by the fact that most people lived in nondescript or revival-style homes and that racial and class inequalities barred many Californians from sharing the state's abundance.

Yet the promise was real in an age of unprecedented American economic growth. California had the highest living standard in the country, and the exuberant claims of its boosters seemed well within reach. Its new technology, materials, and forms would be the harbingers of domestic paradise. A region that, only decades before, had been portrayed as pastoral became a beacon of modernity, as audiences around the world were persuaded to look to California as a portent of a better life. Eudorah Moore echoed the prevailing sentiment when she said that people on the West Coast "are pioneering busily in advance of the national culture."[78] It was this optimistic faith in innovation, in the state's "zestful sense of why not" and the products it generated, that made California loom so large in the American, and indeed the world's, imagination.[79]

10.27. Charles Eames and Ray Eames for Tigrett Enterprises. *Hang-It-All*, 1953. Cat. 81

10.28. Gere Kavanaugh. City-planning toy (prototype), c. 1965. Cat. 147 **Designed for an article in *Progressive Architecture*, the toy was also exhibited in *California Design 10*, 1968, but never went into production.**

NOTES

1 Shulman, quoted in Marylou Luther, "So You Want to Be a Photographer? Know the Negative, Warns Professional," undated article from an unidentified newspaper, Shulman Archives, quoted in Joseph Rosa, *A Constructed View: The Architectural Photography of Julius Shulman* (New York: Rizzoli, 1994), 88.

2 See Beatriz Colomina, *Domesticity at War* (Cambridge, Mass.: MIT Press, 2007); Greg Castillo, *Cold War on the Home Front: The Soft Power of Midcentury Design* (Minneapolis: University of Minnesota Press, 2010); Cynthia Lee Henthorn, *From Submarines to Suburbs: Selling a Better America, 1939–1959* (Athens: Ohio University Press, 2006); and David Crowley and Jane Pavitt, eds., *Cold War Modern: Design, 1945–1970*, exh. cat. (London: V and A Publishing, 2008).

3 *Life*, October 19, 1962; the quote is from the cover of this special issue.

4 "California Scrapbook: West Coast Artists Set Decorative Trends in Motion," *House and Garden*, December 1947, 123.

5 "Our New Kind of Living Calls for Indoor-Outdoor Furniture," *House Beautiful*, October 1952, 311.

6 Edgar Kaufmann, Jr., *What Is Modern Design?* (New York: Museum of Modern Art, 1950), 8.

7 Colomina, *Domesticity at War*, 12.

8 Esther McCoy, *Case Study Houses, 1945–1962*, 2nd ed. (Santa Monica: Hennessey and Ingalls, 1977), 9. See also Susan Morgan, "Being There: Esther McCoy, the Accidental Architectural Historian," *Archives of American Art Journal* 48 (Spring 2009): 19–45.

9 David Gebhard and Robert Winter, *A Guide to Architecture in Southern California* (Los Angeles: Los Angeles County Museum of Art, 1965), 17.

10 Mary Melton, "The Making of an Icon," *LA Magazine*, July 2001, reprinted in Elizabeth A. T. Smith, *Case Study Houses* (Cologne: Taschen, 2002), 314–15.

11 Monica Penick, "The Pace Setter Houses: Livable Modernism in Postwar America" (PhD diss., University of Texas at Austin, 2007).

12 "The Arts of Daily Living," *House Beautiful*, October 1954, 167.

13 Ibid.

14 Edgar Kaufmann, Jr., and Finn Juhl, "Good Design '51 as Seen by Its Director and by Its Designer," *Interiors* 110 (March 1951): 100, quoted in Mary Anne Staniszewski, *The Power of Display: A History of Exhibition Installations at the Museum of Modern Art* (Cambridge, Mass.: MIT Press, 1998), 176.

15 The lamp and textile by Olga Lee were illustrated in Virginia Stewart, "Southern California Work Selected for Good Design Exhibits," *Los Angeles Times*, July 26, 1953, H6 and H7. The table by Gene Tepper was illustrated in Virginia Stewart, "These California Items Selected from the New York and Chicago Exhibition May Be Seen at Long Beach Art Center," *Los Angeles Times*, April 25, 1954, L12.

16 "News Release from the Pasadena Art Institute. First All-California Good Design Exhibition," n.d., box 1, California Design Archive. Oakland Museum of California. For more about the *California Design* exhibitions, see Jo Lauria and Suzanne Baizerman, *California Design: The Legacy of West Coast Craft and Style* (San Francisco: Chronicle Books, 2005).

17 Fulton, quoted in Armin Kietzmann, "Pacific Design: Inventive Yet Conciliatory," *San Diego Union*, February 12, 1956, reprinted as an undated press release by the Pasadena Art Museum, box 2, California Design Archive. Kietzmann is quoting from a speech made by Joseph Fulton at the opening of the first *California Design* exhibition.

18 Elaine K. Sewell, "These Are California Designed," *Los Angeles Times*, August 21, 1955, 118.

19 Letter, Grace McCann Morley to Robert Held (owner of the Pacific Shop), June 12, 1953, folder 20, box 40, Exhibition Records, San Francisco Museum of Modern Art (SFMOMA) Archives. For more on Morley, see Kara Kirk, "Grace McCann Morley and the Modern Museum," in *San Francisco Museum of Modern Art: 75 Years of Looking Forward*, exh. cat. (San Francisco: San Francisco Museum of Modern Art, 2009), 71–82.

20 Allan Adler, invoice to San Francisco Museum of Art, April 20, 1949, for the exhibition *Design in the Living Room*, folder 24, box 31, Exhibition Records, SFMOMA Archives.

21 Richard B. Freeman (assistant director, SFMA), *Design in the Kitchen* (San Francisco: San Francisco Museum of Art, 1949), n.p., folder 2, box 31, Exhibition Records, SFMOMA Archives.

22 Allon T. Schoener to Luther W. Conover, October 8, 1951, folder 17, box 94, Administrative Records, SFMOMA Archives.

23 Arthur Millier, *The Arts in Western Living* (Pomona: Los Angeles County Fair

10.29. Ruth Asawa. Center: *S.250* sculpture, c. 1955. Cat. 14. Left and right: Untitled sculptures, c. 1955, height: 123 in. (315.4 cm); and c. 1968, height: 102 in. (259.1 cm). Fine Arts Museums of San Francisco, Gift of Jacqueline Hoefer

Association, 1955), n.p. The quote cited here is from the first page of the introduction.

24 Ibid. The concluding essay was written by Richard Petterson, the fair's director of Arts and Crafts, who worked under Millard Sheets.

25 Elizabeth F. G. Hanson and Eudorah M. Moore, statement dated June 8, 1961, box 4, California Design Archive. Moore codirected the 1962 exhibition with Hanson; from 1965 to the last *California Design* exhibition in 1976, she was sole director.

26 "California Design IX Progress Report," December 2, 1963, box 4, California Design Archive.

27 "California Design IX Recap," in *California Design 10* (brochure), 1968, box 6, California Design Archive. The California Design Archive contains numerous files of clippings from magazines and newspapers about the exhibitions, attesting to the success of Moore's efforts.

28 Ibid. Copies of these filmstrips and the interpretive brochures are also in the California Design Archive.

29 Lori Ann Lindberg, "California Design Archives, 1955–1984" (master's thesis, San Jose State University, 2000), 20.

30 "Carson Pirie Scott Promotion," September 30, 1965, box 30, California Design Archive.

31 Pasadena Art Museum press release, March 8, 1962, box 4, California Design Archive.

32 Eudorah Moore to "Gentlemen," n.d., box 5, California Design Archive.

33 *California Design 8* (Pasadena: Pasadena Art Museum, 1962), 38.

34 "California Scrapbook," 123. See also Henry Dreyfuss, "California: World's New Design Center," *Western Advertising*, June 1947, 60.

35 Fay Hammond, "Apparel Industry Marks New Step in Style World," *Los Angeles Times*, August 15, 1944, A14; "California's Corridor Is Cooperative," *Retailing Daily*, December 1, 1952, 26.

36 Quote from Harry Jackson's unpublished memoir, "Pacifica Designs: The Pacifica Story," 1994, 2, http://www.rcj.com/PacificaDesigns.pdf. Jackson's passion for Pacifica (which even led him to open Pacifica departments in the Japanese department store chain Takashimaya in 1962) outlived his family business. When Jacksons closed in 1965, Harry Jackson established the smaller Pacifica Designs shop in San Francisco.

37 "Pacifica," *Arts and Architecture*, June 1952, 21.

38 "Pacifica: A New Mood in Decorating," *House and Garden*, April 1952, 98–99. This issue features a number of articles on Pacifica furnishings. See also "Harry Jackson Presents a Distinguished Company," *Interiors*, April 1952, 126–31; "Pacifica," *Arts and Architecture*, June 1952, 20–22; "Eastward Ho: California Home Styles Invade Rest of U.S.," *Life*, March 17, 1952, 131–35; "Trends Pacific Supplement," *Retailing Daily*, December 1, 1952. Thanks to Steve Cabella for providing this reference. For the de Young exhibition, see "Furnishings of the Pacific," *Counterpoint*, May 1952, 24–25.

39 "Gump's Goes Modern," *Time*, May 30, 1949, 78; "Gump's: One of a Kind," *Business Week*, December 21, 1963, 46–53. Richard Gump, *Good Taste Costs No More* (Garden City, N.Y.: Doubleday, 1951).

40 "Gump's Announces New Wholesale Department," *Western Home Furnisher*, November 1947, 9, 24, in box 1, Frank Brothers records, 1929–2005, Research Library, Getty Research Institute.

41 Bob Stocksdale, interview by Signe Mayfield, February 16–March 21, 2001, Archives of American Art, Smithsonian Institution; Edith Heath, "Tableware and Tile for the World, Heath Ceramics, 1944–1994," interview by Rosalie Ross, 1990–92, 1994, Regional Oral History Office, Bancroft Library, University of California, Berkeley.

42 "The Garden on the Cover," *Sunset*, November 1936, 15; "Amberg-Hirth of San Francisco," *Design*, May 1944, 18. Amberg-Hirth was bought out by Cargoes Inc. in 1952. See advertisement, *Counterpoint*, March 1952, 4.

43 "A San Francisco Jewelry Shop: It Buys to Sell," *Craft Horizons*, July–August 1957, 12–13. Thanks to Julie Muñiz for this reference. Merry Renk, interview by Arline Fisch, January 18–19, 2001, Archives of American Art, Smithsonian Institution.

44 Advertisement for Pacific Shop, *Arts and Architecture*, December 1947, 20; *For Holiday Giving for Holiday Living from Pacific Shop* (catalogue), n.d. Thanks to Steve Cabella for this reference.

45 Dorothée Imbert, "Byways to Modernism: The Early Landscapes," in *Thomas Church, Landscape Architect: Designing a Modern California Landscape*, ed. Marc Treib (San Francisco: William Stout, 2003), 42.

46 Advertisement for Aalto designs, *Arts and Architecture*, November 1947, 15.

47 Advertisement for Barker Brothers, *Arts and Architecture*, May 1947, 4. The block-long incarnation was new, but Barker Brothers had already prominently advertised its fifth-floor Modern Shop in several prior issues of *Arts and Architecture*, beginning in 1946.

48 Quote from "Where to Buy Well Designed Objects," *Everyday Art Quarterly*, Spring 1948, 1–5. For a sample of Frank Brothers prices, see their advertisement in *Arts and Architecture*, October 1949, 19. The company that became Frank Brothers was founded by Edward's brother Maurice and their father, Louis; Ron Frank is Maurice's son. Ron began working at the store in 1954 and became president in 1965, when the company split. Edward then headed Moreddi, originally the brothers' separate design import firm.

49 Hector Arce, "Design Success," *Home Furnishings Daily*, March 10, 1969, 9. The Eames and Glenn connections were discussed by Ron Frank with Bobbye Tigerman, April 3, 2007. Glenn of California was founded by Stanley Glenn Young and Harold Rose.

50 Shirley Ray, "Danish Furniture Display Now Here," *Independent Press-Telegram*, December 7, 1961. Ray is referring to *Arts of Denmark: Viking to Modern* at the Metropolitan Museum of Art, New York, October 14, 1960–January 8, 1961. See Rosine Raoul, "The Danish Tradition in Design," *Metropolitan Museum of Art Bulletin*, December 1960, 120–24.

51 For a Frank Brothers' advertisement, see, for example, *Arts and Architecture*, April 1947, 8. And Dan Johnson's furniture line (see p. 4) appeared in photographs by Harry H. Baskerville Jr. of Rodney Walker's Case Study House #17, published in *Arts and Architecture*, July 1947, 40–42.

52 Conrad Brown, "California," *Craft Horizons*, September–October 1956, 11.

53 Esther McCoy, "The Important House," *New Yorker*, April 17, 1948, 54.

54 "New Shells," *Time*, August 15, 1949, 58–62. See also Simon Niedenthal, "'Glamourized Houses:' Neutra, Photography, and the Kaufmann House," *Journal of Architectural Education*, November 1993, 101–12.

55 Melton, "Making of an Icon," 314–15.

56 "Tubular Steel, Cord, and Glass: Van Keppel-Green Combines Them in Furniture," *Interiors*, July 1947, 92–93. "Confidence in Sound Modern Furniture Spurs California Design Team," *Christian Science Monitor*, March 17, 1954, 13; advertisement for Van Keppel-Green, *Arts and Architecture*, November 1948, 20; advertisement for Van Keppel-Green, *Arts*

and *Architecture*, November 1949, 7. In 1956 the store moved again, to an even larger location near Santa Monica and Wilshire Boulevards, on Lasky Drive.

57 "A Merchandiser Stresses Design," *Western Advertising*, July 1947, 43. For the growth of Joseph Magnin, see "J. Magnin Planning 14 Stores in Area," *Los Angeles Times*, February 27, 1964, B9; and "Why Amfac Got Rid of Joseph Magnin," *Business Week*, July 4, 1977, 19.

58 "Practical Principles of Interior Design: An Interview with Rudi Baumfeld, Partner, Victor Gruen Associates," for *Interior Design*, 1967. Rudi Baumfeld file, Gruen Associates, Los Angeles office. For descriptions of some of these interiors, see "Variety with Integration in San Francisco," *Interiors*, June 1961, 106–7; "Graphic Design and Allied Arts Play Important Role in the Design of West Coast Store," *Architectural Record*, May 1967, 184–85.

59 Ellen Magnin Newman, conversation with Wendy Kaplan, May 14, 2010.

60 Conrad Brown, "California," *Craft Horizons*, September–October 1956, 11.

61 Advertisement, *Creative Designs in Home Furnishings*, September 1937.

62 *California Design 8* (Pasadena: Pasadena Art Museum, 1962), 21. *California Design 9* would include a more broadly conceived section called "Accent on Color."

63 Karal Ann Marling, "Imagineering the Disney Theme Parks," in *Designing Disney's Theme Parks: The Architecture of Reassurance*, exh. cat., ed. Karal Ann Marling (Montreal: Canadian Centre for Architecture; Paris and New York: Flammarion, 1997), 144–46. Neal Gabler, *Walt Disney: The Triumph of the American Imagination* (New York: Vintage Books, 2006), 530–37.

64 Kirse Granat May, *Golden State, Golden Youth: The California Image in Popular Culture, 1955–1966* (Chapel Hill: University of North Carolina Press, 2002), 43–44.

65 Gary S. Cross, *Kids' Stuff: Toys and the Changing World of American Childhood* (Cambridge, Mass.: Harvard University Press, 1997), 165.

66 Art Buchwald, "Status Symbols in the Doll House," *Los Angeles Times*, September 1963, D1; Art Buchwald, "Ken Jilts Barbie for Another Doll," *Los Angeles Times*, November 1963, B1. See also M. G. Lord, *Barbie: The Unauthorized Biography of a Real Doll* (New York: William Morrow, 1994), 41–42.

67 Brock Milton, "Case of the Teen-Age Doll," *New York Times*, April 21, 1963, SM43.

68 Eleanor Roosevelt, "My Day," United Feature Syndicate, September 15, 1951, http://www.gwu.edu/-erpapers/myday/. Thanks to Steve Cabella for this reference.

69 Amy F. Ogata, "Creative Playthings: Educational Toys and Postwar American Culture," *Winterthur Portfolio*, Summer–Autumn 2004, 129–56.

70 Quoted in James B. O'Connell, "A Visit with Charles Eames," *Think*, April 1961, 9.

71 Quote from "The Child at Play in a World of Form," *Progressive Architecture*, April 1966, 198. Kavanaugh's toy appears on 197.

72 Reyner Banham, "Klarheit, Ehrlichkeit, Einfachkeit . . . and Wit Too! The Case Study Houses in the World's Eyes," in *Blueprints for Modern Living: History and Legacy of the Case Study Houses*, exh. cat. (Los Angeles: Museum of Contemporary Art; Cambridge, Mass.: MIT Press, 1989), 183, 186.

73 *Tredicesima Triennale di Milano*, exh. cat. (Milan: Palazzo dell'Arte al Parco Milano, 1964), 49.

74 See Roberto Aloi, *Esempi di arredamento moderno di tutto il mondo* (Milan: Ulrico Hoepli), volumes from the 1950s.

75 *Industrie und Handwerk schaffen neues Hausgerät in USA*, exh. cat. (Stuttgart: Landesgewerbemuseum, 1951). See also Gay McDonald, "The 'Advance' of American Postwar Design in Europe: MoMA and the *Design for Use, USA* Exhibition 1951–1953," *Design Issues* 24 (Spring 2008): 15–27.

76 Castillo, *Cold War on the Home Front*, xi; see also Jack Masey and Conway Lloyd Morgan, *Cold War Confrontations: US Exhibitions and Their Role in the Cultural Cold War* (Baden, Switzerland: Lars Müller, 2008).

77 "The Two Worlds: A Day-Long Debate," *New York Times*, July 25, 1959, 1.

78 Eudorah Moore, "The Designer Is Knocking. Are You Listening?" (lecture to the National Home Fashions League and the Fashion Group, Chicago, January 7, 1969), 3, box 35, California Design Archive. In this quote, Moore is paraphrasing a speech by Dr. Howard Mumford Jones of Harvard.

79 Ibid. In this quote, Moore is paraphrasing Henry Dreyfuss.

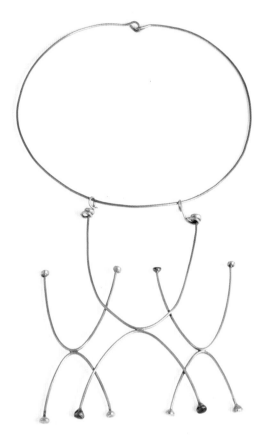

10.30. Claire Falkenstein. Necklace, c. 1948. Cat. 88

Overleaf

James Lovera. Bowl, 1953. Cat. 180

Margit Fellegi for Cole of California. Woman's swimsuit and skirt, c. 1944. Cat. 92

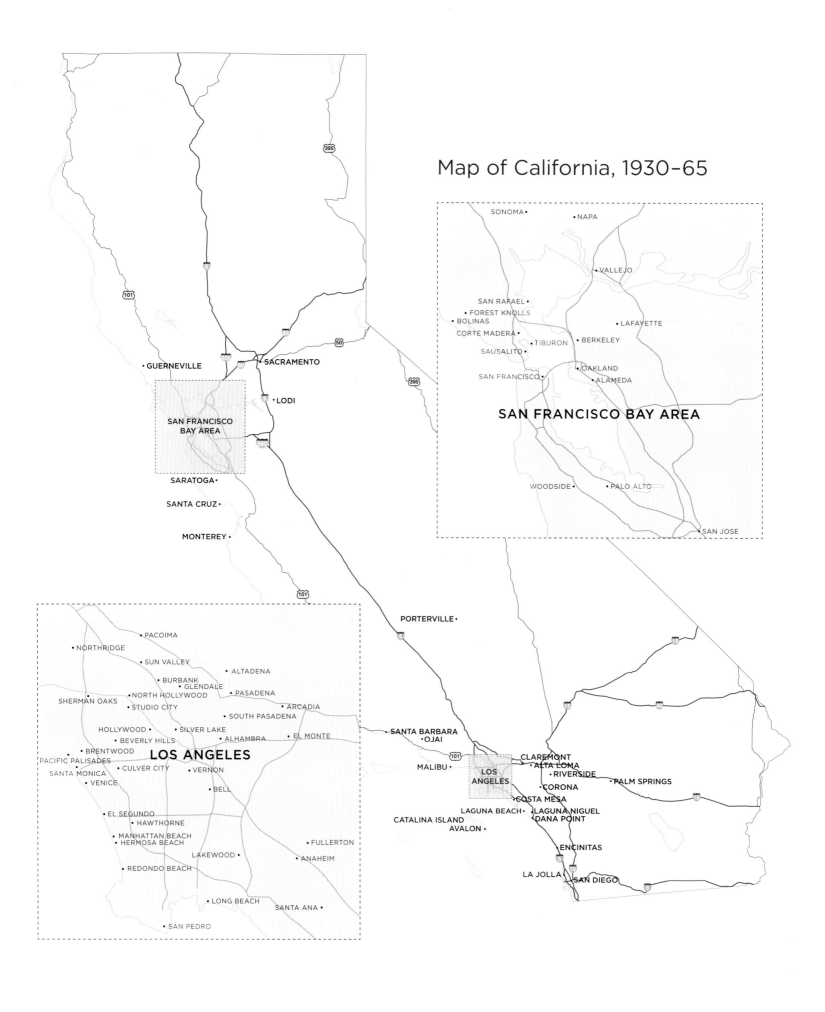

Map of California, 1930–65

SAN FRANCISCO BAY AREA

SONOMA •
• NAPA
• VALLEJO
SAN RAFAEL •
• FOREST KNOLLS
• BOLINAS
CORTE MADERA •
SAUSALITO •
• TIBURON
• BERKELEY
LAFAYETTE
• OAKLAND
SAN FRANCISCO •
• ALAMEDA
WOODSIDE •
• PALO ALTO
• SAN JOSE

• GUERNEVILLE
• SACRAMENTO

SAN FRANCISCO
BAY AREA

• LODI

SARATOGA •

SANTA CRUZ •

MONTEREY •

PORTERVILLE •

LOS ANGELES

• PACOIMA
• NORTHRIDGE
• SUN VALLEY
• ALTADENA
• BURBANK
• GLENDALE
• PASADENA
SHERMAN OAKS •
• NORTH HOLLYWOOD
• ARCADIA
• STUDIO CITY
• SOUTH PASADENA
HOLLYWOOD •
• SILVER LAKE
• BEVERLY HILLS
• ALHAMBRA
• EL MONTE
• BRENTWOOD
PACIFIC PALISADES •
LOS ANGELES
SANTA MONICA •
• CULVER CITY
• VERNON
• VENICE
• BELL
• EL SEGUNDO
• HAWTHORNE
• MANHATTAN BEACH
• HERMOSA BEACH
• FULLERTON
LAKEWOOD •
• ANAHEIM
• REDONDO BEACH
• LONG BEACH
SANTA ANA •
• SAN PEDRO

SANTA BARBARA •
• OJAI
MALIBU •
CLAREMONT •
• ALTA LOMA
• RIVERSIDE
LOS ANGELES
• CORONA
• PALM SPRINGS
COSTA MESA •
LAGUNA BEACH •
• LAGUNA NIGUEL
• DANA POINT
CATALINA ISLAND •
AVALON •
• ENCINITAS
LA JOLLA •
• SAN DIEGO

Checklist of the Exhibition

By Bobbye Tigerman, Staci Steinberger, and Jennifer Munro Miller

Objects are listed alphabetically by designer. For designers with multiple objects, those objects are grouped by manufacturers or collaborators and listed chronologically within each group. Locations refer to places in California, unless otherwise indicated. The "active" location for each designer refers to the place or places in California where the designer worked during the period covered by the exhibition (1930–65). Brentwood, Century City, Hollywood, Hollywood Hills, North Hollywood, Northridge, Pacific Palisades, Pacoima, San Pedro, Sherman Oaks, Silver Lake, Sun Valley, and Venice are neighborhoods in Los Angeles. Model and style numbers, when known, appear after the name of the object. The date specified for each work is the design date; when documented, the date of manufacture is also listed. For groups of objects, dimensions are provided for only the largest one; height precedes width precedes depth. A checklist of the ephemera included in the exhibition begins on p. 341.

The checklist is accurate as of May 2011.

EVELYN ACKERMAN

(b. 1924, active Culver City)

JEROME ACKERMAN

(b. 1920, active Culver City)

ERA Industries (Culver City, 1956–present)

1 *Ellipses* **mosaic**, c. 1958
Made in Mexico
Exhibited in *California Design 4*, Pasadena
Art Museum, 1958
Glass mosaic
12¾ x 60½ x 1 in. (32.4 x 153.7 x 2.5 cm)
Collection of Hilary and James McQuaide
Fig. 7.21

ACME BOOTS

(Clarksville, Tennessee, founded 1929)

2 **Woman's cowboy boots**, 1930s
Leather
Each: 11¼ x 10¼ x 3⅞ in. (28.6 x 26 x 9.8 cm)
Courtesy of Museum of the American West,
Autry National Center; 88.126.3.1-.2

ALLAN ADLER (1916–2002, active Los Angeles)

3 *Teardrop* **coffeepot (173g), teapot (175g),
creamer and sugar (174g)**, c. 1957
Silver, ebony
Coffeepot, height: 10 in. (25.4 cm);
diameter: 9 in. (22.7 cm)
Collection of Rebecca Adler (Mrs. Allan
Adler)
Fig. 7.17

GILBERT ADRIAN

(1903–1959, active Los Angeles)

Adrian Ltd. (Beverly Hills, 1942–52)

4 **Woman's two-piece suit**, 1946–48
Worsted wool twill
Jacket, center-back length: 25¼ in. (64.1 cm);
skirt, center-back length: 26¼ in. (66.7 cm)
LACMA, Purchased with funds provided by
Eleanor La Vove, Maryon Patricia Lears,
Ricki Ring and Gustave Tassell,
M.2003.95a-b
Fig. 8.30

5 **Two-piece dress from** *The Atomic 50s*
collection, 1950
Rayon crepe, rayon faille
Dress, center-back length: 37 in. (94 cm);
bolero, center-back length: 14 in. (35.6 cm)
LACMA, Gift of Mrs. Houston Rehrig,
CR.69.55.5a, b
Fig. 8.31

GREGORY AIN (1908–1988, active Los Angeles)

6 **Dunsmuir Flats**, Los Angeles (exterior
perspective), 1937
Graphite on paper
9¾ x 19¼ in. (24.8 x 48.9 cm)
Gregory Ain Collection, Architecture and
Design Collection, University Art Museum,
UC Santa Barbara
Fig. 4.6

7 **Dunsmuir Flats**, Los Angeles (plan), 1937
Ink on paper
9¼ x 24⅜ in. (23.5 x 61.9 cm)
Gregory Ain Collection, Architecture and
Design Collection, University Art Museum,
UC Santa Barbara
Fig. 4.5

ALEXANDER (n.d.)

8   Plate for Convair Division of General Dynamics, c. 1960
Enamel on copper
Diameter: 7⅞ in. (20 cm)
LACMA, Gift of Wendy Kaplan, M.2010.124
Fig. 6.31

HOBART "HOBIE" ALTER
(b. 1933, active Dana Point)

9   Surfboard, 1961
Owned by Chuck Quinn
Polyurethane foam, redwood, glue,
fiberglass cloth, polyester resin
118 x 22 x 11 in. (300 x 55.9 x 28 cm)
Surfing Heritage Foundation
Fig. 6.17

JOHN ALTOON
(1925–1969, active Los Angeles area)

Pacific Jazz Records (Hollywood, founded
1952), record label
Standard Lithograph (Los Angeles, n.d.), printer

10   Chet Baker Big Band (album cover), 1957
Offset lithography
12¼ x 12¼ in. (31.1 x 31.1 cm)
LACMA, Decorative Arts and Design
Council Fund, M.2010.119.1a-b

LAURA ANDRESON
(1902–1999, active Los Angeles)

11   Bowl, 1940
Earthenware
Height: 8⅞ in. (22.5 cm); diameter: 10¼ in.
(26 cm)
Collection of Forrest L. Merrill
Fig. 7.14

MERLE ARMITAGE (1893–1975, active
Los Angeles), designer and author

E. Weyhe, Inc. (New York, founded 1919),
publisher

12   Elise (book), 1934
Letterpress
13¼ x 10⅛ in. (33.7 x 25.7 cm)
Victoria Dailey and Steve Turner Collection,
Los Angeles
Fig. 9.2

ROBERT ARNESON (1930–1992, active Davis)

13   No Deposit, No Return sculpture, 1961
Made at the California State Fair,
Sacramento
Earthenware
Height: 10¾ in. (27.3 cm); diameter: 5 in.
(12.7 cm)
LACMA, Smits Ceramics Purchase Fund,
Modern Art Deaccession Fund, and the
Decorative Arts Council Acquisition Fund,
M.91.245
Fig. 7.25

RUTH ASAWA (b. 1926, active San Francisco)

14   S.250 sculpture, c. 1955
Exhibited in São Paulo Bienal, 1955
Iron, galvanized steel wire
138 x 17 x 17 in. (350.5 x 43.2 x 43.2 cm)
Fine Arts Museums of San Francisco,
Gift of Jacqueline Hoefer
Fig. 10.29

F. CARLTON BALL
(1911–1992, active Los Angeles)

15   Vase, c. 1966
Stoneware
Height: 59 in. (149.9 cm); diameter: 18 in.
(45.7 cm)
Everson Museum of Art, Gift of Mr. and Mrs.
John D. Williams, 66.64
Fig. 7.10

LOUELLA BALLERINO
(1900–1978, active Los Angeles)

16   Woman's skirt and jacket, 1942
Skirt: rayon faille, grosgrain ribbon,
metallic-yarn trim; jacket: rayon faille
Jacket, center-back length: 17½ in. (44.5 cm);
skirt, center-back length: 43 in. (109.2 cm)
LACMA, Gift of the Fashion Group, Inc., of
Los Angeles, 48.39.30a-b

Jantzen (Portland, Oregon, 1910–present)

17   Playsuit and skirt in Drumbeat pattern, 1947
Printed cotton
Playsuit, center-back length: 27½ in. (69.9 cm);
skirt, center-back length: 27¾ in. (70.5 cm)
LACMA, Gift of Laurel Thornburg,
M.2007.194.5a-b
Fig. 8.16

SAUL BASS (1920–1996, active Los Angeles)

18   Letterhead and envelope for Max Yavno,
c. 1954
Offset lithography
Letterhead: 7 x 8⅜ in. (17.8 x 21.3 cm)
Academy of Motion Picture Arts and
Sciences, Margaret Herrick Library,
Saul Bass papers

Capitol Records (Hollywood, founded 1942),
record label

**19   Frank Sinatra Conducts Tone Poems of
Color** (album cover), 1956
Offset lithography and letterpress
12¼ x 12¼ in. (31.1 x 31.1 cm)
LACMA, Gift of Michael Hodgson
Fig. 9.23

Castle Company (n.d.), printer
Monsen-Los Angeles (Los Angeles, n.d.),
typographer

**20   First Annual Exhibition: Society of
Contemporary Designers** (exhibition
catalogue), 1950
Offset lithography
6 x 8 in. (15.2 x 20.3 cm)
Collection of Louis Danziger

Art Goodman (n.d.), illustrator
Phyllis Tanner (n.d.), illustrator

21   Doggy bag for Lawry's Foods, Inc., 1961
Offset lithography on bleached kraft paper
13 x 4⅞ in. (33 x 12.4 cm)
Academy of Motion Picture Arts and
Sciences, Margaret Herrick Library,
Saul Bass papers

Otto Preminger (b. Romania or Poland,
c. 1906–1986), producer
Carlyle Productions (n.d.)

22   The Man with the Golden Arm
(title sequence), 1955
Film, 1 minute, 20 seconds
Courtesy of Otto Preminger Films Ltd.
Fig. 9.21

23   The Man with the Golden Arm (poster),
1955
Offset lithography
42 x 27⅝ in. (106.5 x 70.2 cm)
Academy of Motion Picture Arts and
Sciences, Margaret Herrick Library,
Saul Bass papers
Fig. 9.22

Otto Preminger, producer
Carlyle Productions
Anderson, Ritchie & Simon (South Pasadena,
founded 1932; formerly Ward Ritchie Press),
printer

24 **The Man with the Golden Arm** (letterhead
and envelope, press-preview invitation,
press-preview survey, album cover), 1955
Offset lithography
Press-preview survey: 12⅝ x 7½ in.
(32.1 x 19.1 cm)
Academy of Motion Picture Arts and
Sciences, Margaret Herrick Library,
Saul Bass papers

MILO BAUGHMAN

(1923–2003, active Los Angeles)

Glenn of California (Arcadia, 1948–92)

25 **Cocktail table**, model 500, c. 1950
Wood, glass, Masonite, aluminum,
stainless steel
14 x 48 x 30 in. (35.6 x 121.9 x 76.2 cm)
Collection of Jill Grey
Fig. 5.23

HARRY BERTOIA (b. Italy, 1915–1978, active
Los Angeles area and La Jolla)

26 **Pin**, 1943–50
Silver, ebony
4¼ x 1⅞ in. (10.8 x 4.8 cm)
Private collection, Miami
Fig. 7.31

PORTER BLANCHARD

(1886–1973, active Los Angeles area)

27 **Clock**, c. 1938
Gold-plated silver
12½ x 11 x 4 in. (31.8 x 27.9 x 10.2 cm)
Collection of Cynthia Adler
Fig. 2.13

28 **Flatware**, c. 1940
Silver
Knife: 9¾ x ⅞ x ⅞ in. (24.8 x 2.2 x 2.2 cm)
Collection of Linda Adler Hughes

29 **Teapot, creamer, and sugar**, c. 1965
Pewter, ebony
Teapot, height: 7½ in. (19.1 cm); diameter:
6¼ in. (15.9 cm)
LACMA, Gift of Cynthia Sikes Yorkin,
M.2009.94.1-.3
Fig. 5.27

MITCHELL BOBRICK

(1921–1979, active Los Angeles)

Controlight Company (Los Angeles, n.d.)

30 **Controlight lamp and bookshelf**, c. 1949
Iron, ceramic, fiberglass
21⅞ x 18¼ x 18 in. (55.6 x 46.4 x 45.7 cm)
LACMA, Purchased with funds provided by
Sam and Gracie Miller, M.2007.236.3
Fig. 6.20

BETTY BRADER

(1923–1986, active San Francisco area)

Fantasy (San Francisco, founded 1949),
record label

31 **Cal Tjader Quintet** (album cover), 1956
Offset lithography
12¼ x 12¼ in. (31.1 x 31.1 cm)
LACMA, Decorative Arts and Design
Council Fund, M.2010.119.3a-b
Fig. 9.24

DURLIN BRAYTON

(1897–1951, active Laguna Beach)

Brayton Laguna Pottery (Laguna Beach, 1927–68)

32 **Dinnerware set**, c. 1930
Earthenware
Dinner plate, diameter: 10 in. (25.4 cm)
Collection of Bill Stern
Fig. 2.18

MARGARET BRUTON

(1894–1983, active Alameda and Monterey)

33 **Mosaic**, c. 1935–40
Concrete, metal, stone
22 x 28 x 1 in. (55.9 x 71.1 x 2.5 cm)
Collection of Teresa and Eric Del Piero
Fig. 1.22

CLARENCE M. BURROUGHS

(1904–1998, active Glendale)

Burroughs Manufacturing Corporation
(Los Angeles area, incorporated 1949)

34 **Pitcher**, c. 1948
Plastic
8½ x 7½ x 3⅝ in. (21.6 x 19.1 x 9.2 cm)
LACMA, Decorative Arts and Design
Council Fund, M.2010.120.1
Fig. 6.3

WALLACE "WALLY" M. BYAM

(1896–1962, active Los Angeles)

Airstream Trailer Company (Los Angeles,
1932–79; Jackson Center, Ohio, 1952–present)

35 **Clipper**, 1936
Aluminum
96 x 228 x 84 in. (243.8 x 579.1 x 213.4 cm)
Auburn Trailer Collection
See p.355

CALIFORNIA HAND PRINTS

(Hermosa Beach, incorporated 1936)

36 **Mexican Sombrero** textile, c. 1941
Cotton
61¼ x 48 in. (155.6 x 121.9 cm)
LACMA, Gift of Esther Ginsberg and Harry
Eden in honor of Bob and Rhonda Heintz,
AC1999.42.1

CARLOS OF PALM SPRINGS (n.d.)

37 **Man's jacket**, c. 1950
Wool tweed
Center-back length: 33 in. (83.8 cm)
LACMA, Gift of Esther Ginsberg,
M.2010.130.1

ARTHUR ESPENET CARPENTER

(1920–2006, active Bolinas)

38 **Rib chair**, 1968
Exhibited in California Design 10,
Pasadena Art Museum, 1968
Laminated walnut, leather
53 x 33 x 35 in. (134.6 x 83.8 x 88.9 cm)
Oakland Museum of California,
Gift of the artist
Fig. 7.34

CATALINA POTTERY (Avalon, 1927–37)

39 **Shrimp cocktail dish**, c. 1934
Earthenware
Height: 4 in. (10.2 cm); diameter: 4½ in.
(11.4 cm)
Collection of Allan and Laurie Carter
Fig. 2.19

40 **Trojan tea set**, c. 1935
Earthenware
Teapot, height: 4⅛ in. (10.5 cm); diameter:
8¾ in. (22.2 cm)
Collection of Dr. Andrew and Deborah Frank
Fig. 2.35

CATALINA/PACIFIC KNITTING MILLS

(Los Angeles, 1907–93; later Catalina Sportswear)

41 Woman's swimsuit, c. 1928
Wool knit
Center-back length: 16½ in. (41.9 cm)
LACMA, Gift of Esther Ginsberg and Linda
Davis in honor of Jackie Olbrychowski,
AC1999.204.7

THOMAS DOLLIVER CHURCH

(1902–1978, active San Francisco)

42 Dewey and Jean Donnell Ranch pool,
Sonoma County, 1948
Photograph taken c. 1948; printed 2011
Inkjet print
16 x 20 in. (40.6 x 50.8 cm)
Thomas Church Collection, Environmental
Design Archives, University of California,
Berkeley
Fig. 1.21

Lawrence Halprin (1916–2009, active San
Francisco), project landscape architect
George T. Rockrise (1917–2000, active San
Francisco area), project architect

43 Dewey and Jean Donnell Ranch pool,
Sonoma County (plan), 1948
Hand-colored lithograph
8 x 10 in. (20.3 x 25.4 cm)
Thomas Church Collection, Environmental
Design Archives, University of California,
Berkeley
Fig. 1.23

WILLIAM CLAXTON

(1927–2008, active Hollywood)

Pauline Annon (b. 1922), illustrator
World Pacific Records (Hollywood, 1957–70),
record label
Standard Lithograph (Los Angeles, n.d.), printer

44 Jazz Canto Vol. 1 (album cover), 1958
Offset lithography
12¼ x 12¼ in. (31.1 x 31.1 cm)
LACMA, Decorative Arts and Design
Council Fund, M.2010.119.5a–b
Fig. 9.24

Pacific Jazz Records (Hollywood, founded 1952),
record label

45 Bud Shank and Three Trombones (album
cover), 1954
Offset lithography
10¼ x 10¼ in. (26 x 26 cm)
LACMA, Decorative Arts and Design
Council Fund, M.2010.119.4a–b
Fig. 9.24

CHESTER COBB (1899–1967, active Burbank)

Division of Information, War Production Board,
Office for Emergency Management
(Washington, D.C., 1942–45), publisher
Hollywood Writers Mobilization (Los Angeles,
founded 1941), publisher
WPA Federal Art Project (Southern California,
1935–43), printer

46 Production Lines Are Battle Lines! (poster),
c. 1942
Screenprint
36 x 24 in. (91.4 x 61 cm)
Lent anonymously
Fig. 1.10

R. COELHO-CORDOZA (n.d.)

Hawk House (Los Angeles, n.d.)

47 Barbecue-brazier, c. 1948
Cast iron
Height: 20 in. (50.8 cm); diameter: 43 in.
(109.2 cm)
Collection of Edith Liu
Fig. 5.2

LUTHER CONOVER (1913–1993, active Sausalito)

48 Chair, c. 1950
Mahogany, iron
30⅞ x 21 x 19¼ in. (78.4 x 53.3 x 48.9 cm)
LACMA, Purchased with funds provided by
Harris & Ruble, M.2010.10
Fig. 6.4

ELSIE CRAWFORD

(1913–1999, active Los Angeles area and Palo Alto)

49 Zipper lamp, 1965; this example made 1997
Form exhibited in California Design 9,
Pasadena Art Museum, 1965
Acrylic
18 x 26 x 26 in. (45.7 x 66 x 66 cm)
LACMA, Gift of the artist, AC1997.259.1
Fig. 10.15 (right)

DAVID CRESSEY (b. 1916, active Los Angeles)

Architectural Pottery (Los Angeles, 1950–71;
thereafter Group Artec)

**50 Glyph screen wall for California state
government building**, Sacramento, c. 1963;
this example made c. 1965
Stoneware
Each totem: 102 x 14 x 24 in. (259.1 x 35.6 x
61 cm)
LACMA, Purchased with funds provided by
Viveca Paulin-Ferrell and Will Ferrell, David
Bohnett and Tom Gregory, Willow Bay and
Bob Iger, and Ann and Jim Gianopulos,
M.2010.111.1–.6
Fig. 1.14

GRANT DAHLSTROM (1902–1980), typographer

Grace Marion Brown (c. 1905–n.d., active Los
Angeles), illustrator
Merle Armitage (1893–1975), author
Jake Zeitlin (1902–1987), publisher

51 The Aristocracy of Art (book), 1929
Offset lithography
10 x 7 in. (25.4 x 17.8 cm)
Victoria Dailey and Steve Turner Collection,
Los Angeles

LOUIS DANZIGER (b. 1923, active Los Angeles)

**52 Fourth Annual: Frances Holmes
Achievement Award for the Los Angeles
Advertising Women** (announcement), 1949
Lithograph
18 x 15⅛ in. (45.7 x 38.4 cm)
Louis Danziger Collection, Graphic Design
Archive, Cary Graphic Arts Collection,
Rochester Institute of Technology
Fig. 9.16

Los Angeles County Museum of Art
(Los Angeles, 1965–present), publisher

53 New York School: The First Generation
(poster), 1965
Offset lithography
22 x 17 in. (55.9 x 43.2 cm)
LACMA, Gift of Don Menveg, M.2010.169
Fig. 9.15

Marvin Rand (1924–2009, active Los Angeles), photographer

54 **Mockup of advertisement for General Lighting Company**, 1949
Ink, photograph, tracing paper, masking tape, matte board
8½ x 11⅛ in. (21.6 x 28.3 cm)
Louis Danziger Collection, Graphic Design Archive, Cary Graphic Arts Collection, Rochester Institute of Technology
See fig. 9.14

J. R. (JULIUS RALPH) DAVIDSON
(b. Germany, 1889–1977, active Los Angeles)

55 **Lamp**, c. 1940
Chrome-plated metal, parchment
14 x 6 x 15½ in. (35.6 x 15.2 x 39.4 cm)
J. R. Davidson Collection, Architecture and Design Collection, University Art Museum, UC Santa Barbara
Fig. 2.11

56 **Table**, c. 1940
Birch, Tufflex glass
24½ x 14 x 18 in. (62.2 x 35.6 x 45.7 cm)
J. R. Davidson Collection, Architecture and Design Collection, University Art Museum, UC Santa Barbara
Fig. 2.11

57 **Case Study House #1**, unrealized (perspective of living room and terrace), 1945
Ink on paper
17½ x 28 in. (44.5 x 71.1 cm)
J. R. Davidson Collection, Architecture and Design Collection, University Art Museum, UC Santa Barbara
Fig. 4.13

DOUGLAS DEEDS (b. 1937, active San Diego)
Architectural Fiberglass (Los Angeles, 1961–71; thereafter Group Artec)

58 **Bench**, model FGB-816, c. 1962
Form exhibited in *California Design 9*, Pasadena Art Museum, 1965
Fiberglass
30 x 84 x 28 in. (76.2 x 213.4 x 71.1 cm)
Collection of Douglas Deeds
See fig. 6.19

RUPERT DEESE (1924–2010, active Claremont)

59 **Cocktail pitcher**, c. 1950
Stoneware
Height: 9⅛ in. (23.2 cm); diameter: 5⅛ in. (13 cm)
LACMA, Decorative Arts and Design Council Fund, M.2010.93
P. 6

60 **Cocktail pitcher**, c. 1950
Stoneware
Height: 8 in. (20.3 cm); diameter: 4½ in. (11.4 cm)
Collection of Dr. Andrew and Deborah Frank

61 **Ashtray**, c. 1951
Stoneware
1½ x 9 x 4⅝ in. (3.8 x 22.9 x 11.7 cm)
Collection of Bill Stern

MARGARET DE PATTA
(1903–1964, active San Francisco area and Napa)

62 **Flatware**, c. 1936
Silver, copper, stainless steel
Knife: 9⅜ x ⅞ x ½ in. (23.8 x 2.2 x 1.3 cm)
LACMA, Decorative Arts Deaccession Fund, M.2007.20.1–.4
Fig. 2.15

63 **Ring**, 1949
White gold, rutilated quartz crystal
⅞ x ¾ x 1 in. (2.2 x 1.9 x 2.5 cm)
De Patta/Bielawski Collection

64 **Pin**, c. 1955
Silver, pebbles
2¾ x 2¾ x ⅝ in. (7 x 7 x 1.6 cm)
Collection of Mark McDonald, Hudson, N.Y.
Fig. 7.7

Designs Contemporary (San Francisco and Napa, n.d.)

65 **Pin**, no. 6, c. 1946–57
Silver, quartz
2 x 3½ x ½ in. (5.1 x 8.9 x 1.3 cm)
LACMA, Decorative Arts and Design Acquisition and Deaccession Funds, M.2010.8
Fig. 7.6

MARY ANN DeWEESE
(1913–1993, active Los Angeles)

Catalina Sportswear (Los Angeles, 1907–93)

66 **Woman's two-piece swimsuit, man's swim trunks, and man's shirt in *California Lobster* pattern from the *Sweethearts in Swim Suits* collection**, 1949
Lastex, cotton
Two-piece swimsuit, center-back length: 14 in. (35.6 cm); swim trunks, center-back length: 15 in. (38.1 cm); shirt, center-back length: 27½ in. (69.9 cm)
Collection of Esther Ginsberg/Golyester Antiques
Fig. 8.27

CARLOS DINIZ
(1928–2001, active Los Angeles), delineator

Killingsworth, Brady & Smith (Long Beach, 1953–67; thereafter Killingsworth, Brady & Associates), architect

67 **Frank Brothers Furniture**, Long Beach (exterior perspective), 1963
Ink on paper
26½ x 27 in. (67.3 x 68.6 cm)
Carlos Diniz Archive
Fig. 10.19

Ladd & Kelsey, Architects (Pasadena, 1958–80), architect

68 **Monarch Bay Homes**, Laguna Niguel (exterior), 1961
Screenprint
20 x 26 in. (50.8 x 66 cm)
LACMA, Gift of Gilbert Ortiz and Edward Cella Art + Architecture, M.2010.76.1

69 **Monarch Bay Homes**, Laguna Niguel (outdoor dining terrace), 1961
Screenprint
20⅛ x 26 in. (51.1 x 66 cm)
LACMA, Gift of Gilbert Ortiz and Edward Cella Art + Architecture, M.2010.76.2
Fig. 1.5

HENRY DREYFUSS

(1904–1972, active Pasadena)

JAMES M. CONNER (b. 1922, active Pasadena)

Henry Dreyfuss (New York, 1929–present; Pasadena, 1944–69), design firm

Polaroid Corporation (Cambridge, Massachusetts, 1937–present)

70 *The Swinger*, Land camera model 20, 1965; manufactured 1965–70
ABS plastic, PVC, cellulose acetate butyrate, steel
4⅝ x 6 x 5⅝ in. (11.7 x 15.2 x 14.3 cm)
LACMA, Decorative Arts and Design Council Fund, M.2011.6
Fig. 6.25

CHARLES EAMES (1907–1978, active Venice)

EERO SAARINEN (b. Finland, 1910–1961)

Marli Ehrman (b. Germany, 1904–1982), textile designer

Haskelite Manufacturing Corporation (Chicago, c. 1917–c. 1957), manufacturer

Heywood-Wakefield (Gardner, Massachusetts, 1897–1979), textile manufacturer

71 **Chair**, 1940
Designed at Cranbrook Academy of Art, Bloomfield Hills, Michigan
Exhibited in *Organic Design in Home Furnishings*, Museum of Modern Art, New York, 1941
Mahogany, wool (replaced)
32½ x 18 x 22 in. (82.6 x 45.7 x 55.9 cm)
LACMA, Decorative Arts and Design Council Fund, M.2008.290.1
Fig. 6.12

CHARLES EAMES

RAY EAMES (1912–1988, active Venice)

Eames Office (Venice, 1941–88)

Molded Plywood Division, Evans Products Company (Venice, 1943–47)

72 **Leg splint**, c. 1941–42; manufactured 1942–45
Molded plywood
42 x 6 x 4½ in. (106.7 x 15.2 x 11.4 cm)
LACMA, Gift of Don Menveg, AC1995.28.1
Fig. 6.13

73 **Body litter (prototype)**, 1943
Molded plywood
8 x 84 x 30 in. (20.3 x 213.4 x 76.2 cm)
Eames Collection, LLC
Fig. 6.14

74 **Elephant**, 1945
Exhibited in *New Furniture Designed by Charles Eames*, Museum of Modern Art, New York, 1946
Molded plywood
16½ x 30¾ x 16¼ in. (41.9 x 78.1 x 41.3 cm)
Eames Collection, LLC
P. 5

Eames Office

Molded Plywood Division, Evans Products Company

Herman Miller Furniture Company (Zeeland, Michigan, 1923–present), distributor

75 *DCW* (dining chair wood), 1946–49
Rosewood, rubber, steel
29 x 19½ x 22 in. (73.7 x 49.5 x 55.9 cm)
LACMA, Decorative Arts and Design Council Fund, M.2008.290.3
Fig. 6.15

Eames Office

Herman Miller Furniture Company

76 *DAX* (dining model), 1948–50; this example made c. 1951–52 in Venice
Fiberglass, steel, rubber
31½ x 25 x 23 in. (80 x 63.5 x 58.4 cm)
LACMA, Purchased with funds provided by Alice and Nahum Lainer, M.2010.13

77 *LAR* (low lounge chair), 1948–50; this example made c. 1951
Form exhibited in *Good Design*, Museum of Modern Art, New York, 1950
Fiberglass, steel, rubber
23 x 24½ x 25 in. (58.4 x 62.2 x 63.5 cm)
Collection of Susan and Michael Rich
Fig. 6.16

78 *ESU* (Eames storage unit), 400 series, c. 1949; manufactured 1950–55
Form exhibited in *Good Design*, Museum of Modern Art, New York, 1951
Zinc-plated steel, birch-faced and plastic-coated plywood, lacquered particle board, rubber
69 x 47 x 16 in. (175.3 x 119.4 x 40.6 cm)
LACMA, Gift of Mr. Sid Avery and Mr. James Corcoran, M.86.105
Fig. 10.21

79 *ETR* (elliptical table rod base), 1951; manufactured 1951–64
Laminated plywood, chromed steel
10 x 88¾ x 29 in. (25.4 x 225.4 x 73.7 cm)
LACMA, Gift of Joel and Margaret Chen of J. F. Chen, M.2010.123
Fig. 5.34

Eames Office

Tigrett Enterprises, The Playhouse Division (Jackson, Tennessee, 1930s–1961)

80 *House of Cards* toy, 1952; this example made c. 1952; manufactured 1952–61
Offset lithography on cardboard, cellophane
4½ x 3⅝ x 2¼ in. (11.4 x 9.2 x 5.7 cm)
Collection of Daniel Ostroff
Fig. 9.17

81 *Hang-It-All*, 1953; manufactured 1953–61
Form exhibited in *Good Design*, Museum of Modern Art, New York, 1953
Enameled steel, wood
30 x 24 x 12 in. (76.2 x 61 x 30.5 cm)
LACMA, Purchased with funds provided by David Bohnett and Tom Gregory, M.2010.27
Fig. 10.27

RAY EAMES

82 *Arts and Architecture* (magazine cover), April 1942
Offset lithography
12½ x 9½ in. (31.8 x 24.1 cm)
Victoria Dailey and Steve Turner Collection, Los Angeles

83 *Arts and Architecture* (magazine cover), May 1943
Offset lithography
12½ x 9½ in. (31.8 x 24.1 cm)
Victoria Dailey and Steve Turner Collection, Los Angeles
Fig. 10.3

Schiffer Prints, a division of Mil-Art Company (New York, founded 1945)

84 *Cross Patch* textile, c. 1945; manufactured 1947–49
Pattern exhibited in *Printed Textiles for the Home*, Museum of Modern Art, New York, 1947
Printed cotton
50 x 54¾ in. (127 x 139.1 cm)
LACMA, Costume and Textiles Deaccession Fund and Decorative Arts and Design Deaccession Fund, M.2009.54.3
Fig. 8.14

GARRETT ECKBO

(1910–2000, active San Francisco area and Los Angeles), landscape architect

John Funk (1908–1993), architect
Joseph Allen Stein (1912–2001), architect
Eckbo, Royston, and Williams (San Francisco and Los Angeles, 1945–58)

85 *Site Plan, Ladera Peninsula Housing Association*, partially realized, 1947
Wax pencil, graphite, and ink on paper
46 x 30 in. (116.8 x 76.2 cm)
Garrett Eckbo Collection, Environmental Design Archives, University of California, Berkeley
Fig. 4.17

CRAIG ELLWOOD

(1922–1992, active Los Angeles)

86 **Gerald Rosen House**, Brentwood (presentation drawing), 1961–63
Ink with Zip-A-Tone on matte board
30 x 40 in. (76.5 x 101.6 cm)
College of Environmental Design, Archives—Special Collections, California State Polytechnic University, Pomona
Fig. 4.26

Laverne Originals (New York, 1940s–1964)

87 **Stereo cabinet for the Gerald Rosen House**, Brentwood, 1961–63
Lacquered wood, chrome-plated steel, wire mesh
36 x 120 x 21 in. (91.4 x 304.8 x 53.3 cm)
Collection of Los Angeles Modern Auctions (LAMA)
Fig. 4.27

CLAIRE FALKENSTEIN

(1908–1997, active San Francisco area and Venice)

88 **Necklace**, c. 1948
Exhibited in *Claire Falkenstein*, San Francisco Museum of Art, 1948
Brass
12 x 6¾ x ½ in. (30.5 x 17.1 x 1.3 cm)
Collection of the Long Beach Museum of Art, gift of the Falkenstein Foundation
Fig. 10.30

89 **Model for garden gate, Peggy Guggenheim Collection**, Venice, 1961
Made in Venice, Italy
Painted copper wire, glass
17½ x 14½ x 1 in. (44.5 x 36.8 x 2.5 cm)
Museum of Fine Arts, Boston. Gift of Mrs. Peggy Guggenheim
P. 9

MARGIT FELLEGI

(1903–1975, active Los Angeles)

Cole of California (Los Angeles, founded 1925)

90 **Woman's swimsuit**, 1936
Printed cotton, elastic (Matletex)
Center-back length: 13 in. (33 cm)
LACMA, Gift of Margit Fellegi, M.74.76.11
Fig. 8.24

91 *Swoon Suit* **woman's swimsuit**, 1942
Acetate satin
Top, center-back length: 8 in. (20.3 cm); shorts, center-back length: 13½ in. (34.3 cm)
LACMA, Gift of Margit Fellegi, M.74.76.7a-b
Fig. 8.25

92 **Woman's swimsuit and skirt**, c. 1944
Glazed cotton chintz, cotton, elastic (Matletex)
Swimsuit, center-back length: 15½ in. (39.4 cm); skirt, center-back length: 43 in. (109.2 cm)
LACMA, Gift of the Fashion Group, Inc., of Los Angeles, 48.39.24a-b
P. 319

93 **Woman's swimsuit and jacket**, c. 1950
Cotton
Swimsuit, center-back length: 19¾ in. (50.2 cm); jacket, center-back length: 30 in. (76.2 cm)
LACMA, Gift of Doris Raymond/The Way We Wore, M.2006.210.1a-b
P. 12

94 **Woman's swimsuit**, 1950–51
Lastex lamé, cotton
Center-back length: 15½ in. (39.4 cm)
LACMA, Gift of Esther Ginsberg and Linda Davis in honor of Jennifer Blake, AC1998.117.9
Fig. 8.34

ARLINE FISCH (b. 1931, active San Diego)

95 *Peacock Tail* **necklace**, 1962
Silver, enamel
9 x 7½ in. (22.9 x 19.1 cm)
LACMA, Gift of Arline Fisch in honor of Dr. Jae Carmichael, M.2010.39
Fig. 7.27

JOHN FOLLIS

(1923–1994, active Pasadena and Los Angeles)

96 *Arts and Architecture* (magazine cover), February 1957
Offset lithography
12½ x 9½ in. (31.8 x 24.1 cm)
Victoria Dailey and Steve Turner Collection, Los Angeles

97 *Arts and Architecture* (magazine cover), June 1962
Offset lithography
12½ x 9½ in. (31.8 x 24.1 cm)
Victoria Dailey and Steve Turner Collection, Los Angeles

JOHN FOLLIS
REX GOODE

(1925–2000, active Pasadena and Los Angeles)

American Crayon Company (Sandusky, Ohio, 1890–2002), publisher

98 *Everyday Art* (magazine), summer 1953
Offset lithography
9 x 6 in. (22.9 x 15.2 cm)
The Mr. and Mrs. Allan Balch Art Research Library, LACMA

Architectural Pottery (Los Angeles, 1950–71; thereafter Group Artec)

99 **Planter**, model E-31, c. 1949
Earthenware, iron
30 x 24 x 24 in. (76.2 x 61 x 61 cm)
Collection of Andy Hackman

JOHN FOLLIS
JAMES REED (n.d., active Los Angeles area)

100 *Arts and Architecture* (magazine cover), April 1953
Offset lithography
12½ x 9½ in. (31.8 x 24.1 cm)
Victoria Dailey and Steve Turner Collection, Los Angeles

101 *Arts and Architecture* (magazine cover), September 1953
Offset lithography
12½ x 9½ in. (31.8 x 24.1 cm)
Collection of Los Angeles Modern Auctions (LAMA)
Fig. 10.4

102 *Arts and Architecture* (magazine cover), June 1955
Offset lithography
12⅝ x 9½ in. (32.1 x 24.1 cm)
Victoria Dailey and Steve Turner Collection, Los Angeles

DANNY HO FONG

(b. China, 1915–1992, active Los Angeles)

Tropi-Cal (Los Angeles, 1936–present; called Fong Brothers Company, 1936–54 and 1985–present)

103 *Wave* chaise, 1966
Manufactured in Hong Kong
Rattan, wrought iron, cotton
16¼ x 84 x 24¼ in. (41.2 x 213.3 x 61.6 cm)
The Museum of Modern Art, New York. Gift of the manufacturer, 1967
Fig. 5.11

MILLER YEE FONG (b. 1941, active Los Angeles)

Tropi-Cal

104 *Lotus* chair, 1968
Manufactured in Hong Kong
Form exhibited in *California Design 10*, Pasadena Museum of Art, 1968
Rattan, wrought iron
33 x 52½ x 40 in. (83.8 x 133.4 x 101.6 cm)
LACMA, Gift of Fong Brothers Co., M.2010.171
Fig. 5.12

PAUL T. FRANKL

(b. Austria, 1886–1958, active Los Angeles)

Frankl Galleries (Los Angeles, 1934–46), retailer

105 **Chair**, c. 1936; manufactured in Manila, 1936–39
Rattan
31 x 31 x 36 in. (78.7 x 78.7 x 91.4 cm)
Collection of Keith Collins
Fig. 2.23

Johnson Furniture Company (Grand Rapids, Michigan, 1908–83)

106 **Console magazine table**, model 5007, 1949; this example made 1949; manufactured 1949–c. 1953
Mahogany, cork
27⅞ x 71½ x 19¾ in. (70.8 x 181.6 x 50.2 cm)
LACMA, Decorative Arts and Design Acquisition Fund, M.2010.109a–c

FRANZ INDUSTRIES (Los Angeles, n.d.)

107 **Candleholders, Aero Art Product**, c. 1948
Aluminum, Micarta
Each: 3 x 5½ in. (7.6 x 14 cm)
Museum of California Design, Los Angeles, Gift of Daniel Ostroff
Fig. 6.2

FUJIYE FUJIKAWA

(1919–1991, active Los Angeles)

108 *See Evil, Hear Evil, Speak to the FBI* (poster design), c. 1942
Made at Heart Mountain internment camp, Wyoming
Gouache on poster board
26 x 18 in. (66 x 45.7 cm)
Collection of Harry Fukasawa
P. 14

KENJI FUJITA (b. 1921, active Los Angeles area)

109 **Condiment bottle**, c. 1960
Porcelain
12¼ x 5⅜ x 2⅝ in. (31.1 x 13.7 x 6.7 cm)
LACMA, Gift of Emily Tigerman, M.2009.114.4
Fig. 5.33

GABRIEL OF PASADENA (Pasadena, n.d.)

110 **Plate, basket, dish, salt, and pepper**, c. 1951
Porcelain
Plate, diameter: 10¾ in. (27.3 cm)
Collection of Steven Ziel and Chase Langford

RUDI GERNREICH

(b. Austria, 1922–1985, active Los Angeles)

111 **Dress**, c. 1953
Wool knit
Center-back length: 41 in. (104.1 cm)
LACMA, Gift of the Fashion Group, Inc., M.73.102.6
Fig. 3.21

112 **Woman's swimsuit**, 1958
Wool knit
Center-back length: 23¾ in. (60.3 cm)
LACMA, Gift of Mrs. Adrienne Kaplan, M.83.185

CEDRIC GIBBONS

(1890–1960, active Los Angeles)

George M. Stanley (1903–1970), sculptor

113 **Academy Award of Merit statuette**, 1927–28
Manufactured in Illinois
Awarded to Cedric Gibbons for *The Bridge of San Luis Rey* (1929)
Bronze, gold, Belgian marble
Height: 12 in. (30.5 cm); diameter: 5½ in. (14 cm)
Academy of Motion Picture Arts and Sciences
Fig. 2.9

GRETA MAGNUSSON GROSSMAN

(b. Sweden, 1906–1999, active Los Angeles)

Glenn of California (Arcadia, 1948–92)

114 **Desk (with storage unit)**, models 6200 (and 6200a), 1952; manufactured 1952–c. 1954
Walnut, iron, Formica
47⅝ x 23¾ x 40 in. (121 x 60.3 x 101.6 cm)
LACMA, Decorative Arts Deaccession Fund, M.2007.37
Fig. 3.11

115 **Screen**, model 6239, c. 1952
Walnut, steel wire
60 x 72 x 3 in. (152.4 x 188.9 x 7.6 cm)
Collection of the family of Richard I. Levine, in loving memory
Fig. 5.17

Ralph O. Smith Manufacturing Company (Burbank, c. 1949–54)

116 **Lamp**, model 831, c. 1949; manufactured c. 1949–54
Iron, aluminum
51 x 14⅞ x 12¼ in. (129.5 x 37.8 x 31.1 cm)
LACMA, Decorative Arts and Design Council Fund, M.2007.236.2
P. 7

117 **Floor lamp**, model 900-F, c. 1952; manufactured c. 1952–54
Iron, aluminum
55 x 11½ x 17 in. (139.7 x 29.2 x 43.2 cm)
LACMA, Decorative Arts and Design Council Fund, M.2009.64
P. 7

VICTOR GRUEN

(b. Austria, 1903–1980, active Los Angeles)

Victor Gruen Associates (Los Angeles, 1950–present)

118 **Lighting fixture from Barton's Bonbonniere**, San Francisco, c. 1952
Painted metal (iron/steel and copper alloy, aluminum)
41 x 36 x 40 in. (104.1 x 91.4 x 101.6 cm)
Brooklyn Museum, Marie Bernice Bitzer Fund, 2005.22
Fig. 3.20

TRUDE GUERMONPREZ

(b. Germany, 1910–1976, active San Francisco)

119 **Calico Cat** textile, 1953
Exhibited in *Modern American Wall Hangings*, Victoria and Albert Museum, London, 1962
Cotton, wool, rayon
18 x 24 in. (45.7 x 61 cm)
Collection of Kay Sekimachi
Fig. 8.5

120 **Sample weaving for Rodef Sholom Synagogue**, San Rafael, 1963–64
Silk, metallic yarn
76 x 37 in. (193 x 94 cm)
Gift of Mr. Eric and Mrs. Sylvia Elsesser, The Trude Guermonprez Archives, Smithsonian Institution, Cooper-Hewitt, National Design Museum, 1993-121-5
Fig. 3.6

ROBERT GUIDI (1922–1977, active Los Angeles)

Tri-Arts (Los Angeles, n.d.), design firm
Contemporary Records (Los Angeles, 1951–84), record label

121 *Lighthouse at Laguna* (album cover), 1955
Offset lithography
12¼ x 12¼ in. (31.1 x 31.1 cm)
LACMA, Decorative Arts and Design Council Fund, M.2010.119.7a-b
Fig. 9.24

122 *Shelly Manne and His Friends* (album cover), 1956
Offset lithography
12¼ x 12¼ in. (31.1 x 31.1 cm)
LACMA, Decorative Arts and Design Council Fund, M.2010.119.6a-b

WILLIAM "BILLY" HAINES

(1900–1973, active Beverly Hills)

123 **Chair for the William Haines, Inc., conference room**, 1954
Walnut, leather
33 x 27 x 25 in. (83.8 x 68.6 x 63.5 cm)
Collection of Peter Schifando
Fig. 1.26

RUTH HANDLER

(1916–2002, active Los Angeles area)

JOHN W. "JACK" RYAN

(1926–1991, active Los Angeles area)

CHARLOTTE JOHNSON (1917–1997, active Los Angeles area), fashion designer

Mattel, Inc. (Los Angeles area, 1945–present)

124 *Barbie Teen Age Fashion Model* **(Barbie #1)**, 1959
Designed in Hawthorne and Tokyo; manufactured in Tokyo
Vinyl, Saran, jersey
11½ x 2⅝ x 1¾ in. (29.2 x 6.7 x 4.4 cm)
LACMA, Gift of Mattel, Inc., M.2010.177.2
P. 24

125 *Ken* **doll**, 1961
Designed in Hawthorne; manufactured in Tokyo
Vinyl, cloth, flocking
12 x 3¼ x 1⅞ in. (31.8 x 8.3 x 4.8 cm)
LACMA, Gift of Mattel, Inc., M.2010.177.1

HARWELL HAMILTON HARRIS

(1903–1990, active Los Angeles)

Wayne Andrews (1913–1987), photographer

126 **John Weston Havens Jr. House**, Berkeley (living room), 1939–41
Photograph taken and printed c. 1950
Gelatin silver print
11 x 14 in. (27.9 x 35.6 cm)
Havens House Collection, Environmental Design Archives, University of California, Berkeley
Fig. 2.32

Man Ray (1890–1976), photographer

127 **John Weston Havens Jr. House**, Berkeley (exterior), 1939–41
Photograph taken and printed 1941
Gelatin silver print
14½ x 11½ in. (36.8 x 29.2 cm)
Havens House Collection, Environmental Design Archives, University of California, Berkeley
Fig. 4.11

EDITH HEATH (1911–2005, active Sausalito)

Franz Bergmann (b. Austria, 1898–1977, active San Francisco), metalsmith
Heath Ceramics (Sausalito, 1946–present)

128 **Teapot**, 1949
Stoneware, silver
Height: 4½ in. (11.4 cm); diameter: 8¼ in. (21 cm)
The Brian and Edith Heath Trust
Fig. 7.8

Heath Ceramics

129 *Coupe* **dinnerware**, 1947
Earthenware
Dinner plate, diameter: 10⅝ in. (27 cm)
Collection of Bill Stern
Fig. 1.13

130 **Teapot**, c. 1960
Owned by Edith Heath
Stoneware
Height: 4½ in. (11.4 cm); diameter: 7½ in. (19.1 cm)
The Brian and Edith Heath Trust
Fig. 7.8

OTTO HEINO

(1915–2009, active Los Angeles and Ojai)

VIVIKA HEINO

(1909–1995, active Los Angeles and Ojai)

131 **Vase**, 1960
Stoneware
Height: 21¼ in. (54 cm); diameter: 7⅜ in. (18.7 cm)
Collection of Forrest L. Merrill

BRUCE HILL (n.d.)

Peter Pepper Products (Los Angeles area, 1952–present)

132 *Starburst* **candelabrum**, c. 1953
Iron, glass
36⅝ x 35½ x 4¼ in. (93 x 90.2 x 10.8 cm)
LACMA, Decorative Arts and Design Deaccession Fund, M.2010.11a-i
Fig. 10.17

JOE HONG (1930–2004, active San Francisco)

Joseph Magnin (San Francisco, 1913–69), client

133 *Arches* **and** *Dome* **gift boxes from the** *Renaissance* **series**, 1966
Offset lithography
Arches box: 18 x 9½ x 5 in. (45.7 x 24.1 x 12.7 cm); *Dome* box: 13½ x 11 x 11 in. (34.3 x 27.9 x 27.9 cm)
Collection of Ellen Magnin Newman
See fig. 9.26

LOUIS IPSEN

(b. Denmark, 1873–1947, active Los Angeles)

Victor F. Houser (1905–1998), ceramics engineer

J. A. Bauer Pottery Company (Kentucky, 1885–
1909; Los Angeles, 1909–62)

134 Stacking storage dishes, c. 1932
Earthenware, wood, steel
Height: 7½ in. (19.1 cm); diameter: 5⅞ in.
(14.9 cm)
LACMA, Decorative Arts and Design
Acquisition Fund and partial gift of Bill
Stern, M.2010.91.6.1–.3
Fig. 2.19

FRANK IRWIN

(1922–2002, active Los Angeles area)

Metlox Manufacturing Company, Poppytrail
Division (Manhattan Beach, 1927–89)

**135 *California Contempora* covered vegetable
dish (3426), beverage server (3480), and
juice cup (3480½) in *Freeform* shape**,
c. 1955
Earthenware
Dish, height: 3⅝ in. (9.2 cm); diameter:
11½ in. (29.2 cm)
LACMA, Decorative Arts and Design
Acquisition Fund and partial gift of Bill
Stern, M.2010.91.2–.4
Fig. 5.28

GEORGE JAMES (c. 1921–2003, active Los
Angeles area), form designer

Mary C. Brown (n.d.), decal designer
Gladding McBean & Co., Franciscan Division
(Glendale, 1875–present)

136 *Starburst* platter in *Eclipse* shape, 1953
Earthenware
1⅞ x 15¼ x 9⅞ in. (4.8 x 38.7 x 25.1 cm)
LACMA, Decorative Arts and Design
Council Fund, M.2010.117
Fig. 6.30

JOHN B. STETSON COMPANY

(Philadelphia, 1865–1970; now part of Hatco)

137 Cowboy hat, c. 1930
Wool, leather, ribbon, felt
8 x 15¼ x 14¼ in. (20.3 x 38.7 x 36.2 cm)
Courtesy of Museum of the American West,
Autry National Center; 98.90.2. Donated by
Warren and Nancy Simms in memory of
John J. Sauer

DAN JOHNSON (1918–1979, active Los Angeles)

Dan Johnson Studio (Rome, c. 1959)

Arch Industries (Los Angeles, n.d.), distributor

138 *Gazelle* lounge chair, model 30B, c. 1959
Bronze, cane
27½ x 21 x 26 in. (69.9 x 53.3 x 66 cm)
LACMA, Purchased with funds provided by
Viveca Paulin-Ferrell and Will Ferrell,
M.2010.86
P. 10

Hayden Hall (Alhambra, n.d.)

139 Desk, 1947
Maple, oak
30¼ x 54 x 24 in. (76.8 x 137.2 x 61 cm)
LACMA, Purchased with funds provided by
The Buddy Taub Foundation, Dennis A.
Roach and Jill Roach, Directors,
M.2008.234.2
P. 4

DEDE JOHNSON

(c. 1912–n.d., active Los Angeles)

140 Woman's two-piece suit, 1946
Wool gabardine
Jacket, center-back length: 23 in. (58.4 cm);
pants, inseam length: 17 in. (43.2 cm)
LACMA, Gift of the Fashion Group, Inc. of
Los Angeles, 48.39.6a-b

141 Playsuit and skirt, late 1950s
Printed cotton
Blouse, center-back length: 16½ in.
(41.9 cm); skirt, center-back length: 31½ in.
(80 cm); shorts, center-back length: 16 in.
(40.6 cm)
LACMA, Gift of Esther Ginsberg and James
Morris in memory of Don Morris,
AC1998.40.1.1–.3
Fig. 8.18

A. QUINCY JONES

(1913–1979, active Los Angeles)

FREDERICK E. EMMONS

(1907–1999, active Los Angeles)

**142 Sofa and table from the Robert and Grace
Spencer House**, Beverly Hills, 1961–64
Wood, cork veneer, upholstery
Large sofa: 30 x 124 x 32 in. (76.2 x 315 x
81.3 cm); small sofa: 30 x 52 x 32 in. (76.2 x
132.1 x 81.3 cm); table: 18½ x 32 x 32 in.
(47 x 81.3 x 81.3 cm)
LACMA, Gift of Mr. and Mrs. Robert
Spencer and Harry W. Saunders,
M.90.177.2.1–.3
Fig. 5.22

J. L. Eichler Associates, Inc. (San Francisco area,
founded 1966), developer

143 *Plan 3.5* (exterior perspective and plan),
c. 1966
Print
42 x 22½ in. (106.7 x 57.2 cm)
Oakland and Imada Collection,
Environmental Design Archives, University
of California, Berkeley
Fig. 4.23

JOSEPH ZUKIN OF CALIFORNIA

(Los Angeles, founded 1916)

144 Playsuit, c. 1945
Rayon blend
Center-back length: 36 in. (91.4 cm)
LACMA, Gift of Esther Ginsberg and Linda
Davis in honor of Cherie Erickson Harris and
Claire E. Erickson, AC1999.204.4
Fig. 5.44

JOHN KAPEL (b. 1922, active Woodside)

145 Chair, c. 1958
Walnut, leather
Made in Saratoga
44¾ x 33¾ x 26½ in. (113.7 x 85.7 x 67.3 cm)
Collection of John Kapel, promised gift to
LACMA
See p. 23

EDWARD McKNIGHT KAUFFER (1890–1954)

146 *American Airlines to California* (poster),
c. 1947
Silkscreen
39¾ x 30¼ in. (101 x 76.8 cm)
LACMA, Gift of Debbie and Mark Attanasio
in memory of Martin Kaplan, M.2010.113.2
Fig. 10.2

GERE KAVANAUGH

(b. 1929, active Los Angeles)

147 City-planning toy (prototype), c. 1965
Exhibited in *California Design 10*, Pasadena
Art Museum, 1968
Painted wood, canvas
Canvas mat: 24 x 24 in. (61 x 61 cm)
Collection of Gere Kavanaugh
Fig. 10.28

HENRY C. KECK (b. 1921, active Pasadena)

Keck-Craig Associates (Pasadena,
1951–present)
Dripcut Starline Corporation (Santa Barbara,
n.d.)

148 Salt, pepper, and sugar shakers,
c. 1955–57
Glass, chromed metal
Sugar shaker, height: 4¾ in. (12.1 cm);
diameter: 3 in. (7.6 cm)
Museum of California Design, Los
Angeles, Gift of Keck-Craig, Inc.
Fig. 6.26

Keck-Craig Associates
Electronic Engineering Company of California
(Santa Ana, n.d.)

149 Roadside barricade light, c. 1963
Form exhibited in *California Design 9*,
Pasadena Art Museum, 1965
Polycarbonate, polyethylene, steel
13¼ x 7⅜ x 2⅞ in. (33.7 x 18.7 x 7.3 cm)
Collection of Eudorah M. Moore
Fig. 6.27

SISTER CORITA KENT
(1918–1986, active Los Angeles)

150 *Enriched Bread* (print), 1965
Screenprint on Pellon
29¾ x 36⅜ in. (75.6 x 92.4 cm)
Collection of UCLA Grunwald Center for
the Graphic Arts, Hammer Museum.
Corita Kent Bequest
Fig. 9.28

BERNARD KESTER
(b. 1928, active Los Angeles)

Crawford & Stoughton (Los Angeles,
c. 1962–64)

151 *Strand* textile, c. 1962
Screenprinted cotton
100 x 55 in. (254 x 139.7 cm)
LACMA, Gift of the artist, M.2010.58.1
Fig. 8.10

ALBERT HENRY KING
(b. England, 1900–1982, active Los Angeles)

Lotus & Acanthus Studio (Los Angeles,
founded c. 1931)

152 Punch bowl, 1951
Exhibited in *Designer-Craftsmen U.S.A.*,
Brooklyn Museum and other venues, 1953
Porcelain
Height: 8½ in. (21.6 cm); diameter: 10 in.
(25.4 cm)
LACMA, Purchased with funds provided
by Howard and Gwen Laurie Smits,
M.90.129

MARIA KIPP
(b. Germany, 1900–1988, active Los Angeles)

153 Textile, c. 1938
Mohair, chenille, Lurex
113 x 45 in. (287 x 114.3 cm)
LACMA, Costume Council Fund,
AC1999.19.1
Fig. 8.3

154 Textiles, c. 1950
Various materials, including wool, cotton,
rayon, linen, and chenille
Largest textile: 116 x 50½ in. (294.6 x
128.3 cm)
Collection of Shannon and Peter
Loughrey

H. KOCH & SONS COMPANY
(Corte Madera, 1909–present)

155 Suitcase, c. 1950
Fiberglass, aluminum
14 x 21 x 5 in. (35.6 x 53.3 x 12.7 cm)
Collection of Steve Cabella
Fig. 6.24

CHARLES KRATKA
(1922–2007, active Los Angeles area)

156 *Arts and Architecture* (magazine cover),
September 1952
Offset lithography
12½ x 9½ in. (31.8 x 24.1 cm)
Victoria Dailey and Steve Turner Collection,
Los Angeles
Fig. 10.3

157 *Arts and Architecture* (magazine cover),
December 1956
Offset lithography
12⅞ x 9⅞ in. (32.7 x 25.1 cm)
Collection of Los Angeles Modern
Auctions (LAMA)

158 *Arts and Architecture* (magazine cover),
January 1957
Offset lithography
12⅞ x 9⅞ in. (32.7 x 25.1 cm)
Victoria Dailey and Steve Turner Collection,
Los Angeles
Fig. 10.3

WALTER LAMB
(1901–1980, active Santa Barbara and other
locations)

Brown-Jordan Company (Pasadena,
1945–present)

159 Chaise, model C-4700, c. 1954
Designed in Honolulu
Brass, PVC (polyvinyl chloride)
34½ x 63½ x 27⅛ in. (87.6 x 161.3 x
68.9 cm)
LACMA, Gift of Joel and Margaret Chen
of J. F. Chen, M.2009.164
Fig. 5.8

WALTER LANDOR
(b. Germany, 1913–1995, active San Francisco)

San Francisco Museum of Art (San Francisco,
1935–present; now San Francisco Museum of
Modern Art), publisher

160 *Space for Living* (poster), 1940
Print
14 x 11 in. (35.6 x 27.9 cm)
San Francisco Museum of Modern Art,
Archives
Fig. 3.15

DOYLE LANE (1925–2002, active Los Angeles)

161 Vase, c. 1960
Stoneware
Height: 5 in. (12.7 cm); diameter: 4½ in.
(11.4 cm)
LACMA, Purchased with funds provided
by Andrea and Steve Stanford,
M.2009.114.1
Fig. 1.27

PAUL LÁSZLÓ
(b. Hungary, 1900–1993, active Beverly Hills)

162 *Atomville, U.S.A.*, 1950
Published in *Paul László* (book), printed by
1958
Offset lithography
4¾ x 9½ in. (28.6 x 24.1 cm)
The Mr. and Mrs. Allan C. Balch
Art Research Library, LACMA
Fig. 5.42

163 **Chair for the McCulloch Corporation
showroom**, c. 1954
Stainless steel, brass, leather
29¼ x 19¾ x 22 in. (74.3 x 50.2 x 55.9 cm)
LACMA, Purchased with funds provided by
Suzanne and Ric Kayne and Colleen and
Bradley Bell, M.2009.18
Fig. 3.18

164 *Paul Laszlo's European Group* **textile**,
1954 or before
Rayon, cotton
105½ x 48⅝ in. (268 x 123.5 cm)
LACMA, Gift of Peter and Shannon
Loughrey, M.2010.163
Fig. 3.1

FREDERICK L. LAURITZEN
(1921–1990, active Northridge)

165 **Box**, 1960
Silver, garnet, rosewood
2 x 2½ x 3 in. (5.1 x 6.4 x 7.6 cm)
Crocker Art Museum, gift of Martha
Lauritzen in Memory of Erik Lauritzen,
2007.84.6
P. 352

JOHN LAUTNER
(1911–1994, active Los Angeles)

166 **Foster Carling House**, Hollywood Hills
(exterior perspective), 1947
Pencil on paper
25⅜ x 42¼ in. (64.5 x 107.3 cm)
Gift of The John Lautner Foundation, The
Getty Research Institute, Los Angeles
(2007.M.13)
Fig. 4.15

LAWSON TIME (Pasadena, n.d.)

167 *Zephyr* **clock**, model P40, style 304, c. 1938
Bronze, brass
3⅝ x 8 x 3⅛ in. (9.2 x 20.3 x 7.9 cm)
LACMA, Purchased with funds provided by
Mark and Maura Resnick, M.2010.125
Fig. 2.8

OLGA LEE (b. 1924, active Los Angeles)

L. Anton Maix Fabrics (New York, 1948–present)

168 *Elements* **textile**, c. 1952
Pattern exhibited in *Good Design*, Museum
of Modern Art, New York, 1952
Linen
33¼ x 51⅜ in. (84.5 x 130.5 cm)
LACMA, Decorative Arts and Design
Deaccession Fund, M.2008.8
Fig. 8.15

Ralph O. Smith Manufacturing Company
(Burbank, c. 1949–54)

169 **Lamp**, c. 1952; manufactured c. 1952–54
Form exhibited at California State Fair,
Sacramento, 1953, and *California Design*,
Pasadena Art Museum, 1954
Aluminum, iron
27½ x 10 x 12 in. (69.9 x 25.4 x 30.5 cm)
LACMA, Decorative Arts and Design
Deaccession Fund, M.2007.186
Fig. 10.9

ROGER LEE
(1920–1981, active San Francisco area)

170 *Residence for Mr. and Mrs. Iain Finnie*,
Oakland (perspectives and elevations), 1959
Pencil on paper
24 x 36 in. (61 x 91.4 cm)
Roger Lee Collection, Environmental
Design Archives, University of California,
Berkeley
Fig. 4.19

MALCOLM LELAND
(b. 1922, active Los Angeles area)

171 **Prototypes of modules**, c. 1952
Earthenware
6 modules, each: 23¾ x 3¾ x 4¼ in. (60.3 x
9.5 x 10.8 cm)
LACMA, Decorative Arts and Design
Council Fund, M.2008.7a-f
Fig. 7.20

Malcolm Leland Ceramics
(El Segundo, c. 1950–c. 1955)

172 **Candlesticks**, c. 1950
Earthenware
Height: 5⅞ in. (14.9 cm); diameter: 4¼ in.
(10.8 cm)
LACMA, Decorative Arts and Design
Acquisition Fund and partial gift of Bill
Stern, M.2010.91.1.1-.2

173 **Centerpiece**, c. 1950
Earthenware
Height: 9¼ in. (23.5 cm); diameter: 9 in.
(22.9 cm)
LACMA, Decorative Arts and Design
Acquisition Fund and partial gift of Bill
Stern, M.2010.91.5

LEVI STRAUSS & CO.
(San Francisco, 1853–present)

174 *Lady Levi's* **jeans**, 1934
Cotton
Inseam: 30 in. (76.2 cm)
Levi Strauss & Co. Archives, San Francisco
Fig. 8.22

175 **Woman's** *Rodeo* **shirt**, late 1930s
Rayon satin
Center-back length: 30¼ in. (76.8 cm)
Levi Strauss & Co. Archives, San Francisco
Fig. 8.22

176 **Man's shirt**, 1950s
Cotton, rayon, snap buttons
Center-back length: 30 in. (76.2 cm)
LACMA, Gift of Esther Ginsberg,
M.2010.130.2
Fig. 8.17

177 **Pants and top**, c. 1955
Cotton
Pants, inseam: 28¼ in. (71.8 cm); top,
center-back length: 3⅜ in. (8.6 cm)
Levi Strauss & Co. Archives, San Francisco
P. 16

DOROTHY WRIGHT LIEBES
(1899–1972, active San Francisco)

Dorothy Liebes Design, Inc. (San Francisco,
1934–48; New York, 1948–c. 1972)

178 *Chinese Ribbon* **textile**, 1940
Cotton, silk, metallic yarn
102 x 45 in. (259.1 x 114.3 cm)
Oakland Museum of California, Gift of the
artist
Fig. 8.2

RAYMOND LOEWY (b. France, 1893–1986)

Studebaker Corporation (Indiana, 1852–1966)

179 *Avanti* **automobile**, 1961; manufactured
1963–64
Designed in Palm Springs
Owned by Dick Van Dyke
Fiberglass body
55 x 71 x 194 in. (139.7 x 180.3 x 492.8 cm)
Petersen Automotive Museum
See fig. 6.23

JAMES LOVERA (b. 1920, active San Jose)

180 **Bowl**, 1953
Earthenware
Height: 7½ in. (19.1 cm); diameter: 8⅜ in.
(21.3 cm)
Collection of Forrest L. Merrill
P. 318

GLEN LUKENS (1887–1967, active Los Angeles)

181 **Bowl**, c. 1937
Earthenware
Height: 4⅞ in. (12.4 cm); diameter: 6⅝ in.
(16.8 cm)
Collection of Forrest L. Merrill
Fig. 2.22

182 **Bowl**, c. 1940
Earthenware
Height: 5⅝ in. (14.3 cm); diameter: 22¾ in.
(57.8 cm)
LACMA, Gift of Gary Keith in honor of his
parents, M.2009.167
Fig. 7.13

183 *Autumn Rose* **charger**, c. 1955
Glass
Height: 2¼ in. (5.7 cm); diameter: 17¾ in.
(45.1 cm)
LACMA, Gift of Mark McDonald, Hudson,
N.Y., M.2010.170
Fig. 7.18

ALVIN LUSTIG (1915–1955, active Los Angeles)

184 **Trade card**, c. 1940
Letterpress
10¾ x 8 in. (27.3 x 20.3 cm)
LACMA, Gift of Elaine Lustig Cohen,
M.2009.135

185 **Letterhead for Lloyd Wright**, early 1940s
Letterpress
11 x 8½ in. (27.9 x 21.6 cm)
Collection of Elaine Lustig Cohen

186 **Letterhead for Sheela's**, 1947
Letterpress
11 x 8½ in. (27.9 x 21.6 cm)
Collection of Elaine Lustig Cohen
Fig. 9.8

187 *Arts and Architecture* (magazine cover),
June 1948
Offset lithography
12½ x 9½ in. (31.8 x 24.1 cm)
Victoria Dailey and Steve Turner Collection,
Los Angeles

188 **Coffee table from the Max and Fanya
Finkelstein House**, Los Angeles, c. 1948
Birch plywood, glass
16 x 42 x 23 in. (40.6 x 106.7 x 40.6 cm)
LACMA, Decorative Arts and Design
Council Fund, M.2007.236.1
Fig. 1.17

189 **Letterhead for UPA**, 1950
Letterpress
11 x 8½ in. (27.9 x 21.6 cm)
Collection of Elaine Lustig Cohen

Weston Bonenberger (1923–2007), editor
Frank Harris (n.d.), editor
Watling & Company (Los Angeles, n.d.), publisher

190 *A Guide to Contemporary Architecture in
Southern California* (book), 1951
Offset lithography
9 x 6 in. (22.9 x 15.2 cm)
The Mr. and Mrs. Allan C. Balch
Art Research Library, LACMA

Capitol Records (Hollywood, 1942–present),
record label

191 *Mark Warnow's Sound Off* (album cover),
1944
Offset lithography
10½ x 12 in. (26.7 x 30.5 cm)
Collection of Elaine Lustig Cohen

Alfred Young Fisher (1902–1970), author
Ward Ritchie Press (South Pasadena, founded
1932), publisher

192 *The Ghost in the Underblows* (book), 1940
Letterpress
9⅛ x 6¼ in. (23.2 x 15.9 cm)
Collection of Elaine Lustig Cohen
Fig. 9.10

Roger C. Johnson (1907–1984), editor
Housing Authority of the City of Los Angeles,
publisher

193 *Homes for Heroes* (book), 1942
Offset lithograph
13⅝ x 10⅛ in. (34.6 x 25.7 cm)
Alvin Lustig Collection, Graphic Design
Archive, Cary Graphic Arts Collection,
Rochester Institute of Technology
Fig. 1.19

Laverne Originals (New York, 1940s–1964)

194 *Incantation* **textile**, c. 1947
Cotton
46 x 51½ in. (116.8 x 130.8 cm)
Collection of Elaine Lustig Cohen
See endsheets

New Directions (New York, 1936–present),
publisher

195 *A Room with a View* (book), c. 1944
The Longest Journey (book), c. 1944
A Handful of Dust (book), 1945
A Season in Hell (book), 1945
Offset lithography
Each: 7¼ x 5 in. (18.4 x 12.7 cm)
Museum of California Design, Los Angeles,
Gift of Mark and Maura Resnick
Fig. 1.16

PETER MACCHIARINI
(1909–2001, active San Francisco)

196 **Brooch**, late 1930s
Silver
3⅞ x 1⅜ x ½ in. (9.8 x 3.5 x 1.3 cm)
Collection of Mark McDonald, Hudson, N.Y.
Fig. 7.33

197 **Pin/pendant**, 1950
Silver, Iconel, brass, copper, ebony, ivory
4⅝ x 1⅝ in. (11.7 x 4.1 cm)
Private collection, Miami
Fig. 7.33

198 **Teapot, sugar, creamer, and tray**, 1950s
Silver, wood
Teapot, height: 5¾ in. (14.6 cm); diameter:
7 in. (17.8 cm)
Collection of Eamescollector.com
Fig. 7.30

SAM MALOOF (1916–2009, active Alta Loma)

199 **Desk for Scripps College**, Claremont, 1959
Walnut, cork
29¾ x 58 x 23⅜ in. (75.6 x 147.3 x 59.4 cm)
Scripps College, Claremont, CA
Fig. 7.5

WILLIAM MANKER
(1902–1997, active Pasadena and Claremont)

200 **Oil jar**, 1940s
Earthenware
Height: 14½ in. (36.9 cm); diameter: 12 in.
(30.5 cm)
Collection of John and Joanne Barrett
Fig. 2.21

DAVID STONE MARTIN

(1913–1992, active Los Angeles)

Mercury Records, Clef Division (1946–56), record label

Polydor Paris (n.d.), record label (reissue)

201 **Bird and Diz, volume 2** (album cover),
c. 1950–51; this example made 1984
Offset lithography
12¼ x 12¼ in. (31.1 x 31.1 cm)
LACMA, Decorative Arts and Design
Council Fund, M.2010.119.9a-b

MAURICE MARTINÉ

(1918–2006, active Orange County)

Maurice Martiné Designs (Orange County, n.d.)

202 **Chair**, 1948
Aluminum, cherry, oak
29 x 22 x 25 in. (73.7 x 55.9 x 63.5 cm)
LACMA, Gift of Daniel Morris and Denis
Gallion, Courtesy Historical Design, Inc.,
M.2009.77.1
Fig. 5.40

203 **Chair**, 1948
Aluminum, cherry, original cord
29 x 25¼ x 24 in. (73.7 x 64.2 x 61 cm)
LACMA, Decorative Arts and Design
Deaccession Fund, M.2009.92
Fig. 5.40

ADDIE MASTERS

(1901–1983, active Los Angeles)

204 **Hostess pajamas**, 1940
Rayon crepe
Center-back length: 62 in. (157.5 cm)
LACMA, Gift of the Fashion Group, Inc.,
of Los Angeles, 48.39.2
Fig. 8.19

MATTEL, INC. (Los Angeles area, 1945–present)

205 **Barbie's Dream House**, c. 1962
Designed in Hawthorne
Offset lithography on cardboard
Open: 13¾ x 26 x 33 in. (34.9 x 66 x
83.8 cm)
Collection of Mattel, Inc.
Fig. 10.25

206 **Barbie Go-Together Furniture Kit
package**, 1964
Designed in Hawthorne
Offset lithography on cardboard
7¼ x 6¼ x 1½ in. (18.4 x 15.9 x 3.8 cm)
Collection of Mattel, Inc.

Carson/Roberts (Los Angeles, 1947–71),
advertising agency

207 **Barbie Look television commercial**, 1965
Film, 1 minute
Collection of Mattel, Inc.

HERBERT MATTER

(b. Switzerland, 1907–1984, active Los Angeles)

208 **Arts and Architecture** (magazine cover),
April 1945
Offset lithography
12½ x 9½ in. (31.8 x 24.1 cm)
Victoria Dailey and Steve Turner Collection,
Los Angeles
Fig. 10.3

209 **Arts and Architecture** (magazine cover),
July 1945
Offset lithography
12½ x 9½ in. (31.8 x 24.1 cm)
Victoria Dailey and Steve Turner Collection,
Los Angeles

210 **Arts and Architecture** (magazine cover),
September 1946
Offset lithography
12½ x 9½ in. (31.8 x 24.1 cm)
Collection of Los Angeles Modern Auctions
(LAMA)
Fig. 9.7

211 **Arts and Architecture** (magazine cover),
December 1946
Offset lithography
12½ x 9½ in. (31.8 x 24.1 cm)
Victoria Dailey and Steve Turner Collection,
Los Angeles
Fig. 9.12

ELIZABETH McCORD

(1914–2008, active Los Angeles area)

212 **Big Pink**, 1951
Exhibited in *Six Portable Murals*,
Los Angeles Art Association, 1951, and
Contemporary Painting in the United States,
Los Angeles County Museum, 1951
Casein and wax on Masonite
31¾ x 48⅛ in. (81 x 122.2 cm)
Collection of the Long Beach Museum of
Art, gift of Alice Henderson
Fig. 5.39

HARRISON McINTOSH

(b. 1914, active Claremont)

213 **Covered jar**, 1961
Stoneware
Height: 9¾ in. (24.8 cm); diameter: 6½ in.
(16.5 cm)
Collection of Forrest L. Merrill
P. 13

MICHAEL MORRISON

(b. 1918, active Beverly Hills)

William Haines, Inc. (Beverly Hills, c. 1945–85)

214 **Cigarette holder**, 1950s
Lucite, brass
Height: 6¾ in. (17.1 cm); diameter: 3⅜ in.
(8.6 cm)
Collection of Peter Schifando
Fig. 5.24

GERTRUD NATZLER

(b. Austria, 1908–1971, active Los Angeles)

OTTO NATZLER

(b. Austria, 1908–2007, active Los Angeles)

215 **Bowl**, 1943
Earthenware
Height: 3½ in. (8.8 cm); diameter: 8½ in.
(21.5 cm)
LACMA, Gift of Rose A. Sperry 1972
Revocable Trust, M.72.105.5
Fig. 3.14

216 **Bowl**, 1958
Earthenware
Height: 11⅛ in. (28.3 cm); diameter:
16⅛ in. (41 cm)
Collection of Forrest L. Merrill
Fig. 7.12

OTTO NATZLER

Guild (Los Angeles, 1940s)

217 **Bowls** (set of 7), c. 1945
Cast earthenware
Each: 6¼ x 4½ x 1½ in. (15.8 x 11.7 x 3.7 cm)
Gail Reynolds Natzler, Trustee of the
Natzler Trust
Fig. 6.8

WALLACE NEFF

(1895–1982, active Los Angeles)

Maynard L. Parker (1900–1976, active Los Angeles), photographer

Unidentified photographer

218 Airform houses, 1934–41
Photographs taken mid-20th century; printed 2011
Inkjet print
11 x 14 in. (27.9 x 35.6 cm)
Wallace Neff Photograph Collection

RICHARD NEUTRA

(b. Austria, 1892–1970, active Los Angeles)

219 Chair, 1931
Made for the Richard Neutra VDL Research House, Silver Lake, 1932; this example made c. 1941
Ash plywood, chromed steel, original leather
25½ x 27½ x 26⅜ in. (64.8 x 69.9 x 67 cm)
LACMA, Decorative Arts Council Fund, M.2002.21
Fig. 2.29

220 Josef von Sternberg House, Northridge (aerial perspective), 1934–35
Ink on linen
24¾ x 31⅝ in. (62.9 x 80.5 cm)
UCLA Library Special Collections. Richard and Dion Neutra Papers, 1925–1970
Fig. 4.2

221 Typical Classr[oo]m, Activity Train[in]g, Corona Avenue School, Bell (interior perspective), 1935
Pastel and graphite on board
15¼ x 24 in. (38.7 x 61 cm)
Private collection, London
Fig. 4.1

222 "Camel" table (prototype), c. 1940
Made for the Richard Neutra VDL Research House, Silver Lake, 1932
Birch plywood
Dining height: 28 x 37½ x 72 in. (71.1 x 95.2 x 182.9 cm)
Collection of Dion Neutra, architect, son and partner
Fig. 6.11

223 Channel Heights Housing Project, San Pedro (interior perspective), 1941–42
Ink on linen
23½ x 13½ in. (59.7 x 34.3 cm)
UCLA Library Special Collections. Richard and Dion Neutra Papers, 1925–1970
Fig. 4.8

224 Chair from Channel Heights Housing Project, San Pedro, 1941–42
Plywood, steel, plastic, fabric cushion
29½ x 25 x 31½ in. (74.9 x 63.5 x 80 cm)
LACMA, Gift of Thomas S. Hines, M.91.142
Fig. 4.7

GORDON NEWELL (1905–1998, active Los Angeles and Monterey peninsula)

Architectural Pottery (Los Angeles, 1950–71; thereafter Group Artec)

225 Sea Lion, model N-2, c. 1961
Earthenware
16½ x 22 x 15 in. (41.9 x 55.9 x 38.1 cm)
Collection of Alan and Nora Jaffe

OPCO COMPANY (Los Angeles, n.d.)

226 Ice gun, c. 1935
Aluminum, chrome-plated steel
6¼ x 10¾ x 2½ in. (15.9 x 27.3 x 6.4 cm)
LACMA, Decorative Arts and Design Acquisition Fund and Decorative Arts and Design Council Fund, M.2010.204
Fig. 2.7

JOHN NICHOLAS OTAR

(b. Russia, c. 1891–1939, active Santa Cruz)

227 Covered box, c. 1933
Copper, brass
Height: 4¾ in. (12.1 cm); diameter: 5¼ in. (13.3 cm)
LACMA, Decorative Arts Deaccession Fund, M.2006.36a-b

PACIFIC CLAY PRODUCTS, PACIFIC POTTERY DIVISION

(Los Angeles, c. 1891–1950s)

228 Hostess Ware cocktail mixer, model 630, c. 1935
Earthenware
Height: 10½ in. (26.7 cm); diameter: 4¾ in. (12.1 cm)
Collection of Bill Stern
Fig. 2.20

PACKARD-BELL (Los Angeles, 1926–78)

229 Radio, model 5 R 3, c. 1947
Polystyrene, cellulose nitrate, nickel-plated steel, brass, PVC (polyvinyl chloride) cord
6⅛ x 9⅜ x 5 in. (15.6 x 23.8 x 12.7 cm)
Collection of Andy Hackman
Fig. 6.32

PHILIP PAVAL

(b. Denmark, 1899–1971, active Hollywood)

230 Creamer, 1947
Exhibited in *The Decorative Arts Today*, Newark Museum, Newark, New Jersey, 1948–49
Silver
Height: 5⅜ in. (13.7 cm); diameter: 2¾ in. (7 cm)
Collection of The Newark Museum, Gift of the Artist, 1948

JOCK D. PETERS

(b. Germany, 1889–1934, active Los Angeles)

231 Table from the sportswear department, Bullock's Wilshire department store, Los Angeles, c. 1929
Mahogany, zebrawood, sycamore, and other woods
30½ x 66 x 30 in. (77.5 x 167.6 x 76.2 cm)
LACMA, Decorative Arts and Design Council Fund in honor of Rose Tarlow receiving the 2010 Design Leadership Award, Michael and Jane Eisner, Bobby Kotick, Ann and Jerry Moss, Jane and Terry Semel, The David Geffen Foundation, Margie and Jerry Perenchio, Lynda and Stewart Resnick, Eli and Edythe Broad, Selim K. Zilkha and Mary Hayley, David Bohnett and Tom Gregory, The Judy and Bernard Briskin Fund, Mimi and Peter Haas Fund, Holly Hunt, Jena and Michael King, Kevin Kolanowski, Alexandra and Michael Misczynksi, Frank Pollaro and Jennifer Dubose, Maggie Russell, Susan and Peter Strauss, Luanne Wells, John M. and Judith Hart Angelo, Douglas S. Cramer and Hugh Bush, Suzanne Kayne, Kelly and Ron Meyer, Susan Smalley, Deborah and David Trainer, Design Alliance LA, Thomas A. Kligerman, Kenneth and Louise Litwack, Elaine Lotwin, Carol and Michael Palladino, Janet Dreisen Rappaport, Patti and Bruce Springsteen, and Lars Stensland Jr. and Kim Baer, M.2011.7
Fig. 2.2

ALICE PETTERSON

(1910–1983, active Claremont)

RICHARD B. PETTERSON

(1910–1996, active Claremont)

232 Plate, 1966
Glass, gold luster
Diameter: 11⅛ in. (28.4 cm)
Scripps College, Claremont, CA

233 Plate, 1966
Glass
Diameter: 11⅛ in. (28.4 cm)
Scripps College, Claremont, CA

ANTONIO PRIETO

(b. Spain, 1913–1967, active Oakland)

234 Vessel, 1959
Stoneware
Height: 12⅛ in. (30.8 cm); diameter: 7⅜ in.
(18.7 cm)
Collection of Forrest L. Merrill
Fig. 7.26

MYRTON PURKISS

(b. Canada, 1912–1978, active Fullerton)

235 Plate, c. 1950
Earthenware
Diameter: 8¾ in. (22.2 cm)
LACMA, Purchased with funds provided by
Martha and Bruce Karsh, M.2008.292
Fig. 1.32

RUTH RADAKOVICH

(1920–1975, active Encinitas)

236 Brooch, 1958
Exhibited in *Sculpture, Jewelry: Toza and
Ruth Radakovich*, Long Beach Museum of
Art, 1961
Gold, red tourmaline
1⅝ x 3 x ¾ in. (4.3 x 7.6 x 1.9 cm)
Collection of Jean Radakovich
Fig. 7.19

SVETOZAR RADAKOVICH

(b. Yugoslavia, 1918–1998, active Encinitas)

237 Brooch, 1963
Gold, aquamarine
1⅝ x 2¾ x ¾ in. (4.3 x 7 x 1.9 cm)
Collection of Jean Radakovich
Fig. 7.19

BARNEY M. REID (1913–1992)

Reidart (San Diego, c. 1950–51)

238 Geodetic textile, c. 1951
Cotton
53 x 24 in. (61 x 134.6 cm)
Collection of Bill Stern
Fig. 8.9

239 Place mat, c. 1951
Cotton
18½ x 13½ in. (47 x 34 cm)
Collection of Bill Stern

MERRY RENK (b. 1921, active San Francisco)

240 Folded hairband, 1954
Silver
Height: 2 in. (5.1 cm); diameter: 6½ in.
(16.5 cm)
LACMA, Decorative Arts and Design
Council Fund, TR.15814
Fig. 10.18

241 Branching comb, 1967
Silver, pearls
Length: 7¼ in. (18.4 cm)
Museum of Fine Arts, Boston. Gift of
Joan Pearson Watkins in honor of
C. Malcolm Watkins

FLORENCE RESNIKOFF

(b. 1920, active San Francisco area)

242 Necklace, c. 1962
Silver, pearls, amethyst prism, vermeil
prism, gold
8 x 9 x 1 in. (20.3 x 22.9 x 2.5 cm)
Museum of Fine Arts, Boston. The Daphne
Farago Collection

VICTOR RIES

(b. Germany, 1907, active San Francisco area)

243 Candelabrum, c. 1957
Silver, wood
14 x 14⅛ x 4½ in. (35.6 x 35.9 x 11.4 cm)
Collection of Forrest L. Merrill
Fig. 3.7

244 Necklace, c. 1969
Gold, silver, pearls, carnelian
8½ x 7½ x ⅜ in. (21.6 x 19.1 x 1 cm)
Oakland Museum of California, Bequest of
Mrs. Dorothea Adams McCoy
Fig. 3.9

ED ROSSBACH (1914–2002, active Berkeley)

245 Reconstituted Commercial Textile, 1960
Printed cotton, polyethylene tubing
35½ x 35 in. (90.2 x 88.9 cm)
Museum of Fine Arts, Boston. The Daphne
Farago Collection
Fig. 8.7

HUDSON ROYSHER

(1911–1993, active Los Angeles)

246 Decanter set (2 decanters, 8 cups, tray),
c. 1948
Silver, Sumatra cane
Decanter, height: 10¾ in. (27.3 cm);
diameter: 4½ in. (11.4 cm)
Collection of the Roysher family
Fig. 5.25

MARION SAMPLER

(1920–1998, active Los Angeles)

Victor Gruen Associates
(Los Angeles, 1950–present)

**247 Two Christmas cards for Victor Gruen
Associates**, c. 1962 and c. 1965
Lithography
1962 card: 3½ x 3½ x 3½ in. (8.9 x 8.9
x 8.9 cm); 1965 card: 5 x 5 x 5 in. (12.7 x 12.7
x 12.7 cm)
Collection of Gruen Associates

ZAHARA SCHATZ

(b. Palestine [now Israel], 1916–1999, active
Berkeley)

248 Lamp, c. 1949
Acrylic, copper, steel, brass, oak, fiberglass
17 x 24 x 9 in. (43.2 x 61 x 22.9 cm)
LACMA, Purchased with funds provided by
Allison and Larry Berg
Fig. 7.16

LANETTE SCHEELINE

(1910–2001, active San Francisco area)

249 Egyptian Garden textile, c. 1939
Airbrushed cotton
65¾ x 52 in. (167 x 132.1 cm)
Gift of Lanette Scheeline, Smithsonian
Institution, Cooper-Hewitt, National Design
Museum, 1984-56-1
Fig. 8.11

R. M. (RUDOLPH MICHAEL) SCHINDLER
(b. Austria, 1887–1953, active Los Angeles)

250 Dresser with mirror from the Milton and Ruth Shep commission, Silver Lake, c. 1934–38
Gumwood, mirror glass
70½ x 105 x 26⅜ in. (179.1 x 266.7 x 67 cm)
LACMA, Gift of Ruth Shep Polen, AC1995.81.19.1–.10
Fig. 2.14

251 T. Falk Apartments, unrealized (aerial perspective), 1943
Graphite on paper
21½ x 21 in. (54.6 x 53.3 cm)
R. M. Schindler Collection, Architecture and Design Collection, University Art Museum, UC Santa Barbara
Fig. 4.9

252 *Typical Apartment*, T. Falk Apartments, unrealized (interior perspective), 1943
Ink on paper
27 x 20 in. (68.6 x 50.8 cm)
R. M. Schindler Collection, Architecture and Design Collection, University Art Museum, UC Santa Barbara
Fig. 4.10

Warren McArthur Corporation (Los Angeles, c. 1930–33; thereafter New York and Connecticut)

253 Chair from Sardi's Restaurant, Hollywood, 1932–33
Aluminum, rubber
34½ x 25 x 23½ in. (87.6 x 63.5 x 59.7 cm)
Collection of Gabrielle and Michael Boyd
Fig. 2.12

JUNE SCHWARCZ (b. 1918, active Sausalito)

254 Bowl, 1964
Enamel on copper
Height: 2¼ in. (5.7 cm); diameter 9¼ in. (23.5 cm)
Collection of Forrest L. Merrill
Fig. 7.32

KAY SEKIMACHI (b. 1926, active Berkeley)

255 *Reflection #2* textile, 1959
Cotton, linen, rayon
21⅞ x 18¼ in. (55.6 x 46.4 cm)
Collection of Kay Sekimachi
Fig. 8.6

256 Room divider, 1960
Linen
87 x 31 in. (221 x 78.7 cm)
Collection of Forrest L. Merrill
Fig. 8.4

SHAWL, NYELAND, AND SEAVEY
(San Francisco, n.d.)
Paul Nyeland (1909–2005); Clyde Seavey (1904–1991); and Louis Shawl (1905–1998)
San Francisco Bay Exposition (San Francisco, n.d.), publisher
Schmidt Lithography Company (San Francisco, n.d.), printer

257 *1939 World's Fair on San Francisco Bay* (poster), 1937
Offset lithography
34½ x 26½ in. (87.6 x 67.3 cm)
Collection of Mark and Maura Resnick
Fig. 1.25

MILLARD SHEETS
(1907–1989, active Los Angeles and Claremont)

258 Screen, 1930s
Oil on canvas on board, wood
88 x 114 x 1½ in. (223.5 x 289.6 x 3.8 cm)
LACMA, Purchased with funds provided by the American Art Council Fund, the Decorative Arts and Design Council Fund, and Barbara and Michael Brickman, M.2009.63
Fig. 2.16

SHELDON OF CALIFORNIA (n.d.)

259 Man's jacket, 1950–52
Rayon
Center-back length: 25¼ in. (64.1 cm)
LACMA, Gift of Esther Ginsberg, M.2010.130.6

OTIS SHEPARD
(1893–1969, active San Francisco)
Wrigley Company (Chicago, 1911–2008; now a subsidiary of Mars, Inc.)

260 *Catalina* (poster), 1938
Designed on Catalina Island; printed in Milwaukee
Lithography
39 x 51 in. (99.1 x 128.5 cm)
Collection of Mark and Maura Resnick
Fig. 9.3

NICOLAS SIDJAKOV
(b. Latvia, 1924–1993, active San Francisco)
Ruth Robbins (1917–2003), author
Parnassus Press (Berkeley, n.d.), publisher
Hogan-Kaus Lithographers (San Francisco, n.d.), printer

261 *Baboushka and the Three Kings* (book), 1960
Offset lithography
6¾ x 7¼ in. (17.1 x 18.4 cm)
The Mr. and Mrs. Allan C. Balch Art Research Library, LACMA
Fig. 9.20

JOSEPH SINEL (b. New Zealand, 1889–1975, active San Francisco area)
Dorothy Wright Liebes (1899–1972), exhibition director
San Francisco Bay Exposition Company (San Francisco, n.d.), publisher
H. S. Crocker Company, Inc., Schwabacher-Frey Company (San Francisco, n.d.), publishers

262 *Decorative Arts: Official Catalog, Department of Fine Arts, Division of Decorative Arts, Golden Gate International Exposition, San Francisco, 1939* (book), 1939
Lithography or letterpress
10¼ x 7½ in. (26 x 19.1 cm)
The Mr. and Mrs. Allan C. Balch Art Research Library, LACMA
P. 347

DON SMITH (1918–1972, active San Francisco)
L. Anton Maix Fabrics (New York, 1948–present)

263 *Fish Fair* textile, c. 1953
Screenprinted linen
34½ x 52 in. (87.6 x 132.1 cm)
LACMA, Purchased with funds provided by the Costume and Textiles Deaccession Fund and the Decorative Arts and Design Deaccession Fund, M.2009.54.5
P. 11

SEWALL SMITH (1904–1988, active Lafayette)
The Golden Age Company (Lafayette, n.d.)

264 *Boom! Or Golden Age!* (board game), 1950
Offset lithography
11 x 20 x 2 in. (27.9 x 50.8 x 5.1 cm)
Collection of Steve Cabella
Fig. 10.26

WHITNEY R. SMITH

(1911–2002, active South Pasadena)

265 **The Garden Wall House for the Barr Lumber Company**, unrealized (elevations), 1946
Graphite and ink on paper
24¼ x 36 in. (61.6 x 91.4 cm)
Smith and Williams Collection, Architecture and Design Collection, University Art Museum, UC Santa Barbara
Fig. 4.18

PAUL SOLDNER (1921–2011, active Claremont)

266 **Vessel**, late 1960s
Earthenware
15½ x 12 x 8 in. (39.4 x 30.5 x 20.3 cm)
LACMA, Gift of Daniel Ostroff, AC1992.293.1

RAPHAEL S. SORIANO

(b. Rhodes [now Greece], 1907–1988, active Los Angeles and Tiburon)

Eichler Homes, Inc. (Palo Alto, 1948–68)

267 **Prototype steel house**, Palo Alto (elevation), 1955
Pastel on vellum
13½ x 15¼ in. (34.3 x 38.7 cm)
College of Environmental Design, Archive—Special Collections, California State Polytechnic University, Pomona
Fig. 4.20

268 **Prototype steel house**, Palo Alto (interior), 1955
Pastel on vellum
9¾ x 15⅛ in. (24.8 x 38.4 cm)
College of Environmental Design, Archive—Special Collections, California State Polytechnic University, Pomona

SOUTHERN PACIFIC COMPANY

(San Francisco, 1865–present; now part of Union Pacific)

269 *Southern Pacific's New Daylight* (poster), c. 1937
Lithograph
Sheet: 22⅞ x 16 in. (58.1 x 40.6 cm)
LACMA, Gift of Debbie and Mark Attanasio in memory of Martin Kaplan, M.2010.113.1
Fig. 9.1

SPENCE AIR PHOTOS (Los Angeles, c. 1918–71)

270 **View of Wilshire and Fairfax, Los Angeles**, 1922
Gelatin silver print
13⅛ x 19⅛ in. (33.3 x 48.6 cm)
LACMA, Decorative Arts and Design Deaccession Fund, M.2010.32.1
Fig. 1.7

271 **View of Wilshire and Fairfax, Los Angeles**, 1929; printed 1930
Gelatin silver print
13⅛ x 19¼ in. (33.3 x 49.1 cm)
LACMA, Decorative Arts and Design Deaccession Fund, M.2010.32.2
Fig. 1.8

ROBERT STACY-JUDD

(b. England, 1884–1975, active Los Angeles)

272 **Howard Hampton Fallout Shelter, Model "C,"** Los Angeles (cutaway perspective), 1961
Graphite and ink on board
15 x 20¼ in. (38.1 x 51.4 cm)
Robert B. Stacy-Judd Collection, Architecture and Design Collection, University Art Museum, UC Santa Barbara

JACK WERNER STAUFFACHER

(b. 1920, active San Francisco)

273 **Two prints from the series Shifting and Inking**, 1963
Made in Pittsburgh, Pennsylvania
Letterpress
Each: 10 x 10 in. (25.4 x 25.4 cm)
San Francisco Museum of Modern Art, Gift of Jack Werner Stauffacher
P. 347 (one print)

Frank Stauffacher (1917–1955), editor
San Francisco Museum of Art (San Francisco, 1935–present; now San Francisco Museum of Modern Art), publisher

274 *Art in Cinema* (book), 1947
Letterpress
8½ x 7¾ in. (21.6 x 19.7 cm)
San Francisco Museum of Modern Art, Research Library
Fig. 9.11

BOB STOCKSDALE (1913–2003, active Berkeley)

275 **Bowl**, 1950s
Black walnut with ebony and other inlays
Height: 5½ in. (14 cm); diameter: 8 in. (20.3 cm)
Collection of Kay Sekimachi

276 **Bowl**, 1958
Exhibited at Brussels World's Fair, 1958
Black walnut
Height: 5½ in. (14 cm); diameter: 6½ in. (16.5 cm)
Collection of Kay Sekimachi
Fig. 7.9

MARTIN STREICH (1926–1999, active Oakland)

277 **Brooch**, c. 1950
Silver, copper, brass
2½ x 2½ x ¼ in. (6.4 x 6.4 x .6 cm)
Oakland Museum of California, Gift of Arlene Streich

ELZA SUNDERLAND

(b. Hungary, 1903–1991, active Los Angeles)

278 *Mexican Pottery* **textile design**, 1939
Gouache on paper
Composition: 22½ x 18½ in. (57.2 x 47 cm)
LACMA, Elza Sunderland Textile Design Collections, M.85.175.140
Fig. 8.12

279 **Textile design**, c. 1946
Gouache on paper
Composition: 16⅞ x 23 in. (42.9 x 58.4 cm)
LACMA, Elza Sunderland Textile Design Collections, M.85.175.318

DEBORAH SUSSMAN

(b. 1931, active Los Angeles area)

Lawrence Alloway (b. England, 1926–1990), author
Los Angeles County Museum of Art (Los Angeles, 1910–present), publisher
Koltun Brothers (Los Angeles, n.d.), printer

280 *Six More* (exhibition catalogue), 1963
Offset lithography
8½ x 5½ in. (21.6 x 14 cm)
The Mr. and Mrs. Allan C. Balch Art Research Library, LACMA
P. 15

LA GARDO TACKETT

(1911–1984, active Los Angeles area)

Architectural Pottery (Los Angeles, 1950–71; thereafter Group Artec)

281 **Garden sculpture**, c. 1955
Earthenware
Largest totem, height: 81 in. (205.7 cm); diameter: 14 in. (35.6 cm)
Collection of the Lawrence family; lent in honor of Max and Rita Lawrence
Fig. 6.18

John Follis, stand designer
Architectural Pottery
282 Planter, model WN-04, c. 1957
Earthenware, walnut
Height: 31¼ in. (79.4 cm); diameter: 18 in.
(45.7 cm)
LACMA, Gift of Joel and Margaret Chen
of J. F. Chen, M.2009.137a-b
Fig. 5.5

Schmid Kreglinger, Inc., Schmid International
Division (Boston, n.d.)
283 *Forma* coffeepot, c. 1959
Manufactured in Japan
Whiteware porcelain
11⅝ x 7¼ x 3½ in. (29.5 x 18.4 x 8.8 cm)
LACMA, Purchased with funds provided by
Candace and Charles Nelson,
M.2009.114.3a-b
Fig. 5.33

GENE TEPPER (b. 1919, active San Francisco)

Tepper-Meyer Associates
(San Francisco, c. 1950-55)
284 Model for *Versitable*, c. 1953
Production version exhibited in *Good
Design*, Museum of Modern Art, New York,
1953, and *California Design*, Pasadena Art
Museum, 1954
Wood, metal
Dining height: 10 x 22 x 11¾ in.
(25.4 x 55.9 x 29.8 cm)
Collection of Gene Tepper
See fig. 6.10

DOROTHY THORPE
(1901-1989, active Glendale and Sun Valley)

Crown Lynn Potteries (New Zealand, 1948-89)
285 *Monterrey* creamer, c. 1965
Earthenware
4⅛ x 5½ x 4⅛ in. (10.5 x 14 x 10.5 cm)
LACMA, Decorative Arts and Design
Council Fund, M.2010.14

286 *Monterrey* sugar bowl, c. 1965
Earthenware
Height: 2½ in. (6.4 cm); diameter: 4¼ in.
(10.8 cm)
Museum of California Design, Los Angeles,
Gift of Daniel Ostroff

ADOLPH TISCHLER (b. 1917, active Los Angeles)
287 *Duo* flatware, c. 1955
Steel, nylon
Knife: 7⅝ x ⅞ x ⅞ in. (19.4 x 2.2 x 2.2 cm)
LACMA, Purchased with funds provided by
Harris & Ruble, M.2009.176.1-.4
Fig. 5.26

NATHAN TURK
(b. Russia, 1895-1988, active Sherman Oaks)
288 Woman's shirt and trousers, 1950s
Wool
Shirt: 24 x 21 in. (61 x 53.3 cm); pants:
43½ x 12½ in. (110.5 x 31.8 cm)
Courtesy of Museum of the American West,
Autry National Center; 2004.88.5.1-.2,
Donated by the Los Angeles County
Museum of Art to the Museum of the
American West
Fig. 8.37

DANIEL GALE TURNBULL
(1886-1964, active Vernon)

Vernon Kilns (Vernon, 1931-58)
289 *Ultra California* coffeepot, c. 1937
Earthenware
Height: 8⅜ in. (21.3 cm); diameter: 8¼ in.
(21 cm)
LACMA, Decorative Arts and Design
Acquisition Fund and partial gift of Bill
Stern, M.2010.91.7a-b
Fig. 2.20

PAUL TUTTLE (1918-2002, active Santa Barbara)

Carson-Johnson, Inc. (El Monte, n.d.)
290 *Z* chair, c. 1964
Form exhibited in *California Design 9*,
Pasadena Museum of Art, 1965
Chrome-plated steel, original leather
28¼ x 26¾ x 32 in. (71.8 x 68 x 81.3 cm)
LACMA, Decorative Arts and Design
Council Fund, M.2008.94
Fig. 10.14

UNKNOWN DESIGNER
291 Belt, 1900-1950
Horsehair, horn, shell, leather
2½ x 43 in. (6.4 x 109.2 cm)
Courtesy of the Museum of the American
West, Autry National Center; 95.15.1

UNKNOWN DESIGNER
292 Belt, 1925-50
Leather, silver
2¼ x 37½ in. (5.7 x 95.3 cm)
Courtesy of the Museum of the American
West, Autry National Center; 2002.57.8.
Dedicated to Bob "Tex" Allen by his son
Ted Baehr and family

UNKNOWN DESIGNER
293 Man's swim trunks and shirt (cabana set),
c. 1963
Made in California
Cotton
Shirt, center-back length: 30 in. (76.2 cm);
trunks, center-back length: 18 in. (45.7 cm)
LACMA, Gift of Esther Ginsberg,
M.2010.130.7a-b
Fig. 8.33

FREDERICK A. USHER JR.
(1923-2009, active Los Angeles area)
294 Design Group invitation cards, 1947-48
Ink and watercolor on paper
9 cards, each: 3¼ x 5½ in. (8.3 x 14 cm)
Collection of Louis Danziger
Fig. 1.15

American Crayon Company (Sandusky, Ohio,
1890-1984), publisher
295 *Everyday Art* (magazine), fall 1956
Offset lithography
9 x 6 in. (22.9 x 15.2 cm)
The Mr. and Mrs. Allan Balch
Art Research Library, LACMA

LYDIA VAN GELDER
(b. 1911, active Lodi, Fresno, and Santa Rosa)
296 *Houses on a Street* textile, 1939
Exhibited at the Golden Gate International
Exposition, San Francisco, 1939
Cotton tapestry weave
83 x 24½ in. (211 x 62.2 cm)
Gift of Lydia Van Gelder, Smithsonian
Institution, Cooper-Hewitt, National Design
Museum, 1996-47-1
Fig. 8.13

JOHN VAN HAMERSVELD

(b. 1941, active Los Angeles area)

Bruce Brown Films (Dana Point, c. 1957–present), producer

297 *The Endless Summer* (poster), 1963;
this example printed in Costa Mesa, 1965
Designed in Dana Point and Los Angeles
Screenprint
60 x 40 in. (152.4 x 101.6 cm)
Collection of Mark and Maura Resnick
Fig. 1.31

HENDRIK VAN KEPPEL

(1914–1988, active Los Angeles and Beverly Hills)

Van Keppel-Green (Beverly Hills, 1939–early 1970s)

298 Lounge chair and ottoman, models 801
and 800, c. 1939; this example made c. 1959
Form exhibited in *Useful Objects*, Museum
of Modern Art, New York, 1946; *Good
Design Is Your Business*, Albright Art
Gallery, Buffalo, New York, 1947; *Design for
Use, USA*, Stuttgart, 1951
Enameled steel, cotton cord (replaced)
Chair: 24½ x 20½ x 33 in. (62.2 x 52.1
x 83.8 cm)
LACMA, Gift of Dan Steen in memory of
Taylor Green, AC1998.31.1-.2
Fig. 6.6

**HENDRIK VAN KEPPEL
TAYLOR GREEN**

(1914–1991, active Los Angeles and Beverly Hills)

Van Keppel-Green

299 *Three-Seater* **sofa**, model 660, c. 1957
Steel, original rattan
30 x 64¼ x 24 in. (76.2 x 163.2 x 61 cm)
LACMA, Decorative Arts and Design
Deaccession Fund, M.2008.234.1
Fig. 5.6

ATTRIBUTED TO VAN KEPPEL-GREEN

300 Lantern, c. 1951
Iron, plastic
Height: 65 in. (165.1 cm); diameter: 8 in.
(20.3 cm)
Collection of Chip Tom and Michael W.
Rabkin

VISTA FURNITURE COMPANY

(Anaheim, n.d.)

301 Counter stool, c. 1952
Mahogany, iron
28⅞ x 14⅝ x 17⅝ in. (73.3 x 37.2 x 44.8 cm)
LACMA, Decorative Arts and Design
Council Fund, M.2010.94
Fig. 5.19

PETER VOULKOS

(1924–2002, active Los Angeles and Berkeley)

302 *Standing Jar*, c. 1954–56
Stoneware
22½ x 16 x 17 in. (57.2 x 40.6 x 43.2 cm)
LACMA, Gift of Howard and Gwen Laurie
Smits in honor of the museum's twenty-
fifth anniversary, M.90.82.55
Fig. 7.3

303 *5000 Feet* **sculpture**, 1958
Exhibited in *Artists of Los Angeles and
Vicinity*, Los Angeles County Museum, 1959
Stoneware
45½ x 21 x 13 in. (115.6 x 53.3 x 33 cm)
LACMA, Junior Art Council Fund, M.59.16
Fig. 7.24

ROBERT WALKER (n.d.), game designer

Walker Products (Berkeley, n.d.), manufacturer
Walter Landor (b. Germany, 1913–1995, active
San Francisco), package designer
Walter Landor & Associates (San Francisco,
1941–present)

304 *Space Spider* (game), 1955
Offset lithography
6 x 6 x 6 in. (15.2 x 15.2 x 15.2 cm)
Collection of Steve Cabella

KEM (KARL EMANUEL MARTIN) WEBER

(b. Germany, 1889–1963, active Los Angeles)

305 Desk and chair, c. 1938
Exhibited at the Golden Gate International
Exposition, San Francisco, 1939
Satinwood, primavera, chrome, aluminum,
resin, leather (replaced)
Desk: 30¼ x 60 x 30 in. (76.8 x 152.4 x
76.2 cm)
LACMA, Purchased jointly with funds
provided by the Decorative Arts and
Design Deaccession Fund, Viveca Paulin-
Ferrell and Will Ferrell, Shannon and Peter
Loughrey, Heidi and Said Saffari, and Holly
and Albert Baril, M.2010.7.1-.2
Fig. 2.28

**306 Walt Disney Studios, Library Reading
Room**, Burbank (presentation drawing),
c. 1939
Watercolor on board
15 x 22 in. (38.1 x 55.9 cm)
Kem Weber Collection, Architecture and
Design Collection, University Art Museum,
UC Santa Barbara
Fig. 2.26

307 Coffee table from Walt Disney Studios,
Burbank, c. 1939
Birch, Bakelite
20 x 30 x 30 in. (50.8 x 76.2 x 76.2 cm)
TFTM, Los Angeles

Airline Chair Company (Los Angeles, 1930s)
308 *Airline* **chair**, c. 1934–35
Birch, ash, original oilcloth
30½ x 34½ x 25 in. (77.5 x 87.6 x 63.5 cm)
LACMA, Purchased with funds provided by
The J. Paul Getty Museum, M.2004.13
Fig. 2.10

KATHERINE WESTPHAL

(b. 1919, active Berkeley)

309 *The Hunt* **quilt**, c. 1963
Cotton with various printing techniques
86 x 64 in. (218.4 x 162.6 cm)
Collection of Katherine Westphal
Fig. 8.8

MARGUERITE WILDENHAIN

(b. France, 1896–1985, active Guerneville)

310 Teapot, creamer, and sugar, c. 1946
Exhibited in the *Eleventh National Ceramic
Exhibition*, Syracuse Museum of Fine Arts,
Syracuse, New York, 1946
Stoneware
Teapot, height: 5 in. (12.7 cm); diameter:
10 in. (25.4 cm)
Everson Museum of Art, Gift of Richard B.
Gump, Purchase Prize 11th Ceramic
National, 1946; 47.515.1-3
Fig. 3.5

311 Vase, c. 1965
Stoneware
Height: 9½ in. (24.1 cm); diameter: 7⅝ in.
(19.4 cm)
Collection of Forrest L. Merrill
Fig. 3.3

BARBARA WILLIS

(b. 1917, active Los Angeles area)

Barbara Willis Pottery (North Hollywood, c. 1942–58)

312 **Pillow vases**, c. 1945
  Earthenware
  Largest vase: 7¼ x 6⅜ x 2¼ in. (18.4 x 16.2 x 5.7 cm)
  LACMA, Decorative Arts and Design Acquisition Fund and partial gift of Bill Stern, M.2010.91.8.1-.3
  Fig. 6.7

BYRON WILSON (1918–1992, active Oakland)

313 **Necklace**, c. 1956
  Form exhibited in the *Second Exhibition of American Jewelry and Related Objects*, Memorial Art Gallery of the University of Rochester, Rochester, New York, 1956
  Silver, ebony, ivory
  8½ x 7 x 1¼ in. (21.6 x 17.8 x 3.2 cm)
  LACMA, Purchased with funds provided by Martha and Bruce Karsh, M.2010.116
  P. 8

BOB WINSTON

(1915–2003, active San Francisco area)

314 **Cuff**, c. 1957
  Silver
  2⅛ x 2¼ x 2¼ in. (5.4 x 5.7 x 5.7 cm)
  Oakland Museum of California, Gift of Grace Stovall

ARNOLD WOLF

(b. 1907, active Berkeley and Los Angeles)

JBL (Los Angeles, 1946–present)

315 *Paragon* speaker, 1957
  Designed in Berkeley; manufactured in Los Angeles, 1957–83
  Walnut veneer
  35¼ x 103⅝ x 24 in. (89.5 x 263.2 x 61 cm)
  Collection of Harman
  See fig. 5.29

JADE SNOW WONG

(1922–2006, active San Francisco)

Woodrow ("Woody") Ong (1916–1985), copper form spinner

316 **Ice bucket**, 1952
  Enamel on copper
  Height: 8 in. (20.3 cm); diameter: 7½ in. (19.1 cm)
  Mrs. Joseph F. Westheimer (Katherine), promised gift to LACMA
  Fig. 7.35

BEATRICE WOOD

(1893–1998, active Los Angeles and Ojai)

317 **Bowl**, c. 1950
  Earthenware
  Height: 6¼ in. (15.9 cm); diameter: 7 in. (17.8 cm)
  LACMA, Gift of Howard and Gwen Laurie Smits, M.87.1.179

WOODY WOODWARD

(1929–1985, active Hollywood)

World Pacific Records, Pacific Jazz Records Division (Hollywood, 1957–70), record label

318 *The Jazz Crusaders, Lookin' Ahead* (album cover), 1962
  Offset lithography
  12¼ x 12¼ in. (31.1 x 31.1 cm)
  LACMA, Decorative Arts and Design Council Fund, M.2010.119.8a-b

ELLAMARIE WOOLLEY

(1913–1976, active San Diego)

JACKSON WOOLLEY

(1910–1992, active San Diego)

319 **Plate**, no. 4126, c. 1951
  Enamel on copper
  Diameter: 8⅛ in. (20.6 cm)
  Collection of The Enamel Arts Foundation, Los Angeles, CA
  Fig. 7.28

320 **Plate**, no. 4755, c. 1952
  Enamel on copper
  Diameter: 8 in. (20.3 cm)
  Collection of The Enamel Arts Foundation, Los Angeles, CA

321 **Bowl**, no. 5259, c. 1953
  Enamel on copper
  Height: 1⅝ in. (4.1 cm); diameter: 8⅛ in. (20.6 cm)
  Collection of The Enamel Arts Foundation, Los Angeles, CA
  Fig. 7.29

FRANK LLOYD WRIGHT (1867–1959)

Esther Born (1902–1987), photographer

322 **Living room, playroom, and exterior, Paul and Jean Hanna House**, Palo Alto, 1937
  Photographs taken c. 1938; printed 2003
  Gelatin silver print
  Three photographs, each: 9½ x 13½ in. (24.1 x 34.3 cm)
  The Getty Research Institute, Los Angeles (2007.R.16)
  Fig. 4.3 (playroom)

WILLIAM WILSON WURSTER

(1895–1973, active San Francisco)

Wurster, Bernardi, and Emmons (San Francisco, 1945–present)

323 *Alterations to Defense Housing Project* (elevations), Carquinez Heights, Vallejo, 1947
  Pencil on tracing paper
  20 x 38½ in. (50.8 x 97.8 cm)
  William W. Wurster/WBE Collection, Environmental Design Archives, University of California, Berkeley
  Fig. 1.18

EPHEMERA

GREGORY AIN (1908–1988, active Los Angeles)

Museum of Modern Art (New York, 1929–present), publisher

324 *The Museum of Modern Art—Woman's Home Companion Exhibition House* (brochure), 1950
  Offset lithography
  7½ x 10 in. (19.1 x 25.4 cm)
  Gregory Ain Collection, Architecture and Design Collection, University Art Museum, UC Santa Barbara
  Fig. 10.7

ART CENTER SCHOOL

(Los Angeles, 1930–present; now Art Center College of Design)

325 **Course catalogue**, 1937
  Offset lithography
  8¼ x 7⅞ in. (21 x 20 cm)
  Courtesy Art Center College of Design
  Fig. 2.17

BARKER BROTHERS (Los Angeles, 1880–1991)

326 *Sunset Hills* (brochure), 1950s
  Offset lithography
  10¾ x 8⅜ in. (27.3 x 21.3 cm)
  Victoria Dailey and Steve Turner Collection, Los Angeles
  Fig. 10.6

ROBERT BROWNJOHN

(1925–1970), cover designer

Conrad Brown (n.d.), editor

327 *Craft Horizons: A Special Issue on California* (magazine), September–October 1956
Offset lithography
11½ x 8⅛ in. (29.2 x 20.6 cm)
American Craft Council Archives

CALIFORNIA COLLEGE OF ARTS AND CRAFTS (Oakland, 1907–present; now California College of the Arts)

328 **Bulletin**, April 1954
Lithography or letterpress
9 x 6 in. (22.9 x 15.2 cm)
California College of the Arts, Meyer Library

CALIFORNIA LABOR SCHOOL

(San Francisco, 1942–57)

329 **Course catalogue**, fall 1948
Offset lithography
5½ x 8 in. (14 x 20.3 cm)
Labor Archives and Research Center, San Francisco State University

CALIFORNIA SCHOOL OF FINE ARTS

(San Francisco, 1871–present; now San Francisco Art Institute)

330 **Course catalogues**, summer 1930, regular session 1930–31, summer 1931
Letterpress
Each: 8 x 5⅜ in. (20.3 x 13.7 cm)
Victoria Dailey and Steve Turner Collection, Los Angeles

CHOUINARD ART INSTITUTE

(Los Angeles, 1921–61), publisher

Martha Rodman (n.d.), illustrator

331 **Course catalogue**, c. 1944–45
Relief print
9¾ x 7¼ in. (24.8 x 18.4 cm)
Victoria Dailey and Steve Turner Collection, Los Angeles

THOMAS DOLLIVER CHURCH

(1902–1978, active San Francisco), landscape architect

Rondal Partridge (b. 1917), photographer

332 *House Beautiful* (magazine), April 1951
Offset lithography
12¾ x 9¾ in. (32.4 x 24.8 cm)
LACMA, Decorative Arts and Design Department library
Fig. 1.29

DARIO DE JULIO

(1916–2010, active Los Angeles)

Western Lithograph Company (Los Angeles, c. 1906–c. 1985), printer

333 *Red Circle* orange-crate label for **McDermont Fruit Company**, Riverside, c. 1938
Offset lithography
9¼ x 10¼ in. (23.5 x 26 cm)
LACMA, Decorative Arts and Design Council Fund, M.2010.118.1
Fig. 9.5

EICHLER HOMES, INC. (Palo Alto, 1948–68)

334 *Eichler Homes Designed to Make Your Everyday a Holiday!* (brochure), c. 1960
Offset lithography
6 x 8 in. (15.2 x 20.3 cm)
Collection of Steve Cabella
Fig. 4.28

GLENN OF CALIFORNIA (Arcadia, 1948–92)

335 **Sales catalogue**, c. 1952
Offset lithography
8¼ x 10¾ in. (21 x 27.3 cm)
Collection of Lloyd and Robert Baron
Fig. 10.10

CLIFF MAY (1908–1989, active Los Angeles)
CHRIS CHOATE (1908–1981, active Los Angeles)

Cliff May Homes (Los Angeles, c. 1953–c. 1959)

336 **Brochure**, 1953
Offset lithography
11 x 8½ in. (27.9 x 21.6 cm)
The Mr. and Mrs. Allan C. Balch Art Research Library, LACMA

MONSANTO CHEMICAL COMPANY

(St. Louis, Missouri, 1901–present)

337 *The Future Won't Wait* (brochure), 1960, showing the "Plastics Home of the Future" at Disneyland, Anaheim
Offset lithography
11 x 8½ in. (27.9 x 21.6 cm)
The Mr. and Mrs. Allan Balch Art Research Library, LACMA
Fig 10.24

PASADENA ART MUSEUM (Pasadena, 1922–present; now Norton Simon Museum)

Clifford Nelson (n.d.), exhibition director
Grant Dahlstrom (1902–1980), typographer
The Castle Press (Pasadena, 1931–present), printer

338 *California Design* (exhibition catalogue), 1954
Letterpress
5½ x 8½ in. (14 x 21.6 cm)
Oakland Museum of California, Paul C. Mills Archive of California Art
Fig. 10.11

Clifford Nelson, exhibition director
Cunningham Press (Alhambra, n.d.), printer

339 *California Design 5* (exhibition catalogue), 1959
Lithography
5⅜ x 8½ in. (13.7 x 21.6 cm)
Oakland Museum of California, Paul C. Mills Archive of California Art

Elizabeth F. G. Hanson (n.d.), exhibition director
Eudorah M. Moore (b. 1918, active Pasadena), exhibition director
Robert Ellis (n.d.), designer
The Castle Press, printer

340 *California Design 8* (exhibition catalogue), 1962
Exhibited in *Western Books Exhibition*, Rounce and Coffin Club, Los Angeles, 1963
Offset lithography
10⅛ x 8¾ in. (25.7 x 22.2 cm)
Oakland Museum of California, Paul C. Mills Archive of California Art

Eudorah M. Moore, exhibition director
Robert Ellis, designer
Cunningham Press, printer

341 *California Design 9* (exhibition catalogue), 1965
Offset lithography
10¼ x 8¾ in. (26 x 22.2 cm)
Oakland Museum of California, Paul C. Mills Archive of California Art

Eudorah M. Moore, exhibition director
Robert Ellis, designer
The Castle Press, printer
Anderson, Ritchie & Simon (South Pasadena, founded 1932; formerly Ward Ritchie Press), printer

342 *California Design 10* (exhibition catalogue), 1968
Exhibited in *Western Books Exhibition*, Rounce and Coffin Club, Los Angeles, 1969
Offset lithography
10¼ x 8¾ in. (26 x 22.2 cm)
Oakland Museum of California, Paul C. Mills Archive of California Art

JOCK D. PETERS
(b. Germany, 1889–1934, active Los Angeles)

343 **Christmas card**, 1930s
Sent to Kem Weber
Relief print
6⅛ x 5 in. (15.6 x 12.7 cm)
Collection of Erika Kem Plack

UNKNOWN DESIGNER
Elizabeth Mock (1911–1998), editor
Museum of Modern Art (New York, 1929–present), publisher

344 *Built in USA, 1932–1944* (exhibition catalogue), 1944
9½ x 7½ in. (24.1 x 19.1 cm)
John Funk Collection, Environmental Design Archives, University of California, Berkeley
Fig. 1.6

UNKNOWN DESIGNER

345 *Lakewood: The Future City, as New as Tomorrow* (brochure), c. 1950
Lithography
4⅝ x 7⅞ in. (11.7 x 20 cm)
Victoria Dailey and Steve Turner Collection, Los Angeles
Fig. 10.6

UNKNOWN DESIGNER

346 *Life* (magazine), April 11, 1949
Offset lithography
14 x 10¼ in. (35.6 x 26 cm)
The Mr. and Mrs. Allan Balch Art Research Library, LACMA

UNKNOWN DESIGNER

347 *Monterrey Hills: Island in the Sky* (brochure), 1950s
Offset lithography
7⅞ x 8 in. (20 x 20.3 cm)
Victoria Dailey and Steve Turner Collection, Los Angeles

UNKNOWN DESIGNER

348 *Popular Mechanics: "The PM California House"* (magazine), October 1958
Offset lithography
9½ x 6½ in. (24.1 x 16.5 cm)
Museum of California Design, Los Angeles, Gift of Bill Stern

UNKNOWN DESIGNER

349 *Sunset* (magazine), November 1936
Offset lithography
11½ x 8¾ in. (29.2 x 22.2 cm)
Collection of Sunset Publishing Corporation
Fig. 1.9

Julius Shulman (1910–2009, active Los Angeles), cover photographer

350 *Sunset* (magazine), March 1950
Offset lithography
11 x 8¼ in. (27.9 x 21 cm)
Collection of Sunset Publishing Corporation
Fig. 9.4

UNKNOWN DESIGNER

351 *Valley Park Mutual Homes in Fabulous Valleywood* (brochure), 1950s
Offset lithography
8⅝ x 6 in. (21.9 x 15.2 cm)
Victoria Dailey and Steve Turner Collection, Los Angeles
Fig. 10.6

VAN KEPPEL-GREEN
(Beverly Hills, 1939–early 1970s)

352 **Sales catalogue**, 1957
Offset lithography
7 x 8½ in. (17.8 x 21.6 cm)
The Mr. and Mrs. Allan Balch Art Research Library, LACMA
Fig. 6.5

WALLACH BUILDERS (North Hollywood, n.d.)

353 *Built to Order* (brochure), 1950s
Offset lithography
4 x 6⅜ in. (10.2 x 16.2 cm)
Victoria Dailey and Steve Turner Collection, Los Angeles
Fig. 10.6

JAMES S. WARD (n.d.)
Jane Fiske McCullough, editor

354 *Industrial Design: Design on the West Coast* (magazine), October 1957
Offset lithography
12 x 9 in. (30.5 x 22.9 cm)
The Mr. and Mrs. Allan Balch Art Research Library, LACMA

WESTERN LITHOGRAPH COMPANY
(Los Angeles, c. 1906–c. 1985), printer

355 *Passport* lemon-crate label for **R. H. Verity, Sons and Co.**, Corona, c. 1930s
Offset lithography
9 x 12⅜ in. (22.9 x 31.4 cm)
LACMA, Decorative Arts and Design Council Fund, M.2010.118.4

356 *Ponca* orange-crate label for Vandalia Packing Association, Porterville, c. 1930s
Offset lithography
9¾ x 10¾ in. (24.8 x 27.3 cm)
LACMA, Decorative Arts and Design Council Fund, M.2010.118.3

LLOYD WRIGHT
(1890–1978, active Los Angeles), logo designer

357 **Christmas card from Jake Zeitlin Bookstore**, c. 1934
Sent to Kem Weber
Letterpress
8⅞ x 5½ in. (22.5 x 14 cm)
Collection of Erika Kem Plack

ROOM SETTINGS CREATED FOR THE *CALIFORNIA DESIGN* EXHIBITION

Because these settings are being presented as ensembles, and most of the craftspeople and designers are represented elsewhere in the exhibition, not all of the objects in the rooms are included in the checklist.

KEM (KARL EMANUEL MARTIN) WEBER (b. Germany, 1889–1963, active Los Angeles)

"Contemporary Living Room," 1939
Original room assembled by Louis Dix Druehl for the John Breuner Company, San Francisco
Exhibited at the Golden Gate International Exposition, San Francisco, 1939–40
See opposite

This room was one of twelve commissioned by Dorothy Wright Liebes and Shepard Vogelgesang for the Decorative Arts Division in the Fine Arts Pavilion at the Golden Gate International Exposition, the 1939 World's Fair in San Francisco. Weber designed a desk and chair specifically for this room (cat. 305) and included other examples of his furniture, such as the *Airline* chair (cat. 308) and coffee table (cat. 307).

CHARLES EAMES (1907–1978, active Venice)
RAY EAMES (1912–1988, active Venice)

Living room from the Eames House (Case Study House #8), Pacific Palisades, built 1949; assembled 1949–88
See fig. 5.37

The home of Charles and Ray Eames was filled with their own designs, gifts from friends, and objects found on their travels. Combining old and new, traditional and contemporary, and familiar and exotic, the house remains an extraordinary example of how one couple lived "in a modern way." All objects in the re-creation have been borrowed from the Eames Foundation, which maintains and preserves the house.

"What Makes the California Look," *Los Angeles Times*, "Home" magazine cover, October 21, 1951

Selected and arranged by Richard B. Petterson (1910–1996, active Claremont)
See figs. 1.1 and 1.30 (key)

This ensemble was created for the cover of the *Los Angeles Times*'s "Home" magazine. Ceramist, teacher, and curator Richard Petterson selected the objects as the epitome of the new "California Look" (see pp. 26 and 55), and many remain icons of modern California design. The following objects that appeared in the rooms are also included in the checklist: cats. 28, 47, 60, 61, 76, 99, 110, 232, 233, 263, 298, 300, 320.

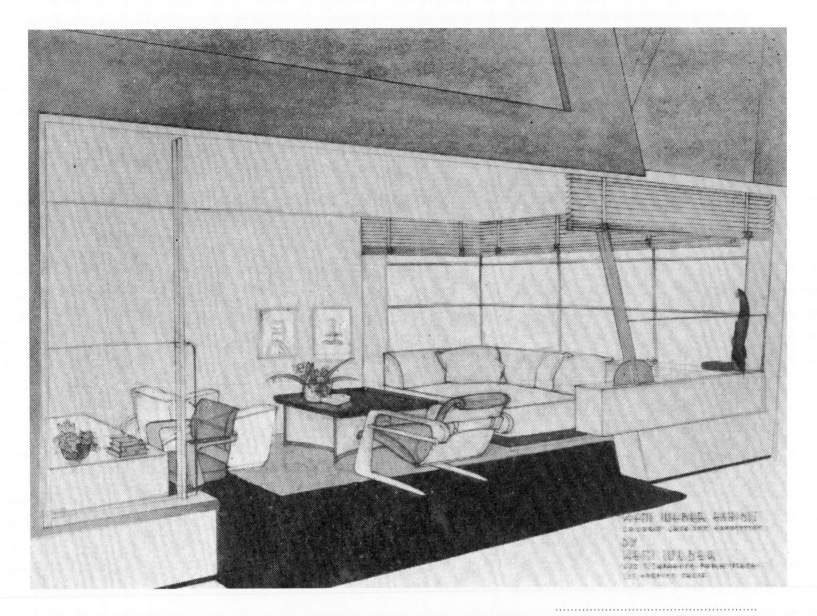

Kem Weber. Drawing and key for
"Contemporary Living Room" for the
Golden Gate International Exposition
(see opposite)
From *Decorative Arts: Official Catalog,
Department of Fine Arts, Division of
Decorative Arts, Golden Gate
International Exposition, San Francisco,
1939*, pp. 11 and 13

★CONTEMPORARY LIVING ROOM

Designed by Kem Weber, Los Angeles. Assembled by Louis Dix Druehl for the John Breuner Co., San Francisco.

Day bed with back cushions.

Low table of Prima-vera with lacquered top.

Table top, transparent photo abstraction by Bob Churchill, Los Angeles, California.

Upholstered chair.

Chair of wood tension construction.

Desk of Prima-vera.

Desk chair.

Floor covering of linoleum.

Hand-tufted rug. Designed by Carston Foge, San Francisco.

Sculpture, "A Study in Wood." By Isamu Noguchi.

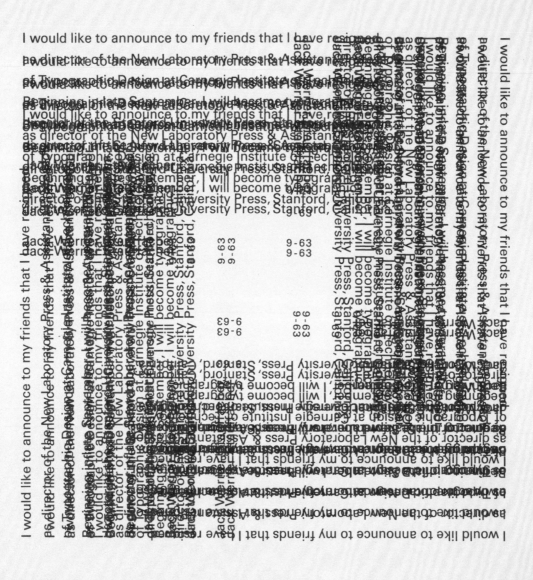

I would like to announce to my friends that I have resigned as director of the New Laboratory Press & Assistant Professor of Typographic Design at Carnegie Institute of Tech. Beginning in late September, I will become typographic director of the Stanford University Press, Stanford, California.

Jack Werner Stauffacher

9-63

Acknowledgments

We are deeply grateful to CEO and Wallis Annenberg Director Michael Govan for his enthusiasm about the exhibition from its initial stages. He championed our goal that LACMA be the first institution to comprehensively explore our state's design history and inspired our efforts not only to produce *California Design, 1930–1965: "Living in a Modern Way"* but also to make building the museum's collections in this area an institutional priority. Nancy Thomas, Deputy Director for Art Administration and Collections, offered encouragement and sage advice every step of the way, for which we extend many thanks.

An exhibition of this scale and scope would not have been possible without the visionary support of the Getty Foundation and its ambitious initiative Pacific Standard Time: Art in L.A. 1945–1980. Two supremely generous grants enabled both the research and the implementation of the exhibition and its catalogue. We are extraordinarily grateful to the lead corporate sponsor, Barbie, which not only supported the exhibition but also donated original Barbie and Ken dolls to the collection. We also express our deep gratitude to the Henry Luce Foundation American Art Program and to the Center for Craft, Creativity, and Design Craft Research Fund for their grants. We are greatly indebted to Debbie and Mark Attanasio, Martha and Bruce Karsh, Viveca Paulin-Ferrell and Will Ferrell, and Shannon and Peter Loughrey for additional essential support.

Our department's support group, the Decorative Arts and Design Council (DADC), led by former chair Marcella Ruble and present chair Oliver M. Furth, fully embraced the mission of acquiring outstanding works of California design. The funds raised by the DADC allowed us to make many key purchases that are included in the exhibition and provided significant support toward exhibition costs. We also thank the Director's Circle, chaired by LACMA Trustee Willow Bay, which hosted a fundraiser at R. M. Schindler's Buck House in June 2010 that enabled us to acquire several more masterpieces of California design. We are especially grateful to LACMA Trustee Viveca Paulin-Ferrell, whose passion for mid-century design contributed so much to the event's success.

The organization of a major exhibition is always a collaborative effort, and the true heroes of this endeavor are the staff of the Decorative Arts and Design

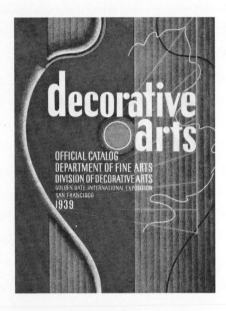

Jack Werner Stauffacher. Print from the series Shifting and Inking, 1963. Cat. 273

Joseph Sinel. *Decorative Arts: Official Catalog, Department of Fine Arts, Division of Decorative Arts, Golden Gate International Exposition, San Francisco, 1939*, cover. Cat. 262

Department. All showed a commitment to the myriad components of exhibition planning far beyond the call of duty. Curatorial Assistant Staci Steinberger was integral to all aspects of the exhibition and catalogue planning. Her extraordinary research prowess, organizational gifts, diplomatic skills, and keen eye were essential to the selection of objects, their documentation for the catalogue, and their installation in the exhibition. Curatorial Administrator Lacy Simkowitz mastered the many details of the exhibition—especially the coordination of photography and loans—with patience, thoroughness, and dedication. Prior to her tenure, we had the capable support of Curatorial Administrators Brittainy Welt and Alexandra Moran. Before his departure for the Museum of Fine Arts, Boston, Curator Thomas Michie's erudition and research played an important role in the initial development of the exhibition.

We are greatly indebted to our resourceful and tireless research team. Research Assistant Jennifer Munro Miller assiduously uncovered vital information about dozens of designers in the exhibition, combing internet databases and traveling to libraries across Los Angeles. In the early stages of the project, Andrea McKenna assisted with biographical and periodical research. Interns Megan Berry, Meagan Blake, Fiona Chen, Maia November, and Aaron Ziolkowski capably conducted many research tasks, from finding period sources to locating images. We also thank Assistant Curator Elizabeth Williams and Decorative Arts and Design Council Assistant Dhyandra Lawson, who kindly took time from other responsibilities to pitch in whenever necessary. And we are grateful to department volunteers Marilyn Gross and Helen de Gyarfas for coming to the museum nearly every week over the five years of planning and keeping our rapidly expanding study files in good order.

The interdisciplinary skills required to examine the breadth and complexity of California design were provided by a number of scholars outside the museum. We are especially grateful to consulting curator Bill Stern for sharing his expertise, advising on object selection, introducing us to many important collectors and designers, and contributing an essay to this publication. We extend heartfelt thanks to the other catalogue authors: Glenn Adamson, Jeremy Aynsley, Pat Kirkham, Melissa Leventon, Christopher Long, and Nicholas Olsberg, who not only recommended objects but also participated in many meetings and countless conversations to ensure that their essays formed a compelling narrative. Jewel Stern contributed her unparalleled knowledge about mid-century metalwork and led us to previously unknown collections. And at LACMA, we salute the incomparable knowledge and collegial generosity of Curator of Costume and Textiles Kaye Spilker, who selected most of the clothing and textiles for the exhibition, oversaw their beautiful photography, and supervised their installation. Without her commitment, we could not have integrated clothing and textiles as fully as this material deserved.

Head of Publications Nola Butler expertly supervised all aspects of catalogue production, coordinating the responsibilities of curators, authors, the editor, photographers, the designer, and the production manager. The book owes a great deal to her wise counsel and commitment to excellence. Monica Paniry, Publications Administrator, provided outstanding assistance in numerous ways. Nancy Grubb skillfully and meticulously edited the manuscript, excising mistakes and inconsistencies, holding us to the highest publication standards, and living up to her international reputation as "the editor's editor." We were fortunate to have the superlative talents of Michael Hodgson, principal of Ph.D, A Design Office, who designed the book with the assistance of Alice Joo. Sue Medlicott and Nerissa Dominguez Vales of The Production Department handled the many details of catalogue production with grace. The stunning photographs of the LACMA objects and local loans are the work of Peter Brenner and Steve Oliver. Robert J. Hennessey's skillful work greatly enhanced all the images in the book. Cheryle Robertson undertook the daunting task of acquiring hundreds of images and permissions and was ably assisted by Stephen Forsling.

We very much appreciate the efforts of the Development department at LACMA, whose outstanding work resulted in much-needed financial support for the exhibition. We are especially grateful to Terry Morello, Melissa Bomes, Chelsea Hadley, Abigail Bangser, Kate Virdone, Stephanie Dyas, and Amanda Lipsey. Zoë Kahr, Liz Andres, and Marciana Broiles in the Exhibition Programs department expertly managed the myriad logistical details of planning, budget, and installation. Stephanie Baker, Erica Franek, Emily Horton, Alexandra Moran, and Suzan Sengöz in the Registrar's office skillfully handled the multitude of tasks related to the borrowing and transportation of objects. Renee Montgomery and Delfin Magpantay advised us on issues relating to insurance and risk management. Barbara Pflaumer, Miranda Carroll, and Annie Carone in the Communications and Marketing department oversaw the press campaign with utmost professionalism.

The broad range of objects in the exhibition required the expertise of every division of LACMA's Conservation Center, and we gratefully acknowledge Director Mark Gilberg for his unstinting support of this project. Special thanks are owed to object conservators John Hirx and Don Menveg for their invaluable advice, masterful treatments of ceramics and furniture, and enthusiasm about the subject matter. Textile conservators Catherine McLean and Susan Schmalz created flattering mounts for the display of fashion and textiles. Paper conservators Janice Schopfer and Soko Furuhata helped us to identify printing techniques, while Dale Davis's frames enhanced all the works on paper. Conservation scientists Frank Preusser and Charlotte Eng identified the material composition of several objects, and Jeff Ono made masterful mounts that showed each object in its best light.

Mary Lenihan in the Education department was involved with the project from the very beginning, contributing to the gallery interpretation and thoughtfully planning a rich, compelling series of public events. Amy Heibel developed an innovative and engaging website and mobile phone application and, together with Alexa Schulz, interviewed many of the designers represented in the exhibition and compiled captivating videos about them and their work. Alexis Curry, Douglas Cordell, Maggie Hanson, Tracy Kerr, and Kristi Yuzuki in the Balch Art Research Library at LACMA tirelessly obtained the many research resources we requested.

Bringing to the project deep knowledge of mid-century California as well as great sensitivity to the interpretation of objects, Craig Hodgetts and Hsinming Fung, together with their staff at Hodgetts+Fung Design and Architecture, especially Anina Weber, created a remarkable exhibition design. They worked closely with Senior Exhibition Designer Victoria Turkel Behner, with invaluable direction by John Bowsher, Director of Art Installations and Facility Planning. Bill Stahl and his Gallery Services staff constructed cases and display equipment with utmost skill, and Jeff Haskin and the Art Preparation and Installation team expertly handled each of the over 350 objects with their customary professionalism. Amy McFarland, Katherine Go, and Daniel Young designed the striking graphics, greatly enhancing the exhibition aesthetic. Peter Kirby of Media Art Services brilliantly managed all things audiovisual, including locating rare and important footage, advising on the integration of media and objects, securing film rights, and installing the equipment.

It is a pleasure to offer thanks to the curatorial staff of the many museums that shared their collections and expertise: Carolyn Brucken at the Museum of the American West, Autry National Center; Barry Harwood at the Brooklyn Museum of Art; Susan Brown at the Cooper-Hewitt National Design Museum; Timothy Burgard at the Fine Arts Museums of San Francisco; Diana Daniels at the Crocker Art Museum; Wim de Wit at the Getty Research Institute; Lynn Downey at Levi Strauss & Co. Archives; Sue Ann Robinson at the Long Beach Museum of Art; Stacie Daniels at the Mills College Museum of Art; Eleanor Gadsden, Kelly L'Ecuyer, and Lauren Whitley at the Museum of Fine Arts, Boston; Julie Muñiz and Inez Brooks-Myers at the Oakland Museum of California; Suzanne Baizerman, formerly of the Oakland Museum of California; Leslie Kendall at the Petersen Automotive Museum; Natasha Johnson at the Phoebe A. Hearst Museum of Anthropology at the University of California, Berkeley; Kirk Delman at the Ruth Chandler Williamson Gallery at Scripps College; Henry Urbach and Jennifer Dunlop Fletcher at the San Francisco Museum of Modern Art; Barry Haun at the Surfing Heritage Foundation; Jocelyn Gibbs, Melinda Gandara, Alexander Hauschild, and Jennifer Whitlock at the University Art Museum at the University of California, Santa Barbara; Kathryn Kanjo, formerly of the University Art Museum at the University of California, Santa Barbara; and Serge Mauduit and Andreas Nutz at the Vitra Design Museum.

We are deeply grateful to the many librarians and archivists who have made their collections available to us for research and loan: Anne Coco and Barbara Hall at the Margaret Herrick Library, Academy of Motion Picture Arts and Sciences; Nancy Sparrow at the Alexander Architectural Archive at the University of Texas, Austin; Robert Dirig at the Art Center Archives; Janice Woo at the Meyer Library, California College of the Arts; Simon Elliott at the Department of Special Collections, Charles E. Young Research Library, University of California, Los Angeles; Waverly Lowell and Miranda Hambro at the Environmental Design Archives, University of California, Berkeley; Lauren Weiss Bricker at the Archives—Special Collections, California State Polytechnic University; Ann Harrison at the Getty Research Institute; Jennifer Watts, Suzanne Oatey, and Erin Chase at the Huntington Library, Art Collections and Botanical Gardens; Catherine Powell at the Labor Archives and Research Center, San Francisco State University; Laura Verlaque at the Pasadena Museum of History; and Barbara Rominski and Peggy Tran-Le at the San Francisco Museum of Modern Art Library & Archives.

The single most rewarding aspect of this project has been the opportunity to meet the extraordinary designers and craftspeople whose work is included in the exhibition. Conversations with them about their work and the design culture in mid-century California were essential to our understanding of the era and to the narrative of the exhibition. They include Jerome and Evelyn Ackerman, Jim Conner, David Cressey, Louis Danziger, Douglas Deeds, Arline Fisch, Miller Fong, John Kapel, Gere Kavanaugh, Henry C. Keck, Bernard Kester, Olga Lee, the late Sam Maloof, Harrison McIntosh, Michael Morrison, Merry Renk, Florence Resnikoff, Victor Ries, June Schwarcz, Kay Sekimachi, Jack Stauffacher, Deborah Sussman, Gene Tepper, Adolph Tischler, the late Frederick Usher Jr., John Van Hamersveld, Katherine Westphal, Barbara Willis, and Arnold Wolf.

We are especially indebted to the family members of the designers and craftspeople included in the exhibition—their memories, collections, and archives were invaluable in helping to preserve these artists' legacies. They include Rebecca and Cynthia Adler; Lisa Aronson; Lucia Dewey Atwood; Tripp Carpenter; Elaine Lustig Cohen; Marjorie, Luther, and Abigail Conover; Donna Cressey; Judy Smith de Barros; Eames Demetrios; Sylvia Elsesser; Grant Follis; Marty and Roy Fujita; Linda Adler Hughes; Susan Landor Keegin; Peter László; Beverly Maloof; Marguerite and Catherine McIntosh; Noa Mohlabane; Gail Reynolds Natzler; Mariah Nielsen; Jeanie Radakovich; Vicki Rand; Martin Roysher and Allison Wittenberg; Tony Sheets; Arlene Streich; Frederick Usher III; Xochitl Usher; Ana Wilson; and Ralph Wise.

The following individuals made outstanding contributions to our research, and we thank them for their patience in fielding our many questions and generosity in sharing information: Julia Armstrong-Totten; Bob and Lloyd Baron; Nancy Berman; Michael Boyd; Chuck Byrne; Edward Cella; Sanders Chase; Joel Chen; Lawrence Converso; Lia Cook; Dale Davis; Sandra Donnell and Justin Faggioli;

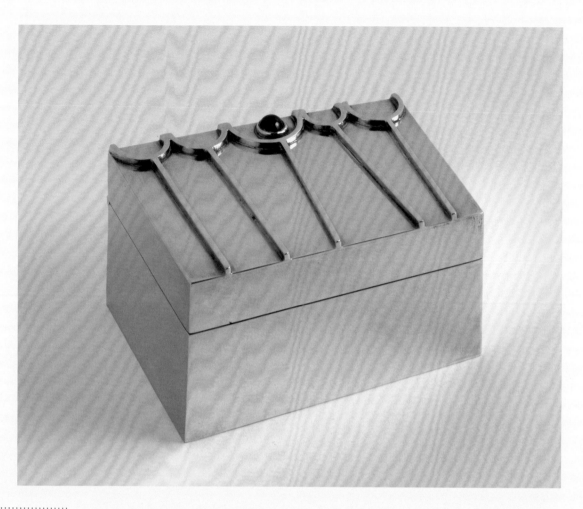

Frederick L. Lauritzen. Box, 1960.
Cat. 165

Brian Eychner; Jeannine Falino; Karen Figilis; Max Finkelstein; Russell Flinchum; Ron and Nancy Frank; Daniel Gregory; Dr. Geoffrey Hacker; Dave Hampton; Jeffrey Head; Catherine Bailey and Robin Petravic of Heath Ceramics; Jim Heimann; Bill Hertel; Rich Jackson; Marian Kovinick; William Krisel; Jo Lauria; Max and Damon Lawrence; Stewart MacDougall; Mark McDonald; SB Master; Jean Mathison; Eudorah M. Moore; Harold Nelson and Bernard Jazzar; Ellen Magnin Newman; Allen Porter; Chuck Quinn; Mark Resnick; Robin Rose; Barry Rosengrant; Lillian Sader; Teresa Sanchez at Gruen Associates; Louise Sandhaus; Peter Schifando; Marbeth Schon; Gail Steele; Jay Stewart; Robert Trout; John Voekel; Dion Warren; Eugene Weston; and James Zemaitis. While we are indebted to them all, we specially acknowledge the extraordinary contributions and matchless expertise of Steve Cabella, Dane Cloutier, Victoria Dailey, Andy Hackman, Eric Haeberli, Shannon and Peter Loughrey, Forrest L. Merrill, Gerard O'Brien, Daniel Ostroff, Evan Snyderman, and Steve Turner, who donated count-less hours of time and generously shared research amassed over many years.

Wendy Kaplan
Department Head and Curator
Decorative Arts and Design

Bobbye Tigerman
Assistant Curator
Decorative Arts and Design

352

Lenders to the Exhibition

Academy of Motion Picture Arts and Sciences

Academy of Motion Picture Arts and Sciences, Margaret Herrick Library

Cynthia Adler

Rebecca Adler (Mrs. Allan Adler)

American Craft Council Archives

Art Center College of Design

Auburn Trailer Collection

Lloyd and Robert Baron

John and Joanne Barrett

Gabrielle and Michael Boyd

Brooklyn Museum

Steve Cabella

California College of the Arts, Meyer Library

California State Polytechnic University, Pomona, College of Environmental Design, Archives—Special Collections

Allan and Laurie Carter

Elaine Lustig Cohen

Keith Collins

Crocker Art Museum

Victoria Dailey and Steve Turner

Louis Danziger

Douglas Deeds

Teresa and Eric Del Piero

De Patta/Bielawski Collection

Carlos Diniz Archive

Eames Collection, LLC

The Enamel Arts Foundation

Everson Museum of Art

Fine Arts Museums of San Francisco

Dr. Andrew and Deborah Frank

Harry Fukasawa

The Getty Research Institute

Esther Ginsberg/Golyester Antiques

Jill Grey

Gruen Associates

Andy Hackman

Hammer Museum, UCLA Grunwald Center for the Graphic Arts

Harman

The Brian and Edith Heath Trust

Linda Adler Hughes

The Huntington Library

Alan and Nora Jaffe

John Kapel

Gere Kavanaugh

The Lawrence Family

Family of Richard I. Levine

Levi Strauss & Co. Archives

Edith Liu

Long Beach Museum of Art

Los Angeles County Museum of Art

The Mr. and Mrs. Allan Balch Art Research Library, LACMA

Los Angeles Modern Auctions (LAMA)

Peter and Shannon Loughrey

Mattel, Inc.

Mark McDonald

Hilary and James McQuaide

Forrest L. Merrill

Eudorah M. Moore

Museum of California Design

The Museum of Fine Arts, Boston

The Museum of Modern Art, New York

Museum of the American West, Autry National Center

Gail Reynolds Natzler

Dion Neutra

The Newark Museum

Ellen Magnin Newman

Oakland Museum of California

Daniel Ostroff

Petersen Automotive Museum

Erika Kem Plack

Private collection, London

Private collection, Miami

Jean Radakovich

Mark and Maura Resnick

Susan and Michael Rich

Rochester Institute of Technology, Cary Graphic Arts Collection

The Roysher Family

San Francisco Museum of Modern Art

San Francisco Museum of Modern Art, Library & Archives

San Francisco State University, Labor Archives and Research Center

Peter Schifando

Scripps College

Kay Sekimachi

Smithsonian Institution, Cooper-Hewitt, National Design Museum

Bill Stern

Sunset Publishing Corporation

Surfing Heritage Foundation

Gene Tepper

Chip Tom and Michael W. Rabkin

University of California, Berkeley, Environmental Design Archives

UCLA Library Special Collections

UC Santa Barbara, University Art Museum, Architecture and Design Collection

Mrs. Joseph F. Westheimer (Katherine)

Katherine Westphal

Steven Ziel and Chase Langford

Illustration Credits

Wally Byam. Airstream *Clipper*, this model c. 1937. See cat. 35

Index